www.brookscole.com

www.brookscole.com is the World Wide Web site for Brooks/Cole and is your direct source to dozens of online resources.

At *www.brookscole.com* you can find out about supplements, demonstration software, and student resources. You can also send e-mail to many of our authors and preview new publications and exciting new technologies.

www.brookscole.com
Changing the way the world learns®

Leadership, Advocacy, and Direct Service Strategies for Professional School Counselors

RACHELLE PÉRUSSE
Plattsburgh State University

GARY E. GOODNOUGH
Plymouth State University

THOMSON
™

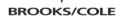

BROOKS/COLE

Australia • Canada • Mexico • Singapore • Spain
United Kingdom • United States

THOMSON

BROOKS/COLE

Publisher: Lisa Gebo
Acquisitions Editor: Marquita Flemming
Assistant Editor: Shelley Gesicki
Editorial Assistant: Amy Lam
Technology Project Manager: Barry Connolly
Marketing Manager: Caroline Concilla
Marketing Assistant: Mary Ho
Advertising Project Manager: Tami Strang
Signing Representative: Linda Larrabee

Project Manager, Editorial Production: Cheri Palmer
Print/Media Buyer: Kris Waller
Permissions Editor: Elizabeth Zuber/Sommy Ko
Production Service: Carlisle Communications
Copy Editor: Carol Kennedy
Illustrator: Carlisle Communications
Cover Designer: Christine Garrigan
Compositor: Carlisle Communications
Printer: Webcom

Printed in Canada
1 2 3 4 5 6 7   07 06 05 04 03

For more information about our products, contact us at:
Thomson Learning Academic Resource Center
1-800-423-0563

For permission to use material from this text, contact us by:
Phone: 1-800-730-2214
Fax: 1-800-730-2215
Web: http://www.thomsonrights.com

Library of Congress Control Number: 2003108356
ISBN 0-534-58933-2

Brooks/Cole—Thomson Learning
10 Davis Drive
Belmont, CA 94002
USA

Asia
Thomson Learning
5 Shenton Way #01-01
UIC Building
Singapore 068808

Australia/New Zealand
Thomson Learning
102 Dodds Street
Southbank, Victoria 3006
Australia

Canada
Nelson
1120 Birchmount Road
Toronto, Ontario M1K 5G4
Canada

Europe/Middle East/Africa
Thomson Learning
High Holborn House
50/51 Bedford Row
London WC1R 4LR
United Kingdom

Latin America
Thomson Learning
Seneca, 53
Colonia Polanco
11560 Mexico D.F.
Mexico

Spain/Portugal
Paraninfo
Calle/Magallanes, 25
28015 Madrid, Spain

Brief Contents

Contents

Chapter 2

Improving Academic Achievement through an Understanding of Learning Styles   34

BRADLEY T. ERFORD, CHERYL MOORE-THOMAS,
AND SHELLEY A. MAZZUCA, LOYOLA COLLEGE IN MARYLAND

Chapter 3

Investigating the World of Work   71

SUSAN SEARS, THE OHIO STATE UNIVERSITY

Chapter 4

Fostering Positive Career Development in Children and Adolescents   102

SPENCER G. NILES AND JERRY TRUSTY, THE PENNSYLVANIA STATE UNIVERSITY, AND NATASHA MITCHELL, UNIVERSITY OF MARYLAND

Chapter 5

Equity, Access, and Career Development: Contextual Conflicts   125

MARY JACKSON AND DALE GRANT, GEORGIA SOUTHERN UNIVERSITY

Chapter 12

School Counselors as Leaders and Advocates in Addressing Sexual Harassment   353

CAROLYN B. STONE, UNIVERSITY OF NORTH FLORIDA

Index   381

Preface

This book is based on the comprehensive developmental school counseling model, as described in the American School Counselor Association (ASCA) National Model for School Counseling Programs (ASCA, 2003), the ASCA National Standards for School Counseling Programs (Campbell & Dahir, 1997) and the Education Trust's Transforming School Counseling Initiative (TSCI) (National Initiative, 1997). In the subsequent chapters, authors use the concepts and ideas inherent in these three national movements to establish direct service strategies based on the current school counseling literature. What follows is a brief synopsis of these national movements, an overview of the book, and suggestions about how counselor educators, preservice, and professional school counselors can use this book.

NATIONAL STANDARDS FOR SCHOOL COUNSELING PROGRAMS

In 1997, ASCA published the National Standards for School Counseling Programs (Campbell & Dahir, 1997). The standards provided the school counseling profession with a nationwide consensus detailing student outcomes—what students should know or be able to do as a result of being in a school having a comprehensive school counseling program. These outcomes are organized by developmental area and comprise academic, career, and personal/social developmental domains.

The structure of the national standards is a logical one, consisting of four levels. At the top are the broad domains (academic, career, personal/social). Under each domain are the standards themselves, nine in all, three within each domain (see Table 1). Contained in the third level, under the standards, are general student competencies. And finally, enumerated after the general student competencies are specific knowledge and skills students will acquire as a result of their participation in a comprehensive school counseling program.

For instance under the domain "Academic Development" are three standards, A, B, and C. Standard A states: "Students will acquire the attitudes, knowledge, and skills that contribute to effective learning in school and across the lifespan."

TABLE 1	THE NATIONAL STANDARDS

Academic Development

Standard A: Students will acquire the attitudes, knowledge, and skills that contribute to effective learning in school and across the life span.

Standard B: Students will complete school with the academic preparation essential to choose from a wide range of substantial postsecondary options, including college.

Standard C: Students will understand the relationship of academics to the world of work, and to life at home and in the community.

Career Development

Standard A: Students will acquire the skills to investigate the world of work in relation to knowledge of self and to make informed career decisions.

Standard B: Students will employ strategies to achieve future career success and satisfaction.

Standard C: Students will understand the relationship between personal qualities, education and training, and the world of work.

Personal/Social Development

Standard A: Students will acquire the attitudes, knowledge, and interpersonal skills to help them understand and respect self and others.

Standard B: Students will make decisions, set goals, and take necessary action to achieve goals.

Standard C: Students will understand safety and survival skills.

Source: Printed and used with permission from the American School Counselor Association.

Student competencies under Standard A support three areas: "to improve academic self-concept, to acquire skills for improving learning, and to achieve school success." Detailed under each of these areas are specific knowledge and skills students will acquire. For example, under "Acquiring skills for improving learning" four specific skills or areas of knowledge students will have as a result of a comprehensive school counseling program are: "apply time management skills and task management skills; demonstrate how effort and persistence positively affect learning; use communication skills to know when and how to ask for help when needed; and apply knowledge of learning styles to positively influence school performance."

The National Standards for School Counseling Programs filled a major gap in the development of the school counseling profession by providing specific information regarding what students should know and be able to do. The standards were written, reviewed, and approved by ASCA members and endorsed by major educational professional associations, including the National Association of Secondary School Principals (NASSP) and the National Association for Elementary School Principals (NAESP).

THE TRANSFORMING SCHOOL COUNSELING INITIATIVE

At approximately the same time the national standards were unveiled, the Transforming School Counseling Initiative (TSCI) was launched. Funded by a grant from the DeWitt Wallace–Reader's Digest Foundation and managed by the Education Trust, TSCI sought to restructure school counselor education by providing money and training to selected counselor education programs around the United States (National Initiative, 1997). By focusing their attention on counselor education programs, the Education Trust sought to make extensive changes in the way professional school counselors were prepared—and from this revamped education, change the way school counselors perceive and implement their roles and jobs. TSCI's main goal was to move the profession away from a mental health focus and toward themes endorsed in the current education reform movement. Central among these themes was to refocus school counselors' energies on the academic development of students. More specifically, TSCI's vision includes school counselors' becoming instrumental players in closing the achievement gap between poor and minority youth and more privileged social classes.

In order to accomplish this robust goal, TSCI put forth a new vision for school counselors that sharpened their focus on academic achievement. Gone were the traditional notions that school counselors' roles were mainly that of counselor, consultant, and coordinator. New roles for school counselors were defined and new foci elaborated upon. Whereas previously school counselors were concerned primarily with helping individual students be successful, TSCI focused on providing systemic change. Such systemic change is to be implemented through newly defined roles involving leadership, advocacy, teaming and collaboration, counseling and coordinating, and assessment and use of data within the framework of multicultural and technological competencies (see Table 2).

National Model for School Counseling Programs

The ASCA National Model for School Counseling Programs was created to help school counselors develop their own comprehensive school counseling programs consistent with the latest educational reform movements. The national model has four elements: foundation, delivery system, management systems, and accountability. Language from the ASCA National Standards and TSCI is incorporated throughout the model. For example, the national standards help form the foundation of the model, while concepts from TSCI are included within the four themes of leadership, advocacy, collaboration and teaming, and systemic change. In addition, the national model encourages school counselors to become users of data to monitor student progress in academic achievement and to demonstrate accountability.

National Model, National Standards, and TSCI

Although the advent of the national model signals a new era for professional school counselors and a leap forward for the profession, the introduction of a new model

TABLE 2	CONSENSUS ON WHAT SCHOOL COUNSELORS SHOULD BE DOING			
Leadership	**Advocacy**	**Teaming and Collaboration**	**Counseling and Coordination**	**Assessment/ Use of Data**
Technology and Multicultural and Diversity Skills (All Areas)				
Promote, plan, implement prevention programs, career/ college activities, course selection and placement activities, social/personal management and decision-making activities	Making available and using data to help the whole school look at student outcomes	Participate/consult with teams for problem solving: ensuring responsiveness to equity and cultural diversity issues as well as learning styles	Brief counseling encounters with individual students, groups, and families	Assess and interpret student needs, recognizing differences in culture, languages, values, and backgrounds
Provide data snapshots of student outcomes, show implications, achievement gaps, and provide leadership for school to view through equity lens	Use data to effect change; calling on resources from school and community	Collaborate with other helping agents (peer helpers, teachers, principal, community agencies, businesses)	Coordinate resources, human and other, for students, families, and staff, to improve student achievement (community, school, home, etc.)	Establish and assess measurable goals for student outcomes from counseling programs, activities, interventions, and experiences
Arrange 1 on 1 relationships for students with adults in school setting for additional support and assistance in reaching academic success	Advocate for student experiences and exposure that will broaden students' career awareness and knowledge	Collaborate with school and community teams to focus on rewards, incentives, and supports for student achievement	Key liaison working with students and school staff to set high aspirations for all students and develop plans/ supports for achieving those aspirations	Assess building barriers that impede learning, inclusion, and/or academic success for all students
Play a leadership role in defining and carrying out the Comprehensive Developmental School Counseling function	Advocate for students' placement and school support for rigorous preparation for all students	Collaborate with school staff members in developing staff training on team response to students' academic, social, emotional, and developmental needs	Coordinate staff training initiatives that address student needs on a school-wide basis	Interpret student data for use in planning for change

Source: Education Trust Transforming School Counseling Initiative, 1999 (www.edtrust.org). Printed with permission from the Education Trust.

can be overwhelming to the already hardworking school counselor. Sometimes the professional school counselor can see new concepts as "something else I have to do" rather than view them as a new way to conceptualize an already existing comprehensive developmental school counseling program. It is our goal in bringing you this book that professional school counselors and school counselors-in-training will begin to understand how to implement the national model, the national standards, and TSCI in their own school counseling programs. Our hope is that current and future school counselors will see that many of the roles and functions of the school counselor in these new initiatives are familiar. That is, school counselors are still expected to perform individual counseling, group counseling, and classroom guidance (Campbell & Dahir, 1997), but the way in which school counselors do their work is changing. School counselors are expected to be leaders, advocates, collaborators, and users of data. It is not enough to work in a solitary manner; school counselors will need to work in collaboration with others and implement programs in a systemic whole-school approach.

The information contained in this book presents to school counselors many ways to incorporate the national model, national standards, and TSCI into practice. Up to now, there has been much discussion about the importance of these concepts, but very little on how to incorporate these concepts into a functional school counseling program. Our book addresses the national standards and the TSCI domains as they pertain to the issue discussed in each chapter and provides readers direction on how to implement and incorporate these standards into the actual practice of school counseling.

OVERVIEW OF THE BOOK

In the chapters that follow, experts in the school counseling field provide details on how school counselors can transform theory and school counseling literature into workable plans for transforming their schools within the context of the national standards. The authors write about twelve topics that span academic, career, and personal/social development. In each chapter, they provide a background of the issue grounded in the professional literature. They then elaborate on how, through leadership and advocacy, professional school counselors can produce systemic change in their schools.

As is clear from the title of the book, we agree with the change in focus elaborated on in the national model. What is different in the provision of classroom, group, and individual counseling in schools today is that it is embedded in the larger endeavor of systemic change and whole-school intervention. We believe that in order to provide change and promote the academic, career, and personal/social development of all students, counselors need to be both change agents and direct service providers.

As a result of this belief, the authors include detailed plans of how professional school counselors, within their comprehensive school counseling programs, can implement their roles as direct service providers to students. Each chapter contains a comprehensive review of the literature, whole-school interventions, and plans for classroom guidance activities and group counseling that comprehensively address central issues facing school counselors. Although we concur with the prevailing thrust of the profession that suggests school counselors' individual counseling be minimized (primarily due to its inefficiency given large caseloads), it is inarguable that at times individual interventions are called for. Thus, each chapter contains individual counseling considerations school counselors should keep in mind as they work with individual students grappling with the specified issue.

The book follows the model of the national standards and incorporates each of the standards within the three domains. The five chapters in Part One detail how, through leadership, advocacy, and direct service, professional school counselors can implement multilevel interventions to help prepare students in each of the academic and career development standards. In Part Two, the authors explore seven issues of importance from the personal/social domain of the national standards: respecting racial and ethnic differences, sexual identity, violence prevention and conflict resolution, loss and grief, alcohol and other substance abuse, stress management, and sexual harassment.

In all of these chapters, the authors show how professional school counselors use traditional skills (for example, individual and group counseling) and new skills (for example, leadership and advocacy) to promote the academic, career, and personal/social development of students within systems. Chapters provide specific information and activities to help school counselors promote the development of all students in ways that provide specificity to the national model, the national standards, and TSCI. Authors help school counselors implement their role as change agent—by providing leadership and advocacy strategies to help change systems. They complement this broader role by elaborating on the direct services that school counselors provide as a result of their expertise in classroom guidance, group, and individual counseling. It is our hope that by providing comprehensive literature reviews, whole-school interventions, classroom guidance lessons, small-group counseling plans, and individual counseling considerations, we will give pre-service and professional school counselors valuable information on transforming their schools and providing effective direct services to the students they serve. In addition, all handouts found in the text can be downloaded to fit an $8\frac{1}{2}'' \times 11''$ page at http://info.wadsworth.com/perusse.

SUGGESTIONS FOR USING THIS BOOK

This book is designed with two separate purposes: (1) to serve as a textbook that can be used in graduate courses to help students see the connection between theory, research, and the practice of school counseling; (2) to serve as a practical tool for professional school counselors who want to adapt their programs to include the emerging schoolwide prevention and intervention stance that is being called for on the national level. This book can be used as a core or supplemental text in graduate-level school counseling courses such as Issues in School Counseling, Introduction to School Counseling, Organization and Administration of School Counseling Programs, Elementary School Counseling, Secondary School Counseling, Program Planning and Management, School Guidance and Counseling, Counseling Children and Adolescents, Practicum, and Internship.

Counselor educators can use the book to help school counseling students envision how a comprehensive developmental program flows from a review of the literature. Once they see several examples of how to implement a prevention/ intervention program in a school system, students could then use the book as a model to develop their own prevention/intervention strategies based on the literature and current thought in the field. Students who are further along in the program, for example in practicum or internship class, can use this book to help them implement intervention/prevention strategies at their site. This hands-on experiential use of the text will allow students to use the information in this book to witness how these strategies can be implemented in a school setting.

ACKNOWLEDGMENTS

The editors would like to gratefully acknowledge the hard work and creativity of the contributing authors. It was an honor to work with such gifted and highly regarded professionals. We thank the reviewers: Donna Henderson, Wake Forest University; Cass Dykeman, Oregon State University; David Duys, Southern Illinois University; Jo Hayslip, Plymouth State College (Professor Emerita); Carolyn Stone, University of North Florida; Denise Worth, California State University–Chico; James O. Fuller, Indiana Wesleyan University; David Srebalus, West Virginia University–Morgantown; Denise Beesley, University of Oklahoma. This book has benefited greatly from their helpful and diligent comments. We are sincerely grateful for the support we received from Julie Martinez, acquisitions editor, Amy Lam and Catherine Broz, editorial assistants, Brooks/Cole Publishing; and Linda Larrabee, executive sales representative, Thomson Learning. Thanks also to Marquita Flemming, acquisitions editor, and Cheri Palmer, senior editorial production project manager, Brooks/Cole Publishing; Trish Finley, project editor, Carlisle Publishers Services; and Carol Kennedy, copyeditor, Carol A. Kennedy Editing Services, for guiding us through the production process. We appreciate their patience and attentiveness through every phase of this project. Finally, we want to thank our families for their love and support.

I am thankful to my many colleagues at Plymouth State University. I am grateful to Lynn, my wife, who has provided me with love and support for over twenty years. Finally, my children, Amy and Jordan, have inspired me in more ways than I can enumerate. In addition, I am thankful for Jordan's technical support and expertise during this project. *GEG*

I am grateful to my school counseling students, who inspired this book. I would like to acknowledge two professionals who have been instrumental in my career: Dr. Richard L. Hayes (The University of Georgia) and Dr. Claire Cole Vaught (Virginia Tech). Thank you for guiding me when I was your student. Most especially, I give thanks and all my love to my husband, Gregg, and our beautiful daughter, Mychael-An. *RP*

REFERENCES

American School Counselor Association (ASCA). (2003). *The ASCA National Model: A framework for school counseling programs*. Alexandria, VA: American School Counselor Association.

Campbell, C. A., & Dahir, C. A. (1997). *Sharing the vision: The national standards for school counseling programs*. Alexandria, VA: ASCA.

National Initiative for Transforming School Counseling. (1997). Retrieved March 1, 2003, from http://www.edtrust.org/.

STRATEGIES FOR ACADEMIC AND CAREER DEVELOPMENT

In Part One, five chapters are designed around the academic development and career development National Standards for School Counseling Programs. In Chapter 1, Peggy LaTurno Hines (Indiana State University) and Teesue H. Fields (Indiana University Southeast) focus on how professional school counselors can intervene to improve the academic functioning of all students. They present a case example of a counselor who uses school achievement data to effect change on a system-wide basis, while offering direct service to students by providing group and individual support. In Chapter 2, Bradley T. Erford, Cheryl Moore-Thomas, and Shelley A. Mazzuca (all from Loyola College in Maryland) explore learning styles— what they are, how counselors can work with students having different styles, and what their impact is on both instruction and student learning. In Chapter 3, Susan Sears (The Ohio State University) explains how school counselors can help all students better understand themselves so they can make healthy career decisions. Spencer G. Niles, Jerry Trusty (both at The Pennsylvania State University), and Natasha Mitchell (University of Maryland) detail in Chapter 4 how school counselors provide leadership and collaborate with multiple systems, in order to promote the career development of students. Finally, Chapter 5, authored by Mary Jackson and Dale Grant (both from Georgia Southern University), explores how career development is complicated by the varying contexts people experience based on their sexual orientation, gender, ability level, and ethnicity. Jackson and Grant provide substantial background information to help school counselors understand these complex phenomena. They then present whole school leadership and advocacy initiatives that promote the fair and equitable treatment of all students so that they have access to the academic programs that foster career development. They follow up these initiatives with classroom and small group activities that help students of diverse backgrounds gain access to important career development information.

School Counseling and Academic Achievement

Peggy LaTurno Hines, Indiana State University, and
Teesue H. Fields, Indiana University Southeast

Introduction

The PK–12 school reform movement of the past fifteen years has significantly influenced American education (Bemak, 2000; Brown, 1999; Perry, 1992). The emphasis on raising student achievement has led to a public demand for schools to be accountable for their students' learning outcomes (Fields & Hines, 2000). As members of the educational team, school counselors need to contribute to the "bottom line" of the school: student mastery of high academic standards. This chapter explores the role of school counselors in facilitating student academic achievement.

Literature Review

Recent Trends in Education

The beliefs that drive education in the United States have significantly changed in the past fifteen to twenty years. The old idea that only some students can learn and that schools are responsible for teaching only motivated students has been replaced with the belief that every student can learn to high standards and that schools have the responsibility for teaching in a way that reaches every student. Schools previously measured their success by the accomplishments of their best students, and most schools were satisfied when students performed better than the state average. In today's current school-reform environment, schools are categorized by the percentage of all students mastering a rigorous curriculum (Hines, 1998). The conviction that all students can and must learn to high academic standards and that schools have the responsibility to teach all students has created a new paradigm through which educators are evaluated (Reynolds & Hines, 2001b; Tucker & Codding, 1998).

Along with this increased emphasis on school accountability, education faces the additional burden of smaller funding allocations. The shrinking education dollar is forcing superintendents and school boards to scrutinize every program for its direct relationship to academic achievement (King & Mathers, 1997; Lockwood & McLean, 1997). With these burgeoning financial and political pressures, school counseling has come under increased scrutiny. If school counselors cannot show that they contribute to the school's academic achievement goals, then counseling programs become expendable (Fields & Hines, 2000). For example, one state went so far as to allow schools to choose between hiring a school counselor or a reading teacher (Guerra, 1997).

Recent Trends in School Counseling

The field of school counseling has also experienced a number of shifts in the past ten to fifteen years. Emphasis has changed to school counseling as a program rather than as a position (Gysbers & Henderson, 2001). School counselors, who previously served only those students who were referred, now create comprehensive school counseling programs designed to serve all students (ASCA, 2003). In addition, the notion that school counseling is a stand-alone, isolated program is being replaced with the belief that school counseling programs must be systemic and delivered through the entire school and community (Green & Keys, 2001; Hines, 1998; Reynolds & Hines, 2001a).

The American School Counselor Association's (ASCA) National Standards for School Counseling Programs (Campbell & Dahir, 1997) created a framework that has been critical to the development of the school counseling field. The standards have helped school counselors begin basing their program on student standards instead of selecting activities based on hunches (Hines & Reynolds, 2001). In addition, ASCA has developed a National Model for School Counseling Programs (ASCA, 2003). The model provides a structure for school counseling programs that brings accountability for student progress to the forefront.

The school counseling literature has also begun to reflect education's focus on raising student achievement. Early heralders of this change called for school counselors to move from being "gatekeepers to advocates" (Hart & Jacobi, 1992) and become facilitators of education reform (Perry, 1992). Others espoused the idea that the skills professional school counselors bring to the educational environment are vital to any effort to raise student achievement (Borders & Drury, 1992; Otwell & Mullis, 1997; Myrick, 1993). However, it was not until the Transforming School Counseling Initiative (TSCI) of the late 1990s that a serious examination of the school counselor's role in raising student achievement began. TSCI, funded by Wallace–Reader's Digest Funds and administered through The Education Trust, Inc., called for school counselors to focus on student academic achievement. Additionally, TSCI recommended that school counselors should be proficient in seven skill domains: (1) advocacy for students, (2) leadership and facilitation of systemic change, (3) counseling and coordination of student assistance services, (4) action research designed to provide data to spur change, (5) teaming and collaboration with educators, parents, students, and communities, (6) use of technology to increase effectiveness and as a tool for advocacy, and (7) application of multicultural and diversity competencies (House & Martin, 1998).

School Counselors' Role in Raising Student Achievement

School counselors have a critical role in facilitating any effort to raise student achievement. First, they use their skills and knowledge in the seven TSCI domains to help the school administration facilitate faculty and community efforts to raise student achievement. Second, school counselors work to align their counseling program priorities with the school's student achievement goals. Finally, counselors facilitate the creation of interventions designed to remove barriers impeding academic achievement.

Using School Counseling Skills to Raise Student Achievement

School counselors hold a distinctive position within the school. They have their fingers on the pulse of the school. They are privy to the opinions and concerns of students, faculty, and administration. In addition, school counselors possess knowledge and skill sets that are unique within the school environment. While both school counselors and administrators receive training in leadership and research, counselors are the only educators skilled in counseling, group facilitation, collaboration and consultation, and advocacy. The uniqueness of their job, coupled with their knowledge and skills, places school counselors in a position to significantly contribute to the school's mission of raising student achievement. Fields and Hines (2000) delineated ways in which the following school counseling skills can be used to help raise student achievement.

COUNSELING SKILLS   The counseling techniques of joining, attending, clarifying, reflecting, and summarizing can be extremely helpful when working with teachers, administrators, parents, and business and community stakeholders who are seeking ways to improve student achievement. School counselors understand that open, honest, two-way communication with students is key to improving their level of achievement. School counselors can also coach educators who are involved in initiating change on how to establish communication lines and keep them open.

GROUP FACILITATION SKILLS   Much of the school improvement process relies on task groups to effectively design and carry out activities. School counselors possess essential group leadership skills. Understanding the importance of group process and the stages of group development allows the counselor to help facilitate the development of a group into an effective work team.

COLLABORATION AND CONSULTATION SKILLS   A great deal of collaboration and teaming must occur in any successful effort to raise student achievement. School counselors know the importance of collaborating with teachers, parents, and the community. They are skilled at networking and know how to utilize a wide variety of resources. Their familiarity with both education and the community makes them a natural liaison in the creation of school/community partnerships.

RESEARCH SKILLS   School counselors' command of basic research skills of data collection, analysis, and dissemination makes them valuable in the analysis of student achievement and related data. Such data include standardized test scores, grades, teacher assessments, and student-management information. In addition, the school counselor understands the importance of disaggregating data by variables such as gender, ethnicity, and socioeconomic status. Disaggregated data help school counselors look for access and equity issues in the school. These data are used to drive interventions, programs, and activities designed to raise student achievement.

ADVOCACY AND LEADERSHIP SKILLS   School counselors are knowledgeable about the forces that influence student achievement, such as school policies, attendance and discipline procedures, parent and community involvement, instruction and assessment, expectations, and guidance standards. School counselors hold a prime position to advocate for interventions designed to help raise one student's achievement level and for programs and experiences that all students need to lower existing barriers to learning. The school counseling skills delineated here are also important advocacy tools for school counselors. They use these skills to work with educators, parents, and community members, at the local, state, and/or national level, to gain the support necessary to implement strategies that lower barriers to student success.

Example: An elementary counselor is an active participant on the school improvement team. The counselor helps the team develop meetings with the faculty and the school's community council to discuss student achievement goals. The counselor presents the school's disaggregated data and facilitates an analysis of the data. Based on the data, the school decides to work to improve third-grade language arts scores on the state achievement test. The counselor then helps in the examination of the variables influencing language arts and advocates for the development of strategies designed to affect those variables. In addition, the counselor coaches team members on improving communication skills and dealing with resistance from faculty or community members.

Aligning Counseling Program Student Standards to Academic Achievement Goals

While using counseling skills to facilitate the school improvement process is important, school counselors need to align their program with the academic goals of the school to truly join the faculty in the work of raising student achievement. The first step is to examine the school's academic achievement goals and ask, "What counseling-related skills and knowledge do our students need in order to help them attain this goal?" Delineate the student standards and competencies believed to directly relate to the academic goal. Then prioritize these standards and competencies to make sure that those with the most promise to help students reach the academic goal receive the greatest attention (Reynolds & Hines, 2001a).

Example: In the previous example, the elementary school's academic goal is to increase third-grade students' language arts scores on the state's standardized test. In a faculty meeting, the school counselor facilitates a discussion with the faculty

TABLE 1.1	NATIONAL STANDARDS AND COMPETENCIES THAT SUPPORT THE MASTERY OF LANGUAGE ARTS CONCEPTS
Standard	**Competency**
Academic Standard A: Students will acquire the attitudes, knowledge, and skills that contribute to effective learning in school and across the life span.	Students will: • Accept mistakes as essential to the learning process • Use communication skills to know when and how to ask for help when needed • Apply time management and task management skills
Academic Standard B: Students will complete school with the academic preparation essential to choose from a wide range of substantial postsecondary options, including college.	Students will: • Learn and apply critical thinking skills • Apply the study skills necessary for academic success at each level

to brainstorm which counseling standards and competencies are important for all students to master in order to score well on the state language arts test. The faculty concludes that to support the mastery of language arts concepts the most important student counseling standards and competencies are as shown in Table 1.1.

Once the prioritized competencies are set, the school counselor then designs activities that will facilitate student mastery of these competencies. These activities may include:

- Collaboration with teachers to integrate the competencies within their curriculum
- Whole-school activities or programs
- Classroom lessons
- Small-group sessions for students having difficulty mastering the competencies
- Individual counseling sessions for students having difficulty mastering the competencies

Intentionally aligning counseling program activities with the school's academic goals places school counselors in the middle of the school's continuous improvement process.

Facilitating the Development of Focused Interventions

School counselors also facilitate the careful analysis of the school's disaggregated data to look for groups of students who may need focused interventions. Counselors help administrators and faculty look for achievement gaps and possible access and equity issues (Hines & Reynolds, 2001; Jerald, 2001). For example, are there groups of students who are not achieving as well as other students? Are there groups of students who are not getting access to rigorous curriculum, quality teachers, or instruction designed to meet their learning styles and needs?

Once groups are identified, school counselors can engage school personnel in a discussion about the barriers preventing these groups from progressing. Appropriate personnel design interventions to remove these barriers to learning. These interventions may be either student- or systems-focused. Student-focused interventions directly affect students. System-focused interventions influence adults or policy. Faculty, school counselors, parents, community members, or others, as appropriate, may implement either student-focused or system-focused interventions.

Example: To continue the elementary school example, the school counselor collaborates with the school principal to facilitate a careful examination of school data. The faculty discovers that low-income students are not scoring as well as their more advantaged peers on the language arts portion of the state achievement test. After a thoughtful review of possible barriers influencing this group's achievement level, the staff decides to implement several strategies. System-focused strategies include the creation of professional development opportunities to help the staff learn about generational poverty, more effective methods to teach students from poverty, and ways to differentiate instruction in the classroom. Student-focused interventions include the creation of a special mentor/tutor program and small-group counseling sessions for identified students to receive additional help with task management and study skills. The school counselor's role in implementing these strategies might be to (1) serve on a committee that will design the professional development experiences and on subsequent faculty study groups that work on the implementation of differentiated instruction, (2) work with business and industry to set up a mentor/tutor program, and (3) conduct small-group counseling experiences for identified students.

The following scenario provides an example of how a high school counselor might work to raise student achievement at her school.

WHOLE-SCHOOL INTERVENTIONS

Robin Lanham is the school counseling director at Community High School (CHS). All CHS students must pass a state standardized test in order to graduate from high school. The test is administered at the beginning of the tenth grade. Robin collaborated with her principal, Sarah Matthews, to design and implement a systematic school improvement process at CHS. Robin helped facilitate small- and large-group experiences designed to help the faculty and school's advisory council think about what they wanted for CHS students and compare this ideal to the current status of CHS students. They specifically focused on ninth-grade data because the state test was administered at the beginning of the tenth grade. A small portion of the school's data that the faculty analyzed is reproduced in Table 1.2. Through this process, the faculty decided that they were concerned about the large number of ninth-graders who did not pass the math section of the state achievement test. Thus, the school decided to work to increase the number of ninth-graders passing the math portion of the test.

TABLE 1.2   **9TH-GRADE DATA DISAGGREGATED BY GENDER, ETHNICITY, AND SOCIOECONOMIC STATUS**

9th-Grade Students	Total Students	% of Students	Passing State Standardized Math Test		9th-Graders Enrolled in Algebra or Above		9th-Graders Passing Algebra or Above		9th-Grade Attendance Rate
			#	% of Total Population	#	% of Total Population	#	% of Those Enrolled	
All students	243	100%	114	47%	164	67%	117	48%	94%
Male	131	54%	43	33%	75	57%	47	36%	91%
Female	113	47%	71	63%	89	79%	70	62%	97%
African American	54	22%	14	26%	29	54%	14	26%	92%
Asian American	14	6%	13	93%	14	100%	13	93%	99%
Euro American	105	43%	73	70%	92	88%	78	74%	97%
Latino American	68	28%	13	19%	29	43%	11	16%	89%
Native American	2	1%	1	50%	1	50%	0	0%	91%
Free/reduced	106	44%	28	26%	49	46%	22	21%	90%
Non–free/reduced	138	57%	86	63%	115	84%	95	69%	96%

Many data concerned the CHS school community:

1. More than one half the students did not pass the math portion of the state test.
2. Male students were much less likely to pass than female students.
3. Students of color were not only less likely to pass the state test but were also less likely to enroll in and pass algebra or higher math.
4. Low-socioeconomic students were also less likely to pass the state test, pass algebra, or even enroll in algebra.

Robin continued to help Sarah with the improvement process by facilitating a school-community examination of the variables related to math achievement, such as curriculum, instruction, assessment, and educational environment. Together, Robin and Sarah joined with the faculty and advisory council in the creation of strategies designed to positively affect those variables critical to increasing math achievement.

As the process unfolded Robin strongly advocated for extra-help and extra-time programs and activities. She also put forth ideas concerning the need for professional development to help faculty understand education-related issues of low-socioeconomic students. In addition, Robin looked at additional data and found that eighth-grade teachers tended to recommend placement in ninth-grade algebra more frequently for white students. Robin brought this to the attention of

TABLE 1.3   NATIONAL STANDARD AND COMPETENCIES THAT SUPPORT ACADEMIC ACHIEVEMENT

Standard	Competency
Academic Standard A: Students will acquire the attitudes, knowledge, and skills that contribute to effective learning in school and across the life span.	Students will: • Apply time-management and task-management skills • Use communication skills to know when and how to ask for help when needed • Demonstrate how effort and persistence positively affect learning

Principal Matthews and the faculty. Due to Robin's advocacy efforts, a dialogue was opened with the feeder middle schools and the central office to look at the issues related to access to algebra in the ninth grade.

While Robin helped facilitate the school's improvement effort and advocate for students at the systemic level, she also knew it was important that the school counseling program be aligned with the school's student achievement goals. She reviewed the school's ASCA National Standards–based student guidance standards and competencies with the faculty and community advisory council. She then asked them to work in small groups to prioritize those guidance competencies that were important for students to master in order to help them pass the math section of the state test. The group identified ten competencies that they believed were critical for the students to master in order to succeed on the test. Three of the competencies were from Academic Standard A (see Table 1.3). This scenario will examine how Robin developed a continuum of programs and services to enable every student to master these three competencies.

Classroom Guidance Activities

To address these competencies with all ninth-grade students, Robin designed a guidance unit for the students. This three-lesson unit addressed time and task management, asking for help, and persistence. After consulting with the faculty, Robin worked with her schedule to deliver the unit in each of the ninth-grade English classes. The lesson plans for the unit are as follow.

Lesson 1: Time and Task Management

Academic Development Standard A: Students will acquire the attitudes, knowledge, and skills that contribute to effective learning in school and across the life span.

Competency: Students will apply time-management and task-management skills.

Learning Objective: After group instruction, students will be able to construct a daily, weekly, and six-weeks' (or other grading period) plan for managing class assignments.

Materials: Planner with semester, month, week, and day divisions.

Developmental Learning Activity

Introduction: The school counselor will inform students that it is usual for ninth-graders to have difficulty deciding how to balance the demands of different classes and teachers and activities (normalizing the situation.) The planner will be a way for all students to deal with the demands of their schedules.

Activity: The first week of school in ninth grade, the counselor and ninth-grade teachers will work with ninth-graders in classroom groups. Each student will receive a planner that includes school activities and holidays.

Each of the core teachers will provide assignments for the first grading period (for example, weekly quizzes, major tests, papers, and so on). If the core teachers work on a team, this will be easier to coordinate, but even if students have some variety of teachers, the counselor can work with teachers to get a list of activities for each class. Core teachers should think about the best way to study for their particular class and to help the students break down assignments based on this information. (For example, a foreign language must be studied daily.)

The students will fill in the due dates in their planner and note weekly events. Students will then be asked to fill in their other activities (sports practices, theater rehearsals, jobs, and so on).

Then students will look at their activities and school assignments for one week and plan how they will study and get assignments finished. Students will translate this into a day-by-day schedule. The counselor will provide some examples, and teachers will furnish approximate times it might take to complete assignments.

Conclusion: Students share their plan with an adult (teacher, coach, tutor, or parent) at the beginning of each week during the first grading period to build in more accountability.

Assessment: Ninth-grade teachers report the number of completed homework and long-term assignments for each week for each class. If daily assignment completions are low, the lesson will be retaught and daily checks made.

Follow-up: Teachers will follow up in each class on a daily basis for the first two weeks of the semester, having students put activities in their planner and checking on the amount of time it took to accomplish tasks. Teachers should also have some discussions about how well students estimated the time that assignments would take and how to plan extra time if a student has problems.

After the first two weeks, teachers will put activities on a special section of the blackboard with a reminder to put notes in their planner. Teachers will check planner on a weekly basis for first grading period, with a follow-up during second grading period and for the first week of the spring semester.

Adjustments for Middle School and Upper Elementary School

This planner activity would also work well for upper elementary school and middle school students. It would be even easier to coordinate when teachers work on teams or plan together. Students can also include in-class study time in the planner. When students start this kind of planning in upper elementary school, the habit is easier to develop and carry through in the higher grades.

LESSON 2: ASKING FOR HELP

Academic Development Standard A: Students will acquire the attitudes, knowledge, and skills that contribute to effective learning in school and across the life span.

Competency: Students will use communication skills to know when and how to ask for help.

Learning Objective: After instruction and practice, students will be able to approach a classmate or teacher to ask for help in each category of need.

Materials: Role-play scenarios (Handout 1.1) "Ask Me" buttons for counselor and teachers.

Developmental Learning Activity

Introduction: The counselor will preview the lesson and the importance of asking for help.

Activity: The counselor will have a brief discussion concerning when to ask for help: "When do you call 911?" After writing some of the responses on the board, the counselor asks, "When do you go to a teacher for help?" The counselor also writes these responses on the board.

The counselor shows an overhead of the following categories and shows how student responses fit into these categories:

> I am confused about an assignment.
> I don't understand a concept.
> I don't understand my grade.
> I need feedback on my work (how am I doing?).

The counselor then asks each teacher, "Do you mind if students ask for help?" As each teacher says "NO, please ask," or some variation, the teacher puts on the "Ask Me" button.

The counselor teaches the formula for asking for help:

ASKING FOR HELP

Excuse me, _____ (teacher's name), I am _____ (verb: lost, unclear, confused, uncertain) about _____ (specific topic) and I would appreciate your help. If you don't have time now, when would be a better time to talk?

Have the following guidelines on a poster to put in the room (may be personalized by teacher):

Ask when the teacher is not busy.

If necessary, write your initial request and put it on teacher's desk or in mailbox in the room. (If willing, teachers could provide a special place for such notes.)

Suggest a time when you are available to work (lunch, study hall, after school, and so on).

Be respectful.

State your need; don't attack the teacher. (*I* message, not *you* message.)

Pursue your request until you get what you need.

Summarize the plan or outcome.

The counselor models asking for help with a teacher, using the rules and formula given above. Next, students are given scenarios (Handout 1.1) to practice asking skills. First, they practice in threes: two students practice the scenarios while the third student completes the evaluation checklist, then they switch until everyone has practiced. Finally, each student does a scenario with a teacher, counselor, or aide. Handout 1.1.

Conclusion: The counselor asks, "What was the hardest thing about asking for help?" "How could the teachers make it easier to ask for help?" (Teachers take notes and bring this back to the team.)

Assessment: When students do a scenario with teacher, a student helper or another teacher completes an evaluation checklist on the role play. If the student completes the role play successfully, the student gets a sticker with a "?" to wear.

Evaluation Checklist

___ Request clearly stated what was needed.

___ Request was an "I need" by student rather than "You did" to teacher.

___ Exchange with teacher was respectful throughout.

___ Follow-up questions or statements by student were clear.

___ A specific plan was agreed to by teacher and student.

___ Student summarized the plan to check for accuracy.

Follow-up: For a few days after this activity, teachers give time in their classes for students to request help. Teacher tallies number of students who request help. Model for asking stays on poster in the room. Teacher also identifies any students who might seem to need help but haven't asked. The school counselor has a private conference with these students, asking them to use the model and specify what they need.

Adjustments for Middle School

Due to the multiple teachers middle school students have, asking for help is also a problem for these students. This activity should work well for middle school.

LESSON 3: TRY, TRY AGAIN

Academic Development Standard A: Students will acquire the attitudes, knowledge, and skills that contribute to effective learning in school and across the life span.

Competency: Students will demonstrate how effort and persistence positively affect learning.

Learning Objective: Using a simulated class assignment, students will receive a variety of tools to master new concept.

Materials: A foreign-language question and several possible answers. The one given here is in Swedish, but you can substitute one in a language a counselor or teacher knows. It is best to choose a language students are unlikely to know. Make separate copies of Handout 1.2 and Handout 1.3 for each student.

Developmental Learning Activity

Students are asked to learn an unfamiliar skill and reach mastery. The main criterion is that the activity be broken down into steps and that students receive praise for small amounts of progress and that they keep track of their progress on a checklist. They can also reinforce each other.

Introduction: The school counselor introduces the lesson and places the students in groups of three. Each student receives a copy of Handout 1.2.

Activity: The counselor or teacher pronounces the parts and explains what they mean. The students then practice for a few minutes without any help, with one person asking the question and the other two each making an answer. The leader says the phrases again and asks how accurate the students were. Then the leader asks, "What might help?" Suggestions are written on the board. (The leader can add things such as saying the words slowly, working one person at a time with the other two reinforcing, and so on.)

The students are given Handout 1.3, which has the sentences with the words spelled phonetically underneath. The leader again pronounces the words and asks the students to practice using some of the suggested tactics. When a group thinks they have each mastered one sentence, they raise their hands and the leader checks on their pronunciation. The leader makes gentle corrections and models again if necessary; the leader also gives lavish praise, and each member is given a sticker to wear when their sentence is correct. Then they are asked to switch sentences until each person has learned all three parts. (The second and third parts should take less time.) Time is called after ten minutes, and the leader asks each group that is ready to raise a hand. The leader decides whether people do part 1, 2, or 3. If the whole group is correct, the group gets a small bag of candy. If a group doesn't want to try, they are asked to work on the sentences at home and try the next time.

Conclusion: After everyone who wants to has tried, the leader asks, "What was the hardest thing about this activity?" "Why didn't you give up when you weren't successful?" "What would make it easier to learn to learn a language?" "How is this activity like learning something hard in another class?"

Assessment: Students correctly pronounce sentences. Note phrases used to encourage students to keep trying.

Follow-up: Have posters for classroom, "You learned Swedish, surely you can learn _____." Teachers can add some of their new concepts in the blank. Also put some signs around the board that include some of the encouragements that students gave each other during the learning exercise.

Teachers use one actual class assignment to break down into parts and give students feedback on each part; individual feedback charts giving progress would also help.

Adjustments for Middle School

This activity should also work for middle school. If desired, parts 2 and 3 could be shortened.

A couple of weeks after completing the guidance lessons, Robin gave the students a unit-assessment survey, which asked about the student's use of the skills taught in the lessons. She also talked with the ninth-grade teachers about how the students were doing in the three areas. The data from these two sources led Robin to the discovery that about forty students were still having problems with these competencies.

SMALL-GROUP COUNSELING PLANS

Robin concluded that these students needed more attention and reinforcement than she and the teachers had provided in the whole classroom setting. Instead of just reteaching the same lessons, Robin assumed that the students had a basic understanding of the concepts from the classroom guidance lessons, but she could use the group setting to explore individual problems with the skills. Students could also benefit from the reinforcement and encouragement provided by the group.

Before forming groups, Robin followed ASCA ethical standards and Association for Specialists in Group Work best-practice guidelines and interviewed each student who was identified by teachers as unsuccessful after the classroom guidance lessons and follow-up. Some of the referred students were not appropriate for group or did not choose to be in the group. Robin made sure that all students understood the purpose of the group, agreed to basic group rules, and agreed to work on their own specific academic goals. Once Robin identified students who were both appropriate for and willing to be in the group, she got written parent permission for the students to participate in the group. After obtaining this permission, Robin formed the students into groups of six to eight students, trying to mix the students by gender, ethnicity, willingness to talk, and type of school problem (Hines & Fields, 2002).

Robin decided to adopt a solution-focused approach with the group. Instead of identifying classes where students were having the most problems, the students would start by looking at classes where they were having success. A key component of the group included a review of skills from the previous week at the start of each session. When skills were linked from each lesson and reviewed each week, the skills received repeated reinforcement. Actual student progress in classes would also be monitored and success celebrated. Robin's plans for each group session are as follows.

GROUP SESSION 1: GOOD TO GO

Academic Development Standard A: Students will acquire the attitudes, knowledge, and skills that contribute to effective learning in school and across the life span.

Competency: Students will apply time-management and task-management skills.

Learning Objective: Students will analyze successful time- and task-management skills that they already have and apply these to the subject they want to improve.

Materials: Poster board, marker.

Activities

Introduction: In this first group session, the leader welcomes everyone, restates the purpose of the group, and reminds the group of the rules they agreed to when they signed the consent form: to keep things said in group confidential, not to make put-down statements, to attend regularly, and to sincerely work on the goals each establishes in group. The leader may also want to establish a rule that members don't interrupt each other.

Students introduce themselves and identify the class where they are the most successful and feel the best about themselves. The leader makes linking statements where appropriate, for example, "So Bob, you feel positive about your experiences in math, just like Renita, even though you have different teachers." The leader writes name and identified class on poster board, leaving space for other information.

Counseling Activity: The leader explains that in this first session, the group will try to identify the successful strategies that members are already using in school. Members go around again and talk about the things that make it easier to be successful in the identified class. The leader writes strategies on the board under name and class. The leader also asks students to identify "On a scale from one to ten, with ten being A+, how successful are you in this class?"

Next the leader asks students to identify a class where they have some success, but would like to have more (this can be the good class identified above if the student only has one class with some success) and to state where they are on a scale from 1 to 10. Then the leader asks students what it would take to move up one notch in that class and what strategies they are already using (or using in their best class) that would help them improve a little. The specific questions are listed below:

> Q: How would you rank your success on a scale of 1 to 10?
> Q: What are you doing in this class to be at that rank?
> Q: How can you do more of this to move up one notch?
> Q: What strategies from your most successful class can you use to reach your goal in this class?
> Q: How will you know if you are successful? What will be different?

Each student writes out a plan for reaching the goal during the next week, by doing more of a specific strategy or using a strategy from their best class. The plan includes how they will know when a goal is met (what will be different?). Students read their plans to the group to get feedback. The leader puts the goals on the poster.

Example: To move from a 4 to a 5 in English this week, I will answer all of the study questions in my notebook, instead of just a few of them. I will know I am successful if I make a C grade instead of a D on the weekly quiz.

Conclusion: Ask students who are willing to respond to the following processing questions: What did you learn about yourself as a student today? What will you be able to use this week?

Assessment: Check the written goal for each student to see if it builds on student strengths and tries to expand already working strategies.

Follow-up: Students will report on their progress in next week's group. (The counselor may also encourage the students to share their goal and strategy with the teacher, but it is important for the teacher to be supportive of the incremental goal.)

GROUP SESSION 2: PLANNING FOR SUCCESS

Academic Development Standard A: Students will acquire the attitudes, knowledge, and skills that contribute to effective learning in school and across the life span.

Competency: Students will apply time-management and task-management skills.

Learning Objective: Students will analyze their individual strengths in using their planner and set goals for improvement.

Materials: Poster from last session with goals and strategies, marker and highlighter, students' individual planners, survey results of "A" students in each goal class.

Activities

Introduction: The leader reminds students about group rules. The leader invites students to share how they did on their goals from the previous week; what is their scale number now? What strategies worked to help them reach their goals? When a student identifies a strategy that worked, the leader highlights it on the poster. The leader asks how this strategy can be extended and used more often. The leader makes linking statements for the group member and asks the other members to do the same.

The leader comments on how well the group did during the week to build on what was working. The leader reinforces the idea that students understood themselves and what worked for them. The leader asks them to extend their goal for the coming week (each student says how they will do this).

Counseling Activity: The leader asks students to take out their planner and share how they use the planner to help in their best class. Then the leader asks students to talk about their goal class and share how they use the planner to help in that class. The group works together to give suggestions to each other on how to increase use of the planner in the goal class and how to extend its use. This will include a discussion about estimating the amount of time that is needed to complete assignments or study for tests.

The leader passes around the results of a survey done with the "A" students in each of the goal classes on the major assignments for the past week—how much time they studied and what they did to study—and asks students to compare this with what they planned.

Conclusion: The leader asks each student to write a goal for improving the use of their planner to manage time and tasks in their goal class during the next week. Again, the emphasis is on expanding what they are already doing with the planner and moving just one notch on the scale.

Assessment: The leader will check each goal to be sure it builds on existing strategies and is an incremental change. Example: I will start studying for my test on Tuesday instead of Wednesday.

Follow-up: Group members will share their progress next week. Give the Survey on Study Skills (Handout 1.4) to teachers of the goal classes selected by students in the group. Ask the teacher to choose an assignment that was due in the last week (a test, homework questions, or paper) and that needed advance study or preparation. Ask the teacher to fill in the name of that assignment, copy the Survey on Study Skills, and then give it to four or five "A" students to complete. Students should not put their name on the survey, and the teacher can give the surveys to the counselor to summarize, so that confidentiality is assured for the students.

GROUP SESSION 3: SOMEBODY HELP!

Academic Development Standard A: Students will acquire the attitudes, knowledge, and skills that contribute to effective learning in school and across the life span.

Competency: Students will use communication skills to know when and how to ask for help.

Learning Objective: After practice, students will identify when they need to ask for help and be able to ask for that help.

Materials: Poster from previous sessions, new poster board, marker, individual planners.

Activities

Introduction: The leader asks students to review the group rules. Then each group member tells how they used their planner in the goal class in the previous week and how they have expanded other strategies. Students identify their number on a scale from 1 to 10, and this is written on the poster. The leader reinforces the strategies they use to move up on the scale. Students then briefly analyze their planner for the week ahead. How will they extend their strategies and study time to be more successful in their goal class?

Counseling Activity: Students identify a time when they asked for help in a class and what made it easy for them to ask for help. Strategies from the group are written on the new poster. Students are then asked to share how often they ask for help in their goal class.

The group helps each student identify strategies in asking for help from their best class that could be used in the goal class. (If students have trouble, the leader can use guidelines from the classroom guidance lesson.) Students then do role plays, with one student being the teacher and the other asking for help. The leader asks the group to point out all the positive things the seeker is doing and then asks them to suggest how the seeker can expand the positive skills to be even more effective.

Note: Students can select something they want to ask, or leader can use the scenarios from the classroom guidance lesson.

Conclusion: Students identify a situation in their goal class where they need help. Students write a goal in their planner of how they will ask for help in the coming week.

Assessment: The leader and group assess the asking skills of each member in the role play. The leader also checks the goal for next week.

Follow-up: The students will report back next week on their success. The leader might want to also alert the teachers involved, in a general way, that the group is focusing on asking for help in the coming weeks.

GROUP SESSION 4: TRYING, TRYING

Academic Development Standard A: Students will acquire the attitudes, knowledge, and skills that contribute to effective learning in school and across the life span.

Competency: Students will demonstrate how effort and persistence positively effect learning.

Learning Objective: Students will identify strategies they use to persist even when things get hard.

Materials: Poster board, multicolored Post-it notes (different color for each student), markers for each participant, individual planners.

Activities

Introduction: Students review goals from last week and report on what happened when they asked for help. The leader and group reinforce the positive skills students used with such questions as "How did you know how to do that?" and "Wow, what a great way to approach that teacher. How did you ever come up with such a great idea?"

The leader also reviews how things are going in the goal class. Where are they now on a scale from 1 to 10? What have they been doing to help them move up the scale or maintain their position? Students set a new goal extending strategies and using planner.

Counseling Activity: Students each receive a pad of colored Post-it notes and a marker. The leader asks them to think of a time in a class when they got discouraged about some assignment or concept and were tempted to give up but didn't. Volunteers share some examples. Then the leader asks students to write on the Post-it note one thing they did to help themselves not give up.

Each student then explains what they wrote, and the leader puts the notes on the poster board in a random order. The leader then asks that they write down something else they did to not give up (it's all right to duplicate what another student said, but don't say this in advance). These notes go on the poster board with like colors grouped. Then the leader asks if anyone can think of one more thing they did, and students write that on a note. Those who come up with three things are praised ("Wow, three things; look at that!"). The leader then asks students to think about something in class right now where they are discouraged but haven't given up. How can they apply the skills they used in other discouraging situations to this situation? Mention that it is also OK to borrow ideas from other students.

Conclusion: Students write down a situation where they are discouraged in their goal class on a Post-it note. Then they choose two things they can do to keep from giving up in the coming week. These situations and the strategies are rearranged on the poster board. (Students can use their own strategies or those of someone else. It might be necessary to write duplicate copies of some strategies on the student's color note.)

Assessment: The leader checks that the goal and strategies are appropriate.

Follow-up: The students will report back next week on their success. Students' planners and goals for the coming week are also evaluated. Students write their goal and strategies for this week in the planner.

GROUP SESSION 5: THIS SQUARE IS TOO HARD TO FOLD

Academic Development Standard A: Students will acquire the attitudes, knowledge, and skills that contribute to effective learning in school and across the life span.

Competency: Students will demonstrate how effort and persistence positively affect learning.

Learning Objective: Students will break a difficult task into manageable pieces.

Materials: A 5-by-5-inch square of paper suitable for folding (bright colors if possible) for each student, directions for origami project, poster and Post-it notes from previous session.

Activities

Introduction: The leader asks students to report on their goal from last week. If students were not persistent, the leader asks how they can use more of the same strategy or add some other strategies to increase their chance of success. Praise is given for "keeping on" or "coming close." In addition, the leader checks to see if students are asking for help, and practices this if needed with particular students.

The group also checks on the goal class: where things are on a scale of 1 to 10 and how effective strategies and planner use are. The leader and the group give reinforcement for maintenance or progress.

Counseling Activity: The leader gives the students a square of paper and asks them to fold it so that it becomes a swan like the one the leader has. The leader urges students to go ahead and try to make the swan and encourages them to use some of the persistence strategies from the last session. It is unlikely that students will be successful, and so the leader explains that sometimes persistence is not enough. It is necessary to break a task down into pieces that can be accomplished one at a time. The leader then shows Handout 1.5, the directions for making the bird, and takes the students through the project step by step. If any student gets discouraged, the leader asks what strategies would help him/her persist. (Point out that this time it is easier to persist because you are working on the task one step at a time.)

Conclusion: The leader asks students to identify a school assignment they would like to improve. The group helps each student break it down into manageable tasks. The steps are written in the planner along with persistence strategies.

Assessment: The leader checks the goals and tasks as the students work on them.

Follow-up: Next time the students will report on the tasks in the assignment that they have accomplished during the week and tell which persistence strategies worked. The counselor could also ask teachers to take one assignment and break it into manageable steps for the whole class. Alternatively, the teacher could ask students how they would break an upcoming assignment into steps.

GROUP SESSION 6: WOW! LOOK AT ME: I'M SUCCESSFUL!

Academic Development Standard A: Students will acquire the attitudes, knowledge, and skills that contribute to effective learning in schools and across the life span.

Competency: Students will apply time-management and task-management skills.

Learning Objective: Students will review the strategies that they have to be successful students and will set new objectives for success.

Materials: Planner, small candy treats such as M & Ms, "I Know I Can Be A Success" sheet (Handout 1.6).

Activities

Introduction: The group will report on their success in the past week in breaking down assignments into manageable steps. Group members will report on their goal class and give a final rating of 1 to 10.

Counseling Activity: The school counselor says that today will be a review of how successful each student has been in their goal class and how much they understand about how to be a successful student. Students are given the "I Know I Can Be A Success" sheet (Handout 1.6) and asked to think about all of the strategies they used to move from their beginning number to today's number in the goal class. Students take turns identifying their strategies and writing it on the sheet as they identify it. To encourage students to share, each time they identify a strategy give them an M & M. The group keeps doing a go-round until the members run out of strategies.

The school counselor then asks the group to give each member some feedback on "what impressed me most about the successful strategies you use." As each member receives feedback, the leader can also add a piece of positive feedback.

Conclusion: The school counselor invites each student to look at a class where they have been a little less successful than in their goal class and to rate their performance in that class on a scale of 1 to 10. The counselor asks them to write out a goal for that class that will move them up one notch and put it in their planner. Then they choose two strategies they will use to achieve that change and write those in their planner. (The counselor and group check these for applicability.) The counselor points out that now that the group members have so many success strategies, they can use them to tackle any class where they want to improve.

Assessment: The counselor asks members to share what has meant the most to them during the group. Then, what will they take from the group that they will be able to use in school? Finally, members share how they have personally changed during the group.

Students fill out a final evaluation sheet (Handout 1.7).

INDIVIDUAL COUNSELING CONSIDERATIONS

At the end of the group process, all but six students were able to demonstrate mastery of the competencies. From her interaction with these students, Robin believed that they had personal/social issues that were interfering with their ability to master the competencies, so she decided to work individually with these students. There were also some students who were not appropriate for group whom Robin worked with individually. There seemed to be two major types of problems that Robin needed to deal with through individual counseling.

Student Type A: This student made some progress after group counseling, but had trouble generalizing the lessons from the one academic class focused on in the group session to other classes. Robin met with this type of student individually to help him or her apply the skills to all the classes where there were problems. She asked teachers to give immediate feedback to the student and to check the planner on a regular basis. Robin also looked at the student's planner and helped the student break down the assignments into manageable parts. In addition, Robin worked with the student's teachers to set up an accountability system with immediate feedback and frequent praise. With some students, Robin needed to give additional reinforcement when the student made progress, such as a check-in with her every Friday and occasionally a special lunch with her.

Student Type B: This type of student seemed to understand the concepts taught in classroom guidance and group, but did not apply them and seemed uninterested in doing so. It seemed likely that something else was going on with this student to affect motivation. Robin decided to have a counseling session to talk about personal issues concerning friends, family situation, or long-term goals with this type of student. For instance, the student's parents were fighting a lot and the student was so afraid the parents would divorce that the student could not concentrate in class. In this case, the student and counselor worked on the personal issues. Often just being able to talk about the problems lifted some of the burden. One strategy Robin used was to brainstorm ways the student could keep class work going while coping with these personal problems.

Another student with a similar personal problem was deliberately doing poorly academically to get parents to pay attention to her. In that case Robin held a conference with the student and parents to suggest ways the parents could focus on positive academic change. Robin also used the conference to discuss ways to help the student and parents deal with the issues together. Robin also made a referral to an outside agency for more extensive family counseling.

SYSTEM-FOCUSED INTERVENTIONS

While Robin was working to help all the ninth-grade students to master the prioritized student guidance competencies, she also looked at the possible systemic impact of the prioritized competencies. She worked with Principal Matthews to design professional development that helped faculty learn to more effectively teach students how to break tasks into manageable parts and how to create an environment that encourages greater student interaction with the teacher. Robin also facilitated a faculty discussion around the development of a whole-school program designed to help students consistently and efficiently use school planners.

CONCLUSION

School counselors play an important role in student achievement. Their knowledge and skills allow them to be significant contributors to the school improvement process. They are able to design their school counseling program with an emphasis on the guidance standards most likely to help students reach the school's academic achievement goals. In addition, through the facilitation of the development of focused interventions, they can work to lower barriers to learning being experienced by groups of students.

RESOURCES

Books

Davis, L., & Sirotowitz, S. (1996). *Study strategies made easy: A practical plan for school success.* Plantation, FL: Specialty Press.

Marshall, M., & Ford, W. (1994). *The secrets of getting better grades.* Indianapolis: Park Avenue Publications.

Silver, T. (1994). *Study smart: Hands-on, nuts-and-bolts techniques for earning higher grades.* New York: Random House, Villard Books.

Videos from Sunburst, Geneva, IL

You can succeed in school. A video and workbook for grades 3–5.
Student workshop: Study skills I; Study Skills II. Video and handouts for grades 5–9.

REFERENCES

American School Counselor Association (ASCA). (2003). *The ASCA National Model: A framework for school counseling programs.* Alexandria, VA: American School Counselor Association.

Bemak, F. (2000). Transforming the role of the counselor to provide leadership in educational reform. *Professional School Counseling, 3,* 323–331.

Borders, L. D., & Drury, S. M. (1992). Comprehensive school counseling programs: A view for policymakers and practitioners. *Journal of Counseling & Development, 70,* 487–498.

Brown, D. (1999). *Improving academic achievement: What school counselors can do. ERIC Digest* (Report No. EDO-CG-99-5). Greensboro, NC: ERIC Clearinghouse on Counseling and Student Services (ERIC Document Reproduction Service No. ED435895).

Campbell, C., & Dahir, C. (1997). *Sharing the vision: The national standards for school counseling programs.* Alexandria, VA: American School Counselor Association.

Education Trust, Inc. (1997). *Specific counseling skills necessary to transform the role of the school counselor for the 90's and beyond.* Washington, DC: Author. Retrieved June 29, 2001 from http://www.edtrust.org/main/school_counseling.asp#specific

Fields, T. H., & Hines, P. L. (2000). School counselor's role in raising student achievement. In G. Duhon and T. Manson, *Preparation, collaboration and emphasis on the family in school counseling for the new millennium.* Lewiston, NY: The Edwin Mellen Press.

Green, A., & Keys, S. (2001). Expanding the developmental school counseling paradigm: Meeting the needs of the 21st century student. *Professional School Counseling, 5,* 84–95.

Guerra, P. (1997). Virginia eliminates elementary school counseling requirement. *Counseling Today, 40,* 6, 1.

Gysbers, N. C., & Henderson, P. (2001). Comprehensive guidance and counseling programs: A rich history and a bright future. *Professional School Counseling, 4*(4), 246–256.

Hart, P. J., & Jacobi, M. (1992). *From gatekeeper to advocate: Transforming the role of the school counselor.* New York: College Entrance Examination Board.

Hines, P. L. (1998, November). *Raising student achievement through systemic guidance.* Paper presented at the annual meeting of the Education Trust, Washington, DC.

Hines, P. L., & Fields, T. H. (2002). Pregroup screening issues for school counselors. *Journal for Specialists in Group Work, 27,* 358–376.

Hines, P. L., & Reynolds, S. E. (2001, July). *Using data to facilitate systemic change.* Paper presented at the annual Education Trust, Transforming School Counseling Summer Academy, Atlanta, GA.

House, R. M., & Martin, P. J. (1998). Advocating for better futures for all students: A new vision for school counselors. *Education, 119,* 284–291.

Jerald, C. (2001, November). *Cooking with data: The inside scoop about how the Education Trust tells the achievement story.* Paper presented at the annual meeting of Education Trust, Washington, DC.

King, R. A., & Mathers, J. K. (1997). Improving schools through performance-based accountability and financial rewards. *Journal of Education Finance, 23,* 2, 47–76.

Lockwood, R. E., & McLean, J. E. (1997). Twenty-five years of data on educational funding and student achievement: What does it mean? *Educational Research Quarterly, 21*(2), 3–11.

Myrick, R. B. (1993). *Developmental guidance and counseling: A practical approach* (2nd ed.). Minneapolis, MN: Education Media Corporation.

Perry, N. S. (1992). *Educational reform and the school counselors. ERIC Digest* (Report No. EDO-CG-92-25). Ann Arbor, MI: ERIC Clearinghouse on Counseling and Personnel Services (ERIC Document Reproduction Service No. ED347491).

Otwell, P. S., & Mullis, F. (1997). Academic achievement and counselor accountability. *Elementary School Guidance & Counseling, 31,* 343–348.

Reynolds, S. E., & Hines, P. L. (2001a). *Guiding all kids: Systemic guidance for achievement focused schools* (2nd ed.). Bloomington, IN: American Student

Achievement Institute. Retrieved March 3, 2002 from the American Student Achievement Institute Web site: http://asai.indstate.edu

Reynolds, S. E., & Hines, P. L. (2001b). *Vision-to-Action: A Step-by-Step Activity Guide for Systemic Educational Reform* (6th ed.). Bloomington, IN: American Student Achievement Institute. Retrievable at http://asai.indstate.edu

Tucker, M. S., & Codding, J. B. (1998). *Standards for our schools: How to set them, measure them, and reach them.* San Francisco: Jossey Bass.

HANDOUT 1.1

SCENARIOS

Give one set of scenarios (an A, B and C) to each trio. Depending on the number of groups, some groups will have the same scenarios.

A. You have just gotten back your first test in this class, and you got a C-. As you look over your answers, you don't understand why some of them were marked wrong. You studied really hard and you think some of the wrong answers are right.

B. You have listened to the instructions for the _____ homework, but there is a part you just don't understand. You think you will sound stupid if you ask for help because the teacher spent a lot of time in class going over this concept.

C. You got a low grade on the last test and talked to the teacher about studying more effectively. You've turned in two homework assignments and have tried to answer questions in class, but you are not sure that the teacher thinks you are doing any better.

A. You have a test in two days and you are not sure what will be covered. Is the test over only the material in the book, or are class notes also included in the test?

B. The essay you wrote did not receive a good grade. Although you did not have any spelling or grammar errors, the teacher wrote that the writing was unclear and that you did not stay on the topic. You are still not sure what was so wrong about your paper.

C. You have been working on the current assignment for two days, but you aren't making much progress. You know you need help, but you are not sure what kind and how to proceed.

A. Your mom has really been on you to improve your grade in this class. She keeps asking when you will have some papers to show her. You've tried to explain that the tests are only once every two weeks, but that the teacher counts class participation and you have been participating. Your mom still isn't satisfied and wants to know how you are doing.

B. When you looked at your class notes, you noticed that they contradicted some of the things that are in the textbook. You would like to know if you got it wrong in your notes or if the teacher is really telling you something different from the book.

C. You've read the chapter twice and taken notes, but you still don't understand what's the most important stuff to know. Do you have to know everything in the chapter?

HANDOUT 1.2

Part 1:   Vad onskar ni?   Nagot annat?
          What would you like?   Anything else?

Part 2:   Jag ska be att fa lite lappstift, lite tval, lite tand-kraim, tack.
          I would like some lipstick, some soap, some toothpaste, please.

Part 3:   Jag ska be att fa en klubba, lite tuggummi, lite chokladbitars, tack.
          I would like a lollipop, some chewing gum, some chocolates, please.

HANDOUT 1.3

Part 1: Vad onskar ni?   Nagot annat?
         vad ern-skar nee   naw-got an-nat
         What would you like?   Anything else?

Part 2: Jag ska be att fa lite lappstift, lite tval, lite tand-kraim, tack.
         ya ska bay aht faw leeter lep-stift, leeter tvawl, leeter tand-kraim, tak.
         I would like some lipstick, some soap, some toothpaste, please.

Part 3: Jag ska be att fa en klubba, en tuggummi, lite chokladbitar, tack
         ya ska bay aht faw en kloob-ba, en toog-goom-mee, leeter shok-la-beetars, tak.
         I would like a lollipop, some chewing gum, some chocolates, please.

HANDOUT 1.4

SURVEY ON STUDY SKILLS

For this week's assignment of _____, please answer the following questions.

When did you start working on this assignment?

What strategies did you use to help you be successful?

How much time do you estimate that you spent each day on the assignment?

How did you use your planner to help you complete this assignment?

Thank you so much for your help!

HANDOUT 1.5

SWAN

1. Make a diagonal crease, then open the square so it lies flat.

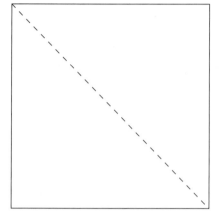

2. Fold two edges (dotted lines) into the center so it looks like 3.

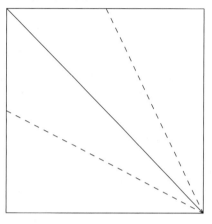

3.

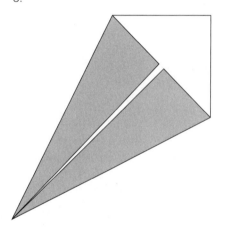

4. Fold the paper in half along the diagonal crease.

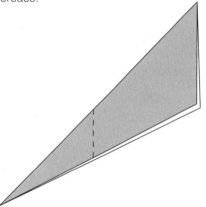

5. Reverse fold the front corner (along diagonal line in 4) so that it is raised like 5.

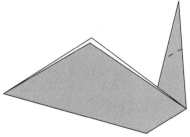

6. Reverse fold the top corner down to make the head.

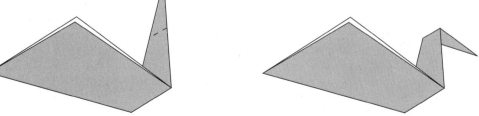

I KNOW

I CAN

BE

A

SUCCESS

IN

SCHOOL

.

SCHOOL SUCCESS GROUP EVALUATION

What was the rank (1 to 10) for your identified goal when you started? _____

What is the rank for your goal now? _____

List the strategies that were the most successful for you:

What are the new or extended ways that you use your planner to be help you be successful?

Check all the types of help you asked for in your goal class or other classes:

_____ Explain homework   _____ Explain class material

_____ Explain what's on a test   _____ Explain grade   _____ Ask for feedback

What are the things you do or tell yourself to keep working when things get hard in school?

What is the next goal for which you will use your new skills?

Improving Academic Achievement Through an Understanding of Learning Styles

Bradley T. Erford, Cheryl Moore-Thomas, and Shelley A. Mazzuca, Loyola College in Maryland

Introduction

With the enactment of federal school reform legislation (for example, Goals 2000, No Child Left Behind), professional school counselors are being called upon to support the academic mission of schools and are held accountable for student achievement more than ever before (Erford, 2003). This chapter provides an overview of the learning-style literature and activities to help students understand their special gifts, as well challenges. Helping students make this connection is key to the leadership and advocacy roles of the professional school counselor. The professional school counselor must take a leadership role to enhance student academic development. Developing faculty and student appreciation of learning strengths and challenges and advocating for students with diverse learning styles is a large part of this leadership role.

Literature Review

What Is a Learning Style?

The term *learning style* refers to the way individual students concentrate on, internalize, process, and retain information (Dunn & Dunn, 1992; 1993; 1999; Dunn, Dunn, & Perrin, 1994). Learning style is a single, important component of the learning process. When students engage in the learning process, their individual learning style interacts with other variables, including the structure and nature of the material to be learned and cognitive activities to process and understand the new information (University of Kansas School of Medicine–Wichita, 1997). While the full extent of biological and environmental contributions to one's learning style is unknown, it is estimated that more than 60 percent of one's learning style is biological, while less than 20 percent is developmental (Restak, 1979;

Thies, 1979). Accordingly, educators should determine and understand student learning styles, even during the elementary years. Learning styles represent learning strengths and weaknesses, and therefore it is more effective to adjust instructional strategies to address the learners' strengths than to relentlessly teach from the teacher's "teaching style" strength.

Numerous learning-style models and theories have been proposed over the past forty years, including reflective/impulsive learners; field dependence/independence; Gregorc's (1979) mindstyle characteristics; learning modalities (Barbe & Milone, 1980; 1981); learning-style elements (Dunn & Dunn, 1992; 1993; 1999); Kolb's (1976; 1984) model of experiential learning; and Gardner's (1993; 1999) theory of multiple intelligences. Together, these models represent a rather comprehensive backdrop from which to understand diverse learner strengths and weaknesses as well as to prepare curriculum to maximize learning. Convincing evidence has been compiled (see Dunn & Dunn, 1999, for a comprehensive summary of extant literature) documenting that teaching through students' learning styles can lead to increased academic achievement. Following are summaries of major theoretical models that have contributed to our understanding of learning style diversity. Table 2.1 also provides a brief summary of learning style models commonly found in the extant literature.

TABLE 2.1   SUMMARY OF SELECTED LEARNING STYLE MODELS

Model	Developer/Researcher	General Concepts
Reflective/impulsive		*Reflective:* Analyzers, *not* risk takers, prefer extra time. *Impulsive:* Risk takers, respond before thinking through thoroughly.
Field dependence/independence		*Field dependent:* Global thinkers, require strategies to comprehend and organize information. *Field independent:* Analytical thinkers, intrinsically motivated, work alone.
Mindstyle characteristics	Gregorc	*Abstract-sequential:* Decode symbols, visualize. *Abstract-random:* Use emotions and imagination in unstructured circumstances. *Concrete-sequential:* Need concrete materials and hands-on instruction. *Concrete-random:* Use trial-and-error, risk takers.
Experiental learning	Kolb	*Accomodators:* Active involvement in concrete situations. *Convergers:* Active experimentation. *Divergers:* Concrete learners who use imagination, reflection, and analysis. *Assimilators:* Abstract thinkers who prefer reflection and options.

(Continued)

TABLE 2.1   SUMMARY OF SELECTED LEARNING STYLE MODELS (CONTINUED)

Model	Developer/Researcher	General Concepts
Learning modalities	Barbe & Milone	Learning style preferences for visual, auditory, tactile, kinesthetic, smell, and taste stimulation. Three biggest categories include visual (learn by sight), auditory (learn by hearing), and tactile/kinesthetic (learn by doing).
Learning style	Dunn & Dunn	Learning is affected by environmental stimuli (sound, light, temperature, and design); emotional stimuli (motivation, persistence, responsibility and structure); sociological stimuli (perception, intake, time, and mobility), and psychological factors (global/analytical, hemisphericity, and impulsive/reflective).
Multiple intelligences	Gardner	Linguistic, logical-mathematical, spatial, bodily kinesthetic, interpersonal, intrapersonal, naturalist.

REFLECTIVE AND IMPULSIVE LEARNERS

Reiff (1992) reported that learning styles have been classified as either reflective or impulsive. *Reflective learners* tend to analyze information and tend not to take risks. Indeed, they often choose not to respond until they are certain of an answer or required to respond. Allowing them to thoroughly examine their learning material and proof their work helps them. Reflective learners' anxiety tends to be lessened when engaging in cooperative learning, learning more efficient test-taking procedures, and being shown that risk taking is a natural process (Reiff, 1992).

Impulsive learners tend to respond before thinking something through thoroughly and have a high capacity for risk taking. Reducing environmental distractions, increasing bodily-kinesthetic activities, and rewarding delayed, thoughtful behavior helps them. Impulsive learners also benefit if instructors structure material and time into smaller segments and provide specific directions and guidelines, especially when the directions require more than one step (Reiff, 1992).

FIELD DEPENDENCE AND FIELD INDEPENDENCE

Field dependence learning style models describe how students, faced with complex problem-solving situations, learn and memorize information (Reiff, 1992). *Field dependent* students are global thinkers who benefit from cooperative learning and require strategies and models for how to organize and comprehend information.

They have difficulty isolating a shape from its surroundings (that is, figure-ground) and experience great difficulty when faced with crowded information and worksheets. Field dependent students find outlines and summaries helpful, as well as tips on how to organize and analyze information. Teacher modeling appears to be very effective.

Field independent students are analytical, cognitively flexible, and intrinsically motivated, and prefer working alone. They have little difficulty isolating a shape from its surroundings and do fine on worksheets and independent mastery programming.

GREGORC'S MINDSTYLE CHARACTERISTICS

Gregorc (1979; Gregorc & Butler, 1984) posited that students basically think along two continua: abstract-concrete and sequential-random. When these two continua are juxtaposed (see Figure 2.1), four "mindstyles" emerge. *Abstract-sequential* students learn by decoding written, verbal, and imagery symbols; listening; and visualizing. *Abstract-random* students learn by using their emotions and imagination through holistic, unstructured learning experiences, group discussions, and "mind webs." *Concrete-sequential* students learn through direct and hands-on instruction in a quiet atmosphere, using concrete materials. *Concrete-random* students learn through divergent experimentation, trial and error, and risk taking.

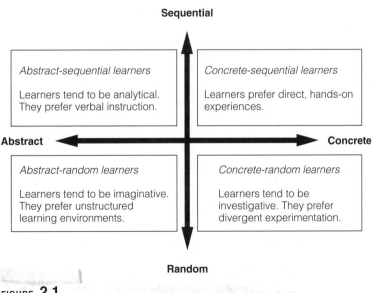

FIGURE 2.1

GREGORC'S MINDSTYLE CHARACTERISTICS

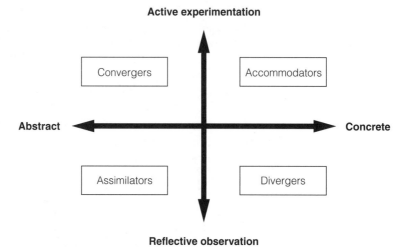

FIGURE 2.2
KOLB'S EXPERIENTIAL LEARNING MODEL

KOLB'S EXPERIENTIAL LEARNING MODEL

Kolb's model of experiential learning (1976; 1984) also juxtaposes two continua: abstract conceptualization–concrete experience; and active experimentation–reflective observation, to arrive at four styles of learning he referred to as accommodators, divergers, assimilators, and convergers (see Figure 2.2). *Accommodators* require active involvement in concrete situations; rely on trial and error; prefer unstructured, experiential learning; and rely on information from others. *Convergers* require active experimentation, constantly test the practical relevance of ideas, and insist on applying theories to practical situations to see how they hold up. *Divergers* require concrete learning situations and use imagination, reflection, and analysis from varying viewpoints. *Assimilators* thrive in abstract situations, prefer reflection and choices to single perspectives, and love to create theoretical models.

LEARNING MODALITIES

Learning modalities are channels through which information is received, given, and stored. These modalities include visual, auditory, tactile, kinesthetic, smell, and taste. Estimates are that in any given classroom, approximately 25–30 percent of students are primarily visual learners (learn by seeing), 25–30 percent are primarily auditory learners (learn by hearing), 15 percent are primarily tactile/kinesthetic learners (learn by doing), and 25–30 percent are of mixed modalities (Barbe & Milone, 1980; 1981).

Obviously, no single-modality instructional approach is likely to reach all students. A modality-based instructional approach simultaneously addressing the learning styles of visual, auditory, and kinesthetic learners is preferable.

LEARNING STYLE ELEMENTS

The learning style elements model, proposed by Dunn and Dunn (1992; 1993; 1999), describes numerous factors that affect how well one learns. Learning style elements include environmental stimuli, emotional stimuli, sociological stimuli, physiological stimuli, and psychological factors.

Each of the five stimuli of the model contains components called elements. Sound, light, temperature, and design are the elements of the *environmental stimuli*. As preferences for these elements are met, an individual's ability to master new and difficult academic information increases. For example, one student may prefer a quiet study room, and another student may study best in a room with low background music. Bright lights may be helpful to some individuals, but others study best with subdued or task lighting. Additionally, meeting individual preferences for temperature and seating (relaxed/comfortable vs. formal) maximizes learning abilities.

Emotional stimuli of the Dunn and Dunn (1992; 1993; 1999) model include motivation, persistence, responsibility, and structure. Although an individual's preference or need for these elements may vary depending on the given situation, the best results come from considering the level of motivation, willingness to persist, desire to conform (responsibility), and need for structure.

The *sociological stimuli* refer to preferences for learning independently, with peers, with an authority figure, or in varied groupings. Individuals who need to process information independently, for example, may actually decrease their ability to take in new and difficult information if forced to work with a group. Conversely, working alone may diminish the learning of those who benefit from group or paired learning experiences. However, some like to learn in a variety of groupings in a variety of ways, such as learning from an authority figure in one situation and from peers in another.

Perceptual preferences, time, intake, and mobility elements make up the *physiological stimuli*. Perceptual preferences determine whether an individual best learns new and difficult information auditorily, visually, tactually (handling manipulatives), or kinesthetically (moving the body). Perceptual preferences also include recognition of one's best time of day for learning. Some individuals refer to themselves as "morning people," "afternoon people," or "evening people," indicating the time of day they are most able to master new material. The intake element describes the need to eat or drink while concentrating. Many adults actually study more effectively when they eat or drink while working (Dunn & Dunn, 1999). Mobility, the final element, refers to the preference for periodic or consistent movement during the learning process. Examples include people who learn through movement and those who prefer to sit while learning but must have the ability to move or change the position of their seat from time to time.

The *psychological stimuli* elements of the Dunn and Dunn (1992; 1993; 1999) model are global versus analytical processing, hemisphericity, and impulsivity versus reflectivity. Global learners process information in large chunks. Often they absorb information randomly and suddenly "get it." Analytic learners gain information step by step, building competence as they go. Research suggests that these preferences for learning correlate with right- and left-brain processing or hemisphericity (Dunn & Dunn, 1999). Finally, although most learners can be both impulsive and reflective at times, many tend to learn new, difficult material best either through impulsive, or active, learning, which requires asking questions, solving problems, or making applications, or through reflective learning, which involves quiet, independent study and large amounts of think or response time.

MULTIPLE INTELLIGENCES

While Gardner would argue that there is a difference between multiple intelligences and learning styles, his theory is helpful in understanding the way students approach learning tasks and in identifying learning strengths and weaknesses. Gardner's theory (1993; 1999; 2000) highlights eight areas in which a student can demonstrate intelligence. *Linguistic intelligence* requires the capacity for using language (native or otherwise) to understand and express ideas. Students with strength in linguistic intelligence often enjoy reading and writing and generally have highly developed language and memory skills. *Logical-mathematical intelligence* requires an understanding of how to use numbers, mathematical operations, or logical, cause-and-effect relationships to solve complex problems. Students with strong logical-mathematical intelligence tend to excel in math, logical reasoning, and scientific experimentation. *Spatial intelligence* requires the ability to represent the spatial world internally in the mind. Spatially intelligent students are usually good at map reading, puzzles, and art activities. *Musical intelligence* involves the capacity to think musically, particularly the ability to hear, recognize, remember, and perhaps even manipulate patterns of sounds. The musically intelligent often excel at composing, playing instruments, singing, and rhythmic memory. *Bodily-kinesthetic intelligence* requires the ability to use one's body (all or parts) to solve complex movement problems. Students with strengths in the bodily kinesthetic area generally enjoy hands-on and eye-hand-coordination activities. *Interpersonal intelligence* involves an understanding of how to relate to other people and solve interpersonal problems. Interpersonally intelligent people enjoy social activities and relationships, and understand the perspectives of others. *Intrapersonal intelligence* involves understanding one's own internal motivations, strengths, and weaknesses. These students are often self-confident, self-motivated, and independent. The *naturalist intelligence* requires an ability to classify and discriminate among objects. Students high in the naturalist intelligence enjoy interacting with plants and animals, and recognizing and classifying objects. Gardner (2000, p. 60) appears poised to add a ninth intelligence, *existential,* which involves a "concern with 'ultimate' issues."

In recent years, Gardner's theory of multiple intelligences has enjoyed growing acceptance. Implications for classroom instruction have changed the way some educators approach and structure curriculum and student learning (Brualdi, 1998). The practicality and flexibility of the theory appears to appeal to many involved in education. The theory is not without controversy, however. Williams (2000) suggested that a critical perspective of the theory is warranted, given the subjectivity or arbitrary nature of Gardner's designated areas of intelligence. Future research on multiple intelligences may answer these questions regarding the conceptual framework of the theory. Future study may also provide additional empirical support.

WHOLE-SCHOOL INTERVENTIONS

This workshop is a professional school counselor leadership activity with faculty, administration, staff, and parents. It involves an experiential introductory lesson on multiple intelligences for the adults who are important in the students' lives. The workshop can be used for educator or parent training at the elementary, middle, or high school level. The lesson requires about forty-five minutes, and professional school counselors are encouraged to modify the PowerPoint slides and activities as necessary to individualize the presentation to their school community, and make it even more engaging.

UNDERSTANDING A STUDENT'S MULTIPLE INTELLIGENCES

Academic Standard A: Adults will acquire the attitudes, knowledge, and skills that contribute to effective learning in school and across the life span.

Competencies: Adults will identify attitudes and behaviors that lead to successful learning and will apply knowledge of learning styles to positively influence school performance.

Learning Objective: After attending an experiential lesson on multiple intelligences, adults will gain an understanding of students' learning styles and the learning approaches each may benefit from.

Materials: PowerPoint slides (projector, computer setup), handouts of the PowerPoint slides (see Handout 2.1), ten toothpicks per participant.

Developmental Learning Activities

Introduction: The school counselor, begins by explaining that many students have different learning strengths and weaknesses. For example, some students like to work alone, others in groups; some would rather think in silence, others out loud; some like to act out how something works, others would rather draw a diagram or picture. Next, solicit several examples of learning strengths from adults (this allows a connection to be made between the current objective and previous knowledge).

Activity: Use the PowerPoint slides to lead a discussion of the multiple intelligences. Directions for the activities in Slides 3, 5, and 7 follow.

Activity, Slide 3: "When I say go, you will have one minute to use these letters to make as many real words as you can. However, to make these words you must use only the letters from boxes that touch each other—whether beside, on top of, or diagonal to. For example, notice on the top line that A and S are beside each other and when combined form the word 'AS.' Likewise, notice that the letters on the bottom two lines can be combined to form the word 'G-R-I-P.' So long as the boxes are touching, you can combine the letters. Any questions?" Answer any questions. Then say, "You have one minute. *Go*—as fast as you can." After one minute say, "Stop. Now give yourself one point for each letter of each real word. For example, 'AS' is worth two points and 'GRIP' is worth four points. Then add up the total number of points you have." Wait a minute for the participants to tabulate. "How many have more than twenty points? Thirty points? Forty points? Fifty points? This is a task that requires word knowledge, flexibility, and verbal ability." Continue to discuss their performance.

Activity, Slide 5: Tell the participants that they will be asked to solve a problem using logic. Read the information from Slide 5 and allow several minutes for participants to determine the answer. Ask participants to discuss the methods they used to arrive at the solution.

Activity, Slide 7: Provide ten toothpicks to each participant. Have them arrange the toothpicks so that the toothpicks look just like the house on Slide 7. Say, "Notice how the house is facing to the left. Now, moving only two toothpicks, change the design so that the house is facing in the opposite direction." After several minutes, have the participants discuss how they accomplished the task.

Conclusion: Lead adults in a brief discussion of the interests and skills related to the intelligences discussed. Challenge the adults to describe what each has done to develop these abilities in themselves and students and what each could do to develop these skills to even higher levels in the future.

Assessment: At the end of the session, have each participant think of at least one student with whom they are familiar and, in writing, identify the student's top two intelligences and at least three strategies they would use to help that student learn more efficiently.

Follow-up: In the future, have adults share what they have been doing to improve student achievement using the new information and strategies.

CLASSROOM GUIDANCE ACTIVITIES

These three classroom lessons increase students' awareness of learning styles in general and enable students to understand their own learning styles in order to experience academic success. These lessons are suitable for either upper elementary, middle, or high school settings.

LESSON 1: WHAT KIND OF LEARNER ARE YOU?

Academic Development Standard A: Students will acquire the attitudes, knowledge, and skills that contribute to effective learning in school and across the life span.

Academic Development Standard B: Students will complete school with the academic preparation essential to choose from a wide range of substantial postsecondary options, including college.

Competencies: Students will apply knowledge of learning styles to positively influence school performance and will articulate feelings of competence and confidence as a learner.

Learning Objectives: (1) After completing an inventory, 80 percent of the students will be able to identify his or her primary intelligence. (2) After comparing the results of the interest inventory to a specific learning situation, 80 percent of the students will be able to describe how a student's primary intelligences affect classroom success.

Materials: Pencils; Teele Inventory of Multiple Intelligences (Teele, 1992) (or TEEN-MIDAS, Shearer, 1994, for teenagers); a preselected short story or passage of information that is difficult to remember; overhead projector and screen; overheads of the objectives and the inventory; overhead "Class Profile of Primary Intelligences" (see Handout 2.2); homework worksheet "What Kind of Learner Am I?" (see Handout 2.3) for each student.

Developmental Learning Activity

Introduction: The school counselor begins the lesson by having a student read the objectives out loud to the class. Discussion should include a demonstration in which the facilitator reads a short story with information that is difficult to remember and asks the class questions about the story. As the students answer the questions the facilitator prompts them by asking, "How could I have made it easier for you to understand and remember details about the story?" or "If you were the classroom teacher, how would you teach this information to a class and why?" This will lead into a short discussion about multiple intelligences.

Activity: The students individually complete and score a multiple intelligences inventory in order to identify their own primary intelligences. On completion of the inventory, students break into small groups and identify and discuss ways in which each student's own primary intelligence provides a benefit in the classroom. Each student then writes a one-paragraph essay on how their primary intelligences affect their academic achievement. Assign the "What Kind of Learner Am I?" (Handout 2.3) worksheet for homework.

Conclusion: As a class, complete the overhead entitled "Class Profile of Primary Intelligences" (Handout 2.2) by listing each student's name underneath their primary intelligence. This will allow students to see the dynamics of the class and identify various student intelligences or styles of learning.

Assessment: Students complete the "What Kind of Learner Am I" worksheet (Handout 2.3) for homework. It asks the student's own primary intelligence, ways in which an intelligence enables success in the classroom, and identification of some limitation and/or difficulties that the student's primary intelligence may have created. If 80 percent of students can identify their own primary intelligence and accurately describe how one's primary intelligence affects one's academic success, the objectives will be met.

Follow-up: The follow-up to this lesson is a discussion about the homework and a review of the class profile. This discussion is the introduction to the second lesson.

LESSON 2: LEARNING ABOUT LEARNING STYLES

Academic Development Standard A: Students will acquire the attitudes, knowledge, and skills that contribute to effective learning in school and across the life span.

Academic Development Standard B: Students will complete school with the academic preparation essential to choose from a wide range of substantial postsecondary options, including college.

Competencies: Students will use knowledge of learning styles to positively influence school performance and will become self-directed and independent learners.

Learning Objective: After completing a graphic organizer, students will be able to provide at least one descriptive word for six of the eight intelligences.

Materials: Overhead projector and screen; overheads of the objective(s), class profile, graphic organizer, and homework worksheet; graphic organizer handout for each student (see Handout 2.4); handouts describing the eight intelligences (see Handout 2.5).

Developmental Learning Activities

Introduction: As a class, read and review the lesson's objectives. Next, discuss the answers to the homework (Handout 2.3, "What Kind of Learner Am I?"), which will be a follow-up and review of the information learned in the previous lesson. Then define the term "learning style" and write it for all students to see (see the text presented earlier in this chapter).

Activities: Each student will receive a graphic organizer (see Handout 2.4). As a class, discuss and name the eight intelligences and label them in the graphic organizer. Next, the class breaks into small groups of students with the same learning style. Once in the group, they discuss the strengths and weaknesses of their own learning style. The students fill in the web with their list of strengths and weaknesses. As a class, discuss each of the groups' findings and complete the web. This gives a second chance for students to add more information to their graphic organizer. After the activity, hand out previously prepared worksheets that describe the eight intelligences (Handout 2.5). Students read and highlight the important facts on the worksheets.

Conclusion: As a class, reflect on what was covered on the overheads about the different intelligences. Select several statements that describe one particular ability, and ask the class to identify which intelligence the statement describes.

Assessment: Collect the web graphic organizer. If 80 percent of the students have listed at least one descriptive word for six of the eight intelligences, the objective is met.

Follow-up: Review this information at the beginning of the next session to help students understand the link between multiple intelligence strengths and academic performance.

LESSON 3: WORKING ON MY STYLE

Academic Development Standard A: Students will acquire the attitudes, knowledge, and skills that contribute to effective learning in school and across the life span.

Academic Development Standard B: Students will complete school with the academic preparation essential to choose from a wide range of substantial postsecondary options, including college.

Competencies: Students will apply knowledge of learning styles to positively influence school performance and will become self-directed and independent learners.

Learning Objectives: (1) After completing the "How to Improve My Style" worksheet (Handout 2.6), 80 percent of students will be able to identify at least two ways to improve on their learning strengths and two ways to compensate for a learning weakness. (2) After completing the "How to Improve My Style" worksheet (Handout 2.6), 80 percent of students will be able to set one goal to improve academic success.

Materials: Overhead projector and screen, overhead of Handout 2.6, "How to Improve My Style," a copy of "How to Improve My Style" for each student.

Developmental Learning Activities

Introduction: As a class, read aloud the objectives and summarize the activities from the previous session.

Activity: Hand out the worksheet "How to Improve My Style" (Handout 2.6) and refer to your overhead as you give instructions on how to complete it. Students then complete the worksheet by identifying ways to improve the strengths and weaknesses they observed in their graphic organizer. This will increase students' awareness of how to increase academic success. Discuss how one's primary intelligences affect school performance. Then instruct students to write on the bottom of the worksheet one goal that will help to improve their academic performance.

Conclusion: Summarize the objectives, activities, and lessons from all three sessions. Explain how constant evaluation of one's strengths and weaknesses, successes and challenges, can lead to increased academic performance and successful goal attainment.

Assessment: Collect and score the student worksheets to determine whether 80 percent of students were able to identify at least two ways to improve on their learning strengths and two ways to compensate for a learning weakness, as well as whether 80 percent of students were able to set at least one goal to improve their academic success. If so, the objectives were met.

Follow-up: Continue to collaborate with teachers to enhance use of the knowledge gained to help students achieve school success.

SMALL-GROUP COUNSELING PLANS

The following lessons make up a small counseling group unit for upper elementary, middle, or high school students. These lessons should be used with groups of six to eight students, referred or self-referred, interviewed, and selected by the professional school counselor to participate in group counseling for increasing academic success through awareness and use of appropriate learning styles. Each session addresses Academic Development Standards A and B and should last about forty-five minutes.

GROUP SESSION 1: LEARNING STYLES: WHAT'S UP WITH THAT?

Academic Development Standard A: Students will acquire the attitudes, knowledge, and skills that contribute to effective learning in school and across the life span.

Academic Development Standard B: Students will complete school with the academic preparation essential to choose from a wide range of substantial postsecondary options, including college.

Competencies: Students will use learning styles to positively influence school performance, identify attitudes and behaviors that lead to successful learning, and share knowledge.

Learning Objectives: (1) Upon completion of this lesson, 80 percent of students will be able to define "learning style" in age-appropriate terms. (2) Upon completion of this lesson, 80 percent of students will describe at least one important facet of each of the five elements of learning style in accordance with the Dunn and Dunn (1992) conceptualization. (See the introduction of this chapter for a brief review of the learning style elements.)

Materials: Chart paper, markers, lined paper, drawing paper, pencils, crayons, handouts of learning style elements (see Handout 2.7).

Activities

Introduction

1. Welcome the students to the group. Brainstorm and chart group rules, including rules of confidentiality.
2. Ask students to imagine they have an upcoming test. How might they best prepare for the test if they really wanted to do well? Discuss the various strategies and factors the students suggest. Link common responses so that the students begin to see their commonalities and feel connected to other group members.
3. Suggest that the various factors and strategies the students suggested are clues to the ways they learn best. Introduce the topic of learning styles. As appropriate, include the following, highlighting items c and d:
   a. Learning style is the way each person processes, internalizes, and retains new and difficult academic information (Dunn & Dunn, 1992; 1993).
   b. Learning style is a set of personal characteristics that makes some ways of learning more effective than others (Doolan & Honigsfeld, 2000).
   c. Accommodating individual learning style preferences results in increased academic achievement (Dunn, Griggs, Olsen, Gorman, & Beasley, 1995).
   d. Learning style is affected by five basic stimuli: environmental, emotional, sociological, physiological, and psychological (Dunn & Dunn, 1992; 1993).
      i. Environmental elements include needs or preferences for sound, light, temperature, and seating.
      ii. Emotional elements include needs for motivation, persistence, responsibility, and structure.
      iii. Sociological elements include needs or preferences for learning alone, paired, with a group of peers, in a team, from an authority figure, or in a variety of groups.
      iv. Physiological elements include needs to be exposed to new information through one's strongest perceptual modality first, food intake requirements, time of day, and mobility preferences.
      v. Psychological elements include analytic versus global processing and hemisphericity (right and left brain).

Counseling Activity: Give each student a piece of lined paper and pencil, point to the written questions on the chart paper (write the questions before the session starts), and ask each to provide a written response:

1. What is a learning style?
2. What is at least one important element of each of the five basic stimuli: environmental, emotional, sociological, physiological, and psychological?

Collect the papers when the students have finished.

Give each student a piece of drawing paper. Have the students title the paper "My Learning Style." Have students begin a drawing of their ideal study environment. Students should consider light, temperature, and seating preferences. Use a go-around technique to allow students to share their drawings and feelings regarding their ideal study environment. Link comments and feelings as appropriate.

Conclusion: Discuss the following:

> What did you learn today about learning styles?
> How do you feel about what you discovered about your learning style?
> What was it like for you to hear from the other group members?
> How might you use what you learned about your environmental elements of learning style to help you in your classes?

Assessment: Score student responses to the questions in the first part of the activity. If 80 percent of the students answered correctly, the objective is met.

Follow-up: For homework, ask students to complete drawings of learning style preferences for the remaining four stimuli. (Prepare a handout with the essential facets of the emotional, sociological, physiological, and psychological elements.) These drawings will be shared next session.

GROUP SESSION 2: I'VE GOT STYLE!

Academic Development Standard A: Students will acquire the attitudes, knowledge, and skills that contribute to effective learning in school and across the life span.

Academic Development Standard B: Students will complete school with the academic preparation essential to choose from a wide range of substantial postsecondary options, including college.

Competencies: Students will use knowledge of learning styles to positively influence school performance, articulate feelings of competence and confidence as a learner, identify attitudes and behaviors that lead to successful learning, and share knowledge.

Learning Objective: After completing the learning styles questionnaire (Handout 2.8), 80 percent of students will identify at least three personal learning style elemental preferences (Dunn & Dunn, 1992).

Materials: Pencils, learning styles questionnaires (see Handout 2.8).

Activities

Introduction/Review: Welcome the students to the group. Review group rules, including rules of confidentiality. Ask group members to briefly summarize the first session. Ask students to share drawings of learning style elemental preferences. Allow students to pass if they are not comfortable sharing. Allow students to identify whom they would like to hear from next. Model socialization techniques through appropriate feedback. Link responses as appropriate to encourage universality.

Counseling Activity: Discuss with students that they began to explore learning styles through their own reflection and drawings. Let students know they can also learn more about learning style preferences through various assessments, including self-assessment. Discuss how responses to questions can help students gain more insight about how they learn.

Let students explore their learning style preferences using the learning styles questionnaire (Handout 2.8). Explain that the questionnaire is related to some of the elements of learning style that the group discussed last session. Students should work independently to complete the self-assessment. Emphasize that the questionnaire is not a test, but a tool to help the group members learn more about their individual learning styles. Use a go-around technique and ask each student to identify at least three personal learning style preferences.

Conclusion: Discuss the following:

> How do you feel about what you discovered about your learning style? Did you learn anything new about yourself or others?
> What was it like for you to hear from the other group members?
> How might you use what you learned about your learning style to help you in your classes?

Assessment: Assessment of students should be made via responses to the go-around questions in the activity. If 80 percent of the students can identify at least three personal learning style preferences, the objective is met.

Follow-up: Ask students to continue to think about the work of the group between sessions. The next group session will begin with members' reflections.

GROUP SESSION 3: STYLE POWER

Academic Development Standard A: Students will acquire the attitudes, knowledge, and skills that contribute to effective learning in school and across the life span.

Academic Development Standard B: Students will complete school with the academic preparation essential to choose from a wide range of substantial postsecondary options, including college.

Competencies: Students will use knowledge of learning styles to positively influence school performance, articulate feelings of competence and confidence as a learner, identify attitudes and behaviors that lead to successful learning, and share knowledge.

Learning Objective: After the creation of a learning style art project, 80 percent of the students will express at least one feeling regarding knowledge about their learning style.

Materials: Drawing paper, markers, notebook paper, clay, pencils, glue, scissors, colored paper, and crayons.

Activities

Introduction/Review: Welcome the students to the group. Review group rules, including rules of confidentiality. Ask group members to briefly summarize last session. Discuss the thoughts and feelings group members had regarding the last session: What did they learn about their individual learning style? What thoughts and feelings emerged since the last session?

Counseling Activity: Connect statements regarding positive feelings about intrapersonal and interpersonal learning. Allow group members to share how others would know when they feel good about their learning.

Ask group members to create "a work of art" that shows how they feel about their learning and what they have learned about their learning style. Members may choose to write a poem, draw a picture, create a rap, compose a song, put together a step or dance routine, or make a sculpture. The form of expression is the student's choice. Allow students to work independently on their projects for twenty to twenty-five minutes. In a go-around technique, encourage members to share their projects and feelings about their learning style with the group.

Conclusion: Discuss the following:

> How did you feel working on your project?
> How do you feel knowing that you have a special way that you learn best?
> How do you feel knowing that your group members also have special ways they learn best?
> How might you use what occurred in group to help you in your classes?
> How might what occurred in group help you to become an empowered student?

Assessment: Accomplishment of the learning objective is completed during the go-around in the activity. If 80 percent of the students express feelings regarding their learning styles, the objective is met.

Follow-up: Follow the students' self-disclosure with recognition of positive feelings and hopefulness. Initiate a discussion of the possibility of improved academic performance now that students know how they learn best.

GROUP SESSION 4: MONITORING MY LEARNING STYLE

Academic Development Standard A: Students will acquire the attitudes, knowledge, and skills that contribute to effective learning in school and across the life span.

Academic Development Standard B: Students will complete school with the academic preparation essential to choose from a wide range of substantial postsecondary options, including college.

Competencies: Students will use knowledge of learning styles to positively influence school performance, articulate feelings of competence and confidence as a learner, identify attitudes and behaviors that lead to successful learning, and share knowledge.

Learning Objective: After successfully completing the learning styles worksheet (see Handout 2.9), 80 percent of students will describe how use of their dominant learning preferences can affect their academic performance.

Materials: Pencils, learning styles worksheets (Handout 2.9), and learning styles homework (Handout 2.10) sheets for each student.

Activities

Introduction/Review: Welcome the students to the group. Review group rules. Ask group members to briefly summarize last session. Use a go-around technique to have students share their works of art again.

Link feelings and commonalities among learning style preferences as appropriate. Emphasize common realizations and feelings. Model appropriate feedback. Encourage students to provide positive feedback.

Counseling Activity: Ask students how they follow or are able to accommodate their learning preferences in the classroom or at home. Have students consider when it is possible to follow preferences and when it is not. Have students share their thinking on ways they can incorporate their preferences into their daily learning. Discourage advice giving. Allow students to come up with their own possibilities.

Pass out the learning styles worksheet (see Handout 2.9). Ask students to identify one new way they can honor their learning preference. Each student should complete the following: "Because I now know I learn best . . . I will. . . ." Sample statements: "Because I now know I learn best by taking a few short breaks, I will take a stretch break every twenty minutes while doing my math homework" or "Because I now know I learn best by working with a partner, I will study my weekly vocabulary words with my friend, Carla." Encourage students to make the statements specific and doable. Using a go-around technique, have students share their responses on the learning style worksheet.

Conclusion: Discuss the following:

Are you willing to try to honor your learning preference? Explain.
How do you feel about your plan?
How do you feel now compared to how you felt at the beginning of the group?

Assessment: During the go-around, evaluate the accuracy of student responses to the learning styles worksheet. If 80 percent of students provide an accurate response, the objective is met.

Follow-up: For homework, ask students to write a brief note on their learning styles homework (see Handout 2.10) each time during the next week that they honor their preference as specified in their statement. Notes should include the event, the student's feelings, and the result/consequence. During the next session the group will review and discuss implementation of their plans.

GROUP SESSION 5: LEARNING WITH STYLE!

Academic Development Standard A: Students will acquire the attitudes, knowledge, and skills that contribute to effective learning in school and across the life span.

Academic Development Standard B: Students will complete school with the academic preparation essential to choose from a wide range of substantial postsecondary options, including college.

Competencies: Students will use knowledge of learning styles to positively influence school performance, articulate feelings of competence and confidence as a learner, identify attitudes and behaviors that lead to successful learning, and share knowledge.

Learning Objective: After completing the learning styles homework, 80 percent of students will be able to describe how their learning style preferences affect academic performance.

Materials: Pencils, learning styles worksheet (see Handout 2.9), and learning styles homework (see Handout 2.10) sheets for each student.

Activities

Introduction/Review: Welcome the students to the group. Review group rules. Remind students that group will be ending next session. Introduce the issue of termination. Ask group members to briefly summarize last session.

Counseling Activity: Use a go-around technique to have students share their experiences with their learning styles homework. Link feelings and commonalities among experiences.

Focus group sharing on the transfer of group learnings to academic settings. Use open questions to assist the group in articulating the connection between honoring learning style preferences and academic achievement.

Allow students to complete a second learning styles worksheet (see Handout 2.9) utilizing insight regarding a different stimuli preference. But this time have each student add a statement about how their learning style preference affects their academic performance. Use a go-around technique to have students share their second learning styles worksheet.

For homework, again ask students to write a brief note on the learning styles homework worksheet each time during the next week that they honor their preferences as specified in their two statements (last and current session). Notes should include the event, the student's feelings, and the result/consequence.

Ask the group for permission to consult with classroom teachers about the group members' learning style preferences. This should be done in order to support the group members' academic progress. Assure members that only preferences will be shared. Confidential group information will not be disclosed.

Conclusion: Discuss the following:

> How might what occurred in group help you to become a more confident learner?
> How might what occurred in group help you to become a more competent learner?
> How do you feel about your learning?

Assessment: The learning objective is accomplished when students complete the second learning styles worksheet and during the go-around. If 80 percent of students are able to describe how their learning styles preferences affect their academic performance, the objective is met.

Follow-up: Next session the group will review and discuss implementation of their plans. The professional school counselor will consult with group members' teachers to inform them of each member's learning style preferences.

GROUP SESSION 6: CELEBRATE LEARNING STYLE!

Academic Standard A: Students will acquire the attitudes, knowledge, and skills that contribute to effective learning in school and across the life span.

Academic Development Standard B: Students will complete school with the academic preparation essential to choose from a wide range of substantial postsecondary options, including college.

Competencies: Students will use knowledge of learning styles to positively influence school performance, articulate feelings of competence and confidence as a learner, identify attitudes and behaviors that lead to successful learning, and share knowledge.

Learning Objective: After group discussion, 80 percent of students will be able to describe how awareness of learning style preferences affected their academic self-confidence.

Materials: Snacks, group member certificates (see Handout 2.11), evaluation forms (see Handout 2.12).

Activities

Introduction/Review: Welcome the students to the group. Review group rules. Remind students that this is the last session. Discuss termination and members' feelings regarding leaving the group.

Counseling Activity: Allow group members to share their experiences and feelings regarding implementation of their learning styles worksheet. Share with the group the contact made with classroom teachers. Highlight any positive responses to group activities.

In a go-around, have each student share how knowing about their personal learning style preferences has affected their self-confidence as a learner. Ask members to share one thing they learned from each group member or one thing they appreciate about each member. Encourage members to address their comments directly to each other. Minimize counselor intervention during this group sharing time.

Then, as the professional school counselor, share one thing that you have learned from or appreciate about each group member. Distribute a participation certificate to each member (see Handout 2.11), complete the group evaluation form (see Handout 2.12), and share snacks.

Conclusion: Discuss the following:

How did it feel to hear positive feedback from the group members?
What did you learn from this group experience?

What will you take with you from this group experience?

How do you feel about yourself as a learner now? Is this different than at the beginning of the group? In what way?

How do you feel about the group members as learners? Is this different than at the beginning of the group? In what way?

Assessment: Assessment of the objective is accomplished in the go-around. As the students are conducting the go-around, determine whether 80 percent of students are able to describe how awareness of learning style preferences affected their academic self-confidence.

Follow-up: Analyze data from the summative evaluation forms.

INDIVIDUAL COUNSELING CONSIDERATIONS

Table 2.2 provides suggested strategies for counseling individuals according to their primary learning styles (summarized from Griggs, 1985, and Hall & Lundberg, in press). A list of Internet resources in the learning styles area appears at the end of the chapter.

TABLE 2.2 SUGGESTED STRATEGIES FOR LEARNING STYLE COUNSELING

Element	Suggested Strategies
Emotionality	For those requiring increased structure and motivation, use behavioral approaches, initiate and provide concrete solutions, and follow up frequently. For those requiring less structure, use person-centered approaches.
Sociological	For those who prefer to work alone or in groups, use individual and group counseling approaches respectively. For those preferring group-oriented work, use peer groups and role playing.
Physiological	Auditory learners prefer to repeat words, recall conversations, and use talking approaches to counseling. Visual learners think using images and pictures and prefer written materials, observation, and imagery. Using books and videos may be helpful. Tactile/kinesthetic learners prefer physical involvement and movement, thriving in "hands-on" activities. Art approaches and manipulation of objects are preferred activities.
Psychological	Analytic processors prefer step-by-step procedures that are concrete and detailed, direct talk, and formal interactions. Global processors prefer to talk in general terms before addressing specific aspects, illustrations, anecdotes, casual environments, and nondirective approaches.

Conclusion

Numerous theories and models of student learning styles have been proposed to describe the diversity of approaches students take when learning and solving problems. Understanding one's learning styles is a K–12 journey with each developmental stage offering new opportunities to achieve. Professional school counselors and educators should consider individual learner differences when instructing students, as well as when requiring students to demonstrate what they have learned. By helping students understand their learning style strengths and weaknesses, professional school counselors can enact their leadership and advocacy roles. As part of the school's leadership team, professional school counselors can influence systemic change to ensure appropriate attention is given to learning style instruction in order to help students become successful learners. Learning styles hold great promise in removing systemic barriers to student performance, from both the instructor and the learner viewpoints. In the short term, educators are encouraging students to use their learning style strengths to maximize academic achievement and problem-solving abilities, requiring students to demonstrate what they have learned. In the long term, when students are given the freedom to access information and knowledge and respond through their learning style strengths, educators are allowing students to succeed in ways that will transfer beyond the classroom to the world of adult socialization and careers—where individuals are nearly always given the freedom to perform with some degree of autonomy.

Resources

Web Sites

Center for Teaching and Learning, Indiana State University (http://web.indstate.edu/ctl/styles/ls1.html). Site includes information on models of learning styles, articles about learning styles, and online inventories.

Chaminade College Preparatory, West Hills, CA (http://www.chaminade.org/inspire/learnstl.htm). Site includes a chart with practical tips for determining one's dominant learning style.

Graduate School of Library and Information Science, Telecommunications for Remote Work and Learning, University of Western Ontario (http://granite.cyg.net/~jblackmo/diglib/styl.html). Site includes information on adult learning styles, a bibliography, diagrams, and gender considerations.

James Madison University, Information Skills Curriculum (http://falcon.jmu.edu/~ramseyil/learningstyles.htm). Site includes resource information, scales, articles, and a glossary of terms frequently used in learning style material.

Learning-Styles Network (http://www.learningstyles.net). Site includes research, information, publications, and other resources *focusing* on learning, teaching, and productivity styles.

State University of New York, Oswego, NY (http://www.oswego.edu/~shindler/lstyle.htm). Site includes inventories, bibliography, glossary, articles, and other resources regarding learning style theory.

National Education Association (http://www.nea.org) (http://www.nea.org/helpfrom/
places/s2000/resource/res28.html). Sites include a general web page and a resource
list of people, books, and other resources regarding learning styles.

Secondary School Educators (http://7–12educators.about.com). Site for secondary school
educators includes information on learning styles assessment, theory, and
instructional strategies.

U.S. Department of Education (http://www.ed.gov). Site contains information and
resources on major topics in education. The site can be searched for specific links on
learning styles.

REFERENCES

Barbe, W., & Milone, M. (1980, January). Modality. *Instructor, 89,* 44–49.

Barbe, W., & Milone, M. (1981). What we know about modality strengths. *Educational Leadership, 35,* 378–380.

Brualdi, A. (1998). Multiple intelligences: Gardner's theory. *Teacher Librarian, 26,* 26–28.

Doolan, L. S., & Honigsfeld, A. (2000, May/June). Illuminating the new standards with learning style: Striking a perfect match. *The Clearing House,* 274–278.

Dunn, R., & Dunn, K. (1992). *Teaching elementary students through their individual learning styles.* Boston: Allyn & Bacon.

Dunn, R., & Dunn, K. (1993). *Teaching secondary students through their individual learning styles.* Boston: Allyn & Bacon.

Dunn, R., & Dunn, K. (1999). *The complete guide to the learning styles inservice system.* Boston: Allyn & Bacon.

Dunn, R., Dunn, K., & Perrin, J. (1994). *Teaching young children through their individual learning styles.* Boston: Allyn & Bacon.

Dunn, R., Dunn, K., & Price, R. (1999). *Learning Style Inventory.* Boston: Allyn & Bacon.

Dunn, R., Griggs, S. A., Olsen, J., Gorman, B., & Beasley, M. (1995). A meta-analytic validation of the Dunn and Dunn learning styles model. *Journal of Educational Research, 88,* 237–247.

Erford, B. T. (Ed.). (2003). *Transforming the school counseling profession.* Columbus, OH: Merrill/Prentice-Hall.

Gardner, H. (1993). *Frames of mind: The theory of multiple intelligences.* New York: Basic Books.

Gardner, H. (1999). *The disciplined mind.* New York: Simon & Schuster.

Gardner, H. (2000). *Intelligence reframed: Multiple intelligences for the 21st century.* New York: Basic Books.

Gregorc, A. (1979). Learning styles: Their nature and effects. *National Association of Secondary School Principals, 63,* 19–26.

Gregorc, A., & Butler, K. (1984, April). Learning is a matter of style. *Vocational Education, 59*(3), 27–29.

Griggs, S. A. (1985). Counseling for individual learning styles. *Journal of Counseling and Development, 64,* 202–206.

Hall, B. S., & Lundberg, D. (In press). Integrating learning styles in multicultural counseling. In B. T. Erford (Ed.), *Handbook of school counseling.* Greensboro, NC: ERIC-CAPS.

Kolb, D. A. (1976). *Learning Style Inventory—technical manual.* Boston: Mcber.

Kolb, D. A. (1984). *Experiential learning.* Englewood Cliffs, NJ: Prentice-Hall.

Reiff, J. W. (1992). *Learning styles.* Washington, DC: National Education Association.

Restak, R. (1979). *The brain, the last frontier.* New York: Doubleday.

Shearer, C. B. (1994). *Manual for the TEEN-MIDAS.* Kent, OH: Multiple Intelligences Research & Consulting, Inc.

Teele, S. (1992). *Teele Inventory of Multiple Intelligences.* Redlands, CA: Citrograph Printing.

Thies, A. P. (1979). A brain behavior analysis of learning style. In J. W. Keefe (Ed.), *Student learning styles: Diagnosing and prescribing programs* (pp. 55–61). Reston, VA: National Association of Secondary School Principals.

University of Kansas School of Medicine–Wichita. (1997). *Learning process: Four variables in the learning process.* Retrieved February 12, 2003 from http:/www.kumc.edu/som/medsos/lp.html.

Williams, K. (2000). Do Howard Gardner's multiple intelligences add up? (book review). *British Journal of Educational Studies, 48,* 107–108.

HANDOUT 2.1

SLIDES FOR "UNDERSTANDING STUDENTS' MULTIPLE INTELLIGENCES" PRESENTATION

The Multiple Intelligences

- Linguistic
- Logical-mathematical
- Spatial
- Musical
- Bodily kinesthetic
- Interpersonal
- Intrapersonal
- Naturalist

1

Linguistic Intelligence

- The capacity to use language, your native language and perhaps other languages, to express what's on your mind and to understand other people. Poets really specialize in linguistic intelligence, but any kind of writer, orator, speaker, lawyer, or a person for whom language is an important stock in trade.

2

A	S	D	B
F	E	N	O
L	R	T	U
G	I	P	H

3

Logical/Mathematical Intelligence

- Understanding the underlying principles of some kind of a causal system, the way a scientist or a logician does; or can manipulate numbers, quantities, and operations, the way a mathematician does.

4

A Logical Dilemma

- Ms. Red, Ms. Blue, and Ms. White each wore a dress and carried a purse, each in different colors not in their name. Who wore and carried what? Use the following clues:
- Ms. Red didn't carry a blue purse.
- Ms. Blue carried a red purse.

5

Spatial Intelligence

- The ability to represent the spatial world internally in your mind (sailor, airplane pilot, chess player, sculptor). If you are spatially intelligent and oriented toward the arts, you are more likely to become a painter (sculptor, architect). Similarly certain sciences (astronomy, topology) emphasize spatial intelligence.

6

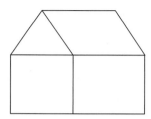

7

Musical Intelligence

- The capacity to think in music, to be able to hear patterns, recognize them, remember them, and perhaps manipulate them. People who have strong musical intelligence don't just remember music easily—they can't get it out of their minds, it's so omnipresent.

8

Bodily/Kinesthetic

- The capacity to use your whole body or parts of your body—your hand, your fingers, your arms—to solve a problem, make something, or put on some kind of production. The most evident examples are people in athletics or the performing arts, particularly dance or acting.

9

Interpersonal Intelligence

- Understanding other people. It's an ability we all need, but it is at a premium if you are a teacher, clinician, salesperson, or politician. Anybody who deals with other people has to be skilled in the interpersonal sphere.

10

Intrapersonal Intelligence

- Having an understanding of yourself, of knowing who you are, what you can do, what you want to do, how you react to things, which things to avoid, and which things to gravitate toward.

11

Naturalist Intelligence

- The human ability to discriminate among living things (plants, animals) as well as sensitivity to other features of the natural world (clouds, rock configurations). In our consumer society this may involve discrimination among cars, sneakers, kinds of makeup, and so on.

12

HANDOUT 2.2

CLASS PROFILE OF PRIMARY INTELLIGENCES

List students' names in appropriate spaces.

Eight Intelligences

Linguistic *Logical* *Spatial* *Kinesthetic* *Musical* *Interpersonal* *Intrapersonal* *Naturalist*

HANDOUT 2.3

Name: _____

Date: _____

WHAT KIND OF LEARNER AM I?

Complete the following sentence starters with information that you learned in your guidance lesson today.

1. My primary intelligence is _____

2. My primary intelligence enables me to be successful in the classroom by _____

   _____

   _____

   _____

3. The following problems have arisen due to my primary intelligence: _____

   _____

   _____

   _____

HANDOUT 2.4

GRAPHIC ORGANIZER

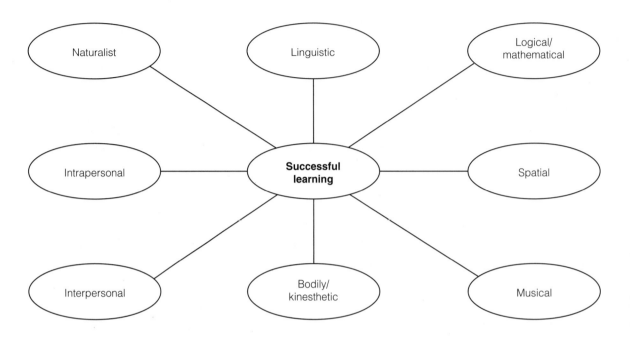

HANDOUT 2.5

THE EIGHT INTELLIGENCES

Intelligence	Description
Linguistic	Requires the capacity for using language (native or otherwise) to understand and express ideas. Students with strength in linguistic intelligence often enjoy reading and writing and generally have highly developed language and memory skills.
Logical-mathematical	Requires an understanding of how to use numbers or mathematical operations, or logical, cause-and-effect relationships to solve complex problems. Students with strong logical-mathematical intelligence tend to excel in math, logical reasoning, and scientific experimentation.
Spatial	Requires the ability to represent the spatial world internally in your mind. Spatially intelligent students are usually good at map reading, puzzles, and art activities.
Musical	Involves the capacity to think musically, particularly the ability to hear, recognize, remember, and perhaps even manipulate patterns of sounds. The musically intelligent often excel at composing, playing instruments, singing, and rhythmic memory.
Bodily-kinesthetic	Requires the ability to use one's body (all or parts) to solve complex movement problems. Students with strengths in the bodily-kinesthetic area generally enjoy hands-on and eye-hand coordination activities.
Interpersonal	Involves an understanding of how to relate to other people and solve interpersonal problems. Interpersonally intelligent people enjoy social activities and relationships, and understand the perspectives of others.
Intrapersonal	Involves understanding one's own internal motivations, strengths, and weaknesses. These students are often self-confident, self-motivated, and independent.
Naturalist	Requires an ability to classify and discriminate among objects. Students high in the naturalist intelligence enjoy interacting with plants and animals, and recognizing and classifying objects.

HOW TO IMPROVE MY STYLE

Name: _____

Date: _____

Reflect on your graphic organizer.

Identify at least two ways to improve on your learning style strengths:

    1.

    2.

    3.

Identify at least two ways to compensate for your learning style weaknesses:

    1.

    2.

    3.

Set at least one goal for yourself to help improve your academic success:

    1.

    2.

HANDOUT 2.7

LEARNING STYLE ELEMENTS

Elements	Description
Environmental	Sound (music, white noise, silence) Light (bright, normal, dim, fluorescent, natural) Temperature (warm, cool, breezy) Design (comfort level, ergonomic, plush, hard)
Emotional	Motivation (intrinsic, extrinsic) Persistence (gives up easily, sticks to it) Responsibility (high, low) Structure (highly structured, low structured)
Sociological	Peers (with, without) Team (with, without) Adult (directed, nondirected) Varied approaches
Physical	Perception (auditory, visual, tactile, kinesthetic) Intake (food, drink) Time of day (morning, afternoon, night) Mobility (stationary, movement)
Psychological	Global/analytical (global learners process information in large chunks, analytic learners process information step by step) Hemisphericity (right brain–spatial, left brain–verbal) Impulsive/reflective (impulsive: active learning, asking questions, problem solving; reflective: quiet, independent, large amounts of think and response time)

HANDOUT 2.8

LEARNING STYLES QUESTIONNAIRE

Name _____   Date _____

Directions: Please circle the letter that most closely describes you. If more than one letter applies, circle the letter that represents your most frequent response. There are no right or wrong answers.

1. When I am learning something new, I prefer to first
   a. learn the details or a small piece
   b. see how what I am learning fits together

2. If I have a big assignment, I prefer to
   a. work on it alone
   b. work with a partner
   c. work with a group

3. When I am studying for a test, I like
   a. to be in a quiet room
   b. to have the television or radio on

4. When I am working on an assignment I like to
   a. work nonstop until it is completed
   b. take a few breaks

5. On long-term projects I like to
   a. have my teacher or parent help me start
   b. start by myself
   c. have my friends start it with me

6. When I get ready to do homework, I am most likely to
   a. get a snack first
   b. play for a while before I get to work
   c. start the assignment right away

7. When I am working on a really tough problem, I prefer to work
   a. at a desk
   b. while lying on the floor or a piece of furniture

8. I learn new things most easily in the
   a. morning
   b. afternoon
   c. evening

9. When I learn a new concept, I like to
   a. read about it first
   b. hear about it first
   c. complete a hands-on activity first

HANDOUT 2.9

LEARNING STYLES WORKSHEET

Name _____   Date _____

Because I now know I learn best _____

_____

I will _____

_____

HANDOUT 2.10

LEARNING STYLES HOMEWORK

Name _____

Event	Your Feelings	Result/Consequence
1.		
2.		
3.		
4.		
5.		
6.		
7.		

GROUP MEMBER CERTIFICATE

(Group Member's Name)

Thank you for your participation in the Learning Styles Group.

You have learned about yourself, others, and strategies that may

enhance your academic success.

Professional School
Counselor's Signature

Date

LEARNING STYLES GROUP EVALUATION

Please circle your response to each question.

	Rarely or not at all	A little	Some	A lot
1. I had the opportunity to express my feelings in group.	1	2	3	4
2. I contributed to the group.	1	2	3	4
3. I felt like I belonged to the group.	1	2	3	4
4. I can define "learning style."	1	2	3	4
5. I know the five stimuli that affect learning style.	1	2	3	4
6. I can describe my learning style preferences.	1	2	3	4
7. I can describe how my learning style affects my academic progress.	1	2	3	4

Comments:

INVESTIGATING THE WORLD OF WORK

Susan Sears, The Ohio State University

INTRODUCTION

Career development includes choosing, entering, adjusting to, and advancing in an occupation. Career development is a lifelong process that interacts dynamically with other life roles (son or daughter, learner, citizen, spouse or partner, leisurite, parent) as well as the environment (Super, 1980). A significant portion of the lifelong career development process occurs during childhood and adolescence. To actively participate in the career development process, students must become aware of their own interests and skills, learn how to collect and evaluate occupational information, and learn how to make effective decisions. Therefore, school counselors have both the opportunity and the responsibility to ensure that their students participate in age-appropriate career-planning activities that result in increased self-awareness, occupational awareness, and effective decision making.

Investigating the world of work is part of the comprehensive and systematic process known as career planning. Career planning requires students to engage in several steps:

- Become aware of the need to plan for their futures
- Learn about their personal characteristics, for example, interests, skills, and values
- Identify occupations that are compatible with their views about themselves
- Collect information about occupational alternatives
- Choose among occupational alternatives
- Act on their occupational choices

This chapter discusses the changing world of work, with a focus on those aspects of career planning that assist students in learning more about themselves (interests, skills, and values), occupations, and ways to connect that information to initial occupational and educational options. Examples of a whole-school intervention, a classroom guidance unit, and a small-group counseling plan are included to guide counselors' design and development of effective school counseling programs. Finally, considerations and suggestions for successful individual career counseling are discussed.

LITERATURE REVIEW

The world of work is changing drastically. The U. S. Department of Labor has charted employment projections through the year 2010 (http://www.bls.gov). These projections include important details about the structure of the economy, the demographic makeup of the labor force, and changes in employment in more than 500 occupations and 260 industries. The following facts and trends seem particularly significant to current and prospective school counselors as they strive to help students plan for their future:

- The U. S. economy is service oriented, with construction and manufacturing less important than a decade ago.
- The number of individuals of Latino and Asian heritage in the labor force will continue to increase faster than will the numbers of African Americans and whites. However, whites will continue to comprise approximately 73 percent of the workers.
- The labor force participation rate for women will continue to increase while men's rate decreases. As a result, women's share of the labor force will increase to 48 percent of all workers by 2010.
- Jobs requiring an associate degree or more education will grow faster than average.
- The median weekly earnings of workers aged 25 to 64 with a bachelor's degree is $834, compared with $507 for workers who hold a high school diploma.
- Unemployment rates throughout workers' lives are lower the more education they have earned.
- The ten fastest-growing occupations are computer software engineers (applications), computer support specialists, computer software engineers (systems software), network and computer systems administrators, network systems and data communications analysts, desktop publishers, database administrators, personal and home-care aides, computer systems analysts, and medical assistants. Most of these occupations require a college degree or advanced training (U. S. Department of Labor, 2002).

Good jobs and higher education seem to go together. Clearly, completing postsecondary education seems to lead to employment in occupations that provide workers with opportunities to earn higher salaries over the course of their lives.

Counselors as Advocates for Higher Education

Given the facts in the preceding bulleted list, middle and high school counselors must encourage every student to consider a two- or four-year college or some type of advanced training after school. The quality of students' future lives may depend on their willingness to continue their education and training after high school. Some argue that school counselors have not advocated effectively enough for advanced education for poor and/or minority students (Martin, 2002). For example, students from low-income families as well as minority groups are less likely to attend college than students from more advantaged backgrounds (The Education Trust, 1999). Those trying to transform school counselors from gatekeepers to student advocates suggest that counselors can collect and/or analyze their schools' course enrollment data to discover the demographics of students enrolled in advanced or college preparatory classes and encourage adjustments to those enrollments where needed (Martin, 2002). Clearly, by monitoring course enrollment data, counselors can intervene and advocate for students who are not meeting their academic potential or who are not receiving enough teacher and parent encouragement and support to register for more rigorous academic courses.

Martin (2002) also proposes that school counselors should be movers and shakers in transforming practices around the use of data in schools. In her opinion, counselors should use data to ask these questions: What students are going on to a two- or four-year college? If students are not succeeding, why aren't they? Are school practices serving as barriers to the achievement and success of some groups of students? To try to find answers to these questions, school counselors can analyze their school data to determine whether some students are being shortchanged. Collecting data on measures of achievement such as test scores, promotion rates, and graduation rates based on student characteristics such as race, gender, and ethnicity can help counselors locate barriers and remove them so all students can be prepared for college.

Self-Awareness

Before students investigate the world of work, they need to identify their interests, skills, and values. In other words, they need opportunities to collect, compile, and reflect on information about themselves.

Interests

An interest is something that holds one's attention or arouses one's curiosity. Interests represent a person's likes and dislikes and are characterized by an individual's intensity of feeling about a subject or thing. The level of intensity may range from mild to strong or passionate (Sears & Gordon, 2000). Students acquire their interests from their parents, schools, friends, and experiences. As they engage in various activities, they react with feelings and develop attitudes. They like or dislike the activity; they feel challenged or bored and competent or clumsy. Their personal reactions and the feedback they receive from parents, family, friends, and teachers shape and focus students' interests.

Many ways to measure or inventory students' interests in elementary, middle, and high school exist. However, measuring students' interests in the elementary school years is not particularly useful. Their interests are immature, are still developing, and will change. On the other hand, helping elementary students define and identify their current interests increases their awareness of the role interests play in their lives. Simply asking elementary students what they like and do not like to do is one way of helping them specify their interests. Hosting career days and inviting speakers representing different occupations to describe what they do and how their interests and skills relate to their occupational choices is another way of providing opportunities for students to see how interests relate to occupations.

Middle and high school students with more experiences and more adult feedback from which to learn are beginning to identify activities that attract them. Eighth-grade or middle school students often take an interest inventory to identify the relationship between their interests and occupational fields and to assist them in designing an educational and career plan for high school. High school students take interest inventories such as the Career Occupational Preference Survey (COPS) published by *Edits* in San Diego, California, which is designed to measure interests in eight career clusters, or the Self-Directed Search (SDS), published by Psychological Assessment Resources in Odessa, Florida, designed to measure personality type and interests in six different occupational groups. Interest inventories can serve as a platform from which counselors can assist students in launching their investigations of the world of work.

Skills

Skills are learned. Some skills help people manage their lives (for example, managing money) and other skills help them earn a living (for example, analyzing data, keyboarding, or performing before an audience). One method of helping students identify their skills is to encourage them to note the subjects in which they excel or the ease with which they learn particular subjects or hobbies. Another way is to help them analyze their achievements. For example, Tanya is in the fifth grade and is very good at using her computer to draw complicated charts and graphs. She first learned that skill from her mother, who is a scientist at a local laboratory. Several of her classmates asked Tanya to teach them how to make charts and graphs. So she has been teaching them during recess and lunch. The teacher who used to praise her for the charts and graphs is now praising her for her excellent teaching skills. Thus, Tanya is using one skill, making charts and graphs via computer, to develop another skill, instructing. This is an opportunity for a teacher or counselor to help Tanya analyze her new skills (that is, giving clear directions, answering questions completely, and displaying patience when others don't learn immediately). She may also recognize that one skill (drawing via computer) can create opportunities to learn another (instructing others).

Values

Values are our preferences or things that are important to us. Values help determine individuals' goals and lifestyles and influence motivation and behavior (Zunker, 2002). Some values hold more meaning than others. Most individuals try to pursue the values that have more meaning to them. Values can motivate individuals to pursue or avoid an activity and can influence what goals people set and act on.

Work values are those activities or attributes associated with work that lead to one activity being appealing while another activity is not. For example, some people value variety in their work; they like being involved in several different activities and having new experiences. Others prefer routine or doing something the same way most of the time. Several examples of work values and their definitions are these:

- Independence: being free to make decisions and plans using one's own personal judgment
- Social: helping others and being concerned about their needs
- Leadership: planning activities and managing the duties of others
- Recognition: achieving acceptance, appreciation, and renown
- Power: being in authority, directing others, and making important decisions
- Prestige: performing work that provides standing in the eyes of others and evokes respect

Students begin to form their values in elementary school and continue their development throughout the remainder of their school years. Activities in the later part of this chapter give counselors suggestions to help students identify their values.

Collecting and Evaluating Occupational Information

Collecting occupational information and interpreting it accurately is an important step in understanding the world of work. Accurate occupational information can help students to:

- Correct stereotypes or faulty beliefs they may hold about specific occupations
- Generate occupational options they have not considered before
- Engage in serious decision making, by introducing them to some of the rewards associated with specific occupations
- Narrow or reduce the number of occupations they are considering

To connect information about themselves to initial occupational and educational options, students need to learn a variety of facts about specific occupations, including the nature of the work performed, the education and training requirements for entry into a career, the earnings and benefits, the personal qualifications and skills needed for success, and occupations related to the field being explored.

Major sources of occupational information include the Internet, computerized information systems, printed materials, audiovisual materials, informational interviews with workers, and direct experiences. In the last decade, the Internet has become a primary source of information as well as one that is easy to access. Counselors who do not use the Internet as a primary source of occupational and educational information are not helping students access the most current information.

The Internet

Access to occupational information is available to anyone who has an Internet connection. Many good Web sites exist, and professional school counselors or school counselors-in-training must learn how to utilize the Internet in their counseling. Most school counselors can benefit from exploring the wealth of information available on the Web. Using a good search engine and entering descriptors such as "occupational information" and "career planning" will generate a rich list of sites. This hands-on approach can help school counselors learn more about occupational information.

OCCUPATIONAL OUTLOOK HANDBOOK (OOH)   The *Occupational Outlook Handbook* Web site (http://www.bls.gov/oco/) is easy enough for upper elementary students and sophisticated enough for high school students to use. The OOH contains information on 35 industries and approximately 250 occupations. The information includes job duties, education and training requirements, earnings, working conditions, places of employment, employment trends, and sources of additional information. Elementary-aged students can simply be introduced to occupational information and encouraged to explore this Web site for their favorite job titles; high school students can be directed to find specific information they need to help them make tentative occupational choices. Students can browse this comprehensive site by occupational category or search using keywords. This Web site also includes charts and graphs providing detailed employment projections that can be used as teaching tools in collaboration with mathematics or other academic classes.

O°NET™   School counselors may remember the *Dictionary of Occupational Titles* (DOT), a publication of the U. S. government for over fifty years. The printed version of the DOT has been retired and has been replaced with an entirely different approach to career information: the Occupational Information Network (O°NET), sponsored by the U. S. Department of Labor's Employment and Training Administration. O°NET (http://www.onetcenter.org) is the now the government's primary source of occupational information. The O°NET database and related products are designed to help employers, workers, educators, and students make informed decisions about education, training, career choices, and work. Students who do not intend to go directly to college or other postsecondary training immediately after high school may find this site useful in their quest for jobs; other students will find that it contains most of the information they need for career exploration and decision making.

Computerized Information Systems

DISCOVER® and SIGI PLUS® are two popular computerized information systems that enable students to take interest and skill assessments online and then match their responses to career clusters. DISCOVER is available through American College Testing and includes modules on learning about work, about yourself, and about occupations, as well as educational choices and making transitions. Several important databases describing two- and four-year colleges, technical and specialized schools, apprenticeship programs, military programs, and graduate professional schools are accessible.

The Educational Testing Service developed the System of Interactive Guidance and Information, SIGI PLUS, and uses values identification and clarification as the basic approach to effective career decision making. Similar to DISCOVER, SIGI PLUS includes modules on self-assessment, search strategies, information, skills, preparing, coping, deciding, and planning.

Printed Materials

The printed version of the *Occupational Outlook Handbook* (OOH) is still one of the best publications available from the U. S. Department of Labor. The printed OOH is revised approximately every two years. *The Guide for Occupational Exploration, Chronicle Guidance's Occupational Briefs,* and the *Encyclopedia of Careers and Vocational Guidance* are other useful resources.

Videos and CDs

Several companies sell commercial videos or compact discs that depict workers in various occupations. Being able to actually see what workers do motivates students to continue their career exploration. One of the most comprehensive reviews of career videos is available from Dr. Richard Feller at Colorado State University. Feller collected a list of 650 career videos and rated 161 of them. Feller can be contacted at feller@condor.cahs.colostate.edu for a list of the ratings.

Informational Interviews

Interviewing workers in different occupational fields can be one of the most stimulating ways for students to collect occupational information. By interviewing actual workers, students can ask specific questions of interest to them and begin to get a better feel for the occupation.

In elementary schools, students can conduct informational interviews with their parents or even with workers in the school (for example, principal, counselor, school psychologist, cafeteria workers, custodian, librarian). When students prepare interview questions and conduct interviews, they are learning about work and about occupations at the same time.

The primary benefit of informational interviews is the firsthand knowledge students gain about the actual work environment and the tasks associated with the occupation. Further, interviews give middle and high school students opportunities to actually visit places of employment. Counselors should help students generate appropriate questions for the interviews before the visits so students will be prepared and will not waste the workers' time. Later in this chapter, the example of a small-group counseling activity includes a list of questions students can use in informational interviews.

Direct Experiences

Job shadowing, internships, and volunteer work are other important ways to gain direct information about occupations. Job shadowing involves following a worker around for a time, usually a day or two. Students need opportunities to discuss their experiences after they occur. Conducting a small group in which five or six students discuss what they learned from their shadowing activity is one way to help students reflect on their experiences. Before participating in job shadowing, students should research the occupations of the individuals they plan to shadow so they will understand what they are seeing and hearing.

Internships for high school students can provide them with real-world experiences in their areas of interest. School counselors can arrange for internships in local businesses, government, and community agencies. Some high schools release students from school to participate in internships. Because internships last longer, they give students a more realistic view of occupations than job shadowing does. In addition, students are able to actually complete work tasks similar to those they would do if employed. Counselors should discuss internship experiences with students to help them integrate their experiences into their career planning.

Students work in large numbers at service stations, fast food restaurants, and retail stores. These are work environments in which students can learn about some aspects of work regardless of their occupational interests. As high school counselors engage in career and educational planning with their students, they should include discussions about the work experiences the students have already accumulated. Schools typically ignore the fact that many students already work and thus overlook an opportunity to build on students' real-life experiences with work.

Evaluating Occupational Information

As students are learning how to search for occupational information, they also must learn how to evaluate it. Robert Hoppock (1976) first suggested that information gathering should focus on these questions:

> When was the information prepared? Is it current?
> Who wrote it? Are the authors reputable?
> Why was it written? Do the authors provide accurate, objective information or are they trying to sell you something?
> How was the information collected? Did it come from reliable sources, such as statistics on employment trends from state agencies or the U.S. Department of Labor?

For information to be truly useful, it must be accurate. Because of the amount of information that is available on the Internet, it is vital for students to make certain the source of their information is reliable. Counselors should display a list of reputable Web sites in their offices as well as providing a handout for students and parents.

Choosing among Occupational Alternatives

Once students have collected information about their interests, skills, values, and related occupations, they need to make a tentative occupational decision that makes sense to them. Choosing among occupational alternatives is a challenging task for students. Sometimes they have to deal with competing interests and values or may not feel confident about their skills. Students also have to consider factors in their environment that impact their decisions. For example, Robert wants to pursue an occupation that will require that he attend a college in another state. That decision would mean extra expenses, and he knows his parents are not financially able to provide the support he needs. Should he compromise and choose another occupation and attend a two-year or four-year college in his local area so he can live at home? Should he plan to go to college part-time and work so he can pay his own expenses? Questions like these can cause stress and confusion for students. They need caring adults to help them generate occupational options, analyze the pros and cons of each option, and design a plan of action to implement their choices.

WHOLE-SCHOOL INTERVENTIONS

School counselors are uniquely prepared to lead schoolwide interventions focusing on students' career development. Usually schools counselors are the only professionals in schools who have taken coursework in career counseling or know anything about occupational information. Thus, they need to help teachers understand why career planning is important for students.

Planning for a schoolwide intervention or program requires some imagination. So, let us imagine a counselor in a middle school in a large urban community has been talking with the principal about ways to increase the motivation and goal directedness of the seventh-grade students. She has read that helping students investigate the world of work may encourage them to set realistic educational and career goals. She convinces the principal to try a career theme for the year: Investigating the World of Work. At the first staff meeting of the year, she explains her ideas to the teaching staff and asks them if they would be willing to participate in activities focusing on work and occupations. They agree, some more enthusiastically than others.

Since the counselor knows how important it is to team and collaborate with teachers, she asks for volunteers to form a committee to develop the career program. At the first meeting of the committee, she shows them the school counseling standards developed by the American School Counselor Association (Campbell & Dahir, 1997). The seventh-grade teachers on the committee suggest that Standard A under the Career Development domain would allow them to utilize technology and to work on a career theme at the same time. The teachers become excited as they talk about ways they can use the World Wide Web to help students investigate occupational information. The counselor distributes a list of student competencies that go with the ASCA Standards, and the committee chooses the competencies they want students to achieve:
Students will:

- Learn about their interests, skills, and values
- Learn how to collect and evaluate occupational information
- Learn to interact and work cooperatively in teams
- Learn about traditional and nontraditional occupations
- Learn to set goals

The teachers report not knowing much about career development and ask the counselor to provide them with information. She agrees to gather resources and to lead them in exploring the Internet on their professional development day scheduled for next week. The teachers like the idea, and the meeting ends on a positive note.

On their professional development day, the teachers on the "Exploring the World of Work Committee" gather together in the computer lab as planned. The school counselor is well prepared and walks the teachers through several Web sites. She actually uses activities she had prepared for a classroom guidance unit she hoped to conduct in cooperation with the technology teacher. First, she instructs teachers to log onto the Internet, go to www.oln.org/explore/interests.html, and complete the Work Interest Quiz. Once they complete their quiz and identify some occupations that are related to their interests, she asks them to investigate those occupations using both the Internet version of the *Occupational Outlook Handbook* and the Occupational Information Network (O°NET). The teachers are amazed. They had no idea that this type of information is so easily available. They spend the entire morning familiarizing themselves with these Web sites and related links. Several teachers mention that they want to expose their own children or nieces and nephews to this information.

After the professional development session with the teachers, the counselor feels she has accomplished her goal. They are very impressed with her knowledge and pick up her enthusiasm as well. They can see why students get excited learning about occupations. The technology teacher who works with seventh-graders is very willing to collaborate with the counselor in delivering the classroom guidance unit (see examples of the activities later in the chapter).

The counselor and teachers develop their plan of action for the unit. First, the counselor will meet with small groups of students in the English classes. Then, the counselor will help the students identify their interests, skills, and values. While the counselor is working with the small groups, the English teacher plans to work on writing skills with others in the class. With a smaller classroom group, the English teacher can give more individual attention to her students. Once all of the students have participated in three small-group sessions and the English teacher has worked to improve their writing skills, the students will begin a career unit with the technology teachers. The technology teachers and the counselor will collaborate in classroom guidance sessions to show the students how to search the Web for occupational information that relates to the interests, skills, and values they have just identified. Students will be expected to take careful notes of their work in the technology class so they will be able to apply it later in their English classes.

Once the technology teachers finish their career unit, the English teacher will assign students an essay. This assignment, a follow-up to the teacher's effort to improve their writing skills, will ask students to use the notes taken from their search of occupational Web sites and turn those notes into an essay to be graded in English class. In addition, since this middle school uses student-led parent conferences, the students will include their essay in a portfolio to be shared with parents during the parent conferences.

The counselor feels she has learned also. She is proud of the results of her leadership. Clearly, the students gained from the experience. Several parents even called her to tell her how excited their children were. She felt a new rapport with the teachers. They could see the students were motivated to learn more about themselves and future options; yet, at the same time, they were able to connect the guidance lessons to academic subjects. The counselor realized that teachers, once they understand how career development concepts and processes can be integrated into their curriculum, are willing to collaborate with her.

CLASSROOM GUIDANCE ACTIVITIES

School counselors need to be effective career and educational advisors if they are to help all students plan for their futures (Education Trust, 1997). Classroom guidance is one intervention in which counselors can share information that is vital to students' career and educational planning. Lessons 1, 2, and 3 are designed to help middle or high school students investigate the world of work. Because students must have access to computers and the Internet to complete the activities, counselors must gain the cooperation of the technology teacher.

LESSON 1: PLANNING FOR THE FUTURE

Academic Development Standard C: Students will understand the relationship of academics to the world of work and to life at home and in the community.

Career Development Standard A: Students will acquire the skills to investigate the world of work in relation to knowledge of self and to make informed career decisions.

Competencies: Students will understand the relationship between learning and work. Students will identify their interests and learn how interests relate to occupations.

Learning Objective: Using their results from an online survey, students will be able to identify their interests and see how interests relate to various occupations.

Materials: Computer lab and access to the Internet, manila folders that the counselor has labeled "Planning for the Future," board or overhead transparencies on which the counselor can write notes or student comments.

Developmental Learning Activities

Introduction: Students begin their activity in a computer lab. The counselor distributes manila folders with five notebook sheets stapled together and labeled "Planning for the Future." The counselor discusses the importance of planning for life after high school. Using the information provided earlier in the chapter, the counselor describes how work is changing. The counselor stresses the relationship between work and education as well as the dim employment prospects for unskilled workers. (Counselors are encouraged to develop a student handout using this information. See Handout 3.1.)

Activity

1. The counselor asks students to write responses to these questions on the first page of their Planning for the Future folders:

   What are your current interests?
   What occupations are compatible with your interests?
   What are your plans once you graduate from high school?

2. The counselor informs the students that they are going to use the Internet to learn more about themselves and more about occupations.
3. The counselor instructs students to log onto a Web site, http://www/oln.org/ explore/interests.html, complete the Work Interest Quiz from the Career Tool Box, and then record the results of the quiz (Work Styles) in their Planning for the Future folders. The counselor moves from student to student to make certain they are accessing the correct Web site and understand the assigned task. The teacher assigned to the class works alongside the counselor.
4. Next, the counselor instructs the students to click on their results (Work Styles categorized under Holland's work environments) from the Work Interest Quiz and read about the occupations that appear on the screen.

Conclusion: The counselor asks students to respond orally to questions such as these:

   What interests did you identify?
   What occupations are related to your interests?
   Which of the occupations that you identified seem most interesting to you?

The counselor reminds the students they will have an opportunity to learn more about the occupations they identified in the next session.

Assessment: The counselor collects the Planning for the Future folders and reviews them before the next session to determine whether the students understood and completed the first activity.

Follow-Up: The counselor asks the teacher for reactions and observations. Did the teacher believe the students were engaged? What were the strengths and weaknesses of the activity?

LESSON 2: INVESTIGATING THE WORLD OF WORK

Career Development Standard A: Students will acquire the skills to investigate the world of work in relation to knowledge of self and to make informed career decisions.

Competency: Students will develop skills to locate, evaluate, and interpret occupational information.

Learning Objectives

- After completing the activity, students can use the Internet to locate occupational information.

- After locating occupational information on the Internet, students will collect and interpret information about several occupations that are compatible with their interests.

Materials: Computer lab, Planning for the Future folders, and Internet access.

Developmental Learning Activities

Introduction: The counselor discusses with students that they will be investigating the Internet version of the *Occupational Outlook Handbook* so they can locate occupational information both now and in the future. The counselor tells them that they will take the title of one of the occupations identified in the Work Interest Quiz and use the Internet to search for information about that occupation as well as information about two or more preferred occupations (www.bls.gov/oco/).

Activity: Students answer each of the questions below and record their responses in their Planning for the Future folder.

- What is the nature of the work in one of your preferred occupations?
- What are the working conditions?
- What kind of education and training is needed?
- What is the job outlook?
- What are other occupations related to the one you are investigating?

Students access O°NET (http://www.onetcenter.org/) and explore three additional occupations that are related to their interests on the Work Interest Quiz.

Conclusion: Students pair up with a classmate and share their findings. The counselor encourages students to share the information they are learning with their parents and/or family members.

Assessment: The counselor collects the Planning for the Future folders and reviews the students' responses prior to the next session. By reviewing the responses, the counselor will know whether students have learned how to use Internet resources to locate occupational information.

Follow-Up: The counselor continues to confer with technology teachers to solicit their feedback about the progress of the guidance lesson and to solicit their assistance for the third session.

Lesson 3: Making a Tentative Choice

Academic Development Standard C: Students will understand the relationship of academics to the world of work and to life at home and in the community.

Career Development Standard A: Students will acquire the skills to investigate the world of work in relation to knowledge of self and to make informed career decisions.

Competencies: Students will understand the relationship between learning and work. Students will learn a decision-making process that can be applied to occupational choices.

Learning Objectives

- After completing the activity, students will learn a decision-making process.
- After completing the activity, students will apply a decision-making process to a scenario similar in nature to the decisions they face.

Materials: Manila folders, Handout 3.2 (Decision-Making Model), and chalkboard or overhead transparencies on which to write students' comments.

Developmental Learning Activities

Introduction: The counselor reviews the first two lessons with the students. The counselor helps them understand the need for a method of making effective decisions.

Activity: Students will learn the decision-making model that appears in Handout 3.2. This example is written directly to students and includes a scenario that will help students understand each step in the process. Counselors can reproduce the model for their classroom unit and use the scenario to teach the model.

The counselor describes each of the decision-making steps in the handout and asks questions such as:

> What goals are you setting for yourselves based on the interests you identified in the first session of the unit?
> What occupational alternatives are you considering based on your explorations on the Internet?
> How do you plan to collect more information through informational interviews or direct experiences such as volunteering or shadowing?
> How do the subjects you are studying at school relate to the occupations that interest you?

Some students will volunteer their thoughts. The counselor can discuss some of the students' responses in the whole group to make certain that all students understand the decision-making process. The counselor asks all students to write brief responses to the questions in their Planning for the Future folders.

Conclusion: The counselor informs the students that they will collect the student folders and review them so they can give students feedback on their planning. The counselor also should set a time with teachers to return the folders to the students during another class session. Giving students feedback on their responses is an important part of this unit and allows counselors to keep brief records on the plans and aspirations of the students. Counselors can reinforce those aspirations whenever possible.

Assessment: Students use their notes about one occupation they explored on the Internet to write a five-hundred-word paper for their computer technology class. The technology teacher will grade this assignment and use it as evidence that students can conduct occupational searches on the Internet.

Follow-Up: The counselor should plan to meet with the technology teachers to discuss possibilities for a follow-up series of classroom guidance activities later in the year, in which students conduct searches for postsecondary options compatible with their tentative occupational choices.

SMALL-GROUP COUNSELING PLANS

Small-group counseling is an effective way to help students learn more about themselves so they will be ready to investigate occupations in high school. These sessions are designed for middle school students and are based on a fifty-minute period with eight to ten students in the group. This plan is designed for six sessions, but processing time depends on the number of students in the group. During the sessions, students will complete handouts that use the Holland types as an organizing rubric to explore occupations.

GROUP SESSION 1: BEGINNING THE CAREER PLANNING PROCESS

Career Development Standard A: Students will acquire the skills to investigate the world of work in relation to knowledge of self and to make informed career decisions.

Competencies: Students will develop an awareness of the importance of career planning. Students will become more aware of their interests.

Learning Objectives

- After being introduced to a career-planning process, students will describe the steps they need to know to engage in career planning.
- Using their results from an interest survey, students will be able to identify their interests.

Materials: Overhead describing the career-planning process described below and Handouts 3.3 and 3.4. (Counselors may want to give a manila folder to each student so they can organize their handouts.)

Activities

Introduction: The school counselor introduces this session by leading students in a discussion of the following questions:

> What do you plan to do after graduating from high school?
> How do you think you will use what you are learning in English class after you graduate from high school?
> What are you learning in math that you think you will use after high school?

The counselor can use any of the students' current subjects (science, social studies, or foreign languages) to generate a discussion about how various subjects are useful in their lives.

The counselor introduces students to the following career-planning process so they begin to realize that making an occupational choice is not a one-time decision.

Career Planning Process for Students

- Students need to become aware of the importance of planning for their futures. They do not need to decide on specific occupations during middle school, but it is helpful for them to begin to explore occupations so they can begin the career-planning process. Students should be reminded that they may be employed in several occupations during their lives, but the occupations may be related, for example, teacher, principal, curriculum director, assistant superintendent.
- Students need to learn about their personal characteristics, for example, interests, skills, and values.
- Students need to identify occupations that are compatible with their views about themselves.
- Students need to collect information about occupational alternatives. They need to learn how to use the Internet and printed information to locate current occupational information.
- Students need to learn how to choose among occupational alternatives. They should learn how to make decisions so they can connect information about themselves to occupational information to make initial occupational decisions.
- Students need to realize they must choose courses in high school so their tentative occupational decisions can become realities.

The counselor explains to students that the six small-group sessions in which they are participating will help them experience the six steps of career planning.

Counseling Activity: The counselor introduces John Holland's theory of types. Holland suggests that the choice of an occupation is an expression of one's personality and that people in the same occupation have similar personalities (Holland, 1992). Holland sees career interests as an expression of individuals' personalities and uses six categories to describe personality types: Realistic, Investigative, Artistic, Social, Enterprising, and Conventional. He also suggests there are six types of work environments: Realistic, Investigative, Artistic, Social, Enterprising, and Conventional. Before the counselor explains Holland's theory, the counselor gives students Handout 3.3 to help them follow the explanation.

Next, the counselor asks students in the group to complete Handout 3.4.

Conclusion: The counselor asks the students to share their interests with the group. The counselor facilitates discussion by asking questions such as these:

Do you use your interests in any hobbies?
Do some of you have similar interests?

Assessment: To determine whether students have completed the activity completely, the counselor collects the students' Handout 3.4 to review before the next session.

GROUP SESSION 2: LEARNING ABOUT MY SKILLS

Career Development Standard A: Students will acquire the skills to investigate the world of work in relation to knowledge of self and to make informed career decisions.

Competency: Students will identify their strongest skills.

Learning Objective: Using the results from a skills survey, students will be able to identify their areas of strength.

Materials: Handout 3.5.

Activities

Introduction: The counselor asks students to define the word "skill" and then asks four or five students to give examples of skills they possess and what they know about skills. This discussion should allow the counselor to make certain that students understand what skills are and also to see whether students make any connections between skills and occupations.

The counselor discusses transferable and functional skills. *Transferable skills* are those that can be utilized in several different occupations. For example, conducting training sessions in business and industry requires many of the same skills that teachers use when instructing students. Communicating, diagnosing, and monitoring are also transferable skills. *Functional skills* are those skills that help people perform tasks required in specific occupations. Programming computers or playing a violin in an orchestra would be examples of functional skills.

The students complete Handout 3.5 (Exploring Your Skills). The counselor asks students to record (on the activity) three skills in which they perceive themselves as above average.

Counseling Activity: The counselor asks students to share their skills with other members of the group. The counselor facilitates the sharing by asking questions such as these:

Are your skills similar to or different from others in the group?
Where did you acquire your skills?
What skills do you acquire at school?

Conclusion: The counselor asks students to reflect on the relationship between this session and the last one.

Assessment: The counselor collects Handout 3.5 and reviews it before the next session to ensure that students have completed it.

GROUP SESSION 3: VALUES

Career Development Standard A: Students will acquire the skills to investigate the world of work in relation to knowledge of self and to make informed career decisions.

Competency: Students will develop an awareness of their values related to work.

Learning Objective: Using their results from a work values inventory, students will be able to identify their work values.

Materials: Handout 3.6.

Activities

Introduction: The counselor asks students these questions: What is a value? What is a value that you hold? The counselor may want to write some of the students' responses on a board or a blank transparency. The counselor then tells students that the activity they do in group today is going to help them learn how values relate to occupations.

Counseling Activity: The counselor leads a discussion with students about the values in Handout 3.6. When the counselor believes the students have an understanding of the values, the counselor asks them to complete the handout. After they have completed it, the counselor asks students to share their choices with other members of the group. In a small group, ask students to discuss their rankings of work values and give examples of how they think the values they choose can be met through work.

Conclusion: The counselor responds to any questions about the three activities that students have completed and concludes with this general question. What have you learned about yourself during the last three sessions?

Assessment: The counselor collects Handout 3.6 and reviews it to see if students have completed it.

GROUP SESSION 4: PULLING IT ALL TOGETHER: YOUR CAREER PROFILE

Career Development Standard A: Students will acquire the skills to investigate the world of work in relation to knowledge of self and to make informed career decisions.

Competency: Students will profile their interests, skills, and values and identify occupations that relate to that profile.

Learning Objective: After completing a career profile, students will recognize the relationship between their interests, skills, and values and occupations.

Materials: Handout 3.7.

Activities

Introduction: The counselor explains to students that today's activity is designed to help them pull together what they have been learning about themselves. The counselor reviews with students what they have learned about interests, skills, and values. Then the counselor asks students to complete Handout 3.7 (Your Career Profile).

Counseling Activity: The counselor asks students to share their results and their reactions to the occupations that are compatible with their Holland types. The counselor should encourage students to share any information they know about the occupations that are compatible with their Holland types. (They may not know much about some of the occupations because they have not been exposed to very much occupational information.)

Conclusion: The counselor goes around and asks the members of the group what they have learned today.

Assessment: Students take a copy of the career profile home to share with parents or other family members.

GROUP SESSION 5: LEARNING MORE ABOUT OCCUPATIONS

Career Development Standard A: Students will acquire the skills to investigate the world of work in relation to knowledge of self and to make informed career decisions.

Competency: Students will learn how to find information about occupations that are compatible with their interests, skills, and values.

Learning Objective: After this group experience, students will know how to find occupational information on the Internet.

Materials: This session must be held in a location (career center, library, computer lab) where at least three computers are available for students to use.

Activities

Introduction: The counselor asks students to share their parents' reactions to the career profile they shared. The counselor may ask questions such as these:

> What did your parents think of your choices?
> Did they have any suggestions to make?

After the introductory discussion, the counselor demonstrates how to use the online version of the *Occupational Outlook Handbook* (http://www_bls.gov/oco/).

Counseling Activity: The counselor asks students to work in teams of two and answer the following questions (on paper) about two of the occupations in which they are interested:

- What is the nature of the work involved in the occupation?
- What kind of education and training is needed?
- What occupations are related to the one you are investigating?

Students share what they found with another person on their team, and they assist each other when needed. They print the information they have found on the Internet, and the counselor encourages them to take the occupational descriptions home and share them with parents or other family members or friends.

Conclusion: The counselor reassembles the small group and asks students to share some of the information they discovered. The counselor should listen carefully to ensure that students are interpreting the occupational information accurately.

Assessment: The counselor moves from team to team to ensure that students are on task and understand the questions as well as to review the students' responses for accuracy.

GROUP SESSION 6: WHAT DID I LEARN?

Career Development Standard A: Students will acquire the skills to investigate the world of work in relation to knowledge of self and to make informed career decisions.

Competency: Students will evaluate what they have learned about themselves as a result of small-group counseling sessions focusing on interests, skills, and values, and related occupations.

Learning Objective: After this session, students will be able to describe their interests, skills, and values, and related occupational choices.

Materials: Student folders or handouts.

Activities

Introduction: The counselor explains that this activity is designed to help students review what they have learned and identify at least one occupation that seems compatible with their interests, skills, and values.

Counseling Activity: The counselor facilitates a discussion with students regarding the following questions:

- Of the occupations you explored, which occupation seems most interesting to you?
- Is that occupation compatible with your interests, skills, and values?
- How do you know?
- How much and what kind of education and training is required to enter the occupation?

- Do you think you could succeed in that occupation? Why or why not?
- Do you think you will locate information about other occupations that may interest you in the future? What processes would you use to find the information?
- Have you learned anything else as a result of participating in these group sessions?

Conclusion: Once all of the students have had opportunities to describe what they have learned, the counselor explains that they might have opportunities to be a part of other group sessions in the future. The counselor should make a positive statement about each of the students' participation, such as these:

> "Your comments showed that you were really thinking about your future."
> "You collaborated so well with the other students."
> "You mastered exploring the Internet so quickly."
> "You followed directions well."

In other words, all students should be leaving the group with a feeling of accomplishment.

Assessment: Prior to the last group session, the counselor prepares a sheet of the questions listed under Counseling Activity for each student in the group. As students are discussing what they have learned, the counselor can take brief notes on their sheets so they have a record of what students say they learned. Once the group has concluded, the counselor reviews the responses to see whether all of the students mastered the learning objectives.

Follow-up: The counselor should meet with the technology teachers to encourage them to introduce students to additional Web sites that provide occupational information. The counselor can provide a list of sites for the teachers to use and offer to help them develop a lesson that will introduce all students to occupational information on the Internet.

INDIVIDUAL COUNSELING CONSIDERATIONS

School counselors can enhance their individual career and educational counseling by setting up a career center. Even one computer with Internet access combined with printed materials such as hard copies of the *Occupational Outlook Handbook* will enable counselors to help students investigate the world of work and plan for their future. However, several cautions are in order. Counselors must recognize that the amount of information on the Internet can be overwhelming. It is difficult and time consuming for individuals to comb through all of the data by themselves. Counselors should prepare a list of the most dependable Web sites for their students to log onto first. Several resources already have been cited in other sections of this chapter, and more appear in the resource list at the end of the chapter.

Appropriately, students like to search databases for additional occupational information. However, depending on the search engine used, there are significant differences in the sources identified. Counselors should become familiar with the capabilities of various search engines so they can advise students.

High school counselors who are fortunate enough to work in schools where the counselor-to-student ratio is reasonable may want to consider holding individual career-planning conferences with parents or guardians and each student. Parent and student conferences permit counselors to involve parents in their child's educational and career planning as early as the eighth or ninth grade. This approach can help parents learn how to support their children's aspirations.

If individual conferences with parents are not feasible, counselors can conduct larger group sessions with parents and students during evening hours. For example, counselors can show parents and their children how to access occupational information on the Internet. Most parent-teacher associations would welcome opportunities to work with counselors to provide information for parents.

Finally, any of the activities described under the classroom guidance and small-group counseling plans above can be adapted for use with individuals as well.

CONCLUSION

This chapter addressed the changing world of work and then focused on those aspects of career planning that assist counselors in helping their students collect information about themselves (interests, skills, and values) and connect that information to initial occupational and educational options. In addition, examples of whole-school, classroom guidance, and small-group counseling and activities were provided to guide counselors in their development of effective school counseling programs. Finally, suggestions for successful individual career counseling were discussed with particular attention given to wise use of the Internet.

RESOURCES

Many resources to assist school counselors in helping students investigate the world of work are available. A few are listed below.

Web Sites

Assessment Systems

These systems give students the option of taking assessments via computer. Examples are:

- The Strong Interest Inventory® is administered from the publisher's Web site at http://www.cpp-db.com/products/strong/index.asp.
- The Self-Directed Search® is administered from the publishers' Web site at http://www.self-directed-search.com.

U. S. Department of Labor

The Department of Labor is one of the most important sources of occupational information. The *Dictionary of Occupational Titles* has been replaced by O°NET at http://www.doleta.gov/programs/onet. This database describes more than 1000 occupations.

A second publication of the Department of Labor is the *Occupational Outlook Handbook* (OOH) at http://www.bls.gov/oco/. It provides extensive data about 250 occupations and includes, on a quarterly basis, the *Occupational Outlook Quarterly*.

The federal government has funded several public Web sites with easily accessible occupational and employment information. CAREER INFO NET (http://www.acinet.org/) helps students search employment trends, occupational requirements, wages, and state-by-state labor market conditions. JOBBANK (http://www.ajb.org/) is a resource for teens and adults who are seeking jobs.

State Career Information Delivery Systems (CIDS)

See the Web site of the Association of Computer-Based Systems for Career Information (http://www.acsci.org) for a listing of state information systems.

Commercial Systems

There are many commercial Web sites. Two worth exploring are:

- http://www.Petersons.com
- http://www.riverpub.com

Books

The most comprehensive source of information in a book can be found in:

Herr, E. L., & Cramer, S. H. (1996). *Career guidance and counseling through the lifespan* (5th ed.). New York: HarperCollins

Holland, J. L. (1992). *Making vocational choices* (2nd ed.). Odessa, FL: Psychological Assessment Resources.

Sears, S. J., & Gordon, V. N. (2002). *Building your career: A guide to your future* (3rd ed). Upper Saddle River, NJ: Prentice Hall.

REFERENCES

Campbell, C., & Dahir, C. (1997). *Sharing the vision: The national standards for school counseling programs.* Alexandria, VA: American School Counselor Association.

Education Trust, Inc., The. (1997). *The national guidance and counseling reform program.* Washington, DC: Author.

Education Trust, Inc., The. (1999, September). *The transforming school counseling initiative.* Washington, DC: Author.

Holland, J. (1973). *Making vocational choices: A theory of careers.* Englewood Cliffs, NJ: Prentice-Hall.

Holland, J. (1992). *Making vocational choices* (2nd ed.). Odessa, FL: Psychological Assessment Resources.

Hoppock, R. (1976). *Occupational information.* New York: McGraw-Hill.

Martin, P. (2002). Transforming school counseling: A national perspective. *Theory into Practice, 41,* 148–153.

Sears, S. J., & Gordon, V. N. (2000). *Building your career: A guide to your future.* Upper Saddle River, NJ: Prentice Hall.

Super, D. E. (1980). A life-span, life space approach to career development. *Journal of Vocational Behavior, 16,* 282–298.

U. S. Department of Labor. (2002). *Occupational outlook handbook, 2002–2003.* Washington, DC: U. S. Government Printing Office.

Zunker, V. G. (2002). *Career counseling: Applied concepts of life planning* (6th ed.). Pacific Grove, CA: Brooks/Cole.

HANDOUT 3.1

- The U.S. economy is service oriented, with construction and manufacturing less important than a decade ago.

- The number of individuals of Latino and Asian heritage in the labor force will continue to increase faster than will the numbers of African Americans and whites. However, whites will continue to comprise approximately 73 percent of the workers.

- The labor force participation rate for women will continue to increase while men's rate decreases. As a result, women's share of the labor force will increase to 48 percent of all workers by 2010.

- Jobs requiring an associate degree or more education will grow faster than average.

- The median weekly earnings of workers aged 25 to 64 with a bachelor's degree is $834, compared with $507 for workers who hold a high school diploma.

- Unemployment rates throughout workers' lives are lower the more education they have earned.

- The ten fastest-growing occupations are computer software engineers (applications), computer support specialists, computer software engineers (systems software), network and computer systems administrators, network systems and data communications analysts, desktop publishers, database administrators, personal and home-care aides, computer systems analysts, and medical assistants. Most of these occupations require a college degree or advanced training (U.S. Department of Labor, 2002).

HANDOUT 3.2

DECISION-MAKING MODEL

1. *Define the problem* or define what you are trying to decide. For example, break down your occupational choice into small components: Rather than asking a general question such as "In what career will I be the happiest?" define the problem as "What groups of occupations give me the best opportunity to use my interest in math?"

2. *State your goal or goals clearly and concisely.* Example of a goal: "I plan to decide what group of occupations will allow me to use my interests, allow me to be independent, and also pay well."

3. *Collect information.* Ask questions such as "What kind of information do I need to make this decision?" "Where can I find the information?" "Should I conduct an informational interview with people from different occupations?" "Should I volunteer during the summer in one or two of the occupational areas that interest me?"

4. *List alternative solutions.* If you hope to work in occupations that use your interests and skills in, for example, math, then you could consider accounting, teaching, business, and actuarial work, to name just a few. Once you list alternatives, another set of questions arises: "Which of these occupations also reflect your values of autonomy and variety?" "What skills do you need to become an accountant?" "Do you have those skills or are you willing to try to acquire them?" "How many years of college do you have to attend to succeed in these occupations?" These questions need to be answered as you move to the next step: choosing among the alternatives.

5. *Choose one of the alternatives.* One alternative may seem particularly inviting to you. For example, after reading about accounting and interviewing an accountant, you decide that is the occupational choice you want to make at this time. In general, the accountants you interviewed indicated they had variety in their jobs. One person who owned her business reported that autonomy was one of the reasons for becoming an accountant. You know you have been getting Bs in math, but you could do better. After reading about accounting and talking to your school counselor, you understand that you must be willing to work harder in math classes. In fact, you have to do more in all of your classes if you want to succeed in college.

6. *Take action on your choice.* Once you have made a commitment to your choice, you need to take action to make your choice a reality. Since your initial choice is accounting, you also know that you will need to attend a four-year college to enter your occupation. That means you need to commit to studying harder during your high school years and to take rigorous courses to increase your chance for success in college.

Description of each of the six personality types (Holland, 1973):

The realistic type prefers activities that are explicit and ordered. They like to manipulate objects, tools, and machines. They have mechanical skills but lack social skills, and they prefer jobs such as auto mechanic, electrician, farmer, or aircraft controller.

The investigative type prefers activities such as observing and investigating physical, biological, and cultural phenomena in order to understand and control such phenomena. They are not particularly fond of social activities but may prefer mathematical and scientific activities. They like jobs such as biologist, chemist, physicist, anthropologist, or medical technologist.

The artistic type likes less structured activities and is good at manipulating materials to create art forms. They may have skills in art, music, drama, and language and are often creative, nonconforming, and expressive. They like jobs such as composer, drama critic, writer, actor, or designer.

The social type likes activities that allow them to inform, teach, or lead others. They do not like explicit, ordered, and systematic activities and usually possess good social and interpersonal skills. They do not like working alone and prefer jobs such as teacher, minister, counselor, and psychologist.

The enterprising type prefers activities that permit them to lead and persuade others to achieve economic gain. They prefer concrete to symbolic activities and are not scientifically oriented. They like jobs such as salesperson, manager, business executive, and sports promoter.

The conventional type prefers activities that are ordered and systematic. They like to manipulate data, keep records, file materials, organize written and numerical data, and operate computers. The do not prefer exploratory or ambiguous activities. They like jobs such as financial analyst, banker, administrative assistant, or tax expert.

Holland's work environments parallel his personality types. The Realistic environment includes the orderly and systematic manipulation of objects, tools, and machines. The Investigative environment is characterized by the systematic investigation of physical, biological, and cultural phenomena. The Artistic environment is free and unstructured, fostering art forms and products. The Social environment includes helping and teaching others and interacting in flexible ways. The Enterprising environment involves leading and manipulating others to achieve economic and/or organizational goals. The Conventional environment requires participation in orderly and systematic activities and the manipulation of data (Holland, 1973).

IDENTIFYING INTERESTS

Note to students: This activity is designed to help you identify your interests. It uses John Holland's occupational classification system to help you identify how your interests relate to occupations. Put a check mark (✓) in front of the activities that you like to do or think you would like to do.

Realistic

____ Take shop in school
____ Fix electrical appliances
____ Repair cars
____ Landscape the yard
____ Build or repair furniture
____ Drive a truck or bus
____ Work with animals
____ Build houses

Investigative

____ Study psychology
____ Do science experiments
____ Design
____ Work in a laboratory
____ Study about oceans
____ Program computers
____ Solve math problems
____ Study animal behavior

Artistic

____ Play in a band
____ Decorate your room
____ Take art classes
____ Write poetry or stories
____ Work on a newspaper
____ Sculpt wood or clay
____ Take modern dance or ballet
____ Act in theatrical productions

Social

____ Teach students
____ Help people solve problems
____ Be a volunteer in a hospital
____ Work with people at church
____ Be a good friend
____ Help people who are ill
____ Supervise workers in a business
____ Help people develop their physical abilities

Enterprising

____ Sell products in a store
____ Manage your own business
____ Run for class officer
____ Manage a group of salespeople
____ Participate on the debate team
____ Set up a law practice
____ Persuade others to do something your way
____ Help others find employment

Conventional

____ Keyboard/Enter data on a computer
____ Work as a bank teller
____ Operate office equipment
____ Supervise a quality control project
____ Work as a teacher's aide
____ Develop an accounting system for a business
____ Perform general office work
____ Work as a library assistant

You can learn more about John Holland and the Self-Directed Search by logging onto http://www.self-directed-search.com.

In which three areas did you have the most check marks? _____, _____, and _____.

EXPLORING YOUR SKILLS

The list of words below identifies work skills associated with different occupations. Put a check mark (✓) in front of those skills you currently possess or plan to acquire.

I am able to:

___	1. Play a musical instrument	___	16. Experiment
___	2. Create	___	17. Solve
___	3. Entertain	___	18. Diagnose
___	4. Draw pictures	___	19. Analyze information
___	5. Sculpt	___	20. Think rationally
___	6. Repair	___	21. Organize/direct
___	7. Drive	___	22. Coordinate
___	8. Build	___	23. Teach others
___	9. Care for plants	___	24. Cooperate
___	10. Protect others	___	25. Counsel others
___	11. Sell	___	26. Follow directions
___	12. Budget money	___	27. Do routine work
___	13. Influence others	___	28. Do well with details
___	14. Work with customers	___	29. Follow rules
___	15. Lead others	___	30. Follow others

Count the number of check marks in each of the six categories and write the totals in the blank spaces:

From 1 to 5 = ____(artistic)   From 16 to 20 = ____(investigative)
From 5 to 10 = ____(realistic)   From 21 to 25 = ____(social)
From 11 to 15 = ____(enterprising) From 26 to 30 = ____(conventional)

In which three of the six categories did you have the most check marks?
_____, _____, and _____.

HANDOUT 3.6

EXPLORING YOUR VALUES

Complete the following activity to clarify your work-related values. From the ten values listed below, choose the four values you believe to be most important to you and rank them from 1 to 4, with "1" being the most important.

___ 1. Achievement: Work that makes me feel as if I have accomplished something important.

___ 2. Security: Work that provides me with the certainty of having a job even in difficult times.

___ 3. Creativity: Work that permits me to invent new things, design new products, or develop new ideas.

___ 4. Prestige: Work that gives me standing and respect in the eyes of other people.

___ 5. Economic returns: Work that pays well and enables me to have what I want.

___ 6. Intellectual stimulation: Work that provides the opportunity for learning how and why things work.

___ 7. Variety: Work that allows me to change from one activity to another.

___ 8. Altruism: Work that permits me to help others.

___ 9. Power: Work that allows me to direct others and make important decisions.

___ 10. Mechanical: Work that involves working with things, objects, and machines.

___ 11. Routine: Work that permits doing something the same way each time.

___ 12. Accuracy: Work that involves doing things in a correct and precise manner.

Review your top four choices and determine which Holland types reflect your current work values. Circle the three types that reflect more of your work values:

Artistic: Creativity, variety, and prestige
Realistic: Achievement, security, economic returns, and mechanical
Enterprising: Achievement, economic returns, variety, and power
Investigative: Variety, prestige, creativity, and intellectual stimulation
Social: Prestige, altruism, and achievement
Conventional: Security, achievement, routine, and accuracy

Write the names of the Holland types here: _____, _____, and _____.

HANDOUT 3.7

YOUR CAREER PROFILE

To students: To summarize what you have learned about yourself by completing all of the previous activities, complete the career profile below. Take a minute and review Handouts 3.4, 3.5, and 3.6 prior to completing the career profile. In each of the areas (interests, skills, and values), circle the Holland types that describe you.

My Career Profile

Interests	Realistic	Investigative	Artistic
	Social	Enterprising	Conventional
Skills	Realistic	Investigative	Artistic
	Social	Enterprising	Conventional
Values	Realistic	Investigative	Artistic
	Social	Enterprising	Conventional

Holland suggests that all occupations can be divided into six work environments using the same descriptors as his personality types. These are examples of occupations in each of Holland's six work environments:

Realistic

Mechanical engineer
Agriculture teacher
Air traffic controller
Designer
Chef

Investigative

Chemist
Pharmacist
Computer programmer
Mathematician
Veterinarian

Social

Social worker
Nurse
Counselor
History teacher
Economist

Enterprising

Banker
Lawyer
Personnel manager
Radio/television announcer
Recreation director

Artistic

Artist
Interior designer
Editor
Musician
Public relations expert

Conventional

Accountant
Finance expert
Payroll clerk
Credit manager
Secretary

Circle occupations that you would like to explore in the Holland categories that best reflect your interests, skills, and values. Write the two that interest you the most here: _____ and _____.

FOSTERING POSITIVE CAREER DEVELOPMENT IN CHILDREN AND ADOLESCENTS

Spencer G. Niles and Jerry Trusty, The Pennsylvania State University, and Natasha Mitchell, University of Maryland

INTRODUCTION

School counselors consider providing career-development interventions as an important job-related responsibility. *The National Standards for School Counseling Programs* (Campbell & Dahir, 1997) identify career development as an essential element of school counseling programs. Indeed, the history of school counseling is inextricably intertwined with career-development interventions. For example, early legislative funding (for example, the National Defense Educational Act) for school counseling positions emerged in response to the perceived need for more concerted efforts directed toward guiding students who were talented in math and science into science-related occupations. Career-education programs, which represent the primary initiative in influencing the career development of school students, were implemented initially in the 1970s as vehicles for helping each student "make work a meaningful, productive, and satisfying part of his or her life" (Hoyt, 1975, p. 5).

LITERATURE REVIEW

Career-Development Tasks Confronting Elementary School Students

Elementary school children, who are typically between the ages of five and ten, face several career-development tasks and concerns. Donald Super's life-span theory outlines children's concerns and the tasks that should be accomplished during this stage to promote success in later stages of the child's career development.

During the growth stage (birth to age fourteen) the child engages in forming a picture of the self. The four major tasks for the child in this stage are developing concern about one's future, developing feelings of personal control over one's life, developing the conviction to achieve in school work, and acquiring competent work habits and attitudes (Super, Savickas, & Super, 1996). Children in elementary school are primarily concerned with the tasks of the fantasy substage of the growth stage. Up until age ten, children are involved in increasing their self-awareness, developing an awareness of how various jobs are valued, and developing feelings of competency and satisfaction from their own activities (Herring, 1998; Super, Savickas, & Super, 1996). Children's development of their self-concept is often accomplished through identification with adults in the family, school, community, and/or public media. In addition, children use fantasy, fueled by an innate sense of curiosity, to act out career roles in their play (Super, Savickas, & Super, 1996). Fantasy-based activity and school experiences lead children to the next career-development stage of determining interests in particular areas or specific careers.

According to Super's life-span theory, around age ten children typically enter the interest substage of the growth stage. While in the interest substage, they develop an awareness of activities they take pleasure in and begin to base their initial career aspirations on the activities they like (Herring, 1998). As children develop interests in and outside school, they are developing an important aspect of being able to engage in sound career decision making in the future (Super, 1990). In many ways, the focus of the growth stage is to help elementary school children develop mastery of general tasks that aid in supporting self-concept development, which is crucial for future career-specific success.

Clearly, during elementary school the foundation for future achievement is established (Herring, 1998). The American School Counselor Association states that the "elementary school years set the tone for developing the skills, knowledge and attitudes necessary for children to become healthy, productive adults" (American School Counselor Association, n.d.). Given this, these years are a crucial time for school counselors to implement activities to assist elementary school-age children in addressing concerns and successfully completing the tasks of the growth stage.

Career-Development Tasks Confronting Middle School Students

Middle school children, who are typically between the ages of eleven and thirteen, also face specific career-development tasks and concerns. Donald Super's life-span theory outlines early-adolescent concerns and tasks that should be accomplished during this stage to promote future career success.

According to Super's life-span theory, middle school children are primarily coping with the tasks associated with the capacities substage of the growth stage. Young adolescents in this stage begin to assess their own abilities or capacities (Super, Savickas, & Super, 1996). Prior to this stage, children primarily focus on building career aspirations based on their interests, without paying much attention to their abilities or capacities. During middle school, children become aware of what their abilities are and how their particular abilities may support or hinder the expression of their interests.

Given this developmental task, the goals for career development during this period involve increasing preadolescents' understanding of their abilities and skills, as well as increasing their awareness of the wide variety of careers. Paisley and Hubbard (1994) state that as their main career-development goals, middle school students confront the tasks of (1) becoming aware of personal characteristics, interests, aptitudes, and skills; (2) developing an awareness of the diversity of the world of work; (3) understanding the relationship between performance in school and future choices; and (4) developing a positive attitude toward work.

Middle school is a pivotal time in early-adolescent career development because during this time period, middle school students begin to establish career directions based on interests, perceived abilities, and knowledge of career options. School counselors, as part of their comprehensive, developmental school counseling programs, can facilitate adolescent development during this period by engaging students in activities that help students become aware of the importance of accurate self-assessment and the world of work information. This information provides the foundation for coping with career-development tasks in high school.

Career-Development Tasks Confronting High School Students

Adolescents in high school typically range in age from fourteen to seventeen years old. During this period, adolescents clarify career interests and make specific plans to achieve stated career goals. Super's life-span theory (Super, Savickas, & Super, 1996) provides an understanding of the career-development tasks adolescents encounter in high school.

According to Super's life-span theory, adolescents in high school enter the exploration stage and are specifically focused on the task of crystallization. "When habits of industriousness, achievement, and foresight coalesce, individuals turn to daydreaming about possible selves they may construct. Eventually, these occupational daydreams crystallize into a publicly recognized vocational identity with corresponding preferences for a group of occupations at a particular ability level" (Super, Savickas, & Super, 1996, p. 132). Therefore, the task of crystallization is characterized by the need for high school adolescents to clarify their self-concepts and connect their self-concepts to appropriate work options (Herring, 1998). Once crystallized and specified, tentative career goals are then translated into postsecondary plans. For example, if a student determines that she wants to become an engineer, she will begin to make career decisions to assist her in reaching that goal. She will determine that she must attend college and begin to investigate colleges that she could attend given her skills, values, and interests. Then she will apply to a selected group of colleges. This short example demonstrates the tasks of this period, which are crystallizing the self-concept and expressing the self-concept through activities and behaviors that will allow the individual to implement the self-concept.

High school counselors must use a wide variety of activities to meet the extensive needs of high school adolescents. Given the importance of this stage of career development, high school counselors have a responsibility to engage students in exploratory activities that will promote the optimal career development of students well beyond their high school years.

WHOLE-SCHOOL INTERVENTIONS

Leading and Advocating for Career Development Requires Systematic Planning

For school counselors to function as leaders and advocates in meeting the career development needs of students, counselors must engage in systematic and coordinated program planning. Walz and Benjamin (1984) offer useful guidelines for school counselors to follow in developing systematic career-development intervention programs. Their guidelines include the following:

- Involve a team of knowledgeable professionals, parents, and representatives from the community in all phases of program planning.
- Use developmentally appropriate interventions.
- Be sure that the program goals and objectives are clearly communicated to all involved in the program.
- Make sure the program is based on student needs.
- Have an evaluation component to determine the degree to which the program goals and objectives have been achieved.
- Make sure that those involved in program delivery are highly competent.

Niles and Harris-Bowlsbey (2002) note that guidelines such as those proposed by Walz and Benjamin (1984) highlight the fact that school counselors must be sensitive to the political climate in which they operate. For example, if school counselors do not adequately communicate the benefits of career interventions, then the probability increases that program resources will be vulnerable to funding cuts (Niles & Harris-Bowlsbey, 2002). If school personnel view career interventions only as a burden, the program has little chance to succeed. Thus, the "marketing" of the program to all stakeholders becomes an important aspect of systematic program development and implementation (Niles & Harris-Bowlsbey).

Another important theme involved in systematic career-development program planning is the need to take a team approach in program development and implementation. Although school counselors have the training and expertise to take the leadership role in career-development programs, one person cannot accomplish all the goals and objectives of an effective career program. Involving others (for example, teachers, parents/guardians, peers, community members, school administrators) requires school counselors to communicate clearly concerning the goals, objectives, roles, and functions of each person involved in delivering career services to students. While we advocate taking a team approach to developing career services and delivering them to students, we also contend that counselors must maintain a leadership role in this process for the following reasons:

1. Counselors are often the only professionals in the school system with specific training in career development.
2. Counselors possess the knowledge of career development theory and practice necessary for formulating appropriate career development program interventions.
3. The processes typically used in program delivery relate to counselors' primary areas of expertise. These processes are counseling, assessment, career information services, placement services, consultation procedures, and referrals. (Niles & Harris-Bowlsbey, 2002, p. 253)

Leading and Advocating for Career Development by Taking a Developmental Systems Perspective

The word *systematic* is used frequently by those promoting comprehensive career-development programs (for example, Campbell & Dahir, 1997; Gysbers & Henderson, 2000; Niles & Harris-Bowlsbey, 2002; Lampe, Trusty, & Criswell, 2001; Starr, 1996). In this use, *Merriam-Webster's* (1996) second meaning of the word *systematic* is conveyed: "presented or formulated as a coherent body of ideas or principles" (p. 1198). That is, comprehensive career-development programs follow a sequence of coherent steps or stages, guided by ideas and principles resulting from research and practical experience, and may be guided by national standards (for example, Campbell & Dahir, 1997). *Merriam-Webster's* (1996) first definition of *systematic* is "relating to or consisting of a system" (p. 1198). When this definition is applied, career-development programs, schools, and students are seen as components and members of related systems and subsystems. From this perspective, the influences of contexts are more visible. Although the application of general systems theory and systems thinking is not new to school counseling programs (for example, see Gysbers & Henderson, 2000) and career-development theory (Vondracek & Fouad, 1994; Vondracek, Lerner, & Schulenberg, 1986), and although the principles of program development and national standards do not ignore contextual influences, we believe that the development of programs and delivery of services can derive benefits from a systems view.

VanZandt and Hayslip (2001) noted that systems thinking helps counselors conceptualize programs in a broader context. Balancing the perspectives of the two definitions of *systematic*—(1) being organized and purposeful in adhering to a coherent set of principles, while (2) accounting for multiple contexts and influences—seems to be a way to understand the career development of young people, to develop programs, and to help young people utilize resources and minimize obstacles.

A Systems Perspective Helps Organization and Structure

VanZandt and Hayslip (2001) asserted that systems thinking helps counselors see how components of counseling programs function together, as subsystems, to create an effective counseling program. Systematic, comprehensive, developmental, and holistic career-development programs are organized around a mission and goals; when subsystems function together, goals are achieved efficiently. A systems perspective also helps various personnel involved in service delivery interface effectively and efficiently with the larger system, the school. For example, school-based data (for example, achievement test scores, attendance data, demographic data) are useful in designing and implementing career-development interventions and psychoeducational activities. If these data, or the information they convey, flow freely to counseling programs, then counselors make more informed decisions and design effective and efficient interventions. Also, counselors can provide feedback to the larger school system regarding needs for data, and counseling programs provide data that are useful to the school.

The Career-Development Program Is an Integral Subsystem

Several authors (Gysbers & Henderson, 2000; Lampe et al., 2001; Myrick, 1997; Schmidt, 2003) argue that career-development programs should be an integral part of the school itself, and should not be seen as ancillary services or support services. Myrick and Schmidt, for example, assert that the career guidance curriculum should be part of the school curriculum, delivered by counselors and teachers. Using the systems metaphor from biological entities, if part of the larger system is not useful or necessary to the functioning of the system as a whole, it is absorbed or it is rejected.

How does a subsystem become ancillary or unnecessary? The concept of *boundaries* from structural family therapy (Nichols & Schwartz, 2001) is useful for addressing this question. Structural family therapy focuses on the systems and subsystems within the family and on the family as a subsystem of the community and the broader social context. Subsystems are maintained by boundaries. Boundaries are invisible barriers that regulate the flow of information among systems and subsystems. Boundaries are conceptualized along a continuum, ranging from diffuse (nonexistent) to rigid (impermeable). Healthy boundaries lie along the middle of the continuum. Healthy boundaries are clear, allowing for free flow of information while maintaining the autonomy of the subsystem. Diffuse boundaries lead to enmeshment and dependence. Rigid boundaries lead to disengagement and isolation.

To apply the concept of boundaries to counseling for career development in schools, if boundaries around the career-development program are diffuse, the program becomes enmeshed with other subsystems in the school and loses its autonomy and identity. In such a school, for example, it may be difficult to distinguish the assistant principal's role from the counselor's role in service delivery. The career-development program is undefined and poorly articulated, and the career development of students is largely ignored. Counselors might also lose autonomy by being absorbed into clerical or testing roles. If boundaries are rigid, the career-development program has autonomy, but connectedness is sacrificed, the program becomes ancillary and disconnected from the larger system, the school, and from other subsystems (for example, students, families, teachers).

The desirable state is clear boundaries. Programs maintain their autonomy and connectedness. The career-development program is integrated into the school curriculum, the entire school is engaged in the career development of students, counselors are important to the mission of the school, and information flows to and from the counseling and career-development program subsystem and various other subsystems, including students, administrators, teachers, parents and families, the community, businesses, agencies, and institutions.

Communication Enhances Ownership

When information readily flows to and from those who have a stake in programs, wide ownership of the program results. Counselors form program advisory committees (Schmidt, 2003), and input is gathered from members and the groundwork is laid for program planning. In the area of career development, advisory groups need stakeholders from businesses. Counselors should also involve adults from the community who are not current parents of students. This population, which is often overlooked, can provide important resources such as employment opportunities, mentors, externships, career-development program input, and other forms of support.

Communication with school administrators is paramount. Administrators' preparation programs often do not address, and therefore many administrators do not understand, counseling programs adequately. Also, there are several possible areas of conflict between administrators and counselors. For example, counselors and principals may have conflicts regarding leadership roles, and principals and counselors may disagree on how counselors and programs should be evaluated (Lampe et al., 2001). In addition, counselors and administrators are likely to take divergent perspectives on the education of children (for example, administrators may not take a holistic and developmental view on career development). Therefore, communication between these two subsystems should come early and often. Again, the concept of clear boundaries, and autonomy with connectedness, applies in developing and maintaining healthy relationships and effective service delivery.

The importance of communication with teachers cannot be overstated. Consultation and collaboration with teachers are major roles for school counselors (Myrick, 1997; Schmidt, 2003). This communication is necessary for the success of any career-development program, and is essential for the effective delivery of many career-development interventions.

Involving Important Subsystems

In preceding sections we underscored the importance of engaging in systematic and coordinated program planning that involves all stakeholders in program development and implementation. Involvement of and communication with people from a variety of entities are necessary for leading (planning, designing, implementing, and evaluating) career-development efforts. Next we focus most on two subsystems in the career development process, students and their families, while recognizing that other systems and subsystems (for example, the economic environment, the community) are important.

Students

No subsystem is more important than the students, and the free flow of information between students and counselors is particularly salient. In comprehensive, developmental counseling programs, the program is designed to provide services for all students in the school (Myrick, 1997). Whereas particular students have particular needs, all students in the school have career-development needs. Even students whose educational and personal-social development has been optimal have needs relative to their continuing career development. One major means of communication from students to counselors is the needs assessment.

Needs assessments, if well constructed and guided by advisory groups, can provide valid direction for career-development programs. From needs-assessment results and other data, counselors develop objectives, competencies, priorities, and desired outcomes. Needs-assessment data guide counselors in formulating program goals, and assessment data provide a basis for evaluation of programs (Russo & Kassera, 1989; Gysbers & Henderson, 2000; Lampe et al., 2001; VanZandt & Hayslip, 2001). Needs-assessment data help make programs valid by virtue of being designed around students' needs. Data help demonstrate counselor and program accountability, and needs assessments encourage students' ownership of the program (that is, program services emerge from student input). Needs-assessment data provide counselors with important information that can be used to guide them in advocating for career services that address students' career concerns.

Needs-assessment data also foster program flexibility. For example, if 40 percent of the students in a particular high school are seeking nonacademic postsecondary educational programs (certificate programs, apprenticeships, and the like), needs of these students will be reflected in the needs-assessment results. Russo and Kassera (1989) point out an important caution in using aggregated needs-assessment data: If certain populations are relatively small, their needs become lost when data are aggregated. For instance, Hypothetical High School is in an upper-middle-class area. However, 10 percent of the students are of relatively low socioeconomic status (SES). Counselors should find a sensitive way to survey those lower-SES students because their career development needs will likely be much different from the needs of most students in the school. If the low-SES students' data are aggregated with data from the entire school, their needs are overshadowed by the needs of the majority group. In a career-development context, needs generally differ for subgroups based on gender, race-ethnicity, culture, SES, disability status, and the postsecondary options available to students. Needs assessments for sub-groups are especially important for schools serving a heterogeneous population.

However, student needs assessments are not the sole means of assessing students' needs. Students in elementary schools, for example, are generally less aware of their needs than are middle or high school students. Although needs assessments administered to elementary students can reveal some information, elementary counselors generally rely more on parents' and teachers' perceptions of students' career needs. Other information used for designing career programs could come from focus groups, interviews, town-hall type discussions, and existing school and community data.

Parents and Families

In designing and implementing career-development programs, counselors should give strong attention to parents and families. Research studies indicate that parents have a pervasive and enduring influence on the career development of their children (for example, Trusty, 1998, 1999). Parental influence is strong for the U.S. population as a whole (Trusty, 2002; Trusty, Plata, & Salazar, 2003). In research investigating students' ratings of various persons (for example, parents, counselors, teachers, peers) as career-development resources (Kotrlik & Harrison, 1989; Peterson, Stivers, & Peters, 1986; Sebald, 1989), students consistently rated parents highest. Also, parents desired to help their children (Laramore, 1984), and parents saw counselors as effective career-development resources for their children (Trusty, Watts, & Crawford, 1996).

Parents have the advantage of being continual resources for their children. In contrast, the influences of counselors, teachers, and schools are each much more temporal. The influence of parents is also more multidimensional than the influence students experience from counselors, teachers, and schools (Trusty & Pirtle, 1998). Given this research, it is not surprising that young people view their parents as important career-development resources—regardless of whether the parents are competent to serve as career resources for their children. Although young people progressively become more independent from parents, they continue to depend heavily on their parents for career-development assistance. Given these conditions, counselors are in an advantageous position for helping parents help their children advance in their career development (Middleton & Loughead, 1993; Peterson et al., 1986; Whiston, 1989).

Two dimensions of parents' influences, identified through research, seem particularly productive for helping children advance in their career development: parental involvement and parents' expectations for their children. Parental involvement means different things to different people, and parental involvement has been conceptualized in many ways in the literature. It has been seen as parents' involvement in school decision making, involvement in school organizations, and involvement with children's learning at home (see Epstein, 1990; Trusty, 1998). The type of parental involvement that seems most influential in young people's career development is home-based involvement (Hickman, Greenwood, & Miller, 1995; Trusty, 1998, 1999, 2002; Trusty et al., 2003). Involved parents regularly communicate effectively with their children regarding school, their studies, their vocational development, and their personal lives.

The other strong parental influence on young people's career development is parents' expectations. The intergenerational educational-goal transmission process is very strong (Smith, 1991, Trusty & Pirtle, 1998). That is, parents' educational goals for their children (for example, vocational certificates, college degrees) and children's educational goals for themselves have strong correspondence. Also, parents tend to agree with one another on goals for their children, and fathers and mothers tend to equally influence sons and daughters. The strong influences of parents' expectations and involvement extend across the years of adolescence. For example, Trusty (2002) used a nationally representative sample of African American adolescents and their parents to study parental influences. When their children were in the eighth grade, parents reported their expectations for postsecondary education for their children. Six years later, when most adolescents were two years beyond high school, adolescents reported the highest level of education that they expected ever to achieve. Parents' expectations from six years earlier had a strong influence on these late-adolescents' expectations. Therefore, counselors should focus on enhancing parents' expectations, and this focus should come early in students' educational careers. At least, parents need to be educated on how they can positively influence their children's career development through expectations and involvement.

CLASSROOM GUIDANCE ACTIVITIES

Many school counselors do not provide career-development programs in a systematic and coordinated fashion (Niles & Harris-Bowlsbey, 2002; Walz & Benjamin, 1984). The piecemeal implementation of career-development interventions obviously limits the degree to which such interventions can positively influence students. Moreover, such an approach often creates confusion, for those not directly involved in their creation and implementation, about the meaning and purpose of career-development programs.

Leading and Advocating for Career Development: A Complex Challenge

Obviously, developing and delivering systematic and coordinated career services to students is a complex task. It requires counselors to play the lead role in advocating for systematic and comprehensive career services for children and adolescents. Such advocacy requires counselors to work effectively with school personnel, students, and parents/guardians, as well as community and business leaders. Often, advocating for systematic and comprehensive career services for students requires counselors to educate others about the connection between career development and academic achievement. It also often requires counselors to educate others as to the developmental and evolving nature of career-development tasks and the competencies students need to cope with these tasks effectively. Convincing others that students in grades K–12 need career services becomes an even greater challenge when resources are limited and school personnel feel pressure to focus on services that have an obvious and direct connection to student performance in state-related testing programs.

The complexity of developing and implementing comprehensive and systematic K–12 career-development programs becomes clearer when counselors realize that addressing students' career concerns requires not only devoting attention to career-development processes (for example, increasing self-awareness, developing decision-making competencies), but also to the contexts that influence those processes (for example, families, peers, communities). Counselors developing systematic and comprehensive career-development programs must address the fact that career-development processes are influenced by multiple contexts. These contexts can facilitate or constrain career development.

In addition to addressing the fact that multiple contexts influence career development, school counselors must acknowledge that career development cannot be completely isolated from other life roles (for example, student, citizen, friend, child). Gysbers and Henderson (2000), in their book on comprehensive school guidance programs, used the overarching concept of *life career development*, a concept encompassing roles throughout life and the various contexts in which people develop. Gysbers and Henderson's life-career-development view is a holistic, developmental perspective, a view that reflects life as people live it. Most contemporary career-development scholars contend that young people's career development is not disconnected from other areas of development (for example, Krumboltz, 1996; McDaniels & Gysbers, 1992; Super, 1990). Career development encompasses the multiple roles young people play, and includes career, educational, and personal-social development. Although these three descriptors of development (career, educational, personal-social) are commonly used in counseling program models, they are inherently related and are not compartmentalized in comprehensive developmental counseling and guidance programs. For example, Stone and Bradley (1994) stated, "We assert that almost everything you do as an elementary school counselor provides career development counseling" (p. 262). Plus, a teleological view of child and adolescent career development acknowledges that young people are being prepared for eventual participation in multiple life roles.

The following classroom guidance and small-group counseling activities are designed to assist the professional school counselor in implementing a comprehensive developmental career-development program in a systematic fashion. By using whole-school, classroom guidance, small-group, and individual counseling as their delivery methods, school counselors ensure that their career-development program is reaching and meeting the needs of all students in their school. The following lessons are suitable for middle school.

LESSON 1: SELF-ANALYSIS

Career Development Standard C: Students will understand the relationship between personal qualities, education and training, and the world of work.

Competency: Students will identify personal preferences and interests that influence career choices and success.

Learning Objective: Students will be able to describe their personal qualities, interests, and skills.

Materials: Self-analysis worksheet (see Handout 4.1).

Developmental Learning Activities

Introduction: The school counselor introduces the importance of developing self-awareness and personal skills (Ragala, Lambert, & Verhage, 1991). The counselor defines what are personal qualities, interests, and skills. The counselor should also provide examples of personal qualities, interests, and skills in the form of help sheets. The counselor tells students that the worksheet will help them to begin to develop an understanding of their personal qualities, which will aid them in future career exploration.

Activity: The counselor gives each student a self-analysis worksheet (Handout 4.1). Students complete the worksheets with the aid of help sheets that list examples of personal qualities, areas of interest, and skills.

Once all the worksheets are completed, the counselor asks students to go around and share something from their worksheets. The counselor should be sure to reflect back to the student and the rest of the group the unique quality that the student shared from their worksheet.

Conclusion: The school counselor concludes the activity with a class discussion that reinforces the idea that each person has unique characteristics that will relate directly to their personal career choices.

Assessment: Students demonstrate their ability to meet the learning objective by completing their worksheets and actively sharing unique personal characteristics with the group. The school counselor should evaluate the presentations and collect the worksheets to review each student's self-analysis.

Follow-up: In a following session, the school counselor will ask students to go around and share a unique personal quality, interest, or skill.

LESSON 2: LEARNING ABOUT REAL JOBS FROM REAL PEOPLE

Career Development Standard A: Students will acquire the skills to investigate the world of work in relation to knowledge of self and to make informed career decisions.

Competency: Students will learn about the variety of traditional and nontraditional occupations.

Learning Objective: Students will enhance their knowledge of the world of work.

Materials: The school counselor makes arrangements for no more than three guest speakers from different professions to address the students. Prior to the presentations, students are told which professions will be represented among the guest speakers so that the students can prepare questions to ask of the guests.

Developmental Learning Activities

Introduction: The school counselor introduces each of the guests on the panel and encourages students to ask questions of the guests during the presentations.

Activity: Each guest should be allowed to introduce themselves and their profession to the students for approximately five minutes. The counselor then invites questions for the guests from the students. The counselor should make an effort to ensure that questions cover the following basic areas: (1) required education for the career, (2) necessary skills and abilities, (3) rewards of the profession, and (4) difficulties associated with the profession.

Conclusion: After the presentation, the school counselor has students process the experience in small groups where students can discuss what they learned and what they found most interesting (Illinois State Board of Education & Association of Illinois Middle-Level Schools, 2000).

Assessment: The counselor circulates during the small-group process and observes what students have learned from the presentations.

Follow-up: In a subsequent meeting, students write down which career each found most interesting. Students then state how their interests and skills are consistent with the career they selected. The school counselor uses these responses to direct future career exploration.

LESSON 3: JOB SHADOWING

Career Development Standard C: Students will understand the relationship between personal qualities, education and training, and the world of work.

Competencies: Students will identify personal preferences and interests that influence career choices and success. Students will apply academic and employment readiness skills in work-based learning situations such as internships, shadowing, and/or mentoring experiences.

Learning Objective: Students will gain a greater understanding of the specific skills and tasks required for their profession of interest.

Materials: The school counselor arranges for students to shadow a volunteer who is in a profession of interest to the student. Volunteers must be willing to allow students to observe the volunteer on the job and be willing to answer numerous questions from the students. Also, this activity requires thank-you cards and envelopes for the follow-up activity.

Developmental Learning Activities

Introduction: Prior to the actual job-shadowing date, each student should talk on the phone to the individual they will shadow. Students are responsible for making arrangements to get to and from the job-shadowing site on the appropriate day.

Activity: Students are responsible for gathering as much specific information as possible about the job during the shadowing process. Students should be actively involved during the job shadowing and ask questions throughout the day.

Conclusion: The job-shadowing experience concludes with an opportunity for the student and the volunteer to meet privately for at least twenty minutes to discuss the experience and determine how this career might fit with the student's interests.

Assessment: Students each write a short reaction paper describing the experience and submit the paper to the school counselor. In the paper, students should be sure to outline what they liked and disliked about the job, how their interests fit with this job, and whether or not they could see themselves doing this job in the future.

Follow-up: In a following meeting, students write a short thank-you note to their volunteer, explaining what they gained from the experience. The school counselor reviews these thank-you notes before sending them out to the volunteers.

SMALL-GROUP COUNSELING PLANS

The following lessons are suitable for high school.

GROUP SESSION 1: WHAT ARE YOUR PERSONAL GOALS?

Career Development Standard B: Students will employ strategies to achieve future career success and satisfaction.

Career Development Standard A: Students will acquire the skills to investigate the world of work in relation to knowledge of self and to make informed career decisions.

Competencies: Students will identify personal skills, interests, and abilities and relate them to current career choices. Students will learn how to set goals.

Learning Objectives

- Students will solidify a personal plan to achieve their career goals within the support of the group context.
- Students will establish rapport with and among group members.

Materials: Notepaper.

Activities

Introduction: The school counselor explains the purpose of the group and helps members to understand that the group process will reflect their expressed career-development needs. The counselor also develops group rules with the group members.

Icebreaker: The counselor facilitates group members' going around and sharing with the group a little-known fact about themselves.

Counseling Activity: The counselor explains what a personal goal statement is and provides examples. Group members then gather in pairs and spend ten minutes discussing their career aspirations with their partner. Each member writes down a draft version of their personal goal statement and then shares it with the large group. The counselor facilitates large-group discussion about the goal statements.

Conclusion: The counselor explains that goal setting is an important step in achieving one's career goals and commends group members for their participation. The counselor concludes by asking group members to bring their draft goal statements to the next group.

Assessment: The counselor notes each group members' stated career goals and level of enthusiasm for those goals during the reporting-out process.

Follow-up: The counselor begins thinking of potential ways to assist group members in their career planning, given their stated goals.

GROUP SESSION 2: DEVELOPING YOUR PERSONAL PLAN

Career Development Standard B: Students will employ strategies to achieve future career success and satisfaction.

Career Development Standard A: Students will acquire the skills to investigate the world of work in relation to knowledge of self and to make informed career decisions.

Competencies: Students will demonstrate knowledge of the career-planning process. Students will understand the importance of planning.

Learning Objective: Students will develop a personal career plan.

Materials: Notepaper.

Activities

Introduction: The counselor asks students to use their draft personal goal statements from the previous group to develop their personal plans during this group. The counselor stresses the importance and necessity of planning in achieving career goals.

Icebreaker: Each member shares the thoughts they have had regarding their personal goal statements since the last group. The counselor facilitates group awareness of similarities and differences between group members' expressed goals.

Counseling Activity: On a sheet of paper, students write down what their career goals are, how they see their interests, skills, and values relating to their career goals, and what education/training is required to achieve those goals.

Conclusion: On completion of this activity, group members engage in a large-group discussion. The counselor facilitates the discussion in a way that allows each group member to receive feedback on their personal plans. The counselor encourages members to write down things they would like to add to their plans as a result of the group discussion.

Assessment: The participation of each member in the group activity and discussion allows the counselor to evaluate each member's personal plan.

Follow-up: The next group session will allow group members to focus exclusively on their educational journey up until the present time and to see how that journey factors into their career goals.

GROUP SESSION 3: WHERE I'VE BEEN

Career Development Standard B: Students will employ strategies to achieve future career success and satisfaction.

Competency: Students will assess and modify their educational plan to support career goals.

Learning Objectives

- Students will review their past educational activities within the context of their career goals.
- Students will increase the cohesiveness of the group by sharing personal histories.

Materials: Notepaper.

Activities

Introduction: The counselor introduces the purpose of the group and uses the icebreaker to start the discussion.

Icebreaker: The counselor asks each group member to identify the educational or training activity with which they have had the most success.

Counseling Activity: Group members share their educational histories, including areas of success and areas for improvement. The counselor facilitates this discussion and encourages members to think about how their educational history impacts their current career goals.

Conclusion: Each group member then spends five to ten minutes writing down their educational successes and areas for improvement. They also begin to note what things they believe they need to work on in order to achieve their career goals.

Assessment: Students will be able to identify one area of educational success and one area for improvement.

Follow-up: During the next group session, members will begin to focus on what they can do in the future to move closer to achieving their goals.

GROUP SESSION 4: HOW CAN I GET WHERE I'M GOING?

Career Development Standard B: Students will employ strategies to achieve future career success and satisfaction.

Competency: Students will demonstrate awareness of the education and training needed to achieve career goals.

Learning Objective: Students will identify two short-term and two long-term tasks that should be accomplished in order to meet their personal career goals.

Materials: Notepaper.

Activities

Introduction: The counselor reviews everything that the group has accomplished thus far, including setting personal goals, developing personal plans, and assessing educational histories. The counselor then helps the group members understand that they should utilize all of the information they have gathered thus far to determine what needs to be done to achieve their goals.

Icebreaker: Each group member should complete the following prompt: "In order to get where I'm going I must . . . "

Counseling Activity: The counselor explains the difference between short-term and long-term tasks and provides examples. Group members engage in a discussion about what short-term and long-term tasks they believe they need to accomplish to meet their goals. The counselor encourages group members to provide suggestions for tasks to their fellow members. In addition, the counselor helps group members to see similarities regarding where they are in their career development processes.

Conclusion: Each group member writes down two short-term and two long-term tasks to accomplish in order to meet their career goals. The counselor goes around to each group member and provides suggestions and assistance where needed.

Assessment: The school counselor assesses each member's progress toward identifying appropriate tasks while circulating around the group.

Follow-up: Students use this material to add to their personal planning process information.

GROUP SESSION 5: OVERCOMING BARRIERS TO CAREER GOALS

Career Development Standard C: Students will understand the relationship between personal qualities, education and training, and the world of work.

Competency: Students will understand the importance of equity and access in career choice.

Learning Objective: Students will discuss personal and environmental barriers to achieving career success, as well as to discuss strategies for overcoming or managing those barriers.

Materials: Notepaper.

Activities

Introduction: The counselor focuses the group on the objective of the group discussion. An explanation and examples of personal and environmental barriers are discussed. The counselor should be proactive and provide examples of the ways in which racism, sexism, and classism act as barriers to career goal achievement (Mitchell, 2000). This will assist members with feeling comfortable to address these types of environmental barriers during the group process.

Icebreaker: The counselor encourages each group member to complete this prompt: "One thing that gets in the way of me achieving my goals is . . . "

Counseling Activity: Group members actively discuss the ways in which personal and environmental barriers impact achieving career goals. Midway through this discussion, the counselor begins to summarize the barriers discussed and then gently shifts the focus of the group to strategies for addressing and/or managing the identified barriers.

Conclusion: Each group member states two strategies that they could use to address their barriers. Group members also write down their identified strategies.

Assessment: The counselor assesses each group member's ability to develop personal strategies for coping with barriers while group members are sharing the strategies they plan to utilize.

Follow-up: Members use this material, as well as information from previous sessions, to add to their personal career plans.

GROUP SESSION 6: STEPPING STONE TO SUCCESS

Career Development Standard A: Students will acquire the skills to investigate the world of work in relation to knowledge of self and to make informed career decisions.

Competency: Students will develop a positive attitude toward work and learning.

Learning Objective: Students will review what has been accomplished through the group and feel empowered to achieve their personal career goals.

Materials: Folders with the phrase "Stepping Stone to Success" on them, markers.

Activities

Introduction: The counselor states that this is the last group session and encourages members to review the group process by discussing what they learned as a result of being in the group.

Icebreaker: Each group member states the most helpful thing they learned in the group.

Counseling Activity: Group members review the group process. The counselor reinforces to group members that the personal planning work they have done in the group is a "stepping stone" toward achieving their goals. The counselor gives each member a folder so that they may keep their notes and utilize them as a reference to guide their career-development process in the future. The counselor passes around markers so each group member can write their name on their folder.

Conclusion: Group members are allowed to discuss their feelings regarding termination of the group. The counselor discusses resources for future career development and career-planning support.

Assessment: The counselor reviews outcomes for each group member, as well as notes the ways in which the group process should be modified for future groups, given feedback from current group members.

Follow-up: Adjustments should be made to this six-session group process to enhance the group experience for future group members.

INDIVIDUAL COUNSELING CONSIDERATIONS

Most career-development concerns can be addressed via classroom guidance and group counseling activities. However, some situations require individual counseling assistance. For example, when students experience career indecisiveness rather than career indecision, counselors should provide individual attention to address the source of the student's indecisiveness. Career indecision occurs when students lack necessary self-knowledge and/or occupational/educational information to move forward in their career and educational planning. When the information is provided, then students proceed to crystallize their plans. Career indecisiveness exists when students possess the requisite information but remain unable to move forward in their planning. Various factors can result in indecisiveness. For example, when students experience excessive pressure from significant others (for example, parents, guardians, teachers, relatives) to consider particular career/educational options, students may feel "stuck" if those options do not coincide with their particular preferences. This sort of pressure can be especially problematic for students from more collectivistic cultural orientations. In this instance, students may feel as though they are letting their family and/or community down if they do not give in to environmental preferences. A systemic approach involving the family in the counseling process often helps in these situations.

Other issues can also cause career indecisiveness. Students who have perfectionist tendencies, who have excessive fears of failing, or who have dysfunctional career beliefs (e.g., "I must choose what I will do for the rest of my life," "My happiness depends solely on my career") may experience the inability to move forward in their career planning. Counselors can use cognitive behavioral interventions to help such students examine their problematic career and/or personal beliefs. Obviously, when career- and educational-planning concerns occur concurrently with other issues (for example, divorce, death, various forms of abuse), then individual counseling assistance is warranted to help students sort through their concerns and situations. Clearly, counselors must assess each student's situation to determine the type of career assistance that will most benefit each student.

CONCLUSION

We have offered a systems perspective for leading and advocating for the career development of young people. Counselors need to be systematic in planning, organizing, implementing, and evaluating programs. A systems perspective helps counselors understand the relationships among the systems and subsystems that influence career-development programs and the career development of young people. Through informed action, the knowledge gained by this perspective translates into goal-directed, efficient, effective leadership and advocacy. Students themselves are rich sources of information for the career-development program subsystem, and the family system has a strong and enduring effect on career development. Communication within and across systems and subsystems is crucial to the efficient functioning of all of the systems and subsystems involved in young people's career development. Effective communication, planning, and service delivery also requires understanding the specific career-development tasks children and adolescents encounter as they move through grades K–12.

Developing and delivering systematic and coordinated career services to students is a complex task, but it is also a central role for professional school counselors (Campbell & Dahir, 1997). Thus, counselors must play the lead role in advocating for systematic and comprehensive career services for children and adolescents. Such advocacy requires counselors to work effectively with school personnel, students, and parents/guardians, as well as community and business leaders.

Career development is a process that occurs from early childhood through adolescence. School counselors, through the use of comprehensive developmental school counseling programs, can facilitate optimal career growth and exploration. It is important that school counselors systematically help students cope effectively with the career-development tasks the students experience. By engaging in systematic planning based on a thorough understanding of the career-development tasks confronting students, school counselors will act as true advocates for young people and empower them to move effectively toward becoming contributing adults in society.

REFERENCES

American School Counselor Association. (n.d.). *Why elementary school counselors?* Retrieved February 27, 2002, from http://www.schoolcounselor.org/content.cfm? L1=1000&L2=44.

Campbell, C. A., & Dahir, C. A. (1997). *The national standards for school counseling programs*. Alexandria, VA: American School Counselor Association.

Epstein, J. L. (1990). School and family connections: Theory, research, and implications for integrating sociologies of education and family. *Marriage and Family Review, 15*, 99–126.

Gysbers, N. C., & Henderson, P. (2000). *Developing and managing your school guidance program* (3rd ed.). Alexandria, VA: American Counseling Association.

Herring, R. D. (1998). *Career counseling in schools: Multicultural and developmental perspectives*. Alexandria, VA: American Counseling Association.

Hickman, C. W., Greenwood, G., & Miller, M. D. (1995). High school parent involvement: Relationships with achievement, grade level, SES, and gender. *Journal of Research and Development in Education, 28*, 125–134.

Hoyt, K. B. (1975). *Career education: Contributions to an evolving self-concept*. Salt Lake City, UT: Olympus.

Illinois State Board of Education & Association of Illinois Middle-Level Schools. (2000, November). *Career development guide: A comprehensive guide for middle level schools from planning through implementation of career development*. Springfield, IL: Author.

Kotrlik, J. W., & Harrison, B. C. (1989). Career decision patterns of high school seniors in Louisiana. *Journal of Vocational Education, 14*, 47–65.

Krumboltz, J. D. (1996). A learning theory of career counseling. In M. L. Savickas & W. B. Walsh (Eds.), *Handbook of career counseling theory and practice* (pp. 55–80). Palo Alto, CA: Davies-Black.

Lampe, R. E., Trusty, J., & Criswell, R. J. (2001). Counseling programs. In G. Schroth and M. Littleton (Eds.), *Administration and supervision of special programs in education* (pp. 125–138). Dubuque, IA: Kendall/Hunt.

Laramore, D. (1984). Parents' role in the education and career decision-making process. *Journal of Career Education, 10*, 214–215.

McDaniels, C., & Gysbers, N. C. (1992). *Counseling for career development: Theories, resources, and practice*. San Francisco: Jossey-Bass.

Merriam-Webster's Collegiate Dictionary (10th ed.). (1996). Springfield, MA: Merriam-Webster.

Middleton, E. B., & Loughead, T. A. (1993). Parental influence on career development: An integrative framework for adolescent career counseling. *Journal of Career Development, 19*, 161–173.

Mitchell, N. A. (2000). Sister friends: A counseling group for Black female undergraduates. *Journal of College Counseling, 3*, 73–77.

Myrick, R. D. (1997). *Developmental guidance and counseling: A practical approach* (3rd ed.). Minneapolis: Educational Media.

Nichols, M. P., & Schwartz, R. C. (2001). *Family therapy: Concepts and methods* (5th ed). Boston: Allyn & Bacon.

Niles, S. G., & Harris-Bowlsbey, J. (2002). *Career development interventions in the 21st century*. Columbus, OH: Merrill Prentice Hall.

Paisley, P. O., & Hubbard, G. T. (1994). *Developmental school counseling programs: From theory to practice*. Alexandria, VA: American Counseling Association.

Peterson, G. W., Stivers, M. E., & Peters, D. F. (1986). Family versus nonfamily significant others for the career decisions of low-income youth. *Family Relations, 35*, 417–424.

Ragala, J. A., Lambert, R., & Verhage, K. (1991). *Developmental guidance classroom activities for use with the national career development guidelines: Grades 7–9*. Madison, WI: Center on Education and Work.

Russo, T. J., & Kassera, W. (1989). A comprehensive needs-assessment package for secondary school guidance programs. *The School Counselor, 36*, 265–269.

Schmidt, J. J. (2003). *Counseling in schools: Essential services and comprehensive programs* (4th ed.). Boston: Allyn & Bacon.

Sebald, H. (1989). Adolescents' peer orientation: Changes in the support system during the past three decades. *Adolescence, 24,* 937–946.

Smith, T. E. (1991). Agreement of adolescent educational expectations with perceived maternal and paternal educational goals. *Youth & Society, 23,* 155–174.

Starr, M. F. (1996). Comprehensive guidance and systematic educational and career planning: Why a K–12 approach? *Journal of Career Development, 23,* 9–22.

Stone, L. A., & Bradley, F. O. (1994). *Foundations of elementary and middle school counseling.* White Plains, NY: Longman.

Super, D. E. (1990). A life-span, life-space approach to career development. In D. Brown & L. Brooks (Eds.), *Career choice and development: Applying contemporary theories to practice* (pp. 197–261). San Francisco: Jossey-Bass.

Super, D. E., Savickas, M. L., & Super, C. M. (1996). The life-span, life-space approach to careers. In D. Brown, L. Brooks, & Associates (Eds.), *Career choice and development* (3rd ed.) (pp. 121–178). San Francisco: Jossey-Bass.

Trusty, J. (1998). Family influences on educational expectations of late adolescents. *Journal of Educational Research, 91,* 260–270.

Trusty, J. (1999). Effects of eighth-grade parental involvement on late adolescents' educational expectations. *Journal of Research and Development in Education, 32,* 224–233.

Trusty, J. (2002). African Americans' educational expectations: Longitudinal causal models for women and men. *Journal of Counseling & Development, 80,* 332–346.

Trusty, J., & Pirtle, T. (1998). Parents' transmission of educational goals to their adolescent children. *Journal of Research and Development in Education, 32,* 53–65.

Trusty, J., Plata, M., & Salazar, C. (2003). Modeling Mexican Americans' educational expectations: Longitudinal effects of variables across adolescence. *Journal of Adolescent Research, 18,* 131–153.

Trusty, J., Watts, R. E., & Crawford, R. (1996). Career information resources for parents of public school seniors: Findings from a national study. *Journal of Career Development, 22,* 227–238.

VanZandt, Z., & Hayslip, J. (2001). *Developing your school counseling program: A handbook for systemic planning.* Belmont, CA: Brooks/Cole.

Vondracek, F. W., & Fouad, N. A. (1994). Developmental contextualism: An integrative framework for theory and practice. In M. L. Savickas & R. W. Lent (Eds.), *Convergence in career development theories: Implications for science and practice* (pp. 207–214). Palo Alto, CA: Consulting Psychologists Press.

Vondracek, F. W., Lerner, R. M., & Schulenberg, J. E. (1986). *Career development: A life-span developmental approach.* Hillsdale, NJ: Erlbaum.

Walz, G. R., & Benjamin, L. (1984). A systems approach to career guidance. *Vocational Guidance Quarterly, 33,* 26–34.

Whiston, S. C. (1989). Using family systems theory in career counseling: A group for parents. *The School Counselor, 36,* 343–347.

SELF-ANALYSIS WORKSHEET

Name: _____

Instructions: Complete your self-analysis by listing up to five personal qualities, five interests, and five skills you possess. Ask your counselor for assistance if you need help completing your self-analysis.

1. Personal Qualities:

2. Interests:

3. Skills:

EQUITY, ACCESS, AND CAREER DEVELOPMENT: CONTEXTUAL CONFLICTS

CHAPTER

5

Mary Jackson and Dale Grant,
Georgia Southern University

INTRODUCTION

A person's level of educational achievement is associated with their career options. In that regard, professional school counselors have a long history of being advocates for students in their pursuit of postsecondary education. The role of counselors focuses on enhancing students' development in schools, including the process of achieving career maturity. The importance of self-esteem and self-assured identities has long been recognized as part of this developmental process; however, the influence of cultural and systemic components on the development of identity and the development of career-guidance programs as an integral part of the educational experience are still relatively new. Changes in the laws that govern our society have facilitated the diversity we have today. Laws have been enacted to remove many of the equity, access, and service-delivery barriers that have existed for generations. However, issues related to equity and access still exist; they are perceived barriers rather than legal barriers. These perceived barriers function effectively in limiting access and maintaining inequities in the development and articulation of career aspirations and upward career mobility. Many of these barriers are embedded in cross-cultural conflicts that are not addressed in schools because of discomfort, fear, ignorance, and silence on the part of educational leaders. This exclusion helps to maintain the preeminence of the dominant group.

For the populations discussed in this chapter, these perceived barriers inhibit students' academic achievement, career development, and career aspirations. Recent research has increased our understanding by going beyond interest and aptitude assessment to include self-efficacy, cultural identity, cultural and contextual influences, and reconceptualizations of career maturity and career development.

The 1992 National Occupational Information Coordinating Committee (NOICC) guidelines provide a comprehensive list of career-development competencies for elementary, middle, and high school levels. These competencies are useful for developing school counseling program objectives related to career development and can enhance the process of career maturity (Super, 1974). However, these competencies and indicators are not designed to address the contextual realities of a significant number of racial, cultural, and ability groups within the schools—groups that have historical and individual factors influencing their career-development process in distinctive ways. Counselors must consider the structural, contextual, cultural, and sociopolitical realities, both real and perceived, of these diverse groups within our educational system. Many embedded assumptions at the systemic level make it difficult, and even painful in some instances, to understand the perspectives of diverse groups.

This chapter focuses on specific equity and access issues in career counseling for target populations identified by three broad categories—ability, gender, and race. For each of these broad groups, barriers are discussed. However, each set of barriers shares systemically based elements. This chapter takes into consideration the mutually interacting influences between people, their behavior, and their environment (Albert & Luzzo, 1999). It also includes some of the racial and cultural themes in career counseling proposed by Helms and Cook (1999), which highlight the impact of race, social class, and subjective culture at the individual, systemic, and work environment levels. It gives suggestions on how to supplement the general NOICC (1992) competencies for the target populations as well as suggestions for counselor development. Specific activities designed to incorporate some of the cross-cultural interactions and complex realities of target populations are also included.

LITERATURE REVIEW

Many people, regardless of their cultural identity, have not critically considered the oppressive restrictions imposed by institutional racism (Helms & Cook, 1999), heterosexism, and sexism. The mantras of "you can be anything you want to be" and "just try harder" are examples of the voices that may unconsciously block cross-cultural interactions. Many people from diverse racial and cultural backgrounds do not experience the world of work as an opportunity structure for themselves (Helms & Cook, 1999). Without recognition and understanding of our own beliefs and values and the implications of them, we have a tendency to distort cultural messages that interfere with our long-held personal beliefs (Sleeter, 1992). Because of the long-established role of schools in transmission of knowledge and preparation for life in society, some critical analyses of school environments are required to determine the subtle messages transmitted to students in the schools' charge. These analyses should address the extent to which the diversity present is celebrated, valued, and articulated in and outside the classroom by students, teachers, administrators, and staff, as opposed to countered, hushed, ignored, used as tokens, discouraged, or excluded. These distortions often reduce the effectiveness of career counselors with diverse populations when the counselor's and the student's frames of reference are not the same and/or the school environment's and the student's frames of reference are in conflict.

Yang (1991) suggests that as an essential step in becoming more aware and effective, counselors should explore the work-related assumptions under which they were socialized as well as those of their students and society in general. Similar arguments can be made regarding achievement expectations and motivation. Being open to the validity of another's reality, exploring the elements of acculturation, and looking at the personal and vocational implications of their multiple heritages and social conditioning all contribute to increasing awareness and effectiveness. By looking at the multiple realities of all groups and recurring cross-cultural themes, we hope to expand opportunities and possibilities for both the school counselor and, ultimately, the students they serve.

Male and Female Students

Clearly there was a time in our history when access to educational and career options was more limited for women than it is today. Historically, the options for men have been relatively unlimited, given sufficient means, ability, ambition, and self-direction. Social change movements over the past few decades have altered society's view of acceptable roles for men and women. These changes have broadened the range of viable lifestyle and career options for both men and women. However, many attitudes and beliefs are so embedded in our society that they continue to require persistent effort to see their influence on "modern" thinking. These persistent attitudes seem to be, at least in part, embedded in the various cultural contexts in which development occurs. A better understanding of these contexts may help to explain some of the long-standing differences attributed to males and females. One of the major contexts in which development occurs is the school setting itself. Josselson's (1987) research on identity development in females identifies different identity statuses, one of which is foreclosure. Females in this status tend to know from an early age what they want to do and never question the basic messages from their families of origin. Becoming a teacher is associated with this status. Therefore, it is critical that school counselors be aware of how their identity influenced their career choices and how other identity statuses associated with the more nontraditional career choices are available to students.

Women are still likely to be employed in sex-typical occupations (Maume, 1999) even though females tend to have higher career-maturity levels than males (Luzzo, 1995). Historically, women have earned less than men and have struggled more with upward mobility opportunities, as seen in the "glass ceiling". From a developmental perspective, insufficient career exploration, role conflicts, and restrictive internalized beliefs are among the barriers for women. These issues are appropriate domains for the school counselor to explore. The role conflicts are related to choosing between family and career or needing to balance the demands of working and those of raising a family. Some of the restrictive beliefs may reflect societal forces that attach negative labels to women who are career oriented or to men who might consider a predominately female occupation. In general, societal forces, including schools, do not encourage challenges to time-honored or irrational beliefs (Richman, 1988).

In the past, many females were socialized to expect that as adults they would be heterosexual, married homemakers who would raise a family in a relationship where the male in their lives would take primary responsibility for the financial support of the family. If they worked, their income would be supplementary. While this may be the dream of some young girls today, the probability of this scenario becoming reality is much less likely. Yet females today still struggle with remnants of these beliefs and traditional role definitions. Many adolescent females limit their career aspirations, giving looks and relationships greater priority. Some literature suggests that this phenomenon may be a result of discrimination in the classroom (Pipher, 1994). These belief systems limit their consideration of a broad range of careers and may affect the timing and completion of career-development tasks. Encouraging females to focus on the attitudes and behaviors that lead to success in our new economy and integrating these into their lives rather than skillful compartmentalization might be helpful to their career development (Williams, 2000). Additionally, both males and females in schools today might benefit from critically exploring their perceptions of the relationship between work and family as well as from learning appropriate career-exploration and decision-making skills.

Students, regardless of gender, benefit from exploring their specific gender-related expectations as they relate to the integration of work and significant others in their lives. The adoption of gender roles without critical analysis or exposure to nontraditional role models can lead to setting artificial limits on career aspirations. Understanding the context of career counseling, decision-making skills, and enhanced career exploration that encourages students to move out of their "gender box" is essential for addressing access and equity issues. At the elementary level, exposure to new and different gender roles and career options is important. For middle school students, beginning to examine the multiple relationships between gender-role expectations and career aspirations from a "what if" point of view can help students better prepare for more informed career decision making. At the high school level, the focus begins to change to an analysis of existing values and expectations in order to help students address how their perceptions of self fit their career aspirations.

GLBT Students

Students' sexual orientation is not always obvious. This factor coupled with the pervasiveness of the heterosexual worldview makes career counseling for gay, lesbian, bisexual, and transgendered (GLBT) students problematic. GLBT students perceive that they receive less support and guidance from others when making academic and career decisions than do heterosexual students (Nauta, Saucier, & Woodard, 2001). Some empirical research reports tendencies for GLBT students to conform less to traditional and gender-related expectations than the heterosexual population (Brooks, 1991; Hetherington & Orzek, 1989; Morrow, Gore, & Campbell, 1996). Yet, heterosexual school counselors and parents tend to discourage the development of such nonconforming behaviors (Chung, 1995). Thus, it may be more difficult for those students to get support and guidance from individuals directly involved in their lives. This may be compounded for those GLBT students who do not have large support groups to sustain them when they make academic and career decisions (Nauta, Saucier, & Woodard, 2001).

The lack of support and the presence of discrimination perceived in the educational system also exist in the world of work. Both limit equity and access. Levine and Leonard (1984) noted two forms of work discrimination. The more formal forms appear in institutional policies and decisions regarding hiring, firing, promotion, salary, and job assignments. Informal forms are embedded in interpersonal dynamics and work atmosphere, leading to verbal and nonverbal harassment, lack of respect, hostility, and prejudice. Additionally, some GLBT students may discount traditionally conservative careers because of fear of discrimination; however, these assumptions need to be critically analyzed before total dismissal of a career option. Discrimination and lack of equity or access needs to be addressed and integrated into the career-counseling process. However, school counselors should explore the impact of sexual orientation in a respectful way, even if a student is sure that it is irrelevant. Assuming sexual orientation, whether heterosexual or homosexual, is inherently disrespectful. The challenge for the school counselor is to avoid focusing on only one issue or identity and to understand the ways in which multiple identities interact (Schneider & McCurdy-Myers, 1999).

A starting point for school counselors is to seek out professional development opportunities, to be willing and able to serve GLBT students, and to have visible evidence that service is inclusive (Schneider & McCurdy-Myers, 1999). This is a tall order for some school counselors and some school environments. However, it is not only necessary but also our ethical and professional responsibility.

Looking at possible strengths and contributions of GLBT students, Schneider and McCurdy-Myers (1999) also offer some perspectives that merit consideration. Because of the lack of acceptance from society, staying "in the closet" may become a way of life. When given the opportunity, through identity development and/or self-determined freedom, to "come out," GLBT students may develop a strong sense of self. Other positive by-products may include empathy for other stigmatized groups, a strong motivation to remain authentic, and a view of one's career as a way of exploring issues that have personal meaning. GLBT students may be needed and sought after in professions in which diversity is valued.

School environments as well as work settings tend to have a heterosexual bias. Most obvious indicators are relationship-building conversations in which students and others talk about what they do in their spare time. For students, especially at the middle and high school levels, at least highlighting underlying heterosexual assumptions and valuing differences in sexual orientation as an aspect of diversity are important. As for individual counseling, the sessions might focus on the student's perceptions, the messages received, and their impact on that student's sense of self and career aspirations.

Students with Disabilities

Historically, people with disabilities were discriminated against in the workplace. Some were unidentified, misidentified, and under-served. Legislation such as the 1990 Americans with Disabilities Act (ADA) brought to our attention many of the access barriers people with disabilities faced. Legislation also mandated changes in service delivery and employment opportunities, thus reducing the access barriers that impact quality of life as well as employment options. Similarly, the 1990 Individuals with Disabilities Education Act (IDEA) addresses the educational needs of students with disabilities. However, challenges still exist. People with disabilities are underrepresented in the workforce and are underemployed (Ochs & Roessler, 2001), and many experience both job-readiness and job-retention issues. For students with disabilities to take full advantage of their legal rights, a realistic assessment of the impact of their disability on employment and better preparation for employment are needed.

Among the major challenges the educational system faces is to adapt the curriculum so that students with disabilities are better prepared for competitive and sustained employment in the world of work (Tomblin & Haring, 1999). More specifically, many students with disabilities are unaware of the problems that lie ahead of them. Generally, schools focus learning on individual achievement, not cooperation; emphasize the manipulation of abstract symbols, not concrete objects and events; and focus on generalized, rather than situation-specific, learning; however, the second alternative in each case is required for on-the-job competency (Strumpf, Friedman, & Equez, 1989). Some areas of emphasis in career development for students with disabilities might be linking of meaning with activity (Tomblin & Haring, 1999), specific instruction in social-skill survival, community participation, and self-advocacy.

Even though students with disabilities tend to recognize the connection between education and success later in life, they lag behind other students in career maturity (Morningstar, 1997; Ochs & Roessler, 2001). These students are less prepared to make informed career decisions because of lower self-efficacy beliefs and career identities, and are less involved in career-exploration activities (Ochs & Roessler, 2001). Thus, starting at the elementary level, students with disabilities need to begin to understand their disability and engage in interventions that enhance all aspects of their career development. As adolescents and young adults they need to anticipate possible expectations within the employment environment (Wolfe, 2000). Students with disabilities need to know what they can do, what their sources of support are, and how to be self-advocates.

Since disabilities are varied, group-counseling efforts might focus on groups with similar disabilities and on the limitations experienced by students with those disabilities. Degree of limitation and impact on job tasks must be explored. For individual students, self-knowledge of limitations associated with a specific disability might be investigated in the context of career exploration, the education path to the career aspiration, and the fit between all aspects of the career aspirations and the student. Specific job training, job shadowing, knowledge of accommodation in individual and work settings, and role models are helpful in preparing students with disabilities for the world of work.

Gifted Students

The belief that gifted students have so many options that they do not need assistance with career decisions is a lingering myth. Paradoxically, one of the barriers facing this population is their multi-potentiality, which may lead to career indecision (Rysiew,

Shore, & Leeb, 1999). Gifted students tend to be able to achieve academically across virtually any subject matter and have a tendency to be involved in numerous activities outside the classroom setting (Rysiew et al., 1999).

When multi-potentiality is defined as multiple abilities and is accompanied by high motivation and multiple interests and opportunities, career indecision is then associated with the barrier referred to as the "overchoice syndrome" (Rysiew, Shore, & Carson, 1994, p. 44). Confusion and anxiety can result from having too many career choices (Pask-McCartney & Salomone, 1998), and delayed planning and multiple changes in career aspirations can also be an outcome (Emmett & Minor, 1993; Fredrickson, 1972; Grant, Battle, & Heggoy, 2000; Jepsen 1981; Perrone & Van den Heuvel, 1981). In addition, perfectionism in seeking one right occupation (Perrone & Van den Heuvel, 1981; Silverman, 1993), choice of safe academic majors (Kerr & Claiborn, 1991), external pressure from others to excel, and sex-role expectations can be among other influences on career choice (Kerr, 1997; Sanborn, 1974). The gifted tend to be interested in making career-related decisions that provide outlets for their multiple abilities as well as making lifestyle rather than "job" choices; their decisions are highly value driven (Kerr & Claiborn, 1991; Rodenstein, Fleger, & Colangelo, 1977). Because of this value-based propensity embedded within the decision-making process, gifted students can benefit from career-guidance efforts that start at the elementary level (Grant et al., 2000; Kerr & Claiborn, 1991). This long-term examination can help identify and clarify their values in such a way that they can make informed choices about their options and channel their multiple abilities into vocational and avocational choices. Early interventions can also enhance the acquisition of career decision-making and career-exploration skills so that change over their lifespan is achievable.

Beginning at the middle school level and continuing throughout the educational process, gifted students can benefit from examination of dimensions of lifestyle and their fit with personal values and career aspirations. This broadened perspective increases their opportunity to examine multiple talents in the context of their anticipated and preferred lifestyle. Gifted students can benefit from being taught a comprehensive career-decision model that facilitates not only their first career decision but those that follow as they progress through the stages of life. Whether in individual or group counseling, effectively working with gifted students includes not only their talents as they relate to specific career aspirations but their values and expectations regarding their future and a holistic, integrated approach to career and lifestyle.

Students of Color

A helpful context for beginning an appreciation of the career-related issues faced by students of color is provided by Ogbu (1993; 1994). He distinguishes between the cultural orientations of various people of color based on their land of birth. Voluntary cultural groups include individuals who lived a sufficient number of their developmental years in a homeland outside of the United States. These students enter the educational system with their culture intact, and therefore their cultural identity intact, and with an orientation toward adaptation. They anticipate some difficulties in adapting to their new environment, and they have hopeful expectations for their futures. Their future orientation includes career aspirations. These students expect to learn the dominant system while maintaining their culture. These voluntary groups have what Ogbu (1993) identifies as primary cultural differences between themselves and the white American mainstream. Thus, designing appropriate interventions for this group of students includes identifying and addressing specific culture-related differences, such as language and communication styles. However, by the third generation, some aspects of their homeland culture are lost, and more aspects of the dominant culture are adopted (Tatum, 1997). By this time their interactions within school and society may resemble that of oppressed people of color.

Involuntary cultural groups differ from voluntary groups in that they have secondary cultural differences between themselves and the mainstream cultural group. These differences develop after the two populations come into contact with one another or after members from one cultural group begin to participate in institutions controlled by the other group (Ogbu, 2001). Some people of color were brought to this country against their will. For many, the purpose was to serve the dominant culture, while others were relegated to minority and less-than positions. Groups who were historically oppressed—for example, African Americans, early Mexican Americans, Native Hawaiians, and Native Americans (Ogbu)—developed secondary cultural differences in order to cope with a contact situation such as, one group being subordinated by another. According to Ogbu, in some cases minority-group members are aware of these developed ways of coping; in other cases the coping methods have taken on a life of their own and people are not aware of them. Since education has been associated with learning the culture and language of white Americans, students from involuntary minority groups can have a very difficult time in school. This perspective begins to provide some insight into the report that "Black, Latino, and Native American students perform well below whites [sic] in all subjects and at all grade levels" (Olson, 1996, p. 31).

Historically, access to educational opportunities was either legally denied or limited, and the contributions of the involuntary group cultures were absent, limited, or misrepresented within the dominant society. Thus, there has been little or no exposure to the valuable contributions made by members from nondominant group cultures in this society. Because an aspect of career development can be "I can grow up to be like (my hero)," an absence of exposure to members from their cultural group who have contributed to society can limit career aspirations. In addition, the historically oppressed groups have clustered in occupations that they were permitted to enter due to the restrictions imposed by white institutional racism (Helms & Cook, 1999).

Assisting nonmajority students to develop to their potential requires more than changes in the curriculum and increased exposure to role models. Over time and within a segregated society, a number of negative images from the dominant group's frame of reference have become associated with these oppressed cultural groups. Although many of these negative images have been challenged today, others still linger in both subtle and overt messages. These negative images remain influential, as internalized oppression, in limiting the achievements of some minority students. Thus, involuntary cultural groups have within them lingering aspects from their homeland cultures as well as limiting aspects remaining from their historical oppression. Many of the negative messages are familiar when we consider some of the race-based stereotypes prevalent in society.

Ogbu (2001), who has researched the interaction of minority and majority cultures and its relationship to academic achievement, argues that we need to understand the nature of different cultures and their influence on the perceptions and expectations of their members. The research of Fordham and Ogbu (1986) sheds some light on this need in a study involving black youth. Their findings indicated that academic achievement of black youth is made more difficult when their black peers identify achieving black students as acting white. Additionally, Tatum (1997) indicates that associating academic achievement with being white came about after desegregation. Black students who do well in school find themselves in a double bind, experiencing difficulty fitting into the black community, where they may be subjected to the perception of acting white, and yet also lacking full acceptance within the white community, where they may be perceived as an exception to the rule.

Positive self-identity has long been valued in our society and associated with career options that provide the opportunity to reach one's full potential. For whites, positive self-identity may be an individual issue, but positive group identity is a given since their culture is the dominant, normative culture. For students of color, the group or cultural identity has not been positively defined. The recognition of membership in a racial minority group as a historical barrier is not new; however, recognizing the role of the perceptions of one's cultural group as an integral and potentially limiting aspect of the development of identity is relatively new and complex.

In order to assist all students in developing not only positive individual identities but also positive cultural group identities, interventions need to address culture-based components from both the minority and the dominant cultures. Critical interpretations vary from one minority group to another and perhaps from one individual to another. Meaningful dialogue about cultural interpretations of behavior is not easy but is worth the effort. Virtually all of the existing racial-identity models (Cross, 1995; Helms, 1993; Phinney, 1990; Scott & Robinson, 2001) include within them developing an understanding of self as a member of a racial group and an identity that can incorporate contributions from and to other racial groups. In addition, one's cultural identity is influenced by exposure to and interactions with members from other cultural groups.

Tatum (1997) argues that both positive self-identity and positive group identity are important, and she describes a process by which messages that contain culture-group inclusion or exclusion information is transmitted. Self-identity develops first and is influenced by the family circle, which is the nucleus for group identity. The interactions with peers and other members of one's community are observed by other members of this identity group, who then interpret those interactions as consistent or inconsistent with the expectations of the broader cultural group. Consider for a moment perceptions associated with white men in menial jobs, male nurses, black or female CEOs, and cross-cultural dating. Those perceptions, as shared with the broader membership, indicate continued acceptance or nonacceptance possibilities, and can serve as a guide to future interactions. When those interactions are among individuals who are from different cultures, interpretations still take place. However, those interpretations then take place in the context of the identity group and can be limiting, biased, or stereotypical, due to the misperceptions that linger in our society. The person involved in cross-cultural interactions, exposed to the misinterpretations of both groups, seems to face no longer belonging to their identity group on the one hand and rejection or being different and isolated on the other. Thus, we have another double bind. The interpretations of interactions are made from different frames of reference. All too often this means that they do not meet the stereotypical expectations that are associated with them by the other cultural group. Thus, students from involuntary cultural groups can benefit from interventions that help them to identify aspects of their cultural identity to be valued and maintained. In addition, interventions that facilitate the separation of a success-identity from an acting-white-identity are necessary. In a similar fashion, students from the mainstream culture need to identify aspects from their cultural identity to be valued and maintained and to separate them from those aspects that limit the opportunities of others.

WHOLE-SCHOOL INTERVENTIONS

School counselors are in a position to take a leadership role and become advocates for the career development of diverse learners. Common themes underlie the lack of equity and access to effective career development for minority groups. These themes show up in historical and media stereotypes and perceptions that permeate our experiences. These limiting perceptions are manifested in career aspirations of children as early as first and second grade. Wahl and Blackhurst (2000) reported that as early as first grade, girls begin to restrict occupational aspirations and boys' aspirations begin to mirror the race and class differences existing in adult job holdings. Thus, career aspirations are influenced by perceptions of self as they relate to factors such as gender, race, ethnicity, socioeconomic status, and ability. Considering these factors, school counselors need to involve all school personnel in critically looking at the school environment and how it mirrors inhibiting forces that are embedded in the community it serves. Some of these inhibiting forces are often messages embedded in passing comments, jokes, unrecognized achievements, and insincere responses.

School counselors can start this critical analysis by helping schools challenge the inhibiting messages that are transmitted in the classroom, on the playground, in student organizations, in the teacher's lounge, and in policy and practice. What happens in the schools to inform young students that some careers are not available to or are not appropriate for females, people of color, people with disabilities? What are the "you can't" messages that become rooted in identity and ultimately inhibit career aspirations? What are the embedded assumptions at a systemic level that support institutional racism, sexism, heterosexism, and able-ism? In particular, how might a school's climate inadvertently uphold those inhibiting beliefs and assumptions that impact identity development and career exploration and development? What level of awareness, knowledge, and skill do school personnel have in supporting the career development process? For example, sexual harassment may be a significant element in making career decisions. The school counselor could help school personnel look at how sexual harassment is handled in their school. Bringing the realities of sexual harassment to a level of greater awareness, increasing the knowledge base about it, and then teaching skills to handle it can impact the system at a meaningful level. Involvement is another aspect that has positive implications for both identity and career development. Are clubs and organizations reflective of the makeup of the school? Do all students have a *realistic* opportunity to become involved? Is diversity welcomed, encouraged, and valued? Do all students have access? School counselors are in an excellent position, based on training and role responsibilities, to take leadership in instituting such an analysis, to look for ways to rectify the inequities, and to assist in the professional development of staff needed to implement policy and practice changes.

Classroom Guidance Activities

"Career development proceeds—smoothly, jaggedly, positively, negatively—whether or not career guidance or career education exists. As such, career development is not an intervention but the object of an intervention" (Herr & Cramer, 1996, p. 32). Historically, career decision making has primarily involved assessment of interests, aptitudes, and values. For effective career development today, the influences of cultural and systemic contexts must be included. The students of today must address in some depth the inhibiting and perceived barriers that persist as well as the enabling messages that are more recently being articulated in segments of our society and in some of our schools.

One of the most common and more easily identified inhibiting forms of message is the stereotype. When the assumptions underlying these messages, as well as the validity of these messages, are not challenged, there is a risk of them becoming institutionalized practices that restrict career development. Therefore it is important to provide opportunities for students to articulate societal messages and perceived barriers and enablers in order to invalidate the stereotypical, biased messages and develop constructive strategies for changing perceptions of self and career aspirations. The following activities are designed to help students understand the relationship among personal qualities, education and training, and the world of work. More specifically, these activities address becoming more aware of the world of work from a holistic perspective. This holistic view includes barriers, real and perceived; the complex relationship between achievement, success, and satisfaction; as well as the effect of work on lifestyle, lifelong learning, and meaning making. Additionally, embedded within these activities is the opportunity to develop conflict-management and cooperation skills.

The following lessons are suitable for middle or high school.

LESSON 1: UNDERSTANDING EQUITY AND ACCESS ISSUES IN CAREER DECISION MAKING

Career Development Standard C: The students will understand the relationship between personal qualities, education, training, and the world of work.

Competency: The students will understand the importance of equity and access in career choice.

Learning Objectives

- After group discussion and counselor-led instruction, students will be able to identify examples of diversity harassment/discrimination in everyday life.
- After regular reflection and abstraction from personal experience, the student will be able to generate broad, useful cross-cultural concepts that influence the career decision-making process.
- Subsequent to group discussions, students will be able to recognize and examine cross-cultural experiences and their influence on actual and perceived barriers to career decision making and choice.

Materials: Paper, pen.

Developmental Learning Activities

Introduction: The school counselor begins a discussion with students about "isms" the school counselor or the students may have experienced in school and society in general. The discussion of these direct, concrete experiences includes the resultant real or perceived barriers and possible ways of dealing with them.

Activity: The counselor asks the students to think of a critical incident in their lives revolving around an "ism" issue and write a paragraph for each item below:

1. Describe the incident and name the issue(s) involved.
2. Who was involved, and what was the outcome?
3. What reaction did you have, and how has it affected you?
4. How could it have been handled differently?

The students share their experience, with the ground rules that this is a place where ideas can be explored and played with, where questions are encouraged, where someone's experience is not denied, and where mistakes are seen as opportunities to learn and develop.

Each student relates their experience of the critical incident without criticism or correction. Others may suggest other perceptions without negating the experience of the student.

Conclusion: After reflecting and abstracting from the students' experiences, the counselor lists the student's new learning from each incident. The counselor explores the connections between incidents and how these experiences might affect the way one makes decisions.

Assessment: Identified examples of cross-cultural inequities and possible impacts on career decision making and choice could be a measure of competency.

Follow-up: In a subsequent meeting, have the students introduce a decision that they have made in the last week (or two weeks) that was influenced by their looking more critically at cross-cultural issues and real or perceived barriers related to one of the "isms." If they are unable to think of one, have the students relate how their perceptions or actions have been impacted by the discussions.

LESSON 2: TALK SHOW

Career Development Standard C: Students will understand the relationship between personal qualities, education, training, and the world of work.

Competencies: Students will describe the effect of work on lifestyles. Students will learn how to use conflict management skills with peers.

Learning Objectives

- Students will gain knowledge about the interrelationship of life roles.
- Students will gain knowledge of different occupations and changing roles.
- Students will be able to describe stereotypes, biases, and discriminatory behaviors that may limit career opportunities for individuals.
- Students will be able to discuss the pros and cons of various life-role options.

Materials: Video camera, dais for guest speakers, mock microphone for moderator, and area for the rest of the group to sit as audience.

Developmental Learning Activities

Introduction: The students or school counselor selects a show host interviewer/moderator and several guests to represent various positions on a controversial issue. The remaining students (audience) are to participate with questions and comments after the guest's initial presentations and as directed by the moderator. The format is based on the more moderate talk shows on television.

Activity: The topic of the program involves a career-related issue such as:

Should women work?
How to balance career and family.
Work place discrimination.

It's not what you know but whom you know.
The key to success is just trying harder.

Conclusion: The moderator has each guest make a concluding remark. Then the moderator or school counselor poses several process-oriented questions to the whole group:

In what ways were positions modified, solidified?
What did it feel like to defend a minority position/majority position?
What allowed you to see another's position more clearly?
What influenced you to change your mind/attitude?
What influenced you to "dig your toes in" even more?
What had you not previously considered or thought about regarding the
    topic or your position on the topic?

Assessment: Competencies can be measured by the quality of responses to the questions in the conclusion section and demonstrated ability to listen in respectful ways to others' ideas within the group setting.

Follow-up: In a subsequent meeting, have the students review the videotape to see what might have been missed when participating in the action. It is also interesting to note the different reactions when participating in the action and watching the action on video.

LESSON 3: IT'S ALL TIED TOGETHER

Career Development Standard C: Students will understand the relationship between personal qualities, education, training, and the world of work.

Competencies: Students will understand that work is an important and satisfying means of personal expression. Students will learn to work cooperatively with others as a team member.

Learning Objectives

- Students will learn how personal expression can be a part of career choice.
- Students will learn how stereotypes can inhibit career choice.
- Students will learn the value of working cooperatively with others.

Materials: Paper, pencils.

Developmental Learning Activities

Introduction: The counselor discusses the relationship between personal expression, expectations of self, and others' expectations of one, and how that impacts career choice. The counselor tells students that looking at our own stereotypes as well as those of others can be helpful in making more informed and satisfying career decisions.

Activity: Students break into equal-sized groups. They count off sequentially to ensure more diversity within each group (sixteen students would be four groups of four by counting off 1 to 4, with 1s in one section of the room, 2s in another, and so on). Each group receives a scenario such as those listed at the end of this lesson. After reading the scenario, group members discuss immediate reactions. Each group member is assigned or chooses an "element" for which they are responsible to write out suggestions made by the group regarding that element. Possible influential elements might include:

- drawbacks or barriers to making this career choice
- coping strategies needed for success
- risks encountered
- critical events and influencing thoughts in making this choice
- expected effects on family, significant others, and the like

Group members list three to five ideas for each element as it pertains to their scenario (three to five drawbacks recorded by one member, three to five coping strategies recorded by another, and so on). Allow ten to fifteen minutes for this process.

Students then regroup so all that recorded drawbacks are in one group, all coping strategies in another, and so on. These reconstituted groups discuss what each recorded from their former group. The task is to come to conclusions about common issues, situation-specific effects, and new ideas or insights. Each group reports back to the whole class, and results are listed on the board for each category.

Conclusion: The group discusses what was learned about stereotyping, possible barriers to be encountered, a variety of coping strategies, factors affecting decision making, and so on.

Assessment: The counselor uses the quality of student responses for each category listed on the board as a measure of competency.

Follow-up: In a subsequent meeting, the counselor focuses on the interpersonal processes involved in teamwork as well as the presence of any stereotyping, barriers, and coping strategies experienced during the activity by asking:

What new ideas did you learn from other group members?
What did it feel like to contribute; what did it feel like when others had
    similar ideas to your group's ideas?
What did you learn about yourself in this exercise?
What stereotyping went on during the initial group activity?
What barriers to effective teamwork were apparent during the initial group
    activity?

Examples of Scenarios

1. You've just moved into a new neighborhood and discover that your next-door neighbors have a rather nontraditional working arrangement—the man stays home all day with two small children while the woman works downtown in one of the large office buildings.

2. New neighbors move in to the apartment next to you, and you discover that they are homosexual.
3. You go to the hospital for surgery, and you find that the head surgeon is from the Middle East.
4. You find yourself in a classroom where all the other students are of another race.
5. You go to a new dentist recommended by a friend and find that she has blue and green spiked hair.

LESSON 4: CAREER DAY: EQUITY AND ACCESS PERSPECTIVES

Career Development Standard C: The student will understand the relationship between personal qualities, education, training, and the world of work.

Competencies

- Students will understand the relationship between educational achievement and career success.
- Students will explain how work can help to achieve personal success and satisfaction.
- Students will understand that the changing workplace requires lifelong learning and acquiring new skills.
- Students will describe the effect of work on lifestyles.
- Students will understand the importance of equity and access in career choice.
- Students will understand that work is an important and satisfying means of personal expression.

Learning Objectives

- Students will be able to identify specific barriers, both real and perceived, encountered during the career development process.
- Students will be able to identify a variety of coping strategies to overcome obstacles to career goals.
- Students will be able to identify some of the risks involved in career development.
- Students will be able to recognize differing decision-making strategies used in the career-development process.

Materials: Desired number of representatives from the community work force that represent multiple cultures and ethnicities, reflect a range of occupations requiring varying levels of academic preparation, and exemplify a nontraditional career selection (for example, black, female military personnel). The counselor prepares the selected participants to talk about the equity and access issues they experienced, observed, and contemplated in their career development.

Developmental Learning Activities

Introduction: The counselor introduces the Career Day speakers, including the career represented, the basic topics to be addressed by the speaker, and any guidelines regarding the students' interactions with the speakers. The guest speakers present their career story with particular emphasis on experiences that limited access and/or maintained inequities in their development of career aspirations and upward career mobility:

> Barriers both real and perceived (subtle, unconscious, or cross-cultural in nature)
> Coping strategies that have worked (or not worked) for them
> Role of risk taking
> Development of decision-making skills
> Critical incidents that impacted career decisions

Activity: After the presentation, the students write a paragraph on what in the presentation was most significant to them. After paragraphs are completed, the counselor places students in discussion groups of four or five based on similarities of reactions to the presentation. Each group compiles a list of major points shared within their group and brainstorms other barriers, coping strategies, risk taking, or decisions that could have existed, along with the pros and cons of those choices.

Conclusion: Each group of students shares their findings with the total class.

Assessment: Measurement of the competencies can be shown by the student's sharing with the group a barrier, a risk, coping strategies, and/or the pros and cons of decisions they have made in their lives.

Follow-up: In a subsequent meeting, the counselor asks the students to generate other questions or concerns they have as a result of hearing the speaker's experiences.

SMALL-GROUP COUNSELING PLANS

Herr and Cramer (1996) remind us that "decision making, the development of self-identity, and life changes . . . occur within political, economic, and social conditions that influence the achievement images and belief systems on which individuals base their actions" (p. 203). With this in mind, it is important to help students look at some aspects of their culture, gender, race, and ability and the influence of these factors on achievement images, belief systems, decision making, and ultimately career choice. These group sessions are designed for high school students to increase both knowledge and skills in dealing with the sociopolitical nature of the world and the bidirectional influences of personal qualities, education, and the world of work.

Because of the sensitive nature of the material to be introduced in these sessions, students should be advised of basic ground rules that encourage respectful behavior and confidentiality. Based on Allport's (1954) theory on prejudice reduction, the following criteria are suggested:

Cooperation rather than competition is promoted.
Group members have equal status.
Group members have shared goals.
Group members are given opportunities for personalized interactions.
The group situation is sanctioned by principals and parents.

GROUP SESSION 1: MESSAGES

Career Development Standard C: Students will understand the relationship between personal qualities, education, training, and the world of work.

Competencies

- Students will explain how work can help to achieve personal success and satisfaction.
- Students will identify personal preferences and interests influencing career choice and success.
- Students will describe the effect of work on lifestyle.

Learning Objectives

- Students will describe how beliefs and attitudes influence career choice.
- Students will describe how work can be a means of personal expression.

Materials: Flip chart.

Activities

Introduction: The counselor tells the group that they are going to talk about some time-honored beliefs about the importance of family or culture in career decision making.

Icebreaker: The counselor has students generate a list of some of the messages they hear directly or indirectly every day from their families, friends, and teachers, such as:

"Work hard and save your money."
"How much you make (study) determines how important you are."
"Women's first responsibility is to the family."
"You're only worth something if you're working hard."

From the list generated, the students select four or five messages that they think affect the way that they look at the world.

Counseling Activity: The counselor has the students generate examples they see in their world that validate or invalidate their beliefs. They may find that their belief is not reflected in their lived experience. How do their beliefs match their behavior in school? How do they see it in others? When does a specific belief or attitude work for them? When does it not? What makes the difference?

Conclusion: The counselor asks students how they might see these beliefs and attitudes at work in the lives of their teachers, parents, doctors, plumbers, electricians, mechanics, and so on. The counselor helps them continue to match beliefs and cultural messages to their perceptions.

Assessment: The counselor has students:

- Describe how culture and family influence beliefs, attitudes, and the way they see the world and the decisions they make
- Describe how work can be a means of personal expression
- Describe how work influences their relationship with their family

GROUP SESSION 2: MORE MESSAGES

Career Development Standard C: Students will understand the relationship between personal qualities, education, training, and the world of work.

Competencies

- Students will identify personal preferences and interests influencing career choice and success.
- Students will understand the importance of equity and access in career choice.

Learning Objectives

- Students will describe the effects of stereotypes, biases, and discriminatory behaviors that may limit career opportunities for individuals.
- Students will describe how personal preferences and interests influence career choice and success.

Materials: Flip chart; paper and pencils for students.

Activities

Introduction: The counselor discusses the previous session's topic of messages students get from others that influence the way they see the world and the decisions they make. The counselor then introduces the topic of messages students get from families, friends, school, and the world around them about what they can and cannot do as well as what they may and may not do.

Icebreaker: Each student lists on a sheet of paper twenty famous women; they have about five minutes to do so. Then each student lists on the other side of their paper twenty famous men. Then the counselor asks what career each represents. The counselor categorizes answers into career clusters.

Counseling Activity: The counselor asks: What are the messages you get from this? How hard was this to do? Which list was easier for the females (males) to do? How do the lists differ? How are they alike? Again, what message do you get from this exercise that tells you what you can and cannot do as a woman (as a man)? What you may or may not do?

Conclusion: The counselor asks: What have these messages and experiences taught you about yourself? The counselor helps the students keep the focus on the internalization of these messages rather than blaming others.

Assessment: Students summarize how these internalized messages might affect career aspirations and decision making.

Group Session 3: Getting Real

Career Development Standard C: Students will understand the relationship between personal qualities, education, training, and the world of work.

Competencies

- Students will understand the importance of equity and access in career choice.
- Students will learn how to use conflict-management skills with peers and adults.

Learning Objectives

- Students will know how to use conflict-management skills with peers and adults.
- Students will understand the influence of bias, stereotypes, and prejudice on career development.

Materials: None.

Activities

Introduction: The counselor reviews the messages students get from the different expectations of males and females and the effects these messages have on the way we look at ourselves. The counselor then introduces the topic of the effects that race has on each of us and how racism impacts everyone and influences career development. The counselor tells students that it is a concept that is difficult to discuss and often treated as a taboo topic (Tatum, 1992). The counselor explains that it is important to learn about the impact racism has on our development—academically, socially, personally, and career-wise.

Icebreaker: The counselor asks students what racism looks like in school, at work, in the media, in life. Examples might include:

- *White students and students of color isolate from one another.*
- *Minorities get special treatment now with affirmative action.*

Counseling Activity: The counselor helps students distinguish between racism, a system of advantage based on race (Wellman, 1977), and prejudice, preconceived judgment or opinion often based on limited information (Katz, 1978). The counselor takes some of their examples and looks at them through the lens of racism and prejudice to see how each might be present:

- *White students and students of color isolate from one another.* How might this just be a natural gravitation toward similarity rather than racism? How might it be a little of both?
- *Minorities get special treatment now with affirmative action.* This sounds like some get privilege and others don't. And it feels awful when you are not the privileged one.

The counselor leads students in examining a few examples of racism through the filters of limits and costs. For example,

- How does racism limit us? *Spend time ignoring and maybe being afraid.*
- What are some of the costs? *Getting angry with each other.*

Conclusion: The counselor asks students about their experience of talking about sensitive subjects in the group:

> What was it like to know that others did not see things exactly as you saw them?
> What did you learn about managing conflict with peers?
> What did you learn today about prejudice and racism and how it limits all of us?

Assessment: Students enumerate some of the costs of racism in respectful and cooperative ways.

Follow-up: The counselor asks students to notice some of the inequities based on race that they see during the week. Students keep notes concerning the incidents and the context within which they occur and bring it to group next time.

GROUP SESSION 4: MORE GETTING REAL

Career Development Standard C: Students will understand the relationship between personal qualities, education, training, and the world of work.

Competencies

- Students will understand the importance of equity and access in career choice.
- Students will learn how to use conflict-management skills with peers and adults.

Learning Objectives

- Students will describe the effects of stereotypes, biases, and discriminatory behaviors that may limit career opportunities.
- Students will know how to use conflict-management skills with peers and adults.

Materials: None.

Activities

Introduction: The counselor reminds students of the group rules.

Icebreaker: The counselor asks:

> What incidents of racism did you observe this past week in school, at work, in life?
>
> What effects did these observations have on you?
>
> What were your reactions? (anger, shame, guilt, despair)

The counselor helps the students name their reactions. It is important to recognize both the cognitive and affective levels of reactions and further recognize that racism has negative ramifications for everyone.

Counseling Activity: After students name some of the reactions, the counselor asks a couple of the students to role-play an incident they noticed during the past week while the rest of the students observe. After the role play, the counselor asks each participant about their experience of the role they played. Then the counselor asks for observations and reactions from the spectators:

> How was having an incident "role played" different than just talking about it?
>
> How might this experience impact your future decision-making process?

Conclusion: The counselor asks the students what they learned about themselves that surprised them. What did they learn about someone else that surprised them?

Assessment: Requesting that responses be specific and behavioral, the counselor asks the students:

> How might this experience impact your future decision-making process?
>
> What did you learn about conflict management from the exercise?
>
> How did you resolve any conflict with others?
>
> What did you learn about your own stereotypes and biases that might limit career opportunities?

GROUP SESSION 5: CAN I DO IT?

Career Development Standard C: Students will understand the relationship between personal qualities, education, training, and the world of work.

Competencies

- Students will explain how work can help to achieve personal success and satisfaction.
- Students will understand that work is an important and satisfying means of personal expression.

Learning Objectives

- Students will understand the influences of personal preferences and interests on choice.
- Students will make the connections of what they are doing now with the future.

Materials: None.

Activities

Introduction: The counselor reminds students that the group has talked about some of the things that influence beliefs and attitudes, as well as some of the external realities such as bias, stereotyping, and prejudice. The counselor tells students they will now look at how "now" connects with "later."

Icebreaker: The counselor has the students take a few deep breaths and get rid of some of the chatter in their heads. The counselor asks them to look at their lives now.

Counseling Activity: The counselor asks students what they are doing that is working for them in school, at home, at work. The counselor helps them be specific and behavioral. For example, "I know that when I finish my homework, I feel a sense of accomplishment. I know that when I keep my mind on what I'm doing what I'm supposed to at work, I might get more hours or a raise."

- How do you know it's working for you? *I usually have a feeling of accomplishment. No one gives me dirty looks.*
- What are you doing now that's not working for you? *When I get mad, I know that things are not going like I want them to. I study and still don't make good grades.*
- How do you know it's not working for you? *Getting mad generally doesn't change things even though I feel justified at the time. I feel guilty. People don't do what I want them to.*
- How does what you're doing now connect with what you might be doing later? *Dirty looks example—Sometimes I need to get feedback from others to keep me on task.*
  Studying—Sometimes I have to work harder than I want to and sometimes I need help in knowing how to do some things.
  Mad at people—Sometimes people really bug me. I may need to look at a job where I don't have to deal with so many people.

Conclusion: The counselor asks: What are the connections you would like to keep between what you're doing now and what you may be doing in the future? What do you want to do more of, less of?

Assessment: Appropriately responding to the questions in the conclusion section can be a measure of competency.

GROUP SESSION 6: PUTTING IT ALL TOGETHER

Career Development Standard C: Students will understand the relationship between personal qualities, education, training, and the world of work.

Competencies

- Students will identify personal preferences and interests influencing career choice and success.
- Students will describe the effect of work on lifestyle.
- Students will understand that work is an important and satisfying means of personal expression.

Learning Objectives

- Students will recognize how personal preferences and interest influence career choice.
- Students will recognize how work can lead to satisfaction and personal expression.

Materials: Flip chart.

Activities

Introduction: The counselor reviews with students that they have spent several weeks together looking at some important factors that affect career aspirations and decision making. Some of the things they already knew, some they might have forgotten, and some they never thought of in that way before. The counselor tells students that today they'll look at what they've learned about themselves and others in the group, and what they might want to do in the future.

Counseling Activity: The counselor models the learning/change process in group sharing time:

> What surprised you most about what happened during this group?
> What did you learn about yourself that you weren't sure of before?
> What have you learned from your family about working?
> What have you learned from school about working?
> What effects do you think that stereotyping, prejudice, and racism have on the way you view the world of work and your place in it?
> How might you look at things differently now?

Conclusion: The counselor records the most important learning each student had during the group sessions.

Assessment: Responding appropriately to the process questions can be a measure of competency.

Follow-up: The counselor asks group members to keep a journal for two weeks on how they are applying what they learned in group to their lives. The counselor reconvenes the group and has the members review the list of most important learning from the final group. The group discusses how their learning has changed and expanded in just two week's time.

INDIVIDUAL COUNSELING CONSIDERATIONS

School counselors can do some seemingly small but significant things to invite more equity and access for individuals within their schools. A beginning point might be a demographic analysis of students who are referred and self-referred for career counseling. This information could provide the counselor with direction and guidance in looking at possible access and equity issues within the school itself. A strategic approach might involve simple changes within the office to display visible signs of inclusion such as ethnic art, resources representing multiple cultures, and the rainbow or triangle sign suggesting a gay-friendly place. School counselors should continually seek professional development opportunities in areas that increase cross-cultural awareness, knowledge, and skills. As an adjunct to the more formalized professional development, counselors should address their cross-cultural awareness by exploring the work-related assumptions that were operative during their own socializing process (Yang, 1991); this is another important contributor to successful interventions. Becoming aware of these embedded beliefs and assumptions can help clarify perceptual filters and ultimately aid the school counselor in more clearly seeing the current contexts in career development. These interventions increase counselor self-awareness, knowledge, and skill.

The following interventions enhance the career-counseling process with students who may encounter issues of equity and access that limit their career development and choice. Just as the classroom teacher can link current learning tasks to the world of work by helping students appreciate the transferable ideas and skills that come from analyzing a piece of literature, such as critical thinking, implied meaning, multiple roles, and differing experiences, the school counselor can help students analyze their experiences and perceptions to develop new "meaning making" and new options. By linking current learning tasks to the world of work, the school counselor may help develop new "meaning-making" for the student.

Because career options begin to narrow for both males and females as early as first grade, the use of fantasy, dreams, and what-if exercises can expand thinking and validate some possible career choices at almost any level in the career-development process. Another potentially powerful intervention involves reframing. This can be implemented by helping the student look at what appears to be a weakness, looking for the positive intent behind that behavior or characteristic, and then reframing a negative into a strength. If the student is viewed as tenacious rather than stubborn, it becomes easier to work with that attribute to the student's benefit. Hillman and Ventura's (1992) contention is that Churchill's early learning and language difficulties in school were a way of becoming the greatest orator of his time. He needed that extra attention and development to become what he already was. A related concept of highlighting a variety of contexts can also be applied to the complexities of career development. By helping the student articulate and elaborate about the barriers they see and experience, the school counselor can more sensitively address the student's concerns. Asking culturally sensitive, open-ended questions might be appropriate, such as What stops you from _____? Under what circumstances would you consider _____? How is what you're doing now mirroring what you expect in the world of work?

The school counselor needs a modicum of soul searching and cognitive flexibility for these interventions to be meaningful. Some of the interventions may look simple, yet their implementation may take a great deal of self-awareness and knowledge of identity and cross-cultural development. This added awareness and knowledge could be applied to enrich a wide range of interventions already within the school counselor's repertoire.

CONCLUSION

Issues of equity and access continue to limit career development and choice. Until all barriers both real and perceived are removed, professional school counselors need to be aware of the cultural, sociopolitical, and systemic influences that limit career development and choice. It is necessary to create an atmosphere where ideas can be entertained, where questions are encouraged, where mistakes are seen as opportunities to learn, and where irrational beliefs or time-honored limiting beliefs are challenged. Not only do career counseling interventions need to help students deconstruct the negative aspects of their cultural identities, but these interventions need to incorporate the broader contexts of systemic and sociopolitical beliefs that influence and limit career decisions. For many professional school counselors this involves expanding self-knowledge, being more open to the validity of another's reality, and further exploring the elements of acculturation and social conditioning so that real and perceived barriers are considered. Included in the process of expanded exploration might be looking at ways of coping with a hostile environment or glass ceiling, initiating meaningful dialogue about cultural interpretations of behavior, and having discussions of all groups' cultural contributions that should be valued and maintained, as well as discussing those aspects of society that limit the opportunities of others. The professional school counselor's task is to implement career-counseling programs that incorporate the influences of cultural, sociopolitical, and systemic components on career identity development and challenge embedded assumptions that limit equity and access for all students.

REFERENCES

Albert, K. T., & Luzzo, D. A. (1999). The role of perceived barriers in career development: A social cognitive perspective. *Journal of Counseling & Development,* 77(4), 431–437.

Allport, G. W. (1954). *The nature of prejudice*. Cambridge, MA: Addison-Wesley.

Brooks, S. E. (1991). Resources. In N. J. Evans & V. A. Wall (Eds.), *Beyond tolerance: Gays, lesbians, and bisexuals on campus* (pp. 213–232). Alexandria, VA: American College Personnel Association.

Cross, W. E., Jr. (1995). The psychology of Nigrescence: Revising the Cross model. In J. G. Ponterotto, J. M. Cases, L. A. Suzuki, & C. M. Alexander (Eds.), *Handbook of multicultural counseling,* (pp. 93–122). Thousand Oaks, CA: Sage.

Chung, Y. B. (1995). Work discrimination and coping strategies: Conceptual frameworks for counseling lesbian, gay, and bisexual clients. *The Career Development Quarterly, 50,* 33–44.

Emmett, J. D., & Minor, C. W. (1993). Career decision-making factors in gifted young adults. *The Career Development Quarterly, 41,* 350–366.

Fordham, S., & Ogbu, J. U. (1986). Black students' school success: Coping with the burden of acting white. *Urban Review, 18,* 176–206.

Fredrickson, R. H. (1972). The multipotential as vocational decisionmakers. In R. H. Fredrickson & J. W. M. Rothney (Eds.), *Recognizing and assisting multipotential youth* (pp. 58–78). Columbus, OH: Merrill.

Grant, D. F., Battle, D. A., & Heggoy, S. J. (2000). The journey through college of seven gifted females: Influences on their career related decisions. *Roeper Review, 22*(4), 251–260.

Helms, J. E. (1993). Toward a model of white racial identity development. In J. E. Helms (Ed.), *Black and white racial identity: Theory, research, and practice* (pp. 49–66). Westport, CT: Praeger.

Helms, J. E., & Cook, D. A. (1999). *Using race and culture in counseling and psychotherapy: Theory and process.* Needham Heights, MA: Allyn & Bacon.

Herr, E. L., & Cramer, S. H. (1996). *Career guidance and counseling through the life span: Systematic approaches* (5th ed.). New York, NY: HarperCollins Publishers, Inc.

Hetherington, C. & Orzek, A. M. (1989). Career counseling and life planning with lesbian women. *Journal of Counseling & Development, 68,* 52–57.

Hillman, J., & Ventura, M. (1992). *We've had a hundred years of psychotherapy and the world's getting worse.* San Francisco, CA: Harper.

Jepsen, D. A. (1981). Annual review: Practice and research in career counseling and development. *The Career Development Quarterly, 41,* 98–129.

Josselson, R. (1987). *Finding herself: Pathways to identity development in women.* San Francisco: Jossey-Bass.

Katz, J. H. (1978). *White awareness: Handbook for anti-racism training.* Norman, OK: University of Oklahoma Press.

Kerr, B. A. (1990). *Career planning for gifted and talented youth.* ERIC Digest # E492. Reston, VA: ERIC Clearinghouse on Disabilities and Gifted Education (ERIC Document Reproduction Service No. ED321497).

Kerr, B. A. (1997). Developing talents in girls and young women. In N. Colangelo & G. Davis (Eds.), *Handbook of gifted education* (pp. 483–497). Needham Heights, MA: Allyn & Bacon.

Kerr, B. A., & Claiborn, E. D. (1991). Counseling talented adults. *Advanced Development, 3,* 75–83.

Levine, M. P., & Leonard, R. (1984). Discrimination against lesbians in the workforce. *Signs: Journal of Women in Culture and Society, 9,* 700–710.

Luzzo, D. A. (1995). Gender differences in college students' career maturity and perceived barriers in career development. *Journal of Counseling & Development, 73,* 319–322.

Maume, D. J., Jr. (1999). Glass ceilings and glass escalators. *Work & Occupation, 26*(4), 483–510.

Morningstar, M. E. (1997). Critical issues in career development and employment preparation for adolescents with disabilities. *Remedial and Special Education, 18*(5), 307–321.

Morrow, S. L., Gore, P. A., & Campbell, B. W. (1996). The application of a sociocognitive framework to the career development of lesbian women and gay men. *Journal of Vocational Behavior, 48,* 136–148.

National Occupational Information Coordinating Committee (NOICC), U.S. Department of Labor. (1992). *The national career development guidelines project.* Washington, DC: U.S. Department of Labor.

Nauta, M. M., Saucier, A. M., & Woodard, L. E. (2001). Interpersonal influences on students' achievement and career decisions: The impact of sexual orientation. *The Career Development Quarterly, 49*(4), 352–362.

Ochs, L. A., & Roessler, R. T. (2001). Students with disabilities: How ready are they for the 21st century? *Rehabilitation Counseling Bulletin, 44*(3), 170–177.

Ogbu, J. U. (1993). Differences in cultural frame of reference. *International Journal of Behavioral Development, 10,* 483–506.

Ogbu, J. U. (1994). Understanding cultural diversity and learning. *Journal of the Education of the Gifted, 17,* 355–383.

Ogbu, J. U. (2001). Understanding cultural diversity and learning. In J. A. Banks (Ed.) and C. A. M. Banks (Assoc. Ed.), *Handbook of Research on Multicultural Education* (pp. 582–593). San Francisco, CA: Jossey Bass.

Olson, L. (1996, December 4). Achievement gap widening, study reports. *Education Week, 16*(14), 1, 31.

Pask-McCartney, C., & Salomone, P. R. (1998). Difficult cases in career counseling: The multipotentialed client. *The Career Development Quarterly, 36,* 231–240.

Perrone, P. A., & Van den Heuvel, D. H. (1981). Career development of the gifted: Horizons unlimited. *Journal of Career Education, 7,* 299–304.

Pipher, M. (1994). *Reviving Ophelia: Saving the selves of adolescent girls.* New York: Ballantine Books.

Phinney, J. S. (1990). Ethnic identity in adolescents and adults: Review of research. *Psychological Bulletin, 108,* 499–514.

Richman, D. R. (1988). Cognitive career counseling for women. *Journal of Rational-Emotive & Cognitive Behavior Therapy: Cognitive-Behavior Therapy with Women* (special issue), *6*(1–2), 50–65.

Rodenstein, J., Fleger, L. R., & Colangelo, N. (1977). Career development of gifted women. *The Gifted Child Quarterly, 21,* 340–347.

Rysiew, K. J., Shore, B. M., & Carson, A. D. (1994). Multipotentiality and overchoice syndrome: Clarifying common usage. *Gifted and Talented International, 92*(2), 41–46.

Rysiew, K. J., Shore, B. M., & Leeb, R. T. (1999). Multipotentiality, giftedness, and career choice: A review. *Journal of Counseling & Development, 77*(4), 423–431.

Sanborn, M. P. (1974). Career development problems of gifted and talented students. In K. B. Hoyt & J. R. Hebeler (Eds.), *Career education for gifted and talented students* (pp. 103–152). Salt Lake City, UT: Olympus.

Schneider, M., & McCurdy-Myers, J. (1999). Academic and career choices for lesbian and gay young adults. *National Consultation on Career Development Papers 1999,* 7–16.

Scott, D. A., & Robinson, T. L. (2001). White male identity development: The key model. *Journal of Counseling & Development, 79,* 415–421.

Silverman, L. K. (1993). Career counseling. In L. K. Silverman (Ed.), *Counseling the gifted and talented* (pp. 215–238). Denver, CO: Love.

Sleeter, C. E. (1992). Restructuring schools for multicultural education. *Journal of Teacher Education, 43*, 141–148.

Strumpf, L., Friedman, P., & Equez, J. (1989, January 15). *Improving workplace skills: Lessons from JTPA*. Paper presented at the 6th Annual Conference of the Partnership for Training & Employment Careers, Phoenix, AZ.

Super, D. E. (1974). *Measuring vocational maturity for counseling and evaluation*. Washington, DC: National Vocational Guidance Association.

Tatum, B. D. (1992). Talking about race, learning about racism: The application of racial identity development theory in the classroom. *Harvard Educational Review, 62*(1), 1–24.

Tatum, B. D. (1997). *"Why are all the black kids sitting together in the cafeteria?"* New York: Basic Books.

Tomblin, M. J., & Haring, K. A. (1999). Vocational training for students with learning disabilities: A qualitative investigation. *Journal of Vocational Education and Training, 51*(3), 357–370.

U. S. Department of Education. (1990). *Individuals with Disabilities Education Act of 1990*. Washington, DC: U. S. Government Printing Office.

U. S. Department of Justice. (1991). *Americans with disabilities handbook*. Washington, DC: U. S. Government Printing Office.

Wahl, K. H., & Blackhurst, A. (2000). Factors affecting the occupational and educational aspirations of children and adolescents. *Professional School Counseling, 3*(5), 367–375.

Wellman, D. (1977). *Portraits of white racism*. New York: Cambridge University Press.

Williams, C. P. (2000). *Helping women shape a career path and a life that works*. Presented at the International Career Development Conference Year 2000, 17th Annual California Career Conference, November 2000, San Francisco, CA.

Wolfe, K. (2000). Critical skills in career advancement for people with visual impairments. *Journal of Visual Impairment & Blindness, 94*(8), 532–535.

Yang, J. (1991). Career counseling of Chinese American women: Are they in limbo? *The Career Development Quarterly, 39*, 350–359.

STRATEGIES FOR PERSONAL/SOCIAL DEVELOPMENT

In Part Two, seven chapters examine the implementation of the National Standards for School Counseling Programs in Personal/Social Development. In Chapter 6, Deryl F. Bailey (The University of Georgia) and Mary Bradbury-Bailey (Cedar Shoals High School, Athens, GA) discuss how respecting diversity means promoting high standards with plenty of support for all students. Bailey and Bradbury-Bailey detail what school counselors can do to transform their school systems, promote respectful relationships between staff and students, and provide specific support and personal growth for all students. Chapter 7, by Shannon D. Smith (University of Akron) and Stuart F. Chen-Hayes (Lehman College/City University of New York) describes ways school counselors can provide leadership and advocacy for sexual minority youth. Focusing on gay, lesbian, bisexual, transgendered, and questioning youth, Smith and Chen-Hayes provide curricular and group counseling resources that will help bring to reality the vision that schools exist to serve all students. Vivian V. Lee (Old Dominion University) in Chapter 8 outlines the components of an effective violence-prevention and conflict-resolution program within the contexts of school systems (for example, policies and curriculum) and comprehensive school counseling programs. She then provides specific guidance to school counselors on implementing violence-prevention curricula and details how to provide group counseling to students who experience repeated difficulty with conflict. In Chapter 9, Susan Norris Huss (Bowling Green State University) gives an overview of grief and loss issues in children and adolescents. She frames these issues as barriers to learning and provides a comprehensive framework in which parents, school systems, and children can healthily resolve the losses they all experience. Based on the latest research on substance-abuse prevention and intervention, J. Kelly Coker (University of Nevada, Las Vegas) in Chapter 10 puts forth a comprehensive model school counselors can use to effectively address alcohol and other drug use in schools. Coker includes a student workbook as part of a 4-Fold Prevention program that was derived from the research literature. In Chapter 11, Vicki Brooks (Lewis and Clark College) explores how school counselors can provide leadership to help school systems, teachers, and all students manage the stressors of contemporary society in adaptive, healthy ways. The book concludes with Chapter 12, written by Carolyn B. Stone (University of North Florida). Stone reviews the legal landscape regarding schools and sexual harassment and provides systems-level guidance to help schools protect students. She ends the chapter by providing school counselors with multilevel interventions to help both perpetrators and victims of sexual harassment.

RESPECTING DIFFERENCES: RACIAL AND ETHNIC GROUPS

Deryl F. Bailey, The University of Georgia, and Mary Bradbury-Bailey, Cedar Shoals High School, Athens, GA

INTRODUCTION

Despite a new school building, it seems to be business as usual for one Southeastern high school. As I walked past classrooms designated as advanced classes, in spite of the school's large percentage of students of color (mostly African Americans and Hispanic Americans), their presence was lacking in these particular classes. However, they were overrepresented in lower-level classes. As in many other schools across the nation, white and Asian American students populated the advanced-level classes. In addition, white and Asian American students were encouraged to fulfill the requirements for an academic diploma seal, while African American and Hispanic students took courses to fulfill the requirements for a technical or general seal. African American and Hispanic American students, especially males, represent the bulk of the 50 percent school dropout rate.

This scenario represents a dilemma faced by many schools today that are not prepared to handle the rapidly changing demographics seen in our society as a whole. As a result, many students feel alienated from the educational system that should represent a key to their future. We have all experienced feelings of alienation, and we all know they stem from feeling like we do not belong or "fit in" to that particular environment. Unfortunately, within the public school system, these feelings of alienation translate into increased truancy rates, discipline referrals, failure rates, and ultimately, dropout rates.

LITERATURE REVIEW

Recent statistics indicate that more than half the U.S. states graduate less than 75 percent of their students, with Georgia and Arizona graduating 58.5 percent and 55.8 percent respectively; only Vermont and Connecticut were at or near the 90 percent mark (Business Roundtable, 2003). While many factors have been cited as potential causes for these alarming statistics, Wong and Wong (2001) suggest that when students take ownership of their learning it has a direct impact on their academic success. Whether on the district, building, or classroom level, ownership depends on the relationship between members of the delivery system (administrators, counselors, and teachers) and the consumers (students, parents, and the community). As with any group, a successful relationship depends on establishing trust and mutual respect through shared experiences.

Once the center of the community, many schools experienced a connection with the community at large through athletic events, plays, and concerts. Unfortunately, schools no longer experience this feeling of connectedness between the school and the larger community. While the faces of those in the delivery system have remained predominantly white, the faces of the students, parents, and community for many public school systems have dramatically changed over the past few decades, thus limiting the number of shared experiences. According to the U.S. Bureau of Census (2000), the Hispanic and African American populations have grown by 53 percent and 14 percent, respectively, while the white population only increased by 6 percent in the past two decades. As a result of these demographic changes and "white flight," the student population served by public schools has dramatically changed over the past few decades. In Texas, California, and Florida alone, minorities comprise 50 percent of the population; in major U.S. cities, ethnic minorities represent more than half the student population (Holcomb-McCoy, 2003). By the year 2020, researchers predict that children from ethnic minority groups will comprise more than 50 percent of public school students (Hodgkinson, 1995). Regardless of these major shifts in student populations, the faces of school professionals are still mostly represented by whites. The majority of professional school counselors are white and female (Erford, House, & Martin, 2003). This discrepancy between the student population and the school counselors hired to serve them may result in services not sensitive to the special needs of a changing student population. Learning to respect differences between racial and ethnic groups is an intentional process and should reflect the overall mission of every school counseling program. This involves the school counselor's willingness to embark on a multicultural journey—a journey that includes an examination of individual beliefs as well as an examination of the schools' counseling program relative to its the overall mission and goals.

Respecting Differences: It's a Journey, Not an Event

Respecting racial and ethnic differences begins with a desire to become a "culturally-responsive and skilled" counselor. As a professional, the school counselor need only look at the position statement adopted by the American School Counselor

Association (ASCA) to understand the importance of developing these skills. According to ASCA (1999), school counselors should "take action to ensure students of culturally diverse backgrounds have access to appropriate services and opportunities which promote the optimal development of the individual." For the school counselor, respecting racial and ethnic differences should be seen as a professional and ethical responsibility that becomes evident in his or her interactions with students of color. ASCA's statement is not one of passivity, but one that represents a "call to action." So what would be the evidence of a culturally responsive and skilled counselor? We (Bailey & Bradbury-Bailey) offer the following as examples of such evidence:

- Names are respected and pronounced correctly. Counselors inquire as to their meaning, origin, and more importantly, the proper pronunciation.
- Genuineness is evident in personal interactions with students of color and their parents.
- Language of respect dominates conversations with students, and more importantly, conversations with other counselors, teachers, and administrators regarding students of color and other culturally different students.
- A level of comfort exists between student and counselor.
- Counselors avoid making students of color feel like "community service projects."
- Mediocrity from students of color is absolutely NOT accepted.
- Encouragement, not pity, is evident in all interactions.

The above points of evidence are based on the beliefs and collective experiences (45 years) of the chapter authors as a public school teacher and secondary school counselor. Although not complete, this list represents "intentional actions" of professional school counselors who understand the essence of respect and who show that respect in their day-to-day interactions with and decisions made regarding students of color and other culturally different students. While there exists no official training for identifying insincere words or actions of school personnel, students of color and other culturally different students have learned to recognize these types of behaviors from teachers, counselors, administrators, and fellow students. First and foremost, a culturally responsive and skilled counselor understands that attending a session at a conference or workshop, or even a semester-long course is only part of the process of becoming a culturally responsive and skilled professional. Becoming a culturally responsive and skilled professional is an ongoing journey (DeLucia-Waack, DiCarlo, Parker-Sloat, & Rice, 1996) that requires a consistent reassessment of one's level of cultural competence based on the three domains of cultural competence: awareness, knowledge, and skills (Sue, Bernier, Durran, Feinberg, Pedersen, Smith, & Vasquez-Nuttall, 1982; Carney & Kahn, 1984; Sue, Arredondo, & McDavis, 1992).

THE MULTICULTURAL JOURNEY: DEVELOPING AWARENESS AND KNOWLEDGE AS A PROFESSIONAL SCHOOL COUNSELOR

Awareness begins with self-examination, and we suggest that counselors use the following questions as a starting point:

- What are my beliefs and attitudes regarding students of color and other culturally different students and their families?
- What are the origins of these beliefs and attitudes?
- Given the work of school counselors, are my beliefs appropriate?
- What can I do to develop the appropriate beliefs and attitudes needed to assist *all* students in their development?

Self-examination can be an uncomfortable and at times painful process, but it is a necessary one for developing a respect for other cultures. The school counselor who has chosen to embark on this journey must become comfortable with feeling uncomfortable. Counselors must avoid being "politically correct" and be willing to challenge others when appropriate. We must honestly assess what we believe about others who are culturally different and be willing to challenge our beliefs. For some, the most challenging question is the question regarding the origins of their beliefs. More times than not we have incorporated our parents' beliefs into our own belief system. Admitting that what our parents believed may not be appropriate for today's counselors, and learning to separate ourselves from an outdated belief system is a difficult but necessary step in the process. Taking that painful step opens up our lives, making change a possibility.

Opening ourselves up to change means becoming knowledgeable about issues we are unaware of or do not understand: lack of understanding and appreciation for differences between cultures, and the fact that most white teachers and counselors do not understand the benefits that come as a result of being a member of the dominant culture. This lends itself to an atmosphere of alienation between the school system and its students. A common comment made by some white teachers and counselors is, "I do not understand why they [students of color] do not succeed by taking advantage of all the opportunities available to them in our schools and in society in general." They seem to believe that by working hard everyone can gain access to a better standard of living, not realizing that at least some of what they have achieved is the direct result of white privilege (McIntosh, 1989) and their being a part of the dominant culture. Even if teachers and counselors never personally shut the door to opportunity because of someone's race, they may not be aware of doors that have been closed for students and families of color and how that affects their self-concept and achievement in school and society.

Understanding racism and prejudice, both unintentional and intentional, and its effects on students of color represents another important component of the awareness part of the journey. Many white Americans assume that as long as they are not advocating for cross burnings or participating in meetings that involve wearing white sheets then they are excluded from participating in racism. The following personal reflection exemplifies this type of thinking.

Personal Reflection from a Veteran White Female Teacher

As a white, protestant American, I did not understand racism or its crippling effect because I made the assumption that many white Americans make, which is "if I don't feel it or see it, then it must not be happening." As a beginning teacher I assumed that everyone had parents like mine. I grew up thinking and believing in the "golden rule."

What a treasure my parents gave me, but like any treasure, it represented either help or a hindrance depending on how it was used. Relative to my own journey of awareness, it became a tool for me to fight to preserve my identity in spite of the crowd's identity.

Ten years later, I still did not "get it" when a group of my African American students gave me a surprise party at the end of the year for being such a "wonderful" teacher. I thought they were acknowledging my lesson plans and teaching strategies! Sadly enough, it was another ten years before I started getting it. I had taken a group of African American students to a science conference for high school students, and on the way back, the conversation turned toward school and their relationship with certain teachers. Temporarily, they forgot I was in the car and described situations in which they were ignored when they asked for help or tried to answer questions or had to endure smart remarks from certain teachers. Because of my naïve racism, I was so tempted to dismiss their remarks and credit them to the hypersensitivity of adolescence; instead, I quietly listened to their conversation and then inquired as to how they deal with such incidents. They shared the coping strategies they had employed and I realized that this explained why they were so successful academically. Needless to say, even though I would not let them use names as part of their

discussion, I was in shock and still found it hard to believe their stories, but I decided I would let my silence validate their experience.

A few weeks later, an African American student came to my room early the morning we were to leave for a biological field study. When I asked him for his permission slip, he informed me that he was not able to get one of his teachers to sign it. I followed him to the room and stood in the hall so that I could see the teacher without her seeing me. The African American student stood quietly by her desk while she helped another student. When the teacher finished, she ignored the African American student and proceeded to grade papers at her desk. Several minutes went by, and she continued to ignore him until I stepped into view. Based on the subject area, I figured out that this was one of the teachers who the students had described as ignoring African American students in her class. Based on conversations I had with this teacher and her intelligent, "classy" persona, I never would have suspected she was capable of such racist acts unless I had seen it myself. I cannot begin to imagine the impact her behavior has had on the academic performance of African American students in her class—an introductory class that is necessary to advance to the next level, both of which are necessary for admission into post-secondary institutions. Teachers like this represent academic barriers for students of color and have the potential to thwart their attempt to advance to their academic career.

Since that time, I have come to understand that my naivety and assumptions had actually worked to discount the reality for many of my students of color. I needed to stop thinking that they were being overly sensitive and instead listen to their experience. As part of my journey

(continued)

Personal Reflection (continued)

as a teacher I needed to learn how to become an advocate for all students, to hear their experiences without immediately dismissing their reality. My students have clearly taught me that "my perception is my reality." I've also learned how to convey to my students that there is an important skill they must develop; this skill involves understanding that *not everyone who looks like them is for them, and not everyone who does not look them is against them,* and they need to be able to distinguish between the two groups of people.

Having someone help students process and work through situations can greatly enhance the educational experience for all students; unfortunately, this is a rare experience for students of color. Culturally responsive and skilled counselors are perfect for situations such as these. These counselors possess both the expertise and opportunity to provide this type of service. By no means does this mean that some teachers or counselors should sit in judgment of their colleagues based on students' perceptions; instead, counselors must be willing to challenge the system and the inappropriate actions of those within the system. We believe that listening to the students' experiences and understanding their realities is critical to the effectiveness of counselors as change agents.

If counselors are willing to change, then gaining culturally relevant knowledge and developing culturally responsive skills becomes a regular part of one's professional growth. An important part of knowledge involves an understanding of one's strengths and weaknesses relative to multicultural competencies. The Professional School Counselor Multicultural Competence Questionnaire (Holcomb-McCoy & Myers, 1999) is an example of an assessment tool that can help counselors with this self-examination. After an honest evaluation, a clearer understanding of one's weaknesses can assist counselors to plan and take advantage of professional development opportunities. According to Holcomb-McCoy (2003), professional development for school counselors should involve a variety of learning experiences, including but not limited to "investigating one's own cultural or ethnic heritage; attending workshops, seminars, and conferences on multicultural and diversity issues; joining organizations that focus on cultural sensitivity; reading literature written by ethnic minority authors or about ethnic cultures; and becoming familiar with multicultural education literature" (p. 324). While these experiences will definitely help the counselor begin to learn about other cultures, they will only provide indirect access to knowledge about other cultures. Gaining knowledge by direct interaction with other cultures or lifestyles must be intentional, especially for white teachers and counselors, since they represent the dominant culture. If a counseling department or school wants to increase parent participation for their students of color, then department members and school representatives need to go out into the community and be willing to meet with parents through local churches or family restaurants owned and operated by that culture. Meetings should be casual at first so that the different groups can learn about and from each other without any educational issues on the table. Different groups making up the school community will be better prepared to work together if given the chance to understand each other. Thus, by increasing knowledge directly, the implementation of skills becomes a logical next step in the multicultural journey for the professional school counselor.

A JOURNEY THAT INVOLVES ACTION

Once a school counselor commits to the journey by increasing awareness and knowledge, then developing a rapport and establishing a relationship with students of color and other culturally different individuals becomes possible. In doing so, the school counselor switches roles from gatekeeper for the status quo to advocate (Bailey, Getch, & Chen-Hayes, 2003; Clarke & Stone, 2000; Hart & Jacobi, 1992; Toporek, 1999). Respecting cultural differences in students and families can translate into the counselor's ability to look past the excuses for low achievement (for example, poverty, number of students on free and reduced lunches, and family backgrounds). An honest examination of the school climate and culture and believing in the academic potential of all students, especially students of color, will assist counselors in removing educational and social barriers to student achievement (Bailey, 2003; Boykin, 1986). Consequently, an important step for counselors involves their willingness to immerse themselves in the most current multicultural research as it pertains to the educational challenges of students of color and the achievement gap. If school data indicate that students of color, especially African American and Hispanic American students, and students from low-income families are overwhelmingly reflected in discipline referrals, in and/or out of school suspensions, school expulsions, vocational courses, and special education placements, as well as being underrepresented in advanced and gifted and talented classes, then culturally responsive and skilled counselors who view themselves as educational advocates must not accept the stereotypical explanations for these dilemmas. Instead, counselors must develop and implement action plans to remedy these situations.

Achievement Gaps: What School Counselors Need to Know

Data for the Education Trust (1998) indicates that academic achievement gaps exist between different cultures, with whites and Asian Americans producing better scores on high-stakes tests that involve reading, vocabulary, and math than African American and Hispanic students. Unfortunately, these high-stakes test scores are used by both middle and high schools to place students in upper level and college-bound classes, thus continuing to widen the achievement gap and lessen the opportunity for admission into a postsecondary institution as the student progresses through school. Too often the school community is too ready to place all the blame on the student's demographics and lack of parental involvement; this viewpoint allows them to walk away from the problem and never invest time or energy in possible solutions. Respecting differences, however, would prevent the school community from accepting these reasons and instead look to the research for viable answers.

Since parental involvement ranks fourth in research investigating the top thirty factors affecting student achievement, and student demographics ranks twenty-eighth (Wong & Wong, 2001), school counselors must ask themselves, what ranks at the top? According to Wong and Wong (2001), classroom management and time on task are the top two determining factors affecting student achievement; thus, it is within the realm of counselors and teachers to reduce if not eliminate the achievement gap. Data from the Education Trust (1998) supports this finding in that students with similar ability levels will test 30 to 50 percentile points different on academic tests depending upon the teacher they are assigned. Teachers with classroom management experience and extensive knowledge of course content have been reported to have a greater impact on student achievement, especially if the teacher holds a degree in that academic area. The reality is that students from low-income families, predominantly African Americans and Hispanic Americans, are more likely to be taught by teachers who are teaching out of field without a major or minor in that subject or by teachers who are just entering the teaching profession, thus lacking extensive teaching experience (Education Trust, 1998). Furthermore, those subjects are usually core subjects (that is, English, math, and science), which are critical for successful high-stakes test performance. So it is no surprise that these students fall further and further behind as they move from elementary to middle to high school, until the achievement gap is so obvious that it makes repair seem impossible (Brennan, 1999; Education Trust, 1998).

Further compounding the achievement gap are the types of educational tracks, namely, vocational and general, that lack academic rigor, where students of color, with the exception of Asian American students, seem to be overrepresented. As a result, African Americans, Hispanic Americans, and students from low-income families receive an education that is both different and inferior compared to that of their white counterparts (Ford, 1996; Irvine, 1991). African Americans, Hispanic Americans, and students from low-income families usually end up in vocational or general-education tracks based on ability grouping in core areas; as a result, many receive a watered-down curriculum with lower academic expectations and poorer instruction from educators who are either new or teaching out of field (Education Trust, 1998; Irvine, 1991; Jones, Van Fossen, & Spade, 1987). Proponents of tracking argue that this pathway will help train students in a skill so they can seek immediate employment after high school; the reality, however, shows these tracking programs are dominated by African Americans, Hispanics, and low-income students who are exposed to a weak curriculum for core courses like reading, writing, and math. Vocational courses, which tend to be skill based (such as business, computers, and health care), are not problematic in and of themselves; however, the perceptions of educators in nonvocational and general courses toward these students are problematic. Teachers who teach in the college prep and advanced courses tend to view and treat African Americans, Hispanic Americans, and students from low-income families as less than capable. Regardless of the diploma type (vocational, general, college prep, or college prep with honors), all students should be held to high expectations, especially in courses that involve reading, writing, math, and other critical-thinking skills. If public schools are to produce a more skilled work force capable of critical thinking it is essential that all parents and educators, including counselors, hold all students to high expectations.

Too often African Americans, Hispanic Americans, and students from low-income families are not involved in the decision-making process regarding the type of curriculum best suited for their needs and postsecondary plans. Instead they are simply assigned by counselors, teachers, and administrators (Irvine, 1991; Jones, Van Fossen, & Spade, 1987; Education Trust, 1998). Unfortunately, these decisions are based more on behavior and past performance rather than the academic capacity of the individual student. Students who are bored with the watered-down curriculum of a vocational or general track tend to display their frustrations and boredom by living down to the low expectations of the adults in their lives (parents, teachers, counselors, and administrators). This behavior, more often than not, results in discipline referrals and lower grades. Relative to the achievement gap, tracking only serves to widen the gap and make it virtually impossible for even a sophomore student to try and prepare for college. By this time, the student has been tracked into lower level classes, especially math and science, and will only be in geometry or biology by the time he or she is a junior, and advanced algebra by his or her senior year. Tracking in these areas alone has severe implications relative to students' preparation for postsecondary options should they choose to switch from the vocational or general track. For example: 1) their PSAT and SAT scores will be lower because they have not had as much advanced math as other students; 2) they will have to delay taking the SAT or ACT in an attempt to have as much advanced math as possible, thereby delaying their application to college; 3) they may not have all the math required by most postsecondary institutions; and 4) math placement often determines science placement, so they also fall behind in this core area as well. Consequently, these students (African Americans, Hispanics, and students from low-income families) are not as competitive as other applicants. This only perpetuates the myth that they are intellectually inferior, which can play a major role in the students' perception of their own academic ability. Instead of seeing themselves as "behind" and maturing later academically than their white counterparts, these students begin to internalize the negative stereotypes and actually perform below their capabilities when challenged in an upper-level class (Irvine, 1991; The College Board, 1999).

Even more disturbing is the data concerning African American students, especially males, and their placement in special education classes. Research indicates that this particular population is three times more likely than their white counterparts to be assigned into special education classes; academic achievement for these students literally grinds to a halt. Unfortunately, the parents of these students feel alienated from the educational system and feel powerless in fighting the placement. Furthermore, many parents often do not understand the ramifications of their child's placement in a special education program. Conversely, African American students along with Hispanic Americans are rarely recommended for gifted and talented programs; gifted programs typically involve the best teachers and usually have a special budget that allows those teachers to do more creative and thought-provoking activities with their students. Whites and Asian American students tend to dominate these classes, so the achievement gap continues to widen between them and their nonwhite and Asian American peers (Carnegie Corporation, 1984/85; Ford, 1996).

Once counselors have examined the research, it is important for them to decide how this information will change their interactions with and advocacy for nonwhite and Asian American students and parents. A logical first step for culturally responsive and skilled school counselors involves recognizing their changing roles. Because educational reform hinges on student achievement, school counselors need to examine their beliefs and their potential role in improving student achievement. Do educators, including counselors, accept the easy answers or should they challenge themselves in search of the truth, which may include acknowledging their past and/or current role in maintaining the status quo rather than advocating for excellence in all students?

A second skill counselors need to develop is the ability to listen to what students have to say about the academic setting as well as creating opportunities to listen. Oftentimes students can provide a helpful assessment of the academic environment if they trust the person listening and if they perceive that change might result because of their input. For example, during a diversity retreat for a small group of new (no previous teaching experience) and beginning teachers (one to three years of teaching experience), a beginning teacher recalled the following incident. Several African American students were eating lunch in her room one day and began discussing what they defined as "lazy teachers." After a few minutes, the teacher's curiosity forced her to ask the students to explain what they had been discussing without identifying teachers by name. The students defined "lazy teachers" as teachers who students could tell did not expect much from them by the way and what they taught. The students could tell that not much thought had gone into lesson preparation because the teacher would walk in and say, "Well, how about we watch a video today," and then a few days later, "Well, how about you write something in your journal about the video and one of its characters." Also, the students indicated that "you never get anything back that you turn in until weeks later, and then you get this low grade, and they cannot even explain how they got it and just get defensive with you and threaten to write you up . . . lazy." The teacher was able to figure out based on the course content that this was a general English class; so even if a particular student wanted to go to college, he or she might never be exposed to any of the critical thinking and writing skills needed for that level, and his or her SAT scores relative to reading comprehension and vocabulary might also be adversely affected.

Finally, respecting differences would translate into the professional school counselor learning how to become an advocate for certain populations of students in their school. These populations could include, but are not limited to, different ethnic groups, students with special needs, and students with disabilities. Advocacy does not equate with pity; pity represents a polite version of racism. Pity only limits the student relative to academic achievement and usually trains them to accept the victim's role of disempowerment. Advocacy, on the other hand, involves listening to the student, helping the student establish a clear plan of action, and making available the necessary resources so the student can enhance his or her academic achievement. This course of action empowers the student so that he or she learns how to work through future problems (Bailey, Getch, & Chen-Hayes, 2003; Toporek, 1999). In addition, advocacy may involve going against the norm for your department, school, and district and finding other advocates who are willing to implement strategies and action plans conducive to reducing the achievement gap for certain minority groups and students from low-income families.

WHOLE-SCHOOL INTERVENTIONS

The professional school counselor's attitude toward respecting differences and implementing steps to make students' goals a reality can be greatly impacted by the attitude and actions of the administration at the district and building levels. Working toward respecting differences requires a vision of what the learning environment would look like if it were a priority. For a culturally responsive and skilled school counselor wanting to make a difference the following question must not only be asked but also answered: What would an individual school, school system, counselor's office or counseling program, and/or classroom look like if respecting differences was the expectation instead of the exception?

As a current teacher and counselor educator (also a former secondary counselor), we offer the following systemwide, schoolwide, and counseling program ideas.

Systemwide Program

- The organization of a multicultural task force composed of community members and representatives of the school district to investigate strengths and weaknesses of the school system relative to respecting differences.
- District-level personnel's participation in a course that promotes cultural awareness and acts as a starting point for future conversations to occur between district officials and community members.
- The completion of a systemwide curriculum audit by an outside group to investigate strengths and weaknesses relative to leveling and gifted programs.
- Human resources' recruitment, hiring, and retention of qualified teachers and administrators who represent the student population.
- Financial support via local funding or grant-writing for enrichment initiatives geared to promote the academic achievement for student populations affected by achievement gaps.

Schoolwide Program

- School personnel's participation in a course that promotes cultural awareness and acts as a starting point for future conversations to occur between school personnel and community members.

- The celebration of diversity among students organized by student government representatives and sponsors.
- The implementation of retreats and/or seminars for students and teachers that promote conversations between different groups to discover similarities and appreciate differences.
- Support for a reading specialist at each school to improve reading skills for students behind by several grade levels as well as collaborate with classroom teachers to implement reading strategies for their content area.
- Support for an in-house SAT prep course designed for students who score less than the national average.
- Support at the building level for the recruitment, hiring, and retention of qualified teachers and administrators who represent the student body.
- Support for career/vocational curriculum that effectively prepares students for real-world experiences.
- Removal of the tracking system used in core courses (English, math, science, social studies) or curriculum revision for vocational or general-level courses that reflect high expectations.
- Participation in staff development that encourages effective classroom management and promotes a variety of teaching strategies.
- Support by teachers via data collection and participation in enrichment initiatives geared to promote the academic achievement for student populations affected by achievement gaps.
- Creating a school environment that welcomes the participation of community members in academic, social, and athletic events.
- Encouraging a learning environment via staff development that promotes effective classroom management, time on task, and a variety of teaching strategies.

Counseling Program

- Support for and participation in system and schoolwide interventions that promote respecting differences.
- Creating an atmosphere in the counseling office that welcomes and celebrates diversity within the student population.
- Promoting the recruitment, hiring, and retention of qualified counselors that are reflective of the student population.
- Provide support for career/vocational tracks that represent quality programs with real-world learning.
- Develop and implement career fairs, job fairs, and college fairs that are open and useful to all students.
- Proactive participation in the registration process that critically examines the placement of students in vocational and general level classes.
- Implementation of counseling practices that mandate meetings between the counselor and the students they serve.
- Collaboration with classroom teachers in an effort to share information pertinent to student academic and social development ranging from study skills to fighting negative peer pressure.

- Acting as a liaison between teachers, students, and parents if racial incidents occur or are suspected.
- Development and implementation of enrichment initiatives geared to promote the academic achievement for student populations affected by achievement gaps.
- Development and implementation of special counseling programs that encourage participation from parents and community members representing different cultures within the student population.

CLASSROOM GUIDANCE ACTIVITIES

The activities that follow have been successfully used in both the classroom and as a component of an enrichment program entitled *Empowered Youth Programs*. *Empowered Youth Programs* were designed to enhance the social and academic development of adolescents of color in schools and communities. The first series of classroom activities was developed as a result of multiple racial incidents on a high school campus. These incidents involved racial slurs written on lockers, name calling, and student protest. Students and teachers wanted to engage in dialogue regarding "differences" and how their difference might be used as a means to start the healing process. After meeting with groups of students, teachers, administrators, and parents these activities were used (via English classes over a three-week period) as a way to create a safe environment for the dialogue to take place, as well as help students identify, talk about, and understand their differences. Upon the completion of the classroom workshops, parent and community forums were held in which students were given an opportunity to discuss what they had learned during the workshops and their continued concerns.

LESSON 1: PEACE AND UNITY

Personal/Social Development Standard A: Students will acquire the knowledge, attitudes, and interpersonal skills to help them understand and respect self and others.

Competencies

- Students will develop a positive attitude toward self as a unique and worthy person.
- Students will identify values, attitudes, and beliefs.
- Students will identify personal strengths and assets.

Learning Objective: The objective of these sessions entitled "Peace and Unity" is to help students begin a dialogue surrounding racial/ethnic differences and to begin to develop respect for those differences.

Materials: Handouts 6.1–6.4.

Developmental Learning Activity

Introduction: The counselor reviews the objective for these sessions, the Guidelines for Developing a Community of Respect (see Handout 6.1), and the Your Perception Is Your Reality (see Handout 6.2).

Activity: In groups of two or three, students write their definitions for "important words" (see Handout 6.3). The counselor writes words across the board and asks each group to share their definition. Students share definitions (see Handout 6.4).

Conclusion: Students return to small groups and compare group definitions with given definitions. They discuss which were similar and which were different. They make note of similarities and differences on sheet.

LESSON 2: RESPECTING DIFFERENCES

Personal/Social Development Standard A: Students will acquire the knowledge, attitudes, and interpersonal skills to help them understand and respect self and others.

Competencies

- Students will develop a positive attitude toward self as a unique and worthy person.
- Students will identify values, attitudes, and beliefs.
- Students will identify personal strengths and assets.

Learning Objective: The objective of these lessons entitled "Peace and Unity" is to help students begin a dialogue surrounding racial/ethnic differences and to begin to develop respect for those differences.

Materials: Handouts 6.3 and 6.4 from Lesson 1.

Developmental Learning Activity

Introduction: The counselor reviews terms from Lesson 1.

In groups of three (the counselor may want to arrange for new groups each day), students react to the following statement:

> Wearing cowboy boots and listening to country music doesn't make a person a redneck, no more than my going into a dog pound makes me a dog.

In groups of three, students connect terms from the previous session to the statement. They explain their reasons for connecting certain terms. Each triad shares thoughts with the class.

Activity: In groups of three, students write a definition for "respect." They share each small group's definition of respect with the whole group.

The counselor asks students to find someone in the room whom they do not know very well, introduce themselves, and discuss the following with the partner:

- What does it mean for someone to show you respect?
- What does it mean for you to show someone else respect?

Students combine partners to form groups of four and answer the following questions:

- State your full name. Who gave you your name? Does it have special meaning? Do you prefer to be called by any other name?
- Are there names that people call you here at school that you would prefer they not call you? Why?
- Where are you originally from?
- Do you know anything about your family history? For example, where did your ancestors come from, when, and why?
- Do you or your family practice any ethnic or cultural traditions (for example, food, social behaviors, holidays, beliefs)?

The counselor asks each member from the groups of four to introduce someone from their group, answering each of the above questions for that person. The counselor makes sure each person in the class has been "introduced" by a classmate.

Conclusion: Students return to groups of four. Each group member shares a few facts they learned concerning differences.

LESSON 3: LEARNING TO RESPECT DIFFERENCES

Personal/Social Development Standard A: Students will acquire the knowledge, attitudes, and interpersonal skills to help them understand and respect self and others.

Competencies

- Students will develop a positive attitude toward self as a unique and worthy person.
- Students will identify values, attitudes, and beliefs.
- Students will identify personal strengths and assets.

Learning Objective: The objective of these sessions entitled "Peace and Unity" is to help students begin a dialogue surrounding racial/ethnic differences and to begin to develop respect for those differences.

Materials: Handout 6.5.

Developmental Learning Activity

Introduction: Students individually respond to the following questions:

- How did you first come to understand that prejudice/racism existed?
- What is the source of most of your views toward members of other racial groups?

- How do your beliefs affect your behavior toward people from other cultural backgrounds?
- When was the last time you befriended someone from a culture different from your own? Why?

The counselor allows individuals to share their responses with the group. The counselor may need to remind them of the guidelines for developing a community of respect.

Activity: In groups of three, students make a list of things that they can do to bring peace and understanding between themselves and those who represent groups different from their own. They share list with the class.

The whole group brainstorms ways that members of this class (as a part of other school organizations) could help other students learn to respect differences.

Conclusion: Each student completes Handout 6.5 and shares.

Assessment: The counselor reviews students' opinions of how the workshop changed their opinions of their classmates.

The counselor asks each student to bring in a dish (food) that is a traditional holiday family favorite, explain why they chose that particular dish, and then share it with members of the class.

The counselor asks students to complete an evaluation of the course. The evaluation should review the contents of each session and ask students' opinion as to its value in examining their understanding and respect for the differences between their classmates and themselves. The counselor asks teachers to complete a brief survey concerning any changes in behavior or attitude for participants in their classroom.

Follow Up: The counselor arranges a Peace and Unity celebration for students and parents. As part of the celebration, students read aloud their personal commitment (from Handout 6.5).

The counselor asks students to identify one friend they would like to invite to complete the workshop.

The counselor asks graduates to help with one activity in the next workshop as co-leaders.

SMALL-GROUP COUNSELING PLANS

The *Strong Black Male* series of group activities was developed to help adolescent African American males examine their perceptions and other images of strong black men and then relate those images to family and community members and finally to themselves. This series was developed to counter the negative stereotypes that exist regarding black men. At the conclusion of the series, school personnel and parents reported seeing positive changes in the young men who participated in the activities. The positive changes included enhanced self-concept, a stronger focus on academics, an increase in positive interactions with classmates at school and with siblings at home. The group participants reported " . . . feeling good about [themselves]," " . . . I'm proud that I'm black," "I want to prove to people that not all black males sell drugs and that we are smart" (Bailey, 2003).

Both the classroom and group activities were used in conjunction with other methods of assisting young people in understanding and appreciating their differences (for example, forums, field trips, guest speakers, a unity march, and community projects). For lasting change, we suggest building these activities into the school experience for all students. This may require modifying the activities to meet the needs of the school, community, and most importantly, the students.

This eight-session counseling group was designed specifically for adolescent African American male students; however, the sessions may be modified for other student populations. Each session takes about sixty minutes. Assessment and follow-up occurs at the conclusion of the eighth session.

GROUP SESSION 1: BECOMING A STRONG BLACK MALE

Personal/Social Development Standard A: Students will acquire the knowledge, attitudes, and interpersonal skills to help them understand and respect self and others.

Competencies

- Students will develop a positive attitude toward self as a unique and worthy person.
- Students will identify values, attitudes, and beliefs.
- Students will identify personal strengths and assets.

Learning Objective: Students will investigate the images of strong black men as portrayed in the film *Cool Runnings*.

Materials: Film *Cool Runnings*, paper and pencil.

Activities

Introduction: In groups of three, students list the first five names that come to mind when the counselor says "Strong Black Men." They also list the men's outstanding qualities. First they share with their smaller group. Then they share with larger group and compare lists.

Counseling Activity: The counselor numbers students 1–4 and assigns each numbered group to one of the four black men in the film. Tell students that after viewing the video, they will be asked to list qualities they think their character exhibits that reflects their image of a strong black male. Then the counselor begins the video.

Conclusion: The counselor stops the movie at a point where students can recall what is happening. Students turn in their lists next session.

GROUP SESSION 2: BECOMING A STRONG BLACK MALE

Personal/Social Development Standard A: Students will acquire the knowledge, attitudes, and interpersonal skills to help them understand and respect self and others.

Competencies

- Students will develop a positive attitude toward self as a unique and worthy person.
- Students will identify values, attitudes, and beliefs.
- Students will identify personal strengths and assets.

Objective: Students will investigate the images of strong black men as portrayed in the film *Cool Runnings*.

Materials: Film *Cool Runnings*, paper and pencil.

Activities

Introduction: The counselor asks students to review highlights from the previous session. The counselor reviews the goal of investigating the characteristics of strong black men in the movie *Cool Runnings*.

Counseling Activity: The counselor reviews numbers and matching characters from the film. The counselor asks students to continue their list of qualities they think their character exhibits that reflects strong black men. The counselor continues the video.

Conclusion: Students divide into smaller groups according to their character. They share lists of qualities and explain when in the movie they observed that quality. Each group comes up with one list (qualities and explanations) to be shared at the next session.

GROUP SESSION 3: BECOMING A STRONG BLACK MALE

Personal/Social Development Standard A: Students will acquire the knowledge, attitudes, and interpersonal skills to help them understand and respect self and others.

Competencies

- Students will develop a positive attitude toward self as a unique and worthy person.
- Students will identify values, attitudes, and beliefs.
- Students will identify personal strengths and assets.

Learning Objective: Students will investigate the images of strong black men as portrayed in the film *Cool Runnings* as well as five black males involved in their lives.

Materials: Board and marker, paper and pencil.

Activities

Introduction: Students return to smaller groups from the previous session. They review the group's list and assign one person from the group to write the group list on the board.

Counseling Activity: The counselor reviews each group's list of character and qualities. The counselor circles commonalities and asks each student to make a list of all the qualities of strong black men observed in the film on the back of their original list.

Conclusion: The counselor asks each student to list five strong black men that are involved in their lives. They explain their relationship and tell what qualities are most evident in "their men" that are shared on their list from the movie.

   The counselor collects lists.

GROUP SESSION 4: BECOMING A STRONG BLACK MALE

Personal/Social Development Standard A: Students will acquire the knowledge, attitudes, and interpersonal skills to help them understand and respect self and others.

Competencies

- Students will develop a positive attitude toward self as a unique and worthy person.
- Students will identify values, attitudes, and beliefs.
- Students will identify personal strengths and assets.

Learning Objective: Students will investigate the images of strong black men involved in their lives.

Materials: Board and marker, paper and pencil.

Activities

Introduction: The counselor reviews lists from the previous week. Students share with their small group list of five strong black men involved in their lives, relationship to them, and qualities of these men.

Counseling Activity: The counselor should make sure the list of all the qualities of strong black men from the video is still on the board (redo if necessary). Then each student shares the five strong black men involved in their lives, relationship to them, and common qualities that make them strong black men. As each student shares, the counselor asks the student who has already shared (the group leader will start) to check off matching qualities from the Cool Runnings list.

The counselor adds any additional qualities that were not on the original list. Students add any new qualities to their list from Session 3.

Conclusion: The counselor asks participants to consider the qualities they have listed for strong black men and check the five that best represent themselves.

GROUP SESSION 5: BECOMING A STRONG BLACK MALE

Personal/Social Development Standard A: Students will acquire the knowledge, attitudes, and interpersonal skills to help them understand and respect self and others.

Competencies

- Students will develop a positive attitude toward self as a unique and worthy person.
- Students will identify values, attitudes, and beliefs.
- Students will identify personal strengths and assets.

Learning Objective: Students will examine their own lives and name the five qualities that best represent their strengths.

Materials: Board and marker, paper and pencil.

Activities

Introduction: The counselor reviews the final list of strong black men qualities. In groups of three, students share the five qualities they selected to represent themselves and explain why they selected each.

Counseling Activity: The counselor erases check marks from the board list. Each student shares the five qualities they consider strengths. As each participant shares, the counselor asks the student who has already shared (the group leader will start) to check off matching qualities from the final list.

Conclusion: The counselor erases the final list from board. The counselor makes columns for "school," "extracurricular," and "family/community." Students make the same list on their paper.

The group brainstorms evidence of their strengths (qualities of strong black men) that could be seen in the coming week for each area of their lives. The counselor charges them to commit to "collect evidence" in the coming week.

GROUP SESSION 6: BECOMING A STRONG BLACK MALE

Personal/Social Development Standard A: Students will acquire the knowledge, attitudes, and interpersonal skills to help them understand and respect self and others.

Competencies

- Students will develop a positive attitude toward self as a unique and worthy person.
- Students will identify values, attitudes, and beliefs.
- Students will identify personal strengths and assets.

Learning Objective: Students will examine their own lives and "evidence" for five qualities of strong black men that best represent their strengths.

Materials: Board and marker, paper and pencil, poster board cut in fourths, many magazines, scissors, and glue sticks.

Activities

Introduction: The counselor reviews "school," "extracurricular," and "family/community" lists of evidence from the previous week as seen on the board. The students share thoughts with group.

Counseling Activity: The counselor asks students, if their life had been in a movie, what evidence would the viewer be able to see concerning their five strengths? Students share examples of evidence from their "lives as a movie" for the five qualities they consider their strengths.

Conclusion: The counselor asks students to use pictures and words from magazines to create a collage that could be titled: "Strong Black Men." (Students use a paper clip to keep their poster board and magazine clippings together. They will not complete poster until Session #8.)

GROUP SESSION 7: BECOMING A STRONG BLACK MALE

Personal/Social Development Standard A: Students will acquire the knowledge, attitudes, and interpersonal skills to help them understand and respect self and others.

Competencies

- Students will develop a positive attitude toward self as a unique and worthy person.
- Students will identify values, attitudes, and beliefs.
- Students will identify personal strengths and assets.

Learning Objective: Students will examine the lives of strong black men from their community.

Materials: A discussion panel (we suggest a group of men who represent different careers and age groups).

Activities

Introduction: The counselor introduces members of panel.

Counseling Activity: The counselor asks each member of the panel:

- To give a brief biographical sketch
- To review why they think they were asked to participate in a panel entitled "Strong Black Men"
- To give an example of a strong black male in their life

Students can ask questions of panel members.

Conclusion: The counselor asks each panel member to share closing thoughts/ recommendations for participants. The counselor charges participants to continue "collecting evidence" in the coming week for characteristics of strong black men as seen through their actions.

GROUP SESSION 8: BECOMING A STRONG BLACK MALE

Personal/Social Development Standard A: Students will acquire the knowledge, attitudes, and interpersonal skills to help them understand and respect self and others.

Competencies

- Students will develop a positive attitude toward self as a unique and worthy person.
- Students will identify values, attitudes, and beliefs.
- Students will identify personal strengths and assets.

Learning Objective: Students will complete collages that represent qualities of strong black men and evaluate their opinions of strong black men.

Materials: Poster board cut in fourths, lots of magazines, scissors, and glue sticks.

Activities

Introduction: In groups of three, students share their thoughts from the panel in Session 7. For example, who had the greatest impact and why?

Activity: Students share who had the greatest impact on them from the panel discussion. Then they complete collages.
The counselor asks each participant to share the highlights of their collage.

Conclusion: The counselor asks students to return to their first list of five strong black men, to review the list and think about why they selected these individuals. The group discusses how this "mini-course" has affected their opinions of strong black men; the counselor asks students to write down their opinions. The counselor charges students to continue collecting evidence for the qualities of strong black men in their lives.

Assessment: The counselor reviews students' opinions of how the group changed their opinion of strong black men. The counselor asks students to complete an evaluation of the group. The evaluation should review the contents of each session and ask students' opinion as to its value in examining the characteristics of strong black men. The counselor asks teachers to complete a brief survey concerning any changes in behavior or attitude for participants in their classroom.

Follow-up: The counselor arranges a dinner ("Strong Black Men Banquet") for participants and a guest (strong black men involved in their lives). In a short presentation, participants introduce their guest and explain why they were chosen to attend.

The counselor asks students to elect a new cohort to participate in the group. The counselor asks graduates to help with one session as co-leaders.

INDIVIDUAL COUNSELING CONSIDERATIONS

Students have always been confronted with challenges as they attempt to make their way through adolescence. In addition, all students experience some difficulty as they navigate their way through the educational system. Today's students, especially poor students and students of color, are challenged in ways that we never could have imagined decades ago. For this reason, counselors must be diligent in assisting teachers and administrators in creating an educational environment that supports all students and contributes to their success.

Here we suggest individual counseling considerations to assist counselors in helping students gain an understanding of and respect for the many differences that exist in schools today. This understanding and respect will result in a "community of respect" and an overall healthy educational environment. Counselors should:

- Acknowledge personal biases and stereotypes of students who come from racial, ethnic, and cultural backgrounds different from their own
- Work to eliminate behaviors that might suggest prejudice and/or racism toward students of color
- Continue to involve themselves in experiences that will challenge their belief systems
- Develop a relationship with someone (preferably a colleague) who will assist them in processing these experiences
- Help students identify ways in which they are similar
- Have high expectations for all students regardless of their socioeconomic status, ethnicity, or family history

CONCLUSION

As advocates and educational leaders, professional school counselors must possess the appropriate beliefs, knowledge, and skills to bring about positive change, thereby creating educational environments that assist students from all backgrounds in excelling. Counselors must use their skills and position to help students, teachers, and parents to develop a respect for the differences that may exist between them and others. Critical to this process, professional school counselors must be willing to represent the change they want to see in others, be it students, teachers, parents, and/or administrators.

RESOURCES

Multicultural Web Sites for Teachers and Counselors

The following Web sites offer excellent classroom activities for elementary, middle, and high school teachers. These activities provide practical ways of engaging students of all ages in acknowledging, respecting, and accepting the differences that may exist between them and their peers. This in and of itself will enhance the educational environment that students and educators find themselves in on a daily basis. We encourage you to browse each site and select the activities that best fit your student population. Enjoy!

http:/ /www.cloudnet.com/~edrbsass/edmulticult.htm
http:/ /curry.edschool.virginia.edu/go/multicultural/teachers.html
http:/ /www.deerlake.leon.k12.fl.us/mcles.htm
http:/ /jeffcoweb.jeffco.k12.co.us/passport/lessonplan/lessonindex.htm
http:/ /faculty.tamu-commerce.edu/espinoza/s/buster-p-657.html
http:/ /www.isomedia.com/homes/jmele/homepage.html
http:/ /www.ed.gov/databases/ERIC_Digests/ed327613.html
http:/ /www.mhhe.com/socscience/education/multi/activities.html
http:/ /www.pwcs.edu/multicultural/activities.htm
http:/ /racismnoway.com.au/classroom/
http:/ /www.wpe.com/~musici/activs.htm
http:/ /www.prel.org/sit/multied.htm

REFERENCES

American School Counseling Association. (1999). *Position statements*. Retrieved from http:/ /www.schoolcounselor.org/content.cfm?L1=1000&L2=26.

Bailey, D. F. (2003). Preparing African American males for postsecondary options. *Journal of Men Studies*, 12.

Bailey, D. F., Getch, Y., & Chen-Hayes, S. (2003). Professional school counselors as social and academic advocates. In B. T. Erford (Ed.), *Transforming the school counseling profession* (pp. 411–434). Upper Saddle River, NJ: Prentice Hall.

Boykin, A. W. (1986). The triple quandary and the schooling of Afro-American children. In U. Neisser (Ed.). *The school achievement of minority children* (pp. 57–92). Hillsdale, NJ: Lawrence Erlbaum Associates.

Brennan, J. (1999). *They can and they do: Low income students and high academic achievement*. Retrieved from http:/ /www.edtrust.org/low_income.html.

Business Roundtable. (2003, February). *The hidden crisis in the high school dropout problems of young adults in the U.S.: Recent trends in overall school dropout rates and gender differences in dropout behavior*. Retrieved July 4, 2003, from http://www.brtable.org/press.cfm/915#top.

Carnegie Corporation of New York. (1984–1985). Renegotiating society's contract with the public schools. *Carnegie Quarterly, 29/30*(1), 1–4, 6–11.

Carney, C. G., &Kahn, K. B. (1984). Building competencies for effective cross-cultural counseling: A developmental view. *The Counseling Psychologist, 12,* 111–119.

Clarke, M. A., & Stone, C. (2000, May). Evolving our image: School counselors as educational leaders. *Counseling Today,* 21, 22, 29, 46.

College Board (1999). *Reaching the top: A report of the national task force on minority high achievement.* New York: Author.

DeLucia-Waack, J. L., DiCarlo, N. J., Parker-Sloat, E. L., & Rice, K. G. (1996). Multiculturalism: Understanding at the beginning of the process, rather than the ending. In J. DeLucia-Waack (Ed.), *Multicultural counseling competencies: Implications for training and practice* (pp. 237–243). Alexandria, VA: Association for Counselor Education and Supervision.

Education Trust. (1998). *Education Watch: The Education Trust state and national data book* (vol. II). Washington, DC: Author.

Erford, B. T., House, R., & Martin, P. (2003). Transforming the school counseling profession. In B. T. Erford (Ed.), *Transforming the school counseling profession* (pp. 1–20). Upper Saddle River, NJ: Merrill Prentice Hall.

Ford, D. Y. (1996). *Reversing underachievement among gifted black students: Promising practices and programs.* New York: Teachers College Press.

Hart, P. J., & Jacobi, M. (1992). *From gatekeeper to advocate: Transforming the role of professional school counselor.* New York: College Entrance Examination Board, American Counseling Association.

Hodgkinson, H. L. (1995). The changing face of tomorrow's student. *Change, 17,* 38–39.

Holcomb-McCoy, C. (2003). Multicultural competence. In B. T. Erford (Ed.), *Transforming the school counseling profession* (pp. 317–330). Upper Saddle River, NJ: Merrill Prentice Hall.

Holcomb-McCoy, C., & Myers, J. E. (1999). Multicultural competence and counselor training: A national survey. *Journal of Counseling and Development, 77,* 294–302.

Irvine, J. J. (1991). *Black students and school failure: Policies, practices, and prescriptions.* New York: Praeger Publishers.

Jones, J. D., Van Fossen, B. E., & Spade, J. Z. (1987, April). *Individual and organizational predictors of high school track placement.* Paper presented at the meeting of the American Educational and Research Association, Washington, DC.

McIntosh, P. (1989, July/August). White privilege: Unpacking the invisible knapsack. *Peace and Freedom,* 8–10.

Sue, D. W., Arredondo, P., & McDavis, R. J. (1992). Multicultural counseling competencies and standards: A call to the profession. *Journal of Counseling and Development, 70,* 477–486.

Sue, D. W., Bernier, J. E., Durran, A., Feinberg, L., Pedersen, P., Smith, E. J., & Vasquez-Nuttall, E. (1982). Position paper: Cross-cultural counseling competencies. *The Counseling Psychologist, 10,* 45–52.

Toporek, R. L. (1999, June). Advocacy: A voice for our clients and communities. Developing a framework for understanding advocacy in counseling. *Counseling Today,* 34, 35, 39.

U.S. Bureau of Census. (2000). *National population projections: Projection of the resident population by race, Hispanic origins, and nativity.* Middle series 1999 to 2100. Washington, DC: Author.

Wong, H. K., & Wong, R. T. (2001). *The first days of school.* Mountain View, CA: Harry K. Wong Publications, Inc.

HANDOUT 6.1

GUIDELINES FOR DEVELOPING A COMMUNITY OF RESPECT

1. Everyone is expected to participate in all activities. At the same time, each person has to make a decision about how much they want to say and what stories about themselves they feel comfortable telling.

2. It is important for everyone to have a turn. It is not fair for one or two people to dominate the discussions.

3. Because "I" would like everyone to take ownership of what you say and feel, please use "I" when sharing what you feel, think, or believe.

4. Do not misjudge or assume certain things about someone because of something they say or believe to be true.

HANDOUT 6.2

YOUR PERCEPTION IS *YOUR* REALITY!!

- In other words, what you think is true is only true in your eyes!!!!

- Once you realize that what you believe is not true, you have a responsibility to find the truth.

- Untruths hurt . . . so make sure you know the truth before you speak what you think is true.

Write your definitions for the following words:

1. Stereotype:

2. Prejudice:

3. Racism:

4. Culture:

5. Discrimination:

HANDOUT 6.4

IMPORTANT WORDS TO KNOW

1. **Stereotypes:** are specific behavioral traits given to individuals on the basis of their apparent membership in a group. Stereotyping is the process by which individuals are viewed as members of groups and the information that is stored in our minds about the group is transferred to the individual.

2. **Prejudice:** means to prejudge someone. It is an attitude that is based on limited information such as stereotypes. Prejudice is usually, but not always, negative; both positive and negative prejudices are damaging because **they deny the individuality of the person.** *No one is free of prejudice.*

3. **Racism:** represents a form of oppression.
    Racism = Power + Prejudice
    Racism is different from racial prejudice, hatred, or discrimination. Racism involves one group having the power to carry out systematic discrimination through the major institutions of society.

4. **Culture:** any group of people who identify or associate with another on the basis of some common purpose, need, or similarity of background.

5. **Discrimination:** an action of behavior based on prejudice.

Note: Teachers/counselors may add terms as needed.

HANDOUT 6.5

PERSONAL COMMITMENT

Date: _____

Write down what you are willing to do to eliminate negative stereotypes and perceptions about other individuals and/or groups of people:

1.

2.

3.

Signature: _____

Leadership and Advocacy for Lesbian, Bisexual, Gay, Transgendered, and Questioning (LBGTQ) Students: Academic, Career, and Interpersonal Success Strategies

CHAPTER

7

Shannon D. Smith, University of Akron, and Stuart F. Chen-Hayes,
Lehman College/City University of New York

Introduction

As professional school counselors implement national school counseling standards (ACA, 1993; ASCA, 1994; Campbell & Dahir, 1997; Dahir, Sheldon, & Valiga, 1998), work to transform school counseling programs (House & Martin, 1998), and collaborate with teachers, parents, guardians, and administrators for leadership that ensures equity for all students (Johnson, 1996), school counselors must demonstrate accountability, document their effectiveness, and advocate for student achievement and educational success (Johnson, 2000). Despite this need, the ASCA national standards, as well as transformative school counseling models, have been relatively silent about the particular awareness, knowledge, and skills that school counselors need to effectively meet the academic, career, and personal/social success needs of lesbian, bisexual, gay, transgendered, and questioning (LBGTQ) students, families, and school staff.

Sexual orientation and gender identity and expression are topics that often confront school counselors in ways that call for expertise in both educational leadership and advocacy (Chen-Hayes, 1997, 2001a, 2001b, 2001c; Reynolds & Koski, 1995; Robinson, 1994). Irrational fears and ignorance (lack of knowledge) coupled with individual, cultural, and systemic bias in the forms of heterosexism and transgenderism contribute to harmful consequences, including violence for LBGTQ students, staff, and families in K–12 settings (Chen-Hayes, 1997, 2001a; McFarland, 1998; Remafedi, 1994; Ryan & Futterman, 1998). A major challenge school counselors face is to advocate against heterosexism and transgenderism and to provide educational leadership that empowers LBGTQ students, staff, and their families in terms of academic, career, and personal and social success.

The term *sexual orientation* generally refers to the direction of one's sexual attraction and desires, and includes elements such as sexual behavior, erotic fantasy, interpersonal affection, and arousal patterns (Suppe, 1984). The term *gender identity* refers to the subjective experience or self-attribution of one's gender, "one's sense of oneself as male or female" (Irvine, 1990, p. 231). And the term *gender expression* refers to one's self-expression of a particular gender or gender trait. It is important to note that we extend the concept of gender beyond the traditional role of male and female to include diverse genderness such as transgender. Therefore, it is important for the reader to include the concept of "transgender" in his or her notion of gender, gender identity, and gender expression. The LBGTQ Definitions Exercise in this chapter provides description of terminology.

School counselors must actively demonstrate advocacy and leadership that is directed toward the specific needs of LBGTQ students, staff, and families. This should be done when providing classroom developmental school counseling lessons, small-group counseling sessions, and individual and systemic interventions with students, parents and guardians, and staff. This requires attending to the entire school climate. The following areas are essential targets where school counselors need to advocate for LBGTQ students, staff, and families: (1) curriculum, and mission and vision statements for the school (Johnson, 1996) and the school counseling program; (2) school-based data and leadership teams (Johnson, 1996); (3) school building and district policies; (4) staff training; and (5) academic, career, and personal/social success interventions for the whole K–12 school community.

Traditionally, LBGTQ students, staff, and families have been attacked, embarrassed, harassed, humiliated, ignored, shamed, and taunted in schools. Two common ways students respond to these acts of oppression are that (1) they decide to focus on overachieving as a way to cope with rejection, heterosexism, and transgenderism; or (2) they simply drop out of school—never to complete a high school education. According to reports of the Gay and Lesbian Task Force, approximately 28 percent of LBGTQ adolescents drop out of school (Bernstein, 1995). Many staff members (and also family members) believe that LBGTQ students simply do not exist in their schools, and further deny the possibility that an LBGTQ student may be one of their own. Such a rigid denial system precludes accepting that LBGTQ students are present in every school. (In Seattle, Washington, of 8,406 respondents in the ninth to twelfth grades, 4.5 percent of respondents described themselves as gay, lesbian, and bisexual [GLB]. Ninety-one percent described themselves as heterosexual. Another 4 percent indicated that they were "not sure" of their sexual orientation [Reis & Saewyc, 1999]; estimates range from 4 percent to 10 percent, with an average estimate of LBGTQ youth population at 6 percent [Ginsberg, 1998].) This prevents staff from taking the opportunity to become effective allies. We should always assume LBGTQ youth and adults are a part of every school as they are a part of every family. Other staff may hold negative beliefs about LBGTQ persons and sometimes act hostile and belligerent toward these students. Fortunately, there are affirmative school personnel who identify the presence of LBGTQ students and treat them with dignity and respect, though not every school across the country is fortunate enough to have such allying people. Therefore, school counselors must be advocates of LBGTQ students, staff, and families and always acknowledge, honor, and respect their presence in the school.

The best practices of ethical school counselors as leaders and advocates for LBGTQ students, staff, and families include awareness, knowledge, and skills in providing a wide range of academic, career, and interpersonal success activities throughout the school setting for K–12 students, staff, and families. Our definition of school counselors as leaders in terms of LBGTQ issues means they collaborate in the development and implementation of a mission, a vision, and goals that support LBGTQ students, staff, and family. Specifically, school counselors as leaders incorporate the needs of LBGTQ persons into individual, group, and systemic counseling, developmental school counseling curriculum, and policy and planning throughout the school. As advocates, they empower others to support and affirm all students, staff, and families of diverse sexual orientations and gender identities and gender expression. Because little data exist on the academic and career success of LBGTQ students, school counselors are able to take a leadership role and collect data that show evidence of the effects of developmental school counseling interventions to help LBGTQ students succeed at the highest possible levels of academic success and preparation for college or other substantial post-secondary options.

Our goal in this chapter is to share new exercises to help school counselors take the lead to promote specific advocacy and leadership for LBGTQ students and allies, particularly related to the ASCA national standards of academic, career, and personal/social success. Professional school counselors face many challenges and have extraordinary abilities, as school leaders and advocates, to create opportunities for success. It is our hope that the material in this chapter will empower school counselors to meet the needs of LBGTQ students, allies, staff, and families.

LITERATURE REVIEW

As the LBGTQ community becomes more visible, students, staff, and parents are increasingly demanding equitable treatment in schools. LBGTQ students are taking an active role toward establishing a secure educational environment. The school counseling literature has called for a positive response to the needs of the LBGTQ population for over a decade (Elia, 1993; Treadway & Yoakam, 1992). However, many school counselors are ill equipped to provide assistance and affirmation with LBGTQ students, staff, and families.

School counselors must recognize the importance of their roles as advocates and leaders in assisting LBGTQ youth during the process of sexual orientation and gender identity/expression development. School counselors have a unique opportunity to affirm the lives of LBGTQ youth in developing a healthy, secure sexual image rather than a shame-based identity plagued with negative feelings and beliefs. Unfortunately for many LBGTQ youth, research has demonstrated that negative stereotypes and misinformation regarding sexual orientation and gender identity and expression have caused extreme conflict during this developmental period. Many youth cope with this negativity by withdrawing from social activities, overcompensating in many areas, remaining emotionally constricted or isolated, and engaging in self-destructive behaviors including suicide (Gonsiorek, 1988; Ryan & Futterman, 1998; Savin-Williams, 1989).

Many adolescents do not reveal their concerns about sexual orientation and gender identity and expression during the most critical period of sexual identity development (typically during adolescence, but earlier for some youth) for fear of rejection and punishment (Hersch, 1991). Instead, they often withdraw at a time when they most need support. It is critical that LBGTQ students develop healthy concepts about their sexual orientation and gender identity and expression, rather than absorb and internalize heterosexist and transgenderist notions. LBGTQ sexual orientation and gender identity/expression formation is often complicated by internalized stereotypic notions and beliefs, even before LBGTQ students develop an awareness of their sexual orientation or gender identity/expression. Unfortunately, heterosexist and transgenderist attitudes and beliefs coupled with myths and stereotypes become internalized at an early age, and as a result, students can become emotionally impaired during this period of questioning. School counselors can play an important advocacy and leadership role during this critical period by disarming transgenderism, heterosexism, and homophobic prejudice (Chen-Hayes, 2001a, 2001c; Logan, 1996) by providing accurate information regarding sexual orientation and gender identity/expression development.

School counselors have a professional obligation to help all students, including the LBGTQ youth population, develop and grow in a safe school environment. School counselors must provide a safe environment where LBGTQ youth can ask questions and find the answers they need to take steps to progress into fully functioning adults.

For a variety of reasons, LBGTQ youth seem to have a difficult time at school and at home. All LBGTQ youth grapple will the process of "coming out" with parents and classmates. The impact of potential ridicule that LBGTQ youth may have to face can lead to a number of devastating consequences. For instance, many LBGTQ youth consider suicide as a way to escape the verbal assault they encounter from those they love and to alleviate the pain of rejection and isolation. A 1999 survey found that 69 percent of LBGTQ youth experienced some form of verbal harassment or violence, and of those, nearly half reported enduring harassment every day (Gay, Lesbian and Straight Education Network, 1999). Others cope by engaging in self-destructive activities, such as chemical abuse and unprotected sex, which may lead to the contraction of sexually transmitted diseases including HIV.

Physical violence is not uncommon to the LBGTQ youth population. In fact, many LBGTQ youth have to deal with physical abuse from their parents and classmates. LBGTQ students have been victims of sexual harassment in various forms, and in several cases it resulted in severe physical assault and even death. As a result of these events, many LBGTQ advocates have taken action against such violent demonstrations of externalized heterosexism and transgenderism.

Part of the work of educators, including school counselors, is to intervene through education and counseling interventions prior to the onset of violence. Many school counselors lack the necessary training to provide an environment for LBGTQ youth to understand themselves and to cope with the harassment they may encounter. But one practical way school counselors can start to help LBGTQ youth is to gather resources to help this school population. Several educators have developed strong anti-heterosexism curricula. (Unfortunately, no evidence of anti-transgenderism curricula or workshops exist in the literature to date.) Blumenfeld (1992) created an anti-heterosexism training outline from which teachers and school counselors can benefit. Griffin and Harro (1997) developed an anti-heterosexism curriculum design utilizing different but equally powerful exercises and course content. Using a social justice education framework, their colleagues Hardiman and Jackson (1997) built a case for an anti-oppression model of social-justice training that roots heterosexism as one of multiple issues of oppression that school counselors, teachers, and students need to address concurrently.

By combining the literature on LBGTQ identity development and anti-oppression curricula and addressing the ASCA national standards and academic career and interpersonal success expectations for all students, professional school counselors can provide outstanding leadership and advocacy for LBGTQ issues K–12. This type of leadership and LBGTQ advocacy is displayed in systemic interventions, developmental school counseling curriculum lessons, group counseling, and individual counseling and consultation with students, parents, guardians, teachers, and administrators.

WHOLE-SCHOOL INTERVENTIONS

In the school setting, professional school counselors must work individually with LBGTQ students and staff, and occasionally families. However, it is equally important for counselors to work proactively and systematically to promote a safe and secure climate for all LBGTQ people and allies in the school setting. Professional school counselors are the school community's main resource to provide positive role models, support groups, LBGTQ-affirming counseling, safe zones, and LBGTQ-specific activities. Therefore, they must advocate for comprehensive sexual education (Sexuality Information and Education Council [SIECUS], 1996), provide staff diversity training, ensure that LBGTQ issues are included in the curriculum and give a voice to the "hidden curriculum," and develop and implement safe-school statements, as well as inclusive school environments. The "hidden curriculum" refers to knowledge and information that is specific to LBGTQ persons, which is often hidden or absent from education literature and curricula, particularly sexual education curriculum.

Further, professional school counselors need to ensure inclusive classrooms, curriculum (Lipkin, 1992), and libraries, as well as co-curricular activities such as proms, dances, assemblies, and guest speakers. The school counseling program should provide LBGTQ-inclusive curriculum, educational materials, and training. Staff training must include LBGTQ persons and their unique needs. The mission of the school should be linked to each of these inclusive activities and programs. School counselors should work systemically to establish safe schools, LBGTQ safe spaces, and a no-harassment policy and procedures. In their direct services, they should provide specialized academic and career-success activities for LBGTQ students.

Establishing safe zones is a fundamental task for the LBGTQ student advocate. We encourage counselors to display safe-zone stickers on their office door and display other LBGTQ material, such as brochures/advertisements, and information about national LBGTQ organizations and events on a bulletin board. The display could include resources that exist within the community, such as local support groups, LBGTQ community events, and gay-affirmative referral sources such as therapists, physicians, and social/support groups. Tangible signs of LBGTQ resources indicate that LBGTQ students and allies are welcome and accepted and that their rights are protected, thus allowing them to feel safe and secure. Further, it is important for LBGTQ persons and allies to have safe zones beyond the counseling office.

In order to effectively meet the needs of LBGTQ students, the school principal, teachers, support staff, and administrators need to participate in the establishment of inclusive school environments. A no-harassment policy and procedures must be firmly defined and implemented. School counselors will have a difficult time being effective without these policies and procedures in place. Once the no-harassment policy and procedures are established, the school counselor can rely on them to back the employment of any systematic strategic interventions. Second, school counselors must gain the support of leadership, including the school principal as well as administrators and influential faculty.

One of the most powerful strategic interventions toward systematically developing an inclusive school environment is to provide accurate information and training for school personnel. For example, staff training and in-services can review the latest information and research available related to sexual orientation and development. A panel of gay leaders can discuss methods of meeting the needs of LBGTQ students and can answer questions that staff may have regarding LBGTQ youth. Expert speakers can be invited to conduct a school assembly or school board meeting. Also, a counselor can develop a community workshop and invite parents and members of the community to attend to educate and develop alliances. Educational material can improve understanding and awareness of LBGTQ persons and help to correct negative attitudes and stereotypes held about LBGTQ persons and communities.

Professional school counselors must recognize that systemic K–12 leadership and advocacy LBGTQ strategies will not always be easy to employ. In fact, school counselors should anticipate a great deal of resistance at many levels of the educational system. School board members, school administrators, teachers, support staff, and family members may fight against the implementation of LBGTQ leadership and advocacy strategies. Therefore, school counselors must be prepared to accept the occasional failure in implementing any of the potentially high-risk strategies that we are proposing. It is equally important that LBGTQ allies and support networks also be prepared to deal with resistance and the ultimate failure of some LBGTQ leadership and advocacy strategies.

Specific leadership and advocacy activities and lessons are outlined in this chapter. We present developmental curriculum for high school levels, which school counselors can directly employ in classroom and group counseling situations. We encourage counselors to modify these lessons as needed to fit specific situations and age groups.

Classroom Guidance Activities

We have developed the following leadership and advocacy activities and lessons as a result of our experiences advocating for the needs of LBGTQ persons for many years. This combined experience has resulted in a rich school counseling curriculum designed to meet the unique needs of this underrepresented population. Each activity emerged from our experience as advocates against oppression, particularly heterosexist privilege, and as advocates for the specific needs of LBGTQ students, staff, and families. Behind each of the following activities are the stories of many people who have experienced the psychological and emotional damage caused by heterosexist privilege and discrimination, the loss of self from being misunderstood and stereotyped, and the struggle to overcome hatred, anger, and acts of violence against LBGTQ persons and advocates. Each activity is also embedded with stories of triumph and success defeating this prejudice, ignorance, and injustice, and ultimately rising above the social illness of homophobia. We intend for these activities to give a voice to the stories of both defeat and triumph of the many LBGTQ persons and advocates who have fought for social justice, tolerance, and acceptance and understanding.

We have employed each of the following activities (in various forms) for professional presentations at conferences, workshops, seminars, and classrooms across various settings (K–12 schools, universities, mental health agencies, businesses, and more) to people of all ages (4–80+). Each audience responded in a positive manner to our presentations, and reported being challenged to think in new ways and become more open to LBGTQ issues. Due to the nature of the materials presented, occasionally some individual members have struggled more than others with specific challenges to overcome internalized oppression. Therefore, we encourage school counselors to be sensitive to their audience during each of the leadership and advocacy activities and lessons, and to make any necessary adjustments. And, we also ask that one does not "water down" the core content so much as to lose the value of challenging various forms of oppression (for example, homophobia) as well as the intended learning objectives.

As a result of these many presentations, we have developed and refined each exercise based upon audience participation and feedback and our own trial and error. Again, these exercises are specifically designed for students at the high school levels, but we encourage counselors to modify these lessons to match the needs of other situations and age groups. We hope that you and your students will find each of these leadership and advocacy activities and lessons as valuable and meaningful as we have in our work.

Lesson 1: LBGTQ Myths and Stereotypes

Personal/Social Development Standard A: Students will acquire the knowledge, attitudes, and interpersonal skills to help them understand and respect self and others.

Competency: Students will identify values, attitudes, and beliefs.

Learning Objectives

- Students will be able to identify myths and stereotypes associated with LBGTQ persons.
- Students will be challenged to examine their values, attitudes, and beliefs regarding myths and stereotypes associated with LBGTQ persons.
- Students will broaden their values, attitudes, and beliefs regarding sexual minorities.

Materials: Chalkboard or whiteboard, chalk or markers, paper, pencils/pens.

Developmental Learning Activities

Introduction: The counselor initiates a discussion about myths and stereotypes. Students are asked to define what these terms mean in their own words, while the counselor writes the definitions on the chalkboard or whiteboard. Students divide a piece of paper into two columns, "A" and "B". They brainstorm and write down in column "A" ten examples of different myths and stereotypes. Afterward, they write down in column "B" how the person or group represented in each might feel about each myth and stereotype. The counselor can pose several questions to the students, such as "How hurtful are myths and stereotypes?"

Activity: The counselor puts on the board the terms *gay men, heterosexuals, lesbians, bisexuals, transgendered persons.* One at a time, the counselor has the class list "everything you know or have heard about" what each group acts like, looks like, and does for a living, gender differences, and so on, under each term. Then the counselor processes with the class—talks about stereotypes and myths and how they can lead to negative consequences. The counselor asks how LBGTQ persons are treated in the school and how they are often perceived by other people, specifically in terms of students and as human beings.

Conclusion: The counselor asks the students to share their thoughts and feelings generated from the exercise. The counselor encourages students to review the myths and stereotypes derived from this exercise and reflect on the feelings of gay men, heterosexuals, lesbians, bisexuals, and transgendered persons.

Assessment: The counselor asks students to write a summary reflection on this lesson. They are to respond to three questions: (1) What did you learn from the Myths and Stereotypes lesson?; (2) What are negative consequences of myths and stereotypes about LGBTQ persons?; (3) What can you do to stop myths and stereotypes about LGBTQ persons?

Follow-up: During the next lesson, students will read aloud their responses to each question.

LESSON 2: LBGTQ DEFINITIONS

Personal/Social Development Standard A: Students will acquire the knowledge, attitudes, and interpersonal skills to help them understand and respect self and others.

Competency: Students will recognize, accept, respect, and appreciate ethnic and cultural diversity.

Learning Objectives

- Students will be able to understand important LBGTQ definitions and terminology.
- Students will be able to recognize, accept, respect, and appreciate the unique socio-linguistic and cultural aspects of LBGTQ persons.

Materials: Fill-in-the-blank exercise (Handout 7.1, questions 1–23), chalkboard or whiteboard, chalk or markers, pencils/pens.

Developmental Learning Activities

Introduction: This lesson begins with students reading their responses from Lesson 1 (LBGTQ Myths and Stereotypes Exercise) to the group members. Depending on the size of the group and time allotted, the counselor may ask students to read only one or two of their responses. After each student reads their answers aloud, the counselor directs the discussion to the culture of LBGTQ persons and communities.

The discussion focus is on increasing awareness of LBGTQ perceptions, terminology, and subcultures. For example, the counselor begins by asking students to identify their knowledge and perceptions of LBGTQ culture and lifestyles (What are the differences between lesbian, bisexual, gay, transgendered, and questioning persons?). Next, the counselor facilitates specific terminology used in LBGTQ subcultures. Finally, the counselor discusses each subculture in an effort to differentiate the various behaviors of each group. The counselor asks students to identify aspects of LBGTQ persons and communities that are unique and distinct. The students then brainstorm words and definitions specific to LBGTQ persons and communities and develop a brief list, which the counselor or a student writes on the board.

Activity: After several minutes of the brainstorming activity, the counselor gives each student a copy of the fill-in-the-blank exercise in Handout 7.1 (questions 1–23) to complete. Students complete the LBGTQ Definitions Questionnaire by matching the correct term to the correct definition. Upon completion, the counselor reviews the student responses and gives students the correct answers.

Conclusion: The counselor asks the students to reflect on their learning experience by discussing any definitions or ideas that are most salient for new learning.

Assessment: Assessment happens at the beginning of the next session, the counselor can give a brief verbal quiz to the group of students. For example, the counselor can read aloud ten questions from the LBGTQ Definitions Questionnaire, and students can answer by raising their hand.

Or at the beginning of the next session, the students divide into equal teams/groups. The counselor has each group draw 4 to 5 (depending on the size of the group) sexual orientation and gender identity and expression terms from a hat, and the group has to provide a definition for each term. The group that comes up with the highest number of accurate definitions wins.

Follow-up: In subsequent sessions, students are encouraged to use the terminology in their work and in discussions. Additionally, the counselor can model the use of sexual orientation and gender identity and expression terms, and encourage students to do the same.

LESSON 3: WHAT IS YOUR LBGTQ IQ?

Personal/Social Development Standard A: Students will acquire the knowledge, attitudes, and interpersonal skills to help them understand and respect self and others.

Competency: Students will recognize, accept, respect, and appreciate individual differences.

Learning Objectives

- Students will be able to test their knowledge and understanding of LBGTQ terminology and facts.
- Students will be able to recognize, accept, respect, and appreciate individual differences of LBGTQ persons.

Materials: Handout 7.2 (What Is Your LBGTQ IQ? Questionnaire), pencils/pens.

Developmental Learning Activities

Introduction: The counselor begins a discussion about the concept of an ally, and provides a brief example of how to be an ally to an LBGTQ student. The counselor asks students to give an example of being an ally to an LBGTQ student.

Activity: After giving examples, the counselor gives each student a copy of Handout 7.2 (questions 1–12) and the matching answers. Students complete the What Is Your LBGTQ IQ? Questionnaire by matching the correct term to the correct question and filling in the blank. Upon completion, the counselor reviews the student responses and gives students the correct answers.

Conclusion: The counselor asks the students to reflect on their learning experience by discussing how to be an effective ally. Students are asked to provide concrete examples of how each one can, or intends to, be a more active LBGTQ ally.

Assessment: Student scores from the What Is Your LBGTQ IQ? Questionnaire can be one form of assessment. An additional form of assessment at the end of this exercise is to ask students to rate this exercise on a scale of 1–10.

At the beginning of the next session, the professional school counselor asks students to give examples of how they behaved as an effective LBGTQ ally.

Follow-up: In subsequent sessions, students are encouraged to use the information learned from this exercise in their work and in discussions. Additionally, students are encouraged to continually act as LBGTQ allies, and share these activities with their classmates.

SMALL-GROUP COUNSELING PLANS

The following small-group counseling sessions are intended primarily for high school students, although with some modification each group can meet the age-appropriate needs of middle school students. It is important to note that this six-session group-counseling format is designed for LGBTQ students, LGBTQ allies, and students who are interested in learning more about LGBTQ people and their unique needs. Therefore, students representing both heterosexual and homosexual orientations are invited to participate in the group.

The small-group counseling sessions are the result of our combined experiences in working with various groups of children and teenagers. We have carefully selected six key sessions for LGBTQ students and allies that deal with the most pertinent developmental issues facing this group during high school. Once again, we have used these small-group exercises with teens in various settings and have revised them specifically for teens in the high school setting.

Selection criteria for this group should be based upon several key factors. First, a potential member must identify as an LGBTQ student, an LGBTQ ally, or a student who is interested learning more about LGBTQ people. Second, informed parental/guardian consent must be obtained for all members. However, this may be problematic for some students who are not "out" to their parents or guardian. Therefore, the informed consent should be clear in stating that this is a group designed for students of all sexual orientations and that the focus of the group is specifically regarding sexual minorities (LGBTQ students), sexual minority allies (LGBTQ allies), and students who are interested learning more about sexual minority (LGBTQ) people and their unique needs. Parents are informed that the nature of this group is primarily psycho-educational, and it is intended for a diverse population. It should be made clear that a group member does not have to be a LGBTQ person in order to participate in this group. If the consent is presented in this manner, LGBTQ students do not have to reveal their sexual orientation. Students representing both heterosexual and homosexual orientations are invited and encouraged to participate in the group in an effort to facilitate cooperative learning and personal growth.

Confidentiality is maintained as in any other group counseling: all participants are required to maintain confidentiality. Parents must be informed of the scope and limits of confidentiality as established by the American Counseling Association (ACA), elected state governing boards, and the school counseling program.

The school counselor should be careful to select group members who meet the stated criteria. Group membership can be established from interested students who are selected by the school counselor or from referrals from teachers, administrators, the school principal/vice principal, or other community agencies or organizations such as PFLAG.

GROUP SESSION 1: TO CHOOSE OR NOT TO CHOOSE: IS IT REALLY A CHOICE?

Personal/Social Development Standard A: Students will acquire the attitudes, knowledge, and interpersonal skills to help them understand and respect self and others.

Competency: Students will recognize, accept, respect, and appreciate individual differences.

Learning Objectives

- Students will learn the positive and negative aspects related to sexual orientation of various types.
- Students will develop knowledge and understanding of sexual orientation in its various forms and the unique process of sexual identity development.

Materials: A surface for writing, such as a dry-erase board and markers, chalkboard and chalk, or easel with flip-pad and permanent markers.

Activities

Introduction: The counselor explains that students are often unclear about sexual orientation and gender identity and expression origins; therefore, they often hold negative perceptions about LBGTQ people. This exercise helps students understand sexual orientation and gender identity and expression, including both the positive and negative beliefs and stereotypes. While people can choose various forms of sexual behavior and/or gender identity behavior, sexual orientation is not a choice.

Counseling Activity: The counselor asks the group to list all the positives to being heterosexual and traditionally gendered (that is, masculine for men and boys, feminine for women and girls). Then students list all the negatives—there are usually only one or two negatives and many positives. They do the same for lesbian, bisexual, gay, and transgendered people. The reverse is usually true in terms of how people list positives (few) and negatives (many) if it's a mostly heterosexual and traditionally gendered group. The counselor then asks the question, "With all of these negatives, why would anyone choose to be lesbian, bisexual, gay, or transgendered?"

Conclusion: The counselor addresses student comments and concerns, and then explains that although people can choose sexual behavior or gender identity and expression behavior, a sexual orientation is not chosen. It has a much more powerful origin than simply making a decision. Gender identity and expression is also not necessarily a choice but a product of both a person's internal feelings and identity about gender and the extent to which that matches (or doesn't match) their body (external expression of identity).

Assessment: At the end of the group session, the counselor reviews the major themes learned during this session. Each student reflects on a major theme that stands out most in their mind.

At the beginning of the next session, the counselor asks members to begin the group with a brief review of the major themes and to discuss any new insights gained since the last session.

Follow-up: In subsequent sessions, members are encouraged to continue discussion of "choice" as it relates to sexual orientation and gender identity and expression.

GROUP SESSION 2: DEVELOPING A SELF-PORTRAIT

Personal/Social Development Standard A: Students will acquire the attitudes, knowledge, and interpersonal skills to help them understand and respect self and others.

Competency: Students will acquire the attitudes, knowledge, and interpersonal skills to help them understand and respect self and others based on sexual orientation and gender identity and expression.

Learning Objectives

- Students will identify values and beliefs about their sexual orientation and gender identity and expression.
- Students will learn to express feelings related to their sexual orientation and gender identity and expression.

Materials: Magazines, poster board, glue sticks, scissors, markers, colored pencils.

Activities

Introduction: The counselor asks students to begin the group with a brief review of the major themes from Session 1 (To Choose or Not to Choose: Is It Really a Choice?) and discuss any new insights gained since the first session. The counselor discusses with the students what sexual orientation and gender identity and expression mean. Each student considers the people who have influenced their beliefs and values about sexual orientation and gender identity and expression. They should consider both people who are close to them and those who are famous.

Counseling Activity: The counselor tells students to clip pictures of people who have influenced the development of their sexual orientation and gender identity and expression. Students then describe their clip art choices to the class. Each student should consider the following questions:

- Would you have made the same choices for your poster if you had completed this assignment two years ago?
- Would you make the same choices if you were asked to complete this assignment again in two years?
- How are persons who are perceived as LBGTQ treated differently from heterosexuals or traditionally gendered persons in your family, at school, in your community, and so on?

- What can you do to support all persons in terms of their sexual orientation and gender identity and expression differences?
- How can you be an ally to LBGTQ persons?

Conclusion: The counselor discusses this activity with the group members. The students should be encouraged to express their feelings in response to hearing positive and negative descriptions surrounding sexual orientation and gender identity and expression.

Assessment: Students complete a comment card stating what they liked/disliked about the activity.

At the beginning of the next session, the counselor asks each person to state what impacted them the most from this session.

Follow-up: Students keep a journal of reactions to the activities, including any changed beliefs and attitudes about their own sexual orientation and gender identity and expression.

GROUP SESSION 3: FEELING PROUD: YOU BET-CHA "I" AM PROUD TO BE LBGTQ OR AN LBGTQ ALLY!

Personal/Social Development Standard A: Students will acquire the attitudes, knowledge, and interpersonal skills to help them understand and respect self and others.

Competency: Students will develop a positive attitude toward self as a unique and worthy person. They will identify strengths and assets as individuals and as a group of LBGTQ persons and LBGTQ allies.

Learning Objectives

- Students will develop a positive and affirming attitude toward self as a unique and worthy person, and develop a sense of pride in being LBGTQ, LBGTQ ally, or person interested in learning about LBGTQ people.
- Students will identify their personal strengths and assets.

Materials: LBGTQ magazines/stickers, and other materials, poster board, glue sticks, scissors, markers, colored pencils.

Activities

Introduction: The counselor asks each person to state what impacted them the most from the previous session (Developing a Self-Portrait). The counselor introduces the topic of worth and discusses self-respect, self-esteem, and self-worth with the group. The counselor explains the process of building a collage, and asks the students to respond to the questions by building a collage.

Counseling Activity: The counselor asks members to reflect on the following questions while building their collage:

- What does being LBGTQ, LBGTQ ally, or interested person in learning about LBGTQ people mean to you? How has this changed over your lifetime? How do you think it may change in the future?
- What does it mean to you in terms of family? religion/spirituality? career?
- What are advantages for you personally of being LBGTQ, LBGTQ ally, or interested person in learning about LBGTQ people? What are disadvantages?
- What positive messages do you hear? Which of these do you believe? Repeat for negative messages (from media, family, socialization in general).
- What do you imagine your future will look like?
- How would you identify your sexual orientation and gender identity and expression? What impact does this have?
- How would you like to see society change? What pictures in magazines would you like to be able to put here but couldn't find?

Conclusion: The counselor encourages students to share their collage with the other group members, explaining what it means and reflecting on their responses to the questions.

Assessment: Students complete a reflection survey that asks the participants to describe what they gained from this experience.

Students rate (scale 1–10) their self-respect, self-esteem, and self-worth before and after the exercise to determine whether they experienced an increase in any of the three areas, and if so, in which way(s) this occurred.

Follow-up: Students journal about their reactions to the activities and about any changed beliefs and attitudes regarding their own sense of self-respect, self-esteem, and self-worth.

GROUP SESSION 4: UNDERSTANDING SEXUAL ORIENTATION, GENDER IDENTITY, EXPRESSION DEVELOPMENT, AND MYTHS

Personal/Social Development Standard A: Students will acquire the attitudes, knowledge, and interpersonal skills to help them understand and respect self and others.

Competency: Students will recognize, accept, respect, and appreciate individual differences.

Learning Objectives

- Subsequent to group discussions, students will describe myths and facts about sexual orientations and gender identities and expression.
- Students will clarify their knowledge and understanding of sexual orientations and gender identities and expression.

Materials: Chalkboard and chalk (or other board), overhead, transparencies, directions and related charts, pencils/pens, Heterosexual Questionnaire and Traditional Gender Identity and Expression Questionnaire (Handout 7.3).

Activities

Introduction: Many students, including LBGTQ persons and allies, have internalized the ideas that surround heterosexuality and traditional gender identity and expression. The counselor leads students in a discussion about what they think it is like for an individual to be heterosexual and then about what it means to be traditionally gendered.

Counseling Activity: The counselor asks students to complete the Heterosexual Questionnaire and the Traditional Gender Identity and Expression Questionnaire (Handout 7.3). The counselor explains that a person does *not* have to be of a heterosexual orientation in order to complete the questionnaires required for this group exercise. The purpose of this group exercise is to employ these questionnaires in an effort to uncover various forms of heterosexism that LBGTQ students and allies are often are exposed to and may have internalized. The counselor asks LBGTQ students to respond to the questionnaires in one of two ways: (1) respond as a person with a heterosexual orientation (they can pretend, momentarily, or "act as if" they are heterosexual for the purpose of this exercise only); (2) respond to the questionnaires in the manner in which they believe a heterosexual person would "typically" respond.

The counselor asks students how they can create an environment where they can safely share their ideas. Then the counselor has the group share their ideas with each other.

Conclusion: The counselor reviews briefly the discussions about myths and facts about heterosexuality, bisexuality, and being lesbian or gay, as well as traditional and nontraditional forms of gender identity and expression (transsexuals, cross-dressers, intersex persons, drag queens and drag kings, two-spirits). Students list some of the ideas covered during the discussion and things they have seen and heard in school and at home.

Assessment: The counselor can see how many of the myths and facts students can give back at the end of the session.

Follow-up: The counselor asks students to look for examples of heterosexist stereotypes (that is, in sexual orientation and gender identity and gender expression) during the next week. These examples may come from magazines, radio, television, Web sites, and social interactions.

GROUP SESSION 5: FAMOUS LBGTQ PERSONS AND THEIR PLACE IN HERSTORY AND HISTORY: IMPLICATIONS FOR EVERYONE'S CAREER SUCCESS

Personal/Social Development Standard A: Students will acquire the knowledge, attitudes, and interpersonal skills to help them understand and respect self and others.

Competency: LBGTQ students will acquire the skills to investigate the world of work in relation to knowledge of self and to make informed career decisions.

Learning Objectives

- Students of all sexual orientations and gender identities will see the wide range of LBGTQ persons and allies in career paths of all different types.
- Students will develop knowledge and understanding of unique barriers and challenges LBGTQ persons and allies may experience in career paths, as well as the unique opportunities.

Materials: Chalkboard and chalk (or other board), overhead, or computers with the ability to create lists of students' knowledge, and Handout 7.4, a list of LBGTQ persons in various academic/career paths.

Activities

Introduction: Students often have few if any ideas of the role of LBGTQ persons and LBGTQ allies in history, particularly across academic and career types. This exercise allows students to fill in the blanks and see how many LBGTQ persons and allies they can list from herstory/history and today. The counselor explains the meaning of "herstory"—a way of pointing out heterosexual privilege in society and language. The term "herstory" was developed in response to the sexist term "history." The use of the male gender adjective/pronoun "his" as found in the noun "history" implies male dominance, and subsequently denotes women as powerless and weak as compared to men. Therefore, in an effort to promote equality among women and men, we use the term "herstory" here as an educational supplement in cooperation with this lesson.

Counseling Activity: The group brainstorms as many LBGTQ persons and allies as possible from the present and the past. They should try to list at least one hundred. After the list is completed, the group breaks down the list of LBGTQ persons and allies into their level of academic success (if known) and their career types. In addition, the counselor asks about the various cultural identities of persons on their lists. Who is missing—for example, people of color, persons with disabilities, older persons? If so, why? If students get stuck, the counselor can hand out the list of LBGTQ famous persons and allies from the past and present.

Conclusion: The counselor discusses with the students the myths and stereotypes that LBGTQ persons and allies can't succeed academically or that they do so only in certain careers. The counselor asks students to think about the people they know who are LBGTQ and about whether they fit into stereotypical career categories or not. How are LBGTQ students and allies viewed in the school and the larger community? How might all students be harmed by narrow myths and stereotypes about what makes for strong academic and career success based on what is "masculine or feminine" or seen as "gay" or "lesbian" career choices? What about bisexuals? What did students learn about the diversity and variety of LBGTQ persons and allies in various academic and career paths after they have received the handout? How will they think differently about LBGTQ persons' and allies' academic and career paths after this exercise? What are the strengths that LBGTQ persons and allies have in different academic and career choices? What unique barriers and challenges do LBGTQ persons and allies face in different careers, and how can they overcome those barriers and challenges?

Assessment: Students will be able to list multiple examples of LBGTQ persons and allies in a full range of academic and career paths.

Follow-up: The counselor asks students one thing they learned from this exercise. How will that affect their perception of LBGTQ persons and allies in their academic and career success? How will they avoid making assumptions about persons based on their academic success or career interests?

GROUP SESSION 6: "READY OR NOT, HERE WE COME!": CHALLENGING HETEROSEXISM AND TRANSGENDERISM

Personal/Social Development Standard A: Students will acquire the attitudes, knowledge, and interpersonal skills to help them understand and respect self and others.

Personal/Social Development Standard B: Students will make decisions, set goals, and take necessary action to achieve goals.

Personal/Social Development Standard C: Students will understand safety and survival skills.

Competencies

- Students will understand change as a part of growth (as LBGTQ and LBGTQ ally).
- Students will recognize personal (LBGTQ and LBGTQ ally) boundaries, rights, and privacy needs.
- Students will identify and discuss changing (LBGTQ and LBGTQ ally) personal and social roles.

Learning Objectives

- Students will develop knowledge and understanding of the process of "coming out."
- Students will develop safety and survival skills related to the process of coming out.
- Students will make decisions, set goals, and take necessary action regarding expression of their sexual orientation and gender identity and expression, including coming out (the counselor will not ask students to come out).
- Allies will make decisions, set goals, and take necessary action regarding their role as an advocate for LBGTQ persons during the process of coming out.

Materials: A variety of materials may be chosen for this group exercise. Members are asked to be creative by bringing their own items, and the counselor may also utilize materials from the school drama club. Materials may include any type of clothing and costumes, makeup, jewelry and beads, hats, and the like.

Activities

Introduction: The counselor introduces the topic of "coming out" and sets clear boundaries (students will not be asked to reveal their sexual orientation—"come out"—at any time) for the group members regarding this topic. Further, the counselor discusses the positive and negative aspects involved in coming out to family and friends, and encourages students to share their concerns related to this process. The unique role of being an ally is discussed in the process of coming out.

Counseling Activity: The counselor instructs the group members to create a skit about coming out and dealing with aspects of heterosexism and transgenderism. For the process of coming out, the counselor proposes two different skits options: (1) coming out to a best friend or a trusted peer (no matter what their gender or gender identity); (2) coming out to parent(s) or guardian(s). The counselor suggests that students give attention to issues regarding the potential danger(s) related to coming out, such as taunting/harassing—verbal and/or physical—from peers in school or on the street, and to the potential benefits. The counselor emphasizes that violence can occur even in "safe" communities, and suggests direction as to methods of obtaining safety in this kind of a situation.

For a transgendered skit, the counselor directs some students to change their name (a male name to female and vice versa), asking students to refer to each other using the new names. Students display a variety of positive and negative responses to the name change (for example, using different pronouns, deciding whether to go into the men's or women's room, trying on clothes in a store, and so on). After each skit stops, group members provide feedback, such as ways to rework the skit into positive or otherwise different outcomes. Students reenact each skit as time allows. The counselor encourages students to have fun conducting this exercise, and also to focus on the seriousness involved in each skit.

Conclusion: The counselor leads the members in a discussion regarding the positive and negative aspects of coming out and of being an effective ally. The counselor must process any questions and concerns of the group members. Specific concerns may include dealing with the impact on self and others, developing productive ways to come out (for example, not doing it in a fit of anger or as a way to get back at parents), and preparing for any negative results. The counselor emphasizes the point that coming out must be a planned, clearly thought-out action, where a support system is established with trustworthy people prior to following through.

The counselor could use the following questions in the concluding discussion:

- What was it like to be in a skit? What was it like to play a "targeted" character?
- How can you relate to these skits in your own life?
- What do you think would be helpful for you personally if you were in that situation? What kinds of social dynamics do you think you could help change?

- Are there ever situations where it would be safer for an LGBTQ person to "pass" as heterosexual or traditionally gendered, despite their own sense of wanting to be out of the closet all the time? For example, when would the potential consequences be too great to come out in public, or to hold hands with a same-gender person?
- How do you find support from adults and peers when needed?
- What are the benefits and disadvantages of coming out? Which of these consequences (positive or negative) is more pressing for you now? Why? How might this be different in a few years from now?
- What is the role of being an advocate like? What unique aspects of being an ally stand out? What are some challenges or difficulties of being an ally?

Assessment: Students complete a comment card stating what they liked/disliked about the activity. If a final closing session beyond the sixth session is required, students begin the seventh session with a review of Session 6, and discuss any new insights or experiences gained.

Follow-up: Students keep a journal of reactions to the skits, including any changed beliefs, attitudes, and experiences about their own coming-out process.

INDIVIDUAL COUNSELING CONSIDERATIONS

We address individual counseling and consultation with students, parents and guardians, teachers, and administrators last for a specific reason. To truly provide leadership and advocacy for all students, school counselors must be outside their office, working in large-group settings as often as possible. To that end, we encourage school counselors to limit their time in individual counseling and consultation in order to focus services toward larger numbers of students, staff, and faculty in group and systemic interventions. However, all school counselors do some individual counseling and consultation. Ten essential areas of attention are necessary for successful leadership and advocacy with LBGTQ students, staff, and families in K–12 schools:

1. A thorough understanding of the LBGTQ identity development processes (Chen-Hayes & Banez, 2000)
2. Knowledge of violence and safety issues for LBGTQ students and the ability to teach safety skills and provide safe spaces and zero tolerance in policies for LBGTQ students, staff, and families
3. Assurance of confidentiality for coming-out discussions
4. Thorough knowledge of the similarities and differences between sexual orientation and gender identity/expression issues (Chen-Hayes, 2000, 2001a)
5. The ability to distinguish between heterosexual and traditional gender identity privilege (Chen-Hayes, 2000)
6. Knowledge of the increasing legal liability that school districts are under for not providing safe spaces for LBGTQ youth and the ability to ensure that the school has a sexual harassment policy that includes LBGTQ youth

(U.S. Department of Education, 1997; U.S. Department of Education Office for Civil Rights, 1999)

7. Knowledge of local and national print, video, and internet LBGTQ resources
8. Ally skills—knowing how to advocate, become an ally, model advocacy for others, and promote LBGTQ issues as heterosexual and traditionally gendered persons (Gelberg & Chojnacki, 1996)
9. Constant self-reflection and examination of one's own heterosexism and transgenderism
10. Use of inclusive language ("partner" or "significant other" and "spouse," when appropriate), and not assuming anyone's sexual orientation or gender identity/expression

CONCLUSION

School counselors can provide outstanding leadership and advocacy to LBGTQ students, staff, and families through the use of group, systemic, and individual counseling, consultation, and developmental school counseling lessons to empower all members of the school community. In expanding upon the ASCA national school counseling standards (Campbell & Dahir, 1997; Dahir, Sheldon, & Valiga, 1998) for LBGTQ students and integrating progressive educational transformation theory supportive of all students learning at high levels with high teacher and counselor expectations (Johnson, 1996), this chapter provides strategies and resources to promote the academic, career, and interpersonal success of all students, including LBGTQ students. The resource section includes print, video, and Internet resources on LBGTQ issues for students, staff, and families.

RESOURCES

Videos

Numerous videos that address a broad range of sexual orientation and gender identity/expression issues can be purchased online from GLSEN, PFLAG, or Microtraining Associates. The following is a brief list of recommended videos for school counselors, teachers, parents and guardians, administrators, and students.

> *All God's Children*, produced by Woman Vision, the National Gay and Lesbian Task Force, and the National Black Lesbian and Gay Leadership Forum (1996), purchase item #VHS-AGC-WV2.
> *All God's Children* is a documentary regarding the Black Church's acceptance of African American lesbian women and gay men as a unique component of the church body. This video highlights the role of the church and its members' commitment to equal rights and social justice for all people. A classroom study guide accompanies the video.

Both My Moms Are Named Judy: Children of Lesbians and Gays Speak Out,
produced by the Lesbian and Gay Parents Association (1994), purchase
item #VHS.BMM.PR1.

Designed for elementary school educators and administrators, this video
presents a diverse group of children (ages 7–11) who have lesbian and/or
gay parents. These children openly discuss their family relationships and
their feelings about being teased because of their parents' homosexual
orientation. They reveal insights regarding issues of secrecy and silence
about homosexuality in the classroom, and they provide practical
suggestions on how to effect positive change.

Gay Youth: An Educational Video, produced by Pam Walton (1995),
purchase item #VHS-GAY-PW.

This video contrasts the unfortunate suicide of 20-year-old Bobby Griffith
with the remarkable life of 17-year-old Gina Guiterrez. It demonstrates
how LBGTQ youth are at great risk in our society. More importantly, it
shows that through proper education and information coupled with
acceptance and support, that LBGTQ youth can overcome the obstacles
faced by sexual minorities.

I Just Want to Say, produced by GLSEN (1998), purchase item #VHS-
JWS-GL1.

Tennis champion Martina Navratilova discuses the antigay climate in
schools across the nation and its devastating impact on gay youth. She
reveals how educators and school personnel can effectively teach respect
and dignity for all students. Two very important public service
announcements with Judy Shepard follow the main feature.

*Youth OUTLoud!: Addressing Lesbian, Gay, Bisexual and Transgender Youth
Issues in Our Schools*, produced by Sun & Moon Vision Productions
(2000), purchase item #VHS-YOL-GL1.

Promoting safety is a must for all students, particularly for lesbian, gay,
bisexual, transgender, and questioning youth of color in our schools. This
documentary reveals the stories of several high school students who
initiate positive change from local school district policies to state and
federal laws.

Counseling LBGT Youth in Schools and Families: I, II, produced by
Microtraining Associates (www.emicrotraining.com) (2000).

Video series by two counselor educators (Stuart Chen-Hayes and Lynn
Banez) that teaches professional counselors how to work effectively with
LBGT issues in schools. Multiracial vignettes throughout; leader guide
and transcript in addition to the two videotapes.

It's Elementary, produced by Women's Educational Media (1995), purchase
item #VHS-YOL-GL1, or the educational training version #VHS-
IEM-HC.

It's Elementary gives real-life examples of school activities, faculty
meetings, and classroom discussions about lesbian and gay issues. An
accompanying viewing guide facilitates open, constructive dialogue among
the adults in school communities.

LBGTQ Organizations and Web Sites

AGLBIC: The Association for Gay, Lesbian, and Bisexual Issues in Counseling (also includes transgender issues): www.aglbic.org

BINET: Bisexual Network of the United States: www.binetusa.org

Bisexual Resource Center: www.biresource.org

Children of Lesbians and Gays Everywhere: www.colage.org/

Dignity USA: www.dignityusa.org/

IFGE: The International Foundation for Gender Education: www.ifge.org

International Lesbian and Gay Association: www.ilga.org/

Intersex Voices: www.qis.net/~triea/

PFLAG: Parents, Families, and Friends of Lesbians and Gays (and bisexuals and transgendered persons): www.pflag.org

GLAD: Gay & Lesbian Advocates & Defenders: www.glad.org/

Gender PAC: www.gpac.org/

GLAAD: Gay & Lesbian Alliance Against Defamation: www.glaad.org/org/index.html

GLSEN: Gay, Lesbian, and Straight Education Network: www.glsen.org

Human Rights Campaign: www.hrc.org/

The International Gay and Lesbian Human Rights Commission: www.iglhrc.org/

Lambda Legal Defense and Education Fund: www.lambdalegal.org

Lesbian.com: www.lesbian.com

LesbiaNation.com: www.lesbianation.com/

National Black Gay and Lesbian Leadership Forum: www.nblglf.org

National Center for Lesbian Rights: www.nclrights.org

National Gay and Lesbian Taskforce: www.ngltf.org/

National Latina/ø Lesbian, Gay, Bisexual, and Transgender Organization: www.llego.org

NYAGRA: New York Association for Gender Rights Advocacy: www.nyagra.org

OUTPROUD: National Coalition of Gay, Lesbian, Bisexual, and Transgender Youth: www.outproud.org

SIECUS: Sex Education and Information Council of the United States: www.siecus.org

Triangle Foundation: www.tri.org/

REFERENCES

American Counseling Association (ACA). (1993). *The crisis in school counseling.* Alexandria, VA: Author.

American School Counseling Association (ASCA). (1994). *The school counselor's role in education reform.* Alexandria, VA: Author.

Back, G. G. (1985). *Are you still my mother? Are you still my family?* New York: Warner Books.

Bernstein, R. (Ed.). (1995). *Straight parents, gay children.* New York: Thunder's Mouth Press.

Blumenfeld, W. J. (Ed.). (1992). *Homophobia: How we all pay the price.* Boston, MA: Beacon Press.

Campbell, C. A., & Dahir, C. A. (1997). *Sharing the vision: The national standards for school counseling programs.* Alexandria, VA: American School Counselor Association.

Chen-Hayes, S. F. (1997). Counseling lesbian, bisexual, and gay persons in couple and family relationships: Overcoming the stereotypes. *Family Journal: Counseling and Therapy for Couples and Families, 5*(3), 236–240.

Chen-Hayes, S. F. (2000). Social justice advocacy with lesbian, bisexual, gay, and transgendered persons. In Lewis, J., & Bradley, L. (Eds.), *Advocacy in counseling: Counselors, clients, and community* (pp. 89–98). Greensboro, NC: Caps publications (ERIC/CASS).

Chen-Hayes, S. F. (2001a). Counseling and advocacy with transgendered and gender-variant persons in schools and families. *Journal of Humanistic Counseling, Education, and Development, 40*(1), 34–48.

Chen-Hayes, S. F. (2001b). The social justice advocacy readiness questionnaire. *Journal of Lesbian and Gay Social Services, 13*(1/2), 191–203.

Chen-Hayes, S. F. (2001c). Systemic anti-oppression strategies for school counselors as allies affirming queer children, youth, and families of multiracial experience. In Kumashiro, K. (Ed.), *Troubling intersections of race and sexuality: Queer students of color and anti-oppressive education* (pp. 163–178). Lanham, MD: Rowman & Littlefield.

Chen-Hayes, S. F., & Banez, L. (2000). *Lesbian, bisexual, gay, and transgendered counseling 1: Affirmative practice*. Videotape, transcript, and leader guide. Amherst, MA: Microtraining Associates.

Dahir, C. A., Sheldon, C. B., & Valiga, M. J. (1998). *Vision into action: Implementing the national standards for school counseling programs*. Alexandria, VA: American School Counselor Association.

Elia, J. P. (1993). Homophobia in the school: A problem in need of a resolution. *High School Journal, 77,* 177–185.

Gay, Lesbian, and Straight Education Network. (1999). *National school climate survey*. New York: Author.

Gelberg, S., & Chojnacki, J. T. (1996). *Career and life planning with gay, lesbian, and bisexual persons*. Alexandria, VA: American Counseling Association.

Ginsberg, R. W. (1998). Silenced voices inside our schools. *Initiatives, 58,* 1–15.

Gonsiorek, J. (1988). Mental health issues of gay and lesbian adolescents. *Journal of Adolescent Health Care, 9,* 114–122.

Griffin, P., & Harro, B. (1997). Heterosexism curriculum design. In Adams, M., Bell, L. A., & Griffin, P. (Eds.), *Teaching for diversity and social justice: A sourcebook* (pp. 141–163). New York: Routledge.

Hardiman, R., & Jackson, B. W. (1997). Conceptual foundations for social justice courses. In Adams, M., Bell, L. A., & Griffin, P. (Eds.), *Teaching for diversity and social justice: A sourcebook* (pp. 16–29). New York: Routledge.

Hersch, P. (1991, Jan.–Feb.). Secret lives: Lesbians and gay teens in fear of discovery. *Family Networker,* 36–39, 41–43.

House, R. M., & Martin, P. J. (1998). Advocating for better futures for all students: A new vision for school counselors. *Education, 119*(2), 284–291.

Irvine, J. M. (1990). *Disorders of desire: Sex and gender in modern American sexology*. Philadelphia: Temple University Press.

Johnson, L. S. (2000). Promoting professional identity in an era of educational reform. *Professional School Counseling, 4,* 31–40.

Johnson, R. S. (1996). *Setting our sights: Measuring equity in school change*. Los Angeles: Achievement Council.

Klein, F., Sepekoff, B., & Wolf, T. J. (1985). Sexual orientation: A multi-variable dynamic process. In Klein, F., & Wolf, T. J. (Eds.), *Two lives to lead: Bisexuality in men and women* (pp. 35–49). New York: Harrington Park Press.

Lipkin, A. (1992). *Looking at gay and lesbian literature: Gay/Lesbian secondary schools curriculum project*. Cambridge, MA: Harvard Graduate School of Education.

Logan, C. (1996). Homophobia? No. Homo-prejudice? Yes. *Journal of Homosexuality, 31*, 31–53.

McFarland, W. P. (1998). Gay, lesbian, and bisexual student suicide. *Professional School Counseling, 1*(3), 26–29.

QueerTheory.com. Web page. Retrieved November 11, 2001, from http://www.queertheory.com.

Reis, B., & Saewyc, E. (1999). *Eighty-three thousand youth: Selected findings of eight population-based studies as they pertain to anti-gay harassment and the safety and well-being of sexual minority students.* Seattle, WA: Safe Schools Coalition of Washington.

Remafedi, G. (Ed.). (1994). *Death by denial: Studies of suicide in gay and lesbian teenagers.* Boston, MA: Alyson.

Reynolds, A., & Koski, M. J. (1995). Lesbian, gay, and bisexual teens and the school counselor: Building alliances. In Unks, G. (Ed.), *The gay teen: Educational practice and theory for lesbian, gay, and bisexual adolescents.* New York: Routledge.

Robinson, K. E. (1994). Addressing the needs of gay and lesbian students: The school counselor's role. *School Counselor, 41*, 326–332.

Ryan, C., & Futterman, D. (1998). *Lesbian and gay youth: Care and counseling.* New York: Columbia University Press.

Savin-Williams, R. (1989). Gay and lesbian adolescents. *Marriage and Family Review, 14*, 197–216.

Sexuality Information and Education Council of the United States (SIECUS) National Guidelines Task Force. (1996). *Guidelines for comprehensive sexuality education: Kindergarten–12th grade* (2nd ed.). New York: Author.

Suppe, F. (1984). Classifying sexual disorders: The diagnostic and statistical manual of the American Psychiatric Association. *Journal of Homosexuality, 9*(4), 9–28.

Treadway, L., & Yoakam, J. (1992). Creating a safer school environment for lesbian and gay students. *Journal of School Health, 62*, 352–357.

U.S. Department of Education. (1997). *Revised Sexual Harassment Guidance: Harassment of Students by School Employees, Other Students, or Third Parties.* 62 Fed. Reg. 12,034.

U.S. Department of Education Office for Civil Rights. (1999). *Protecting students from harassment and hate crime: A guide for schools.* Washington, DC: Author.

HANDOUT 7.1

Sexual Orientation and Gender Identity and Expression Terms

allies, biological sex, bisexuals, coming out, cross-dressers, drag queens and drag kings, gay men, gender, gender blenders, gender expression, gender identity, gender role, heterosexism, heterosexuals, intersex, lesbians, queer, questioning, sexual orientation, transgendered, transgenderism, transsexuals, two-spirit

LBGTQ DEFINITIONS EXERCISE

1. A person's capacity for sexual and emotional attractions, fantasies, and behaviors toward other persons is referred to as _____. Klein, Sepekoff, and Wolf (1985) proposed that sexual orientation is a multivariable dynamic that includes past, present, and ideal feelings about who is attractive and/or desirable in sexual and/or romantic ways. It can include one's sexual attractions, behaviors, fantasies, gender emotional preference, gender social preference, sexual identity in a community (lesbian, bisexual, gay, heterosexual), and use of a sexual orientation self-label. There is no definitive answer for how sexual orientation occurs in humans; it is on a continuum and can be fluid or fixed over a person's lifetime. The term *sexual preference* is vague and unhelpful because it implies that people can choose their _____, which is not the case for most persons. While anyone may choose various sexual behaviors, _____ is much more than behavior. Cultures and languages vary in the terms used to describe _____.

2. Women who are romantically and sexually attracted to other women and who may or may not act on those attractions are known as _____.

3. People of any gender who have the potential to be romantically and sexually attracted to people of any gender and who may or may not act on those attractions are known as _____.

4. Men who are romantically and sexually attracted to other men and who may or may not act on those attractions are known as _____.

5. People who are romantically and sexually attracted to persons who differ from them in gender identity (that is, boys and girls; women and men) are known as _____.

6. People of various nondominant sexual orientations and gender identities who challenge the traditional categories of sexuality and choose not to label their sexual orientation or gender identity in rigid terms are known as _____. They may include persons whose behavior and attractions are similar to lesbian, bisexual, gay, and transgendered persons. The term still has some controversy surrounding it as once it was used solely as a pejorative or put-down.

7. People who are not clear about their sexual orientation or gender identity and are seeking answers about themselves are known as _____.

8. _____ is an indigenous term that honors persons who are nontraditional in their sexual orientation and/or gender identity expressions and identities. Christian missionaries worked diligently to stop their practices and affirmation in many indigenous nations. However, the traditions and people have lived on underground. They have recently gained much publicity and affirmation in modern indigenous and queer communities as a backlash to colonization and imperialism.

9. A person's internal, subjective experience of how they feel and choose to express self as a "gendered" person in terms of gender roles, attitudes, and behavior is known as _____. A person's internal _____ is like a worldview; it may or may not match the person's external gender expression in terms of clothing or other gendered signals and cues. It may be experienced by some persons as their masculinity, femininity, and/or the combination of their personal and cultural experience and expressions of masculinity and femininity. Persons may choose to live with their internal and external _____ congruent or incongruent based on a variety of personal, social, cultural, spiritual, and political factors.

10. The external or outward appearance and/or presentation of one's gender identity in a sociocultural context is known as _____.

11. _____ is the manner in which a person displays his/her masculinity, femininity, or a combination of multiple gender identities based upon culture definitions and social expectations. There is a continuum of _____ and expression in cultures around the world.

12. A person's genetic composition and physical body, including genitalia and secondary sex characteristics at birth and/or later in the life cycle developed through the use of hormones or surgical procedures, is known as _____. It is not necessarily fixed over a person's lifetime.

13. _____ is a cultural term that societies apply in various ways to classify the attitudes, behaviors, social functioning, and power relations between women, men, girls, boys, cross-dressers, transsexuals, intersex persons, gender blenders, drag queens and drag kings, and other transgendered persons. Certain cultures maintain a rigid dichotomy of either/or in _____; other cultures recognize and celebrate a _____ continuum.

14. _____ is an umbrella term including all members of the nondominant gender identity communities, who have nontraditional gender identity and/or expression, including transsexuals (pre-, post-, and non-operative), cross-dressers, gender blenders, drag queens and drag kings, and intersex persons.

15. People whose external gender identity may not match their internal gender identity are known as _____. In other words, the external genitalia and gender role socialization/expression do not necessarily correspond with internal gender role identity. **Male-to-female** (MtoF) _____ have internal female gender identity and seek to alter their biologically male body characteristics to match an internal female gender identity. **Female-to-male** (FtoM) _____ have internal male gender identity and seek to alter their biologically female body characteristics to match an internal male gender identity. **Pre-operative** (pre-op) _____ await **sex reassignment surgery** (SRS). **Post-operative** (post-op) _____ have completed SRS and are known as **transwomen** or **transmen. Non-operative** (non-op) _____ elect not to alter their bodies through physical surgery. _____ have a range of sexual orientations from heterosexual to bisexual to lesbian or gay.

16. People born with both traditional male and female genitals are known as _____. Many people in industrialized countries have been altered surgically at birth by physicians to fit a traditional gender identity. This assigned "gender" has often been inaccurate.

17. Heterosexual men who dress in traditionally gendered women's clothing are referred to as _____. _____ may find it erotic to wear women's clothing. Persons may cross-dress part-time or full-time. Their community is often secretive and more hidden than the transsexual community. Major concerns for heterosexual male _____ are the ability to pass successfully as women and the ability to be affirmed by other _____ in the community. The term *transvestite* is seen as outdated, unhelpful, and stigmatizing.

(continued)

18. _____ are people who have an external gender identity reflecting a combination of traditionally feminine and masculine attire and/or accessories. _____ question traditional gender dichotomies by replacing them with a continuum.

19. Gay and bisexual men who wear traditional women's clothing are known as _____, and _____ are lesbian and bisexual women who wear traditional men's clothing to celebrate gay pride, to question traditional gender and sexual orientation roles in lesbian, bisexual, gay, and heterosexual communities, to express nontraditional gender identities, to challenge authority, and/or to perform and entertain.

20. Prejudice multiplied by power used by members of the dominant sexual orientation (heterosexual) toward members of nondominant sexual orientations (lesbian, bisexual, and gay) to restrict their access to resources (individual, cultural, and institutional/systemic) is _____. When lesbian, bisexual, and or gay persons believe the myths, stereotypes, and lies about who they are and act accordingly to denigrate themselves and other LBG persons as less worthy than heterosexuals, it is internalized _____. Externalized _____ occurs when heterosexuals use violence, threats, coercion, myths, stereotypes, and other forms of power and control to keep lesbian, bisexual, and gay persons in a position of subordination, ensuring that LBG persons do not have equal access to the same resources that heterosexuals do.

21. Prejudice multiplied by power used by traditionally gendered persons toward nontraditionally gendered persons (transgendered, transsexual, cross-dressers, intersexuals, drag queens and drag kings) to restrict their access to resources (individual, cultural, and institutional/systemic) is _____. When transgendered persons believe the myths, stereotypes, and lies about who they are and act accordingly to denigrate themselves and other transgendered persons as less worthy than traditionally gendered persons, it is internalized _____. Externalized _____ occurs when traditionally gendered persons use violence, threats, coercion, myths, stereotypes, and other forms of power and control to keep transgendered persons in a position of subordination, ensuring that transgendered persons do not have equal access to the same resources that traditionally gendered persons do.

22. _____ are heterosexual and traditionally gendered persons who take on the struggles of challenging the oppressions of heterosexism and transgenderism through developing reciprocal relationships with LBGT persons. These relationships involve a great deal of listening and learning on the part of dominant culture group members toward LBGT persons to challenge heterosexism and transgenderism on individual, cultural, and systemic or institutional levels. This frees up LBGT persons' energies to focus on other issues of oppression.

23. Unlike heterosexuals and traditionally gendered persons, LBGT persons must constantly make decisions about to whom and where they will disclose their sexual orientation and gender identity/expression identities, which is also referred to as _____. It is never anyone else's job to coerce someone to _____. _____ is NOT a universal process, and in some cultures it is done in indirect as opposed to direct ways. Many persons may choose to _____ in some aspects of their life but not in others. It is a life-long process, and there is great variation in it for LBGT persons over time.

Answers

1. sexual orientation 2. lesbians 3. bisexuals 4. gay men 5. heterosexuals 6. queer 7. questioning
8. two-spirit 9. gender identity 10. gender expression 11. gender role 12. biological sex 13. gender
14. transgendered 15. transsexual 16. intersex 17. cross-dressers 18. gender blenders 19. drag queens and drag kings 20. heterosexism 21. transgenderism 22. allies 23. coming out

Source: Adapted from Chen-Hayes, 2000, 2001b.

WHAT IS YOUR LBGTQ IQ? QUESTIONNAIRE

1. Originally used as an epithet and a slur, LBGTQ activists have turned this term around to emphasize what LBGTQ persons have to offer as different and unique: _____

2. The medical process whereby a pre-operative transsexual person receives hormones and alters their body physically is also known as: _____

3. The process of sharing one's LBGTQ identity with self and others: _____

4. Being in the closet or hiding one's sexual orientation or nontraditional gender identity/expression is also known as: _____

5. The use of gender-nonconforming pronouns and sometimes drag to entertain and/or create a subcultural identity that challenges traditional gender values: _____

6. The first lesbian and gay social/political groups in the United States: _____

7. The modern LBGT civil rights movement was born during the summer of 1969 in a civil rebellion inside and out of this gay bar in Manhattan, where the patrons attacked police on a routine visit to harass gay people: _____

8. Activist group that started in the gay community and now includes persons of all sexual orientations and gender identities/expression to challenge unfair HIV/AIDS policies and practices: _____

9. U.S. states that guarantee some form of LBG rights by legislation: _____

10. The percentage of youth suicide attempts that researchers have shown to be made by LBGTQ youth dealing with heterosexism and transgenderism: _____

11. The percentage of runaway youth who identify as LBGTQ: _____

12. The number of U.S. high schools with a LBGTQ student group and/or a gay-straight alliance: _____

Scoring Guide

1 point for each correct answer.
11–12 correct = Very STRONG LBGTQ Ally
9–10 correct = STRONG LBGTQ Ally
7–8 correct = LBGTQ Ally
6 or fewer correct = LBGTQ Information-challenged Ally

(continued)

HANDOUT 7.2 *(continued)*

Answers

1. queer
2. sex reassignment surgery
3. coming out
4. passing
5. camp or "camping it up"
6. the Daughters of Bilitis and the Mattachine Society
7. Stonewall
8. ACT-UP: Aids Coalition To Unleash Power
9. WI, MA, CN, NJ, VT, MN, NH, RI, HI, CA all passed legislation that supports LBG persons in some form; MN was the only state to also include gender identity and expression. ME passed LBG-supportive legislation and then voters rescinded it.
10. Estimates vary from 30 to 50 percent.
11. Estimates vary from at least 50 percent up.
12. under 1000

HETEROSEXUAL QUESTIONNAIRE

1. What do you think caused your heterosexuality?

2. When and how did you first decide you were heterosexual?

3. Is it possible that your heterosexuality is just a phase you will grow out of?

4. Do you hate or are you afraid of people of the same sex?

5. If you have never dated someone of the same sex, is it possible that you just haven't met the right person?

6. To whom have you disclosed your heterosexual tendencies, and how did they take it?

7. Why do heterosexuals feel compelled to seduce others into their lifestyles?

8. Why do heterosexuals insist on flaunting their sexuality? Can't they just be who they are and keep quiet about it?

9. Would you want your children to be heterosexual, knowing the problems they would face?

10. Why do heterosexuals place so much emphasis on sex?

Source: Adapted from Back, G. G. (1985). *Are You Still My Mother? Are You Still My Family?* New York: Warner Books. Questionnaire attributed to Martin Rochlin, Ph.D., West Hollywood, CA.

TRADITIONAL GENDER IDENTITY AND EXPRESSION QUESTIONNAIRE

1. What do you think caused your being traditionally gendered as a masculine man/boy, feminine woman/girl?

2. When and how did you first decide you were traditionally gendered as a masculine boy or a feminine girl?

3. Is it possible that your traditional gender as a masculine boy or a feminine girl is just a phase you will grow out of?

4. Do you hate or are you afraid of masculine boys and men and feminine girls and women?

5. If you have never dated a masculine male or a feminine female, is it possible that you just haven't met the right person?

6. To whom have you disclosed your traditional masculinity or femininity, and how did they take it?

(continued)

7. Why do traditionally masculine men and boys and feminine women and girls feel compelled to seduce others into their lifestyles?

8. Why do masculine men and boys and feminine women and girls insist on flaunting their gender identity and expression? Can't they just be who they are and keep quiet about it?

9. Would you want your boy children to be traditionally masculine and your girl children to be traditionally feminine, knowing the problems they would face?

10. Why do masculine men and boys and feminine women and girls place so much emphasis on conformity in gender identity and expression?

Source: Adapted from Chen-Hayes, 2002.

LIST OF FAMOUS LBGT PERSONS FROM HISTORY/HERSTORY AND TODAY

NOTE: Because the terms *lesbian, bisexual, gay,* and *transgendered* are English-language terms that have been used only in the last five decades, there is no way to accurately use these terms for historical figures. However, there is evidence that many historical figures had same-gender relationships or sexual behavior. Different cultures and different times have used different language and terminology to describe persons whom we now identify as LBGT. The list includes persons who have at one time identified publicly as LBG or T.

Academics: composer John Corigliano; counselor-educators Sari Dworkin, Bob Barrett, Ron McLean, Reese House, Sue Strong, Joy Whitman; historians John Boswell, John D'Emilio, Martin Duberman, Lillian Faderman, Jonathan Ned Katz; sociologists Paisley Currah, Paula Rust-Rodriguez (Bi); teacher-educators Pat Griffin, Jim Sears, Kevin Kumashiro

Activists: Gloria Anzaldua, Elizabeth Birch, Pat Califia, Dallas Denny (TG), Andrea Dworkin, Leslie Feinberg (TG), Harry Hay, Amber Hollibaugh, Cleve Jones, June Jordan (Bi), Lani Ka'ahumanu (Bi), Audre Lorde, Phyllis Lyon, Del Martin, Kate Millet (Bi), Cherrie Moraga, Simon Nkoli, Pauline Park (TG), Sophia Pazos, Minnie Bruce Pratt, Donna Red Wing, Alan Rockaway (Bi), Eleanor Roosevelt, Bayard Rustin, Gertrude Stein, Moonhawk River Stone, Alice B. Toklas, Urvashi Vaid

Actors: Marlon Brando, Wilson Cruz, Rupert Everett, Will Geer, John Gielgud, Rock Hudson, Nathan Lane, Sir Ian McKellen, Sal Mineo, Robert Reed, Dick Sargent, B. D. Wong, multiple cast members from MTV's *The Real World*

Actresses: Amanda Bearse, Ellen DeGeneres, Marlene Dietrich (Bi), Angelina Jolie (Bi), multiple cast members from MTV's *The Real World*

Ambassador: James Hormel

Anthropologist: Margaret Mead (Bi)

Artists: Chrystos, Leonardo da Vinci, Keith Harring, Jasper Johns, Frida Kahlo, Robert Mapplethorpe, Andy Warhol

Athletes: Babe Didrikson, Betty Dodd (golf); Martina Navratilova, Billie Jean King (Bi), Renee Richards (TG) (tennis); Greg Louganis (diving); Bob Paris (body building); David Kopay, Esera Tualo (football); Dick Button, Rudy Galindo (ice skating); Tom Waddell (decathlon, founder of "Gay Games"); participants at the Gay Games

Authors: Paula Gunn Allen, Gloria Anzaldua, Reinaldo Arenas, W. H. Auden, Rita Mae Brown, James Baldwin, Ellen Bass, Kate Bornstein (TG), Pat Califia (TG), Truman Capote, Willa Cather, John Cheever, Quentin Crisp, Mary Daley, Samuel R. Delany, Leslie Feinberg (TG), E. M. Forster (Bi), Jewelle Gomez, Christopher Isherwood, June Jordan (Bi), Jonathon Katz, D. H. Lawrence (Bi), Audre Lorde, Armistead Maupin, Paul Monette, Cherrie Moraga, Anaïs Nin (Bi), Christopher Rice, Anne Rice (Bi), David Sedaris, Michelangelo Signorile, Kitty Tsui, Gore Vidal (Bi), Alice Walker, Oscar Wilde, Virginia Woolf

(continued)

Business leaders/Consultants: David Geffin (billionaire recording producer/executive), David Mixner (consultant/political strategist), Rich Tafel (politics), Mary Cheney (alcohol marketing)

Cartoon characters: Akbar and Jeff from "Life in Hell," Laurence in "For Better or for Worse," most of the characters in "Dykes to Watch Out For"

Cartoonist: Alison Bechdel

Chefs: Craig Claiborne

Clergy: Elias Farajaje-Jones, Carter Heyward, Roger Jones, Troy Perry, Dusty Pruitt, Starhawk, Lynn Ungar, Mel White

College students: Matthew Shepard, U.S. Naval Academy student Joe Steffan

Comedians: Tom Ammiano, Pomo Afro Homos

Comediennes: Sandra Bernhard, Kate Clinton, Lea Delaria, Marga Gomez

Composers: Aaron Copland, John Corigliano, Cole Porter, Stephen Sondheim, Peter Tchaikovsky

Conductor: Leonard Bernstein

Dancers/Choreographers: Alvin Ailey, Bill T. Jones, Arnie Zane, Jin Xing

Doctors: Sheila Kirk (TG), Fritz Klein (Bi), Tom Waddell

Economist: John Maynard Keynes

Editors/Publishers: Sasha Alyson, Pat Califia (TG), Barbara Smith

Fashion designers: Perry Ellis, Isaac Mizrahi, Gianni Versace

Filmmakers: Pedro Almodovar, Gregg Araki, Pratibha Parmar, Marlon Riggs, Gus Van Sant, Rose Troche, John Waters

Historians: Martin Duberman, Lillian Faderman, Jonathon Katz

Illusionists: Siegfried and Roy

Journalists: Tracy Baim, Michael Bronski, Mubarak Dahir, Donna Minkowitz, Deb Price, Randy Shilts

Lawyers: Roberta Achtenberg, Roy Cohn, Fernando Gutierrez, Glenn Magpantay, Jill Metz, Kelly Donovan, William Singer, Urvashi Vaid, Evan Wolfson

Military personnel: Cliff Arnesen (Bi), Miriam ben-Shalom, Margarethe Cammermeyer, James Holobaugh, Keith Meinhold, Leonard Matlovich, Dusty Pruitt, Joe Steffan, Tracy Thorne, Perry Watkins, Jin Xing, Jose Zuniga

Model: Rod Jackson

Nurse: Margarethe Cammermeyer

Philanthropist: James Hormel

Philosophers: Michel Foucault, Jean Paul Sartre

Photographers: Robert Mapplethorpe, Herb Ritts

Playwrights: Kate Bornstein (TG), David Drake, Lorraine Hansberry, Harvey Firestein, Larry Kramer, Tony Kushner, Federico García Lorca, Paul Rudnick, Oscar Wilde

Poets: Lord Byron, Countee Cullen, Allen Ginsberg, Essex Hemphill, Federico García Lorca, Adrienne Rich, Audre Lorde, Edna St. Vincent Millay, Sappho

Politicians: Texas legislator Glen Maxey, New York representatives Deborah Glick and Tom Duane, New York city councilwoman Margarita Lopez, Maryland congressman Robert Bauman, Minnesota legislator Karen Clark, Illinois state representative Larry McKeon, Wisconsin congresswoman Tammy Baldwin, former Massachusetts congressman Gerry Studds, current Massachusetts congressman Barney Frank, Massachusetts state legislator Elaine Noble, Seattle city councilwoman Sherry Harris, former Mississippi congressman Jon Hinson, former San Francisco city supervisor Harvey Milk, San Francisco supervisor and mayoral candidate Tom Ammiano, Washington state legislator Cal Anderson, Clinton administration assistant secretary of housing and urban development Roberta Achtenberg

Public health administrators: Dee Mosbacher, Phill Wilson

Publisher and entrepreneur: Malcolm Forbes

Sexologist: Magnus Hirschfeld

Singers and composers: Joan Baez (Bi), Andy Bell of Erasure, Blackberri, Chastity Bono, David Bowie, Boy George, Neneh Cherry, Alix Dobkin, Melissa Etheridge, Ferron, the Flirtations, Indigo Girls, Sophie B. Hawkins, Janis Ian, Janet Jackson (Bi), Mick Jagger (Bi), Elton John, Holly Johnson (Frankie Goes to Hollywood), Janis Joplin (Bi), k. d. laing, Freddie Mercury (Queen), George Michael (Wham), Meshell Ndegeocello, Holly Near, Pet Shop Boys, Toshi Reagon, Lou Reed, Romanovsky & Phillips, RuPaul, Paul Rutherford (Frankie Goes to Hollywood), Bessie Smith, Jimmy Somerville, Michael Stipe (REM), Kris Williamson

Social worker/Immigrant rights activist: Jane Addams

Talk show host: Rosie O'Donnell

Teachers: Tom Ammiano, Kevin Jennings, Minnie Bruce Pratt

Source: www.queertheory.com, retrieved on November 11, 2001, and personal communications.

VIOLENCE-PREVENTION AND CONFLICT-RESOLUTION EDUCATION IN THE SCHOOLS

Vivian V. Lee, Old Dominion University

INTRODUCTION

The tragic events of September 11, 2001, forever vanquished any innocence, real or illusory, the United States and much of the world may have held regarding the potential magnitude of violent terrorism. As people watched the fatal images of violence, they desperately struggled to make sense of the loss and trauma left behind in the wake of smoldering rubble. Several years earlier, violence had produced numerous fatalities in the 1995 bombing of the Oklahoma City federal building. In between these events, the worst school shooting in American history occurred at Columbine High School in Littleton, Colorado in 1999. As a result of these tragic events, children and youth have become all too familiar with the profile of violence and unacquainted with the face of peace. While these large-scale incidents received widespread media coverage, other hidden and more common forms of violence continue to occur everyday in schools. These may include theft, larceny, and fights that disrupt the learning environment of schools, creating a culture and climate marked by a lack of safety, where conflict ends in violence. Notions of a peaceful learning environment become an abstraction as the tangible incidents of violence carve lasting images into developing minds (Bickmore, 1999). To create a safe and peaceful learning environment characterized by the nonviolent management of conflict requires structured opportunities for staff and students to practice confronting conflict in schools (Bickmore, 1999). Moreover, the unrest in schools caused by violence interferes with students' ability to master cognitive skills (Harris, 2001).

Literature Review

Violence in Schools

Violence in schools has touched many and diverse communities across the United States, as violent victimization among youth reaches unprecedented levels (Farrell, Meyer, & White, 2001). In its wake, schools and communities struggle to find effective solutions to the senseless acts that leave physical and psychological scars on youth and society. Some authors feel the violence of today reflects a greater lack of conscience and focus, striking in a more random fashion and involving increasingly younger perpetrators (Farrell et al., 2001; Jones, 1998). Across our country, large numbers of children grow up in chronically violent neighborhoods, and by their middle years many inner-city children are exposed to serious acts of violence (Schwartz & Proctor, 2000). This increased exposure among disenfranchised groups within urban America creates a greater familiarity with violence, resulting in a lower expectation of peace than in other groups traditionally less directly affected by violence (Flaherty, 2001; Hazler, 1998). New trends in white, rural, and suburban communities, such as the school shootings over the past decade, are shattering previously held expectations of safety and dispelling myths of where, how, and who regarding violent acts among children and adolescents (Stanley, 2000). Despite these new trends of violence, the overall incidence of serious crimes involving weapons in schools is decreasing (Flaherty, 2001; Glasser, 2000).

To understand violence in schools it is helpful to examine the societal and school-based antecedents of violence, the continuum of violent behavior in schools, and risk factors of violent youth. Social disparities and injustices are recognized as the fuel for most forms of school violence (Casella, 2001; Coleman & Deutsch, 2000; Nieto, 1999). Some of these injustices include poverty, disintegrating families, child abuse, romanticized violence, and pressure to achieve (Jones, 1998). Casella (2001) suggests race, gender, social status, sexual identity, prejudice, and fear are also central to varying forms of violence. Other societal factors that are associated with students involved in violent acts include alcohol and drug abuse (Peterson & Skiba, 2001; Sandhu, 2000) and gang affiliation (Sandhu, 2000). Violence associated with drugs and gangs can easily find its way from the streets into the schools. Factors within the school that contribute to violence include a culture and climate of disrespect, large school and class size, strained teacher-student relationships, lack of clarity and follow-through in rules and policies, poor or inconsistent administrative support, few allowances for individual differences, a code of silence, and a lack of school connectedness (Christle, Jolivette, & Nelson, 2000; Farrell & Smith, 2000; Flaherty, 2001). As societal and school-based issues collide, the likelihood of school violence escalates. If left unchecked, the underlying injustices breed conflict; then the destructive management of these conflicts encourages violence, creating a cyclical pattern. When violent behavior does surface it can be considered the ultimate act of disrespect on a continuum that includes many forms of "dissing" ranging from the sensational to more common forms (Flaherty, 2001; Hazler & Carney, 2000).

Some common types of violence in schools include forms of physical aggression without weapons such as fights, theft, larceny, and vandalism. Other lesser forms of disrespect on the violence continuum are equally damaging and may include daily incidents of pushing, shoving, hitting, kicking, obscene language, name calling, and insulting others (Flaherty, 2001; Hazler & Carney, 2000). Significantly, these incidents are not limited to a particular grade level. Violent incidents are evident in preschool and continue with greater likelihood in middle and secondary school as adolescents face multiple developmental challenges that can encourage conflict (Farrell et al., 2001). Additionally, a number of risk factors associated with those who commit violent behavior have been identified. They include: an early onset of delinquency or violence; involvement in frequent, varied, and serious delinquent acts; social-cognitive deficits; risk taking; poor social skills; drug abuse; lack of responsibility; involvement in gangs; no sense of guilt; poor family relations and a lack of parental discipline and monitoring; peer rejection during childhood; association with delinquent peers during adolescence; and exposure to violence and other major stressors (Christle et al., 2000; Minden et al., 2000; Sandhu, 2000). While no one factor or characteristic is a determinant of violent behavior, attention to patterns or clusters may inform interventions. Unfortunately, adults often ignore many common forms of disrespect and consider them child's play (Hazler & Carney, 2000). This lack of monitoring students' behavior leads to victimization in schools (Hanish & Guerra, 2000). As victimization increases, violence becomes part of the accepted mores of the school's culture and climate, blurring the line between violence and nonviolence and making it easier to cross (Flaherty, 2001). The devastating result of this culture of school violence is not limited to the victim; rather it disrupts the learning environment for all members of the school community, negatively impacting student achievement. This insidious picture suggests that no act of violence is an isolated incident and that prevention and education needs to be conceptualized as systemic and sequential along a K–12 continuum.

In the struggle to counteract violent behavior among children and adolescents, many school communities resort to measures such as zero-tolerance policies, in-school police, metal detectors, expulsion from school, and surveillance cameras (Casella, 2001; Harris, 2001). These *negative peacekeeping* measures are designed to deter violence by threatening students with severe punishments (Harris, 2001). While security measures to ensure school safety are important, some believe these measures are merely a stopgap (e.g., Sandhu, 2000). Rather, comprehensive measures, such as those described later in this chapter, are needed to prevent continued violence and reduce the deleterious effects of previous violence.

Conflict in Schools

Before we can address how conflict manifests in schools, we must understand the nature of conflict. Conflict is a natural part of life resulting from interactions that consist of disagreements (Coleman & Deutsch, 2000; George et al., 1996). These conflicts can be resolved either constructively or destructively. Because of the potential for constructive resolution, conflict can be embraced as an opportunity to learn and grow beyond the present situation by increasing awareness and knowledge of self and others, thereby challenging the status quo of violence that impacts the learning environment (Coleman & Deutsch, 2000).

To realize the growth potential of conflict, it is helpful to understand the context in which it occurs, the characteristics of conflict, and the potential types of conflict. Conflict can be conceptualized within four contexts: conflicts occur within the self (intrapersonal), between two or more people (interpersonal), between two or more within a group (intragroup), and between groups (intergroup) (Perlstein & Thrall, 1996). Translated into the school setting, a potentially violent situation can begin at any of these points of conflict. These conflicts are not limited to student interactions. They can occur between teacher and student or teacher and teacher, or can even involve administrators and parents (Carter, 1999). Due to the highly interpersonal nature of conflicts, the potential for the situation to escalate to involve others is likely. For example, an intrapersonal conflict not resolved constructively may lead to an interpersonal conflict and escalate further to involve an intergroup or intragroup conflict. At any point in these interactions the potential for violence exists.

Conflict can be conceptualized as either tractable or intractable. Tractable conflicts are usually minor disputes occurring as a result of incomplete or inaccurate information or multiple stressful events. They are usually easily resolved. Intractable conflicts are more deeply rooted in a competitive, win/lose societal structure and revolve around differing attitudes, values, and beliefs based in contrasting worldviews, limited resources, and unmet needs. These conflicts often arise as a result of groups' differences in religion, race, ethnicity, gender, sexual orientation, and socioeconomic status. Some intractable conflicts occur as disenfranchised populations disproportionately face limited resources and experience unmet needs. Human need is a motivating factor in intractable conflict, as human needs are not negotiable (Conflict Research Consortium, 1998c).

Translated into the school setting, conflict over unmet needs is most often seen in the struggle for identity and belonging, security, esteem, or survival or in disputes with a long history of contentiousness (Conflict Resource Consortium, 1998a; Deutsch, 2001). Implicit in these conflicts are issues of dominance that reflect a hierarchical structure giving one group power over another, thus rejecting the rights, needs, and personhood of the other (Nieto, 1999). This structure of dominance and competition fuels ongoing conflict as students confront the structures that hamper the fulfillment of their needs (Conflict Research Consortium, 1998b). Students feel rejected, and a coercive power dynamic is established. Coercive power dynamics such as rejection, shaming, humiliation, and contempt are a wellspring for the epidemic of violence in the schools (Tremlow, Fonagy, & Sacco, 2001). Moreover, the types of power struggles inherent in intractable conflicts are key factors in continued violence in children and adolescents. To combat this culture and climate that breeds violence, Nieto (1999) suggests reframing the power structure of domination from one of control to one of empowerment, which is used to liberate. In this sense empowerment means increasing all parties' ability to increase control over their lives through the acquisition of skills to actively mediate their own lives and conflicts. This assists individuals and groups to clarify goals, identify options and preferences, and access resources without usurping the rights and dignity of others (Conflict Research Consortium, 1998d). One primary cause of intractable conflict is students' lack of understanding of the attitudes, values, and beliefs of others different from themselves. Recognition, acknowledgement of others, and empathy for others' perspectives lay the foundation for honoring the needs of others in the face of self-interest (Conflict Research Consortium, 1998d). Research indicates that empowered students who were given leadership opportunities were found to be less violent (Harris, 2001).

Liberation through empowerment is not limited to students. All members of the school community need to redefine their relationships to ensure access and equity to meaningful experiences and educational opportunity (Nieto, 1999). If empowerment is to go beyond student-to-student relationships, teachers need to believe in the ability of all students to acquire the knowledge and skills necessary to achieve. Nieto defines this transformation as *empowered pedagogy*, which encourages the cooperative and collaborative efforts of all students to use their power to become active participants in their educational achievement. Moreover, empowered school climate and pedagogy promotes an experiential democratic learning environment that promotes the rights and responsibilities of full citizenship that can be generalized beyond the classroom walls (Nieto).

WHOLE-SCHOOL INTERVENTIONS

Violence and negative forms of conflict resolution compromise the vision, mission, and goals of the overall educational program (Ripley, 2003a). The unique ways in which the culture and climate of violence and conflict are manifest in a particular school can be understood by examining current and longitudinal data available in the school. For example, data that depict discipline referrals, attendance patterns, and dropout rates offer an initial picture. Schools often code discipline offenses to assist in keeping frequency data on each type of offense. These data can also be cross-tabulated with academic achievement to add another dimension in creating a profile of violence in a school. For a more incisive examination, additional disaggregation of data by grade level, race/ethnicity, gender, and socioeconomic status can paint a striking mural of the school and its students that serves to inform systemic interventions. Interventions developed in response to this information ensure that school counseling programs are data driven. In this way, systemic interventions can counteract the negative effects of violence by enhancing the educational mission and academic achievement of all students.

Systemic interventions can be conceptualized at four levels; cultural, disciplinary, curricular, and pedagogical (Coleman & Deutsch, 2000). This systemic model involves all members of the school community and is designed to "promote empowerment, positive social independence, nonviolence and social justice" (Coleman & Deutsch, p. 3). Using this four-level model, the following section examines system-wide violence prevention and conflict resolution strategies.

Changing the Culture and Climate

The key goal of creating a safe culture and climate is to promote the healthy psychosocial development and academic achievement of all students. To accomplish this goal, initiatives need to move beyond a solitary focus on students. Transformation in schools is complex and multilayered and necessitates the cooperative involvement of the entire school community. As a part of this process, counselors' understanding of the interrelationship between empowerment and advocacy as the basis for change is essential (Lee & Walz, 1998). As advocates, counselors are instrumental in assessing and challenging the institutional norms expressed through policies, practices, and procedures that sustain the injustices that fuel violence. Counselors are called upon to implement a systemic change model that translates awareness and knowledge into action through the comprehensive initiatives in a developmental school counseling program. Initiatives aimed at constructive conflict resolution promote cognitive, social, and affective development, increased achievement, cooperative interpersonal relationships, and a healthy expression of emotions (Johnson & Johnson, 1996; Johnson, Johnson, Dudley et al., 1995).

Despite the benefits of systemic change, it must be recognized that transformation is difficult. To ease the uncertainty of change, all stakeholders need to gain ownership in the assessment, planning, and implementation of the change process. Schools should ensure comprehensive assessment by extending their stakeholder involvement beyond the school to involve community members (Coleman & Deutsch, 2000). This ensures the assessment is representative of the diverse needs of the school community. This model stimulates collective and cooperative power from a variety of perspectives useful in forming solutions, because community resources, such as human resource agencies and law enforcement, are often involved in the aftermath of school violence. Teachers, parents, support staff, and community members need to understand their role in clearly defined and personalized strategies that continue throughout the change process (Hazler, 1998). These roles need to be acknowledged, validated, and maintained as part of the new structure of the school (Coleman & Deutsch, 2000; Hazler, 1998). Successful change through a careful redefinition and expansion of existing roles and structures maintains a sense of security as participants become familiar with new practices and procedures (Opffer, 1997). Significantly, within the school, garnering administrative support and leadership is essential. As leaders of the educational team, administrators are charged with ensuring that the mission and goals of the school are achieved and enhanced by systemic change initiatives.

Evidence indicates that teachers who model constructive conflict management and exhibit strong collegial relationships are the most important factors associated with student achievement. Additionally, departments that demonstrate high levels of collegiality produce higher levels of student achievement than departments with lower levels of collegiality within the same school (Opffer, 1997). We can conclude from this research that teacher training and training for all stakeholders is a foundational component in the success of any systemic change model. Before this process can begin we must recognize that most adults in the school and community are not specifically trained to work cooperatively to constructively manage conflict and thus are ill prepared to serve as leaders and role models to students. Essentially, adults cannot model positive relationships and promote knowledge and skills they do not possess (Ripley, 2003a). Thus, when advocating for systemic change, counselors need to first encourage the development of well-planned strategies coupled with adequate time and training for all stakeholders rather than attempting to dismantle existing policies and procedures, which can worsen the situation (Opffer, 1997). Transformation to an empowered culture is a slow process that requires patience and careful assessment, but is well worth the effort (Ripley, 2003).

The Disciplinary Structure and Peer Mediation Programs

Discipline can be defined as the management of student behavior (Bickmore, 1999). Discipline policies are a powerful force in the socialization of students as they observe, internalize, and imitate the ways violence and conflict are managed and by whom (Bickmore, 1999). Therefore, prior to planning and implementing a violence prevention program, it is essential to understand what the disciplinary tone of a school is, what is viewed as a discipline offense, and what is accepted or tolerated in the school. As noted earlier, the disciplinary tone of many schools is characterized by sweeping disciplinary negative peacekeeping measures (Bickmore, 1999). Concern lies in policies that can disproportionately impact marginalized populations, further excluding them from the more autonomous democratic opportunities in the school (Bickmore, 1999; Nieto, 1999). This exclusion can limit access to learning roles and skills for handling conflict afforded to their more privileged peers (Bickmore, 1999). When this happens the same injustices that fuel violence become institutionalized within the system (Casella, 2001). These forms of *systemic violence* then become an extension of societal oppression (Bickmore, 1999; Flaherty, 2001). Implementation of these polices can lead to practices and procedures that can demean and devastate some students (Flaherty, 2001). Some students see these types of discipline policies as a means of rationalizing a prison mentality that denies or restricts educational opportunities and the use of resources for all students (Casella, 2001). This is not to say that measures to maintain students' safety are not needed. Rather, by understanding their impact on students, the learning process, and the relationship between school members, school officials can adopt safety measures that serve to humanize the culture and climate of the school.

Understanding the type of offenses that are addressed by discipline policies and those behaviors that are accepted or tolerated is essential in creating initiatives for change. Unacceptable behaviors that are tolerated, ignored, or go unreported are known as *hidden violence* (Burstyn, 2001; Casella, 2001). These include sexual harassment, assault, and bullying. The reasons these forms of violence are not reported include fear and embarrassment and a belief that the act was not really violent or is not as serious as other acts of violence (Casella, 2001). To unveil hidden violence, students and staff need safe and simple methods of reporting, codified in policy, that are fair and equitable to all students. Students and staff learn that sexual harassment, assault, and bullying are forms of violent disrespect and that they have alternatives for handling these types of situations (Casella). Proactively uncovering hidden violence weakens the root of other forms of violence that can erupt as an outgrowth of earlier acts. As with more overt forms, hidden violence can be observed as early as preschool, highlighting the need for systemic and sequential programming that is both preventative and remedial (Hazler, 1998).

Student involvement in changing the disciplinary structure to prevent violence is especially critical. These opportunities redefine and encourage active school citizenship and promote the rights and responsibilities of renegotiated relationships and roles between students and school personnel (Hazler, 1998; Nieto, 1999). School and community input are essential in these efforts to ensure representation of all constituents and the multiple perspectives necessary for the development of collaborative solutions (Hazler, 1998). This process engenders respect and trust as all members of the school community are recognized as vital and gain the opportunity to influence the establishment of peace in the schools.

One of the ways students can become active participants is through peer mediation programs. A schoolwide model offers conflict resolution and peer mediation training to the entire school population, allows every stakeholder to learn skills and concepts, and encourages all students to serve as a mediators (Tyrrell, Scully, & Halligan, 1998). While peer mediation does not replace traditional discipline, it can be used as a schoolwide first-level intervention to constructively manage conflict and prevent violence (Coleman & Deutsch, 2000). The expansion of disciplinary structures opens opportunities for students to engage in self-discipline and self-regulatory experiences (Stomfay-Stitz, 1994; Sweeney & Carruthers, 1996). Additionally, this reframes students as no longer broken and frees them to become "valuable resources who actively contribute to their school and community" (Thompson, 1996, p.152). Bickmore (1999) defines this reframe as *positive liberty* that involves students as active participants in the democratic process.

All students should receive training and serve as peer mediators to create an inclusive environment where all groups share in the rights and responsibilities of creating a safe learning environment. Mediation is a process whereby a neutral third party or team known as mediators assist two or more individuals experiencing a conflict. The goal of mediation is to confidentially assist disputants in finding their own solutions through collaborative and equitable means to reach a win–win resolution. The process employs skills such as critical thinking, problem solving, and self-discipline (Johnson, Johnson, Dudley et al., 1995; Lane & McWhirter, 1992; Leviton & Greenstone, 1997; Morse & Andrea, 1994; Sweeney & Carruthers, 1996). Peer mediation is used when disputants cannot (1) move beyond the disagreement, (2) see beyond their own perspective, (3) negotiate due to a lack of skills, (4) find a way to maintain the relationship after the conflict, and (5) find a solution that will benefit both parties (Leviton & Greenstone, 1997). The underlying goal is to encourage socially appropriate self-regulatory behavior in the absence of an adult authority figure (Lane & McWhirter, 1992).

As an expansion of traditional disciplinary measures, there are situations in schools when peer mediation is not advised (Lane & McWhirter, 1992; Perlstein & Thrall, 1996). For example, peer mediation should not be employed when disputants:

- Have committed a crime
- Are not rational
- Are using illegal drugs and alcohol

- Engage in violent acts
- Use weapons
- Are possible victims of child abuse (Lane & McWhirter, 1992; Perlstein & Thrall, 1996; Wilburn & Bates, 1997)

Mediation is advised when disputants have relational conflicts that interfere with classroom functioning. Appropriate peer mediation conflicts include:

- Spreading of rumors
- Gossip
- Name calling
- Racial put downs
- Bullying
- Disputes over property

Because any of these disputes can escalate, early attention combined with peer mediation offers an alternative to violence. This underscores the need for training to address the issues of both tractable and intractable conflict. While tractable conflicts can be temporarily resolved through peer mediation, if the underlying differences are not addressed, the conflicts will inevitably resurface, leaving mediation strategies open to suspicion (Burgess & Burgess, 1996). Thus the dynamic and cultural complexity of a school community argues for the inclusion of diversity training as both an institutional objective and a peer mediation training objective (D'Andrea & Daniels, 1996; Day-Vines et al., 1996; Sweeney & Carruthers, 1996). The goal of training is to address differences and assist all school members in recognizing diversity as a "resource rather than a point of contention" (Tyrrell et al., 1998, p. 3). A cautionary note: schoolwide training programs that engage all students as peer mediators sometimes de-emphasize the need for diversity training and multicultural sensitivity (Day-Vines et al., 1996). Inclusion of this element is critical in that students will not and should not mediate only those conflicts with students from their own racial/ethnic background (Day-Vines et al.). Essential to this training is familiarity with the stages of racial/ethnic identity of students of color and white students (Day-Vines et al.). Exposure to this information allows all students to learn culturally contextual perspectives about others' attitudes, values, beliefs, and behaviors and the ways in which individuals and groups other than themselves view conflict and mediation. The multicultural counseling model of awareness, knowledge, and skills can form the foundation of the training and assist in highlighting the unique needs of the entire school population. (For additional information on culturally sensitive selection, training, and implementation of peer mediation programs, see Day-Vines et al.).

The mission of peer mediation training and programming should be aligned with the mission of the school. For example: the Colorado School Mediation Project (2000) developed the following mission:

> The mission of our conflict resolution program is to teach students to resolve conflicts productively, to promote mutual understanding of individual groups throughout the school, and to enhance the climate of the school through integrated curriculum, classroom models and teaching strategies. (pp. 1–2)

This mission is easily integrated into the structure of the school, as it not only targets an overall programmatic philosophy but also provides specific vehicles for intervention strategies. To accomplish this mission, a series of activities are necessary: conflict resolution training through curriculum infusion and integration, classroom conflict resolution process and teaching strategies, and a peer mediation process (Colorado School Mediation Project, 2000). Additionally, the focus on assessment and evaluation of school programs necessitates the translation of the mission into goals and competencies with measurable outcomes. These competencies state what the school community will learn by participating in the program. The Colorado School Mediation Project offers five goals from which content competencies can be developed and implemented:

1. To empower students and teachers with skills necessary to resolve conflict productively without resorting to violence or perpetual estrangement
2. To further develop emotional intelligence
3. To create and uphold social justice
4. To aid in the development of responsible citizenship
5. To create a caring and cooperative school environment (p. 4)

Once goals and competencies are developed and plans for curricular infusion are underway, it is helpful to offer informational seminars to parents and the community through the PTA, open houses, and workshops. Keeping stakeholders informed through strategic public relations events helps maintain support for the transformation process (Lupton-Smith, 1996). School counselors can take a leadership role in developing training teams to assist teachers in presenting curricular content and conducting public relations seminars.

Curricular Structures and Content

With the mission and goals in place, infusion of violence prevention and conflict resolution content into the core curriculum can begin. Curricular integration is a proactive and preventive approach that delivers both content knowledge and experiential practice to actively and constructively engage students in confronting and managing conflict. This process contrasts with negative peacemaking's conflict avoidance, blaming others, and diverting the underlying causes of conflict. Instead, students engage in positive liberty initiatives that encourage skill development as:

- They learn conflict resolution by serving on a student government committee
- They learn about power and problem solving by contributing to a service project
- They learn about peacemaking by serving as peer facilitators or conflict mediators
- They learn about analyzing multiple perspectives on public questions by studying problems of war, peace, or controversial issues (Bickmore, 1999, pp. 235–236).

An understanding of negative peacemaking and positive liberty as it operates in the school parallels the concepts of competition versus collaboration. Schools often lack a collaborative framework for policy formation that is translated into curricular practices and content. Henderson and Milstein (1997) suggest that competitive structures foster individualism rather than collaborative and collective achievement. They believe that competitive structures discourage change and diversity. When a competitive, win-lose environment exists within the curricular structure, conflict resolution and peer mediation become ineffectual because one student or group has to lose to serve the needs of the other (Johnson & Johnson, 1995a). Competition and negative peacemaking therefore promote self-interest, disregarding the needs and perspectives of others, while cooperation and positive liberty promote mutual goals and positive relationships that honor and respect diverse needs and interests (Bickmore, 1999; Johnson & Johnson, 1995a).

One curricular structure that can undermine positive liberty is tracking, which creates inequities in educational opportunities for disenfranchised populations. For example, state and national data reveal that poor and minority students (African American and Latino) are less likely to be placed in a rigorous college preparatory track than white and Asian students (Education Trust, 1998). Though these practices are unacceptable, efforts to dismantle tracking in isolation from the underlying issues are ineffectual (Nieto, 1999). Unless "the way students are thought about and treated by society and consequently by the schools they attend and the educators who teach" changes, the potential benefit of conflict resolution and peer mediation will be topical at best (Nieto, 1999, p. 167). In other words, when conflict arises, students may agree to stop fighting based on the content they have learned in conflict mediation, but if their underlying needs have not been addressed conflict will inevitably resurface. If school and curricular practices are to be transformed, it is critical that the school community believes not only that all students have the right to be trained in peer mediation and conflict resolution but that they have the right to participate in these collaborative positions as equals. This type of positive liberty is aimed at improving the emotional climate of the school and creating a healthy learning environment (Bickmore, 1997; Opffer, 1997).

With transformed beliefs operating in a school, curricular content can focus on several points that assist students in understanding themselves and others. For example, students can learn the physiological and behavioral responses to conflict, such as confronters, avoiders, compromisers, and minimizers (Coleman & Deutsch, 2000; Johnson & Johnson, 1996; Morse & Andrea, 1994). Students also learn active listening, communication skills, decision making, using humor in conflict, the peer mediation process, perspective taking, how to manage anger and hostility and express positive feelings, how to distinguish interests from positions, and how to develop healthy relationships (Coleman & Deutsch, 2000; Johnson & Johnson, 1996; Johnson & Johnson, 1995b). As classroom conflicts arise, opportunities to experientially self-discipline and practice democratic citizenship replace restrictive, unexplained, and rigid classroom rules (Bickmore, 1999). These curricular changes are further enhanced through shifts in traditional pedagogical practices.

Pedagogical Strategies

Despite the benefits to incorporating positive liberty into the core curriculum, new pedagogical strategies can meet with resistance. Teachers, administrators, students, and parents may question the value and relevance of new strategies to educational theory and practice. This concern can in part be ameliorated by proper training and systemic and sequential programs with developmentally appropriate content and teaching strategies. For example, Cutrona and Guerin (1994) suggest a sequential stage process from K–12: K–3 emphasizes sharing feelings, self-affirmation, and cooperation; 4–6 focuses on anger management, creative problem solving, and negotiation; and 7–12 addresses violence prevention and peer mediation models.

Some of the pedagogical strategies that can be used to deliver the curriculum are cooperative, student-centered strategies, including: cooperative grouping, journaling, reflection time, paired sharing, role-playing, creative controversy, Socratic questioning, service learning projects, quote reflection and discussion, historical recreations, perspective taking, storytelling, and mnemonics (Coleman & Deutsch, 2000; Compton, 2000; Michlowski, 1999; Prutzman & Johnson, 1997). Michlowski (1999) uses mnemonics to assist in conflict resolution training, for example, "The Seven C's of Conflict Resolution (communication, cooperation, caring, compromise, choice, change and congruence)" (p. 4).

These methods can be infused into language arts, civics, and social studies through end-of-unit projects, a series of workshops, and semester-long training events. Additionally, opportunities for content infusion are appropriate in any subject area that focuses on human interaction, communication, and problem solving (Bickmore, 1997). Infusion of these types of pedagogical strategies into classroom activities across the curriculum encourages the acquisition of knowledge and skills that may assist in improving the school culture and climate. Ideally, these strategies complement schoolwide interventions to create a comprehensive approach to conflict resolution and violence prevention. Additionally, these strategies can be adjusted for use in small-group counseling initiatives and in individual sessions to reflect a more therapeutic and remedial application. To demonstrate the application of these concepts and strategies, the following section will present a three-session classroom unit, a six-session group counseling intervention, and strategies for individual counseling.

CLASSROOM GUIDANCE ACTIVITIES

The three-session classroom unit presented in this section uses concepts, strategies, and pedagogical techniques that directly reflect the literature. This unit can be adjusted for use at the middle or secondary level. Additionally, teachers and counselors can adjust the lessons to emphasize specific concepts that address the unique needs of a classroom or school. To implement curricular integration requires a close collegial and collaborative relationship between school counselors and teachers. School counselors need to be familiar with the standards-based curriculum in each academic discipline in order to coordinate their efforts in the planning and implementation of targeted competencies.

The school counselor's role in the integration of these types of initiatives into a standards-based curriculum in the classroom can occur in several ways. First, counselors can visit classrooms and offer lessons that they teach; second, they can co-teach a lesson or series of lessons with teachers; finally, they can serve as a consultant to teachers in their preparation of daily lessons (Goodnough & Pérusse, 2003; Ripley, 2003).

The three lessons presented below are designed to be taught collaboratively between the teacher and counselor. This method can highlight the collegial relationship between professionals. Students are often quick to detect the level of cooperation between adults, and thus this method of infusion serves as experiential modeling for students.

These lessons are suitable for upper middle school students and can be incorporated into any unit focused on a conflict between individuals, groups, and/or countries. These lessons are sequential and developmental in nature. They can be used as a prevention strategy to strengthen a positive climate or as an initial step in creating a knowledge base to alter the classroom climate.

LESSON 1: PERSPECTIVE TAKING

Personal/Social Development Standard A: Students will acquire the knowledge, attitudes, and interpersonal skills to help them understand and respect self and others.

Personal/Social Development Standard B: Students will make decisions, set goals, and take necessary action to achieve goals.

Competencies

- Students will respect alternative points of view (Standard A).
- Students will identify values, attitudes, and beliefs (Standard A).
- Students will demonstrate a respect for individual and cultural differences (Standard B).

Learning Objectives

- Students will learn the difference between empathy and sympathy.
- Students will learn how to examine alternative points of view.

Materials: Newsprint paper, markers, and tape.

Developmental Learning Activity

Introduction: The teacher and counselor introduce and lead a discussion on the concepts of empathy, sympathy, and perspective taking in conflicts. The class focuses on the relationship between these concepts and the unit they are studying.

Activity: First the teacher or counselor writes the names of the key figures in the conflict on the board. Students are asked to identify the figure, group, or country whose perspective they oppose the most. Students are placed in groups based on their selection.

Group members brainstorm ideas about the experiences, values, and needs that shaped the perspective. They write their ideas on the newsprint. Group members then brainstorm the types of feelings they believe may be associated with the experiences, values, and needs.

Each group shares their work with the other groups.

The teacher and counselor lead students in a discussion on the process of understanding alternative perspectives by recognizing that empathic understanding necessitates looking beyond the surface to understand the roots of conflict. The teacher and counselor encourage students to note any similarities as well as differences on their lists. Special attention is given to the similarities as a place to form bridges of resolution.

Conclusion: The teacher and counselor have students reflect on any insights they gained as a result of the experience. Possible questions for discussion may include:

- What types of experiences did the individual, group, or country live through that shaped their perspective?
- What values do you feel are associated with these types of experiences?
- What kinds of feelings did you associate with these types of experiences and values and why?
- In what way does their perspective help them meet their needs?
- What needs do you feel they are trying to meet in this conflict?
- How has this process helped you to understand a point of view that you disagree with?
- How do you feel about this point of view now?
- In what ways does this process help dispel myths and stereotypes about individuals and groups?

Assessment: Both objectives are met by having students engage in the activity. The second session will begin by having students respond to questions based on the concepts discussed in the first session.

Follow-up: In the next session students will use the insights gained to engage in the decision-making/problem-solving process.

LESSON 2: RESOLVING THE CONFLICT WITHOUT VIOLENCE

Personal/Social Development Standard B: Students will make decisions, set goals, and take necessary action to achieve goals.

Competency: Students will use a decision-making and problem-solving model.

Learning Objectives
- Students will demonstrate the ability to incorporate alternative points of view into decision making and problem solving.
- Students will learn the decision-making and problem-solving model.
- Students will apply the model to a given conflict situation.

Materials: Lists on newsprint from the previous class session.

Developmental Learning Activity

Introduction: The counselor and teacher review the key concepts of empathy and how to examine an alternative point of view. Next they teach the decision-making and problem-solving model. For each step in the process, they guide the discussion with questions such as the following:

- Identify the problem—What is the conflict? Who is involved?
- Gather information—What else do you need to know? What needs are the disputants trying to meet? What is the sequence of events? What are the underlying issues, such as values, attitudes, and beliefs?
- Generate possible solutions—How can this be peacefully resolved? What is the potential responsibility of each disputant in creating a peaceful solution? What are the similarities between disputants?
- Brainstorm potential consequences of each potential solution—What will happen if this action is taken? What knowledge and skills do the disputants need to make this potential solution work? In what ways will this course of action promote social justice?
- Choose a course of action—What is the choice? How is the course of action justified?
- Monitor the results—What is happening to each disputant and their environment as a result of the decision?
- Reevaluate the results—What criteria will be used to assess the outcome as successful? How can the decision be revised to achieve a more just outcome?

Next, students return to their original groups and apply this model to the conflict situation they examined in the first session. The lists they generated may be used to assist them.

Students write their work on newsprint to share with the class.

Conclusion: The teacher and counselor lead a discussion that asks students to reflect on the process and how their solutions are similar to or different from other groups'. Attention is given to similarities as possible starting points to lead to collaborative problem solving. Students are asked to continue to reflect on the process in preparation for the next session.

Assessment: The three objectives can be met through participation in the activity. The counselor and teacher will begin the next session by asking students to identify the steps in decision making and problem solving.

Follow-up: In the next session students will apply the model to the culminating activity.

LESSON 3: COLLABORATIVE PROBLEM SOLVING

Personal/Social Development Standard B: Students will make decisions, set goals, and take necessary action to achieve goals.

Competency: Students will identify alternative solutions to a problem.

Learning Objectives

- Students will engage in collaborative decision making and problem solving using the model.
- The student will consider alternative perspectives to the problem-solving process.

Materials: Newsprint from previous sessions if desired.

Developmental Learning Activity

Introduction: The counselor and teacher have students reassemble in their previous groups. Students choose one group member to serve as their ambassador at the roundtable for peace activity. The room is arranged in two semicircles with the ambassadors forming one smaller semicircle and the other groups facing the ambassadors in a larger semicircle.

Activity: The activity is designed to bring representatives from each perspective to the table to design a peaceful solution to the conflict that is agreeable to all parties. As the process progresses, ambassadors can take one time-out to consult with their groups. The group members serve as observers and recorders of the process. Once a decision is reached, the members of the groups and the ambassadors discuss the process. Some possible ideas to have students reflect on include:

- How these decisions may have changed the course of history
- How it felt to work cooperatively to reach a decision
- What kinds of things they learned about themselves and their peers
- How the process challenged them to "think outside of the box"
- How learning these skills can help contribute to creating a more just and peaceful society

Conclusion: Students discuss their personal reflections and how this process can be applied to the situations they face everyday in school. The teacher and counselor ask students to reflect on how they can empower themselves to resolve conflict and create positive change in their lives nonviolently.

Assessment: The two objectives can be accomplished by participating in the activity. Leaders incorporate the decision-making and problem-solving model into the formal unit assessment.

Follow-up: To measure the impact of the unit on student behavior and the classroom climate requires some preparation prior to the intervention. Because one of the goals of the comprehensive school counseling program is to use initiatives that promote academic achievement, teachers and counselors may begin by collecting baseline data that are indicators of improved achievement or climatic conditions that support academic achievement. These may simply include the number of occurrences of verbal conflict in the classroom that result in a disruption or discipline referral. Other data may include numbers of missing assignments for each student, absences, and unit or marking-period grades. Integration of strategies should continue within the classroom. Four weeks after the activity or at the end of the marking period, the counselor and teacher can revisit the baseline data and compare it with any gains students have made in those areas. Anecdotal data can also be collected from students as teacher and counselor engage the students in a follow-up discussion of how they have used empathy to understand alternative perspectives and to make decisions and solve problems in a peaceful way since the last meeting. These data can then be evaluated to suggest whether additional use of this intervention in this subject area is warranted, more widespread curricular integration is desired, alterations in content and presentation are necessary, skill training for school personnel is desirable, and other more intensive interventions such as small-group counseling may be useful.

SMALL-GROUP COUNSELING PLANS

This section will examine the use of small-group counseling in conflict resolution education and violence prevention. Group counseling offers an intensive and therapeutic form of service through the use of psychoeducational groups. Psycho-educational groups can be offered to all students and/or can target specific students with recurring conflictual patterns of behavior. Group counseling provides a venue to support and challenge students, helps them examine their behavior and learn new skills, and assists them in making productive and nonviolent choices.

The group sessions that follow provide secondary school students a personal and experiential opportunity to gain new skills to alter their behavior and empower their lives in a positive way. The content and process of the group addresses complex underlying issues, such as intractable conflict, that often lead to violence. The content of the group draws directly from the literature and is presented at a developmental level consistent with secondary school students. Each session offers participants the opportunity to gain information and engage in personal reflection. Because of the complexity of the group and the material, counselors may find it more efficacious to co-lead the group. The group is voluntary and meets once a week for approximately fifty minutes or one standard class period. If block scheduling is in place, it is advisable for the group to start at the beginning of the block period. Some of the questions used in the classroom activity are applicable in the group. Counselors should use their judgment in selecting appropriate questions.

The focus of this group is remedial in nature and targets students who have experienced repeated difficulty with conflict. Counselor familiarity with in-house data sources that can highlight either students with recurring incidents of negative behavior or those who are showing a change in behavior patterns through documented incidents can be useful in identifying students in need. Potential participants can also be identified through a needs assessment, formal or informal referrals from teachers, parents, or administrators, or individual contact with the counselor. Once students are identified, established procedures for screening and securing parental permission can be used.

GROUP SESSION 1: WHAT IS CONFLICT?

Personal/Social Development Standard A: Students will acquire the knowledge, attitudes, and interpersonal skills to help them understand and respect self and others.

Personal/Social Development Standard B: Students will make decisions, set goals, and take necessary action to achieve goals.

Competencies

- Students will understand consequences of decisions, choices, and goals (Standard B).
- Students will demonstrate cooperative behavior in groups (Standard A).

Learning Objectives

- Students will be oriented to the group counseling process.
- Students will begin to examine the relationship between conflict and violence.
- Students will gain knowledge of the nature of conflict.

Materials: Newsprint, students' folders, easel, markers, Handouts 8.1 and 8.2 (What Is the Coolest? and What Is Conflict?).

Activity

Introduction: The counselor welcomes the group members and asks members to introduce themselves. The counselor covers group ground rules, confidentiality, and the preestablished group schedule. The counselor has each member sign the ground rules and places it in an individual folder for each member. The counselor will retain the folder for member use and add handouts as the group progresses. Students have the option to keep their folders with their work at the conclusion of the group.

Icebreaker: Students work in pairs to complete What's the Coolest? (Handout 8.1). They then present their findings together, noting any similarities and differences in their responses. As each pair responds, the group gives attention to group similarities and differences. Note: One of the steps in the conflict-resolution process is finding and building on similarities among the disputants. This method in the icebreaker is an attempt to help members begin to see ways in which they can share and find common ground, as conflict is based on the differences that divide. Possible reflections may include: How does this exercise help us understand each other better? What new things did you learn about each other?

Counseling Activity: First the counselor initiates a discussion on what members hope to gain from the group and what led the members to select this group counseling experience. Again, the counselor draws on similarities between group members and points out and honors differences as additional learning for members. Note: It is not uncommon for some students to indicate that they chose the group experience to avoid attending class. The counselor should not be dismayed by this response. Students may experience difficulty articulating their reasons for attending group, and some may feel vulnerable, thus choosing to save face by offering an evasive response. Others may really just want to get out of class. While the reasons may be varied, the counselor has an opportunity to engage students for an hour a week and is wise to make the most of the time.

Next the counselor invites students to discuss current-event situations where the decisions made about conflictual issues lead to violence. The counselor may need to assist students by giving some general information about current events or making newspapers available.

The counselor invites students to share their ideas about what conflict means to them and why it happens. Then students reflect on what conflict means to them and how and why conflicts become violent. The counselor encourages members to examine how decision making in conflict situations can lead to violence. The counselor can write members' responses on newsprint, again noting similarities. This point is important to help members begin to talk about conflict in a safe, supportive, and nonjudgmental environment. Note: It is essential for counselors to model desired behaviors.

At this point the counselor distributes Handout 8.2, What Is Conflict? The counselor is informative and supportive in assisting members to begin to gain a cognitive framework in which to understand conflict. Members discuss some of the types of issues that may occur in each category of conflict and how some situations may involve multiple types of conflict.

Conclusion: The counselor asks members to reflect on the session and offer one particular point that was most important to them in the session. The counselor encourages members to be observant throughout the week when they encounter conflict or observe it in school, their neighborhoods, or the media.

Assessment: The first two objectives can be met by participating in the activity. The third objective is partially met by the activity, and the next session will begin with a review of the handout on conflict.

Follow-up: The counselor will be available to members if conflict arises throughout the week.

GROUP SESSION 2: UNDERSTANDING THE ROOTS OF CONFLICT

Personal/Social Development Standard B: Students will make decisions, set goals, and take necessary action to achieve goals.

Competencies

- Students will understand consequences of decisions and choices.
- Students will know when peer pressure is influencing a decision.
- Students will demonstrate a respect and appreciation for individual and cultural differences.

Materials: Student folders, easel, newsprint, markers, Handout 8.3 (Conflict Occurs When Our Needs Are Not Met)

Learning Objectives

- Students will recognize personal needs.
- Students will recognize the influence of peers in attempts to meet needs.
- Students will recognize all individuals as having needs.

Activity

Introduction: The counselor begins the session with a check-in to give members a chance to report on the events of their week and reflect on their observations of conflict situations over the course of the week.

Counseling Activity: The counselor reviews the types of conflict from the previous session handout. The counselor asks members to share any insights they may have gained as a result of this information.

Next the counselor begins a discussion about human needs. Students receive the handout Conflict Occurs When Our Needs Are Not Met. The group discusses the role of needs in our lives. The counselor emphasizes that even in conflict situations, we all have needs we are trying to meet. The counselor invites members to discuss:

- How they would define these different types of needs
- How they see these needs active in their lives or the lives of those around them
- How peers influence the choices individuals make in meeting their needs
- Both positive and negative ways in which they observe needs being met, and the consequences of those decisions

Note: Inviting members to discuss these issues allows the counselor to draw on their perspectives at their developmental level. Counselors need to slowly help members incorporate new language into their discussion. The counselor encourages members to brainstorm positive alternatives to negative or violent means of meeting their needs. The counselor encourages members to:

- Consider the perspectives of other group members
- Observe their ability to share different perspectives respectfully
- Avoid blaming

The counselor puts up the newsprint from the previous session that identified conflicts and asks members to identify the types of needs they feel the disputants were trying to achieve. Note: It is essential that the counselor maintains a safe and supportive environment during the session and models nonjudgmental active listening.

The counselor again draws attention to any overlap of similarity in needs. The counselor helps members recognize that multiple unmet needs are often present in conflict situations.

Members have the opportunity to share personal or observed conflict situations; the counselor asks them to identify the type of conflict and the unmet needs in the situation. It is essential for the counselor to provide an environment where members can be vulnerable and save face.

Conclusion: The counselor asks members to reflect on the session and offer a closing thought and to reflect throughout the week on how they can meet their needs in positive ways without depriving anyone else of their needs.

Assessment: The counselor will begin the next session by asking members to describe the nature of conflicts and human needs.

Follow-up: The counselor will be available to students throughout the week if necessary.

GROUP SESSION 3: TYPES OF CONFLICTS

Personal/Social Development Standard A: Students will acquire the knowledge, attitudes, and interpersonal skills to help them understand and respect self and others.

Personal/Social Development Standard B: Students will make decisions, set goals, and take necessary action to achieve goals.

Competencies

- Students will demonstrate a respect and appreciation for individual and cultural differences (Standard B).
- Students will recognize that everyone has rights and responsibilities (Standard A).
- Students will demonstrate cooperative behavior in groups (Standard A).
- Students will respect alternative points of view (Standard A).

Learning Objectives

- Students will gain knowledge of tractable and intractable conflicts.
- Students will gain knowledge of how biases and stereotypes contribute to conflict.
- Students will understand the importance of empowerment in resolving conflict.

Materials: Students' folders, easel, newsprint, Handout 8.4 (The Characteristics of Conflict and Types of Conflict)

Activity

Introduction: The counselor begins the session with a check-in. The counselor reviews the previous two sessions with an emphasis on types of conflicts, unmet needs, and characteristics of conflicts.

Counseling Activity: The counselor introduces the characteristics of conflict and the concepts of tractable and intractable conflict. The counselor invites members to consider:

- The ways that characteristics of conflict surface in tractable and intractable conflict
- The role of biases and stereotypes (underlying values, attitudes, and beliefs) against individuals and/or groups in fueling intractable conflicts
- The use of domination and coercive power in intractable conflicts
- The ways intractable conflicts can lead to violence
- The importance of exploring underlying issues that fuel conflict
- Their own views of intractable conflict in society and the consequences
- The relationship between social justice and intractable conflict

Members may want to share personal reflection or observed situations of intractable conflict.

Next the counselor introduces the concept of empowerment. Members brainstorm their perception/definition of empowerment in situations. The counselor draws attention to the use of power in negative ways to dominate and encourages reflection on positive uses of power to liberate. The counselor encourages members to consider issues of intractable conflict and empowerment to prevent violence in which all sides can:

- Have their needs met
- Have their differences respected
- Learn to consider alternative viewpoints in solving problems
- Work cooperatively based on similarities and common mission

Note: This discussion may yield strong opinions and viewpoints. It is essential that all group members are offered the opportunity to be respected for their viewpoints. This session has the potential to be a powerful experiential exercise in actually confronting different alternative viewpoints. The counselor must ensure that group members can save face in sharing ideas. This session may also need to be extended to two sessions. The counselor can use their judgment in altering the structure of the sessions that follow to allow for needed time. Paying attention to these issues should be given priority over finishing all of the sessions as they are presented.

Conclusion: The counselor invites members to reflect on the issues discussed this session and offer a closing thought. The counselor encourages members to practice self-awareness of their personal responses to these issues.

Assessment: The counselor will begin the next session by asking members to lead the review of the previous session.

Follow-up: The counselor will be available to members throughout the week if necessary.

GROUP SESSION 4: CONFLICT-RESOLUTION MODEL

Personal/Social Development Standard A: Students will acquire the knowledge, attitudes, and interpersonal skills to help them understand and respect self and others.

Personal/Social Development Standard B: Students will make decisions, set goals, and take necessary action to achieve goals.

Competencies

- Students will apply conflict-resolution skills (Standard B).
- Students will demonstrate cooperative behavior in groups (Standard A).

Learning Objectives

- Students will gain knowledge of and apply conflict-resolution model.
- Students will demonstrate ability to cooperatively apply the conflict-resolution model.

Materials: Students' folders, easel, newsprint, markers, Handout 8.5 (Conflict-Resolution Model).

Activity

Introduction: The counselor conducts a check-in with members and asks them to take the lead in reviewing the material from the previous session.

Counseling Activity: The counselor introduces the conflict resolution model (Handout 8.5) and goes through each step with members. The counselor encourages them to apply the knowledge they have gained during the discussion.

Members choose one conflict situation that involves an intractable conflict. They are then divided into two groups and as a subgroup work through the conflict-resolution process. Members record their process on newsprint to share with the larger group.

Subgroups then reassemble to share their work. They discuss similarities and differences. Members discuss any insights they gain from the other subgroups' work. The counselor points out that conflict can be solved in multiple ways and emphasizes respect for varying viewpoints.

Conclusion: The counselor has members reflect on their work and helps them recognize and appreciate their new knowledge and skills and those of their peers. The counselor reminds members that they have two more meetings before they terminate.

Assessment: The objectives are completed by participating in the activity. The counselor will begin the next session by having students describe the steps in the conflict resolution model.

Follow-up: The counselor will be available to members throughout the week as necessary.

GROUP SESSION 5: APPLYING THE CONFLICT-RESOLUTION MODEL

Personal/Social Development Standard A: Students will acquire the knowledge, attitudes, and interpersonal skills to help them understand and respect self and others.

Personal/Social Development Standard B: Students will make decisions, set goals, and take necessary action to achieve goals.

Competencies

- Students will know how to apply conflict-resolution skills (Standard B).
- Students will identify personal strengths and assets (Standard A).

Learning Objectives

- Students will identify personal strengths as assets in resolving conflicts.
- Students will apply the conflict resolution model to their personal lives.

Materials: Students' folders, easel, newsprint, markers, Handout 8.6 (Personal Inventory).

Activity

Introduction: The counselor begins the session with a check-in. Students share any experiences or insights they have gained regarding the material covered in the group. The counselor gives additional time in this session as the content of the last session was more extensive. The counselor invites members to reflect on tractable and intractable conflicts and how the conflict resolution model offers a framework in which to work with these conflicts.

Counseling Activity: The counselor invites members to take a few minutes to reflect on and discuss how this new knowledge and skill can be applied to their lives at school. The counselor then introduces the concept of a personal inventory (see Handout 8.6) to assist members in identifying the types of conflicts they find themselves in most often, the characteristics of the conflicts they are involved in, the needs they most often have difficulty meeting without conflict, and what biases they may hold that add to conflict. Members also inventory the strengths they feel they possess that help them in each of these areas. The counselor invites members to share their responses.

Next, students apply this awareness and knowledge to the conflict resolution model to examine their profile as a "conflict resolver," and they share their findings. Based on their findings, the counselor helps members identify some strategies to strengthen their skills. The counselor emphasizes helping members to empower themselves to grow and have their needs met in nonviolent ways.

Conclusion: Members reflect on the session and any insights they have gained and share. The counselor reminds members that the next session they will terminate the group experience. The counselor asks members to reflect on the group experience as they prepare to end: to think about what they have gained, what they have learned from each other, what they have learned about themselves, and how they can use what they have learned.

Assessment: The objectives are completed by participating in the activity. The counselor asks each member to recall a personal strength and how it assists them in conflict resolution.

Follow-up: The counselor will be available to members throughout the week as needed.

GROUP SESSION 6: GROUP TERMINATION— TYING IT ALL TOGETHER

Personal/Social Development Standard A: Students will acquire the knowledge, attitudes, and interpersonal skills to help them understand and respect self and others.

Personal/Social Development B: Students will make decisions, set goals, and take necessary action to achieve goals.

Competencies

- Students will identify personal strengths and assets (Standard A).
- Students will demonstrate cooperative behavior in groups (Standard A).
- Students will know how to apply conflict-resolution skills (Standard B).
- Students will distinguish between appropriate and inappropriate behaviors (Standard A).

Learning Objectives

- Students will end their group experience.
- Students will display appropriate leave-taking behaviors.
- Students will be able to demonstrate an understanding of generalizing their learning to other areas of their life.
- Students will give feedback to other group members regarding the group experience.

Materials: Students' folders, easel, newsprint, markers, colored paper, pencils or pens, Handout 8.7 (As We Close).

Activity

Introduction: The counselor checks in with members regarding the events of their week and any reflections on the group process. The counselor distributes member's folders to them with their work and handouts for them to keep if desired.

Counseling Activity: Members choose a personal conflict they are presently experiencing that they feel comfortable sharing. Members work in pairs and explain the conflict situation to each other. Members then work together to resolve one conflict at a time. One person will be the voice of the person they are in conflict with, and their partner will be the voice of the other person. After they have explored the conflict from alternative perspectives, the person whose conflict is presently being explored will assume their own voice and the partner will be the other person in the conflict. Then they repeat this process with the partner's conflict, so that each person explores conflict from their own voice and that of the person with whom they are having the conflict.

Partners share with the group what they learned about themselves and about taking the perspective of the person they are currently in conflict with. The counselor invites members to discuss how they might actually implement the plan they developed. The counselor asks members to reflect on and share how the strengths they identified can assist them in this conflict and in conflicts they may encounter in the future. The counselor helps members develop a personal plan that draws on their strengths and helps them brainstorm ways they can improve.

Note: Be sure to stress to members that they have learned new knowledge that the individual/group they are in conflict with may not possess. They should be aware that not everyone they encounter will know this material or respond favorably to them. This is not to discourage them but to help them be realistic in their expectations. Members can brainstorm ways they can share their new awareness, knowledge, and skills through their daily behavior.

Conclusion: To draw the group experience to a close, the counselor asks members to take a moment and consider what they have gained from the group, what they have gained from each other, what is the most important thing they will remember, and how they will use the knowledge they learned. The counselor asks members to share their insights.

As a closing activity the counselor passes around a packet of multicolored paper and has members choose the color they prefer. They draw their hand on the paper. They pass their hand paper around and each member writes what they have gained from the member on that member's hand. Members may want to share some of the feedback they receive or choose to keep it confidential.

The counselor then offers his/her feedback to the group, drawing on the growth the group has achieved.

Assessment: The counselor will distribute a short questionnaire (Handout 8.7) to members.

Follow-up: The counselor will be available for students as needed. The methods to determine the outcome of this intervention can be similar to the follow-up used after the completion of the classroom unit. To reiterate, gathering baseline data that includes but is not limited to discipline referrals, grades, absences, race/gender, socioeconomic levels, and participation in co/extracurricular activities can provide invaluable insights into the needs of students. After four weeks or the end of a marking period, the counselor can update the data to determine student gains. Again, anecdotal information can also be of help through a short survey (Handout 8.8) or personal interview to assess how students are using the knowledge they have gained. Ongoing assistance and support to these students through schoolwide initiatives is ideal.

INDIVIDUAL COUNSELING CONSIDERATIONS

Violence-prevention and conflict-resolution strategies can be offered to students through individual counseling as part of a systemic approach. Within a comprehensive school counseling program, these one-on-one interventions may be viewed as the reactive side of responsive services in situations of immediate conflict. Counselor reliance on this venue is not recommended due to large caseloads. Other initiatives such as small-group counseling, classroom and grade-level activities, and schoolwide initiatives are more time efficient and reach larger numbers of students. As with all other methods of intervention, individual strategies and techniques clearly reflect accepted concepts and constructs in the conflict-resolution literature and are delivered at a developmentally appropriate level. Similar to group counseling, specific counseling techniques are selected to match the needs of the student, ensure culturally responsive practice, and enhance the counseling relationship.

When school counselors do engage students individually, they should keep several factors in mind. First, before counseling begins, it is essential that students are apprised of the limits of confidentiality involving safety issues. Second, most conflicts students bring to the counseling session are usually long-standing disputes that have erupted. When conflicts reach a breaking point there is usually an activating event. Counselors should help students to tell their story and then to look beyond the event to the underlying issues. This not only helps students understand the conflict from a broader perspective, it also gives the counselor insight into the pervasiveness of the issue and the potential impact on the culture and climate of the school. Third, counseling techniques should demonstrate to students that the counselor is willing and able to explore underlying issues in a safe environment. A counselor's attempts to provide quick fixes will undermine counselor credibility, as students will detect that their needs cannot be met by seeking assistance from the school counselor. Fourth, if appropriate, counselors can offer the student the opportunity to engage in the mediation process with the other disputant. This should be a voluntary process for both students, so that the counselor does not become an agent in supporting potential underlying power dynamics. For example, the counselor must maintain a neutral stance when offering mediation to a student even if a student refuses mediation. Favoritism to any student or group can align the counselor with societal "isms," thereby supporting disproportionate distributions of power. The counselor's role in mediation is to help both disputants equalize power and create the conditions for both to be empowered and constructively resolve their conflicts. Finally, the counselor should also assess whether the conflict has escalated, or is in immediate danger of escalating, into violence. Counselors need to involve other school personnel if safety measures are necessary to protect students. It is essential that comprehensive safety strategies or crisis intervention plans be in place in all schools to ensure the safety of all students. The school counselor is in a pivotal position to take a leadership role in developing collaborative teams to respond to the immediate needs of students in conflict situations.

CONCLUSION

As violence reaches unprecedented levels in schools across the United States, many school communities struggle to find effective solutions. To effectively target these issues requires interventions and initiatives that have both an individual and a systemic focus within the school. School counselors are in a unique position to serve as a leader and advocate in the development and implementation of such initiatives within a comprehensive school counseling program that addresses violence prevention and conflict resolution.

Well-planned programmatic initiatives that school counselors can deliver collaboratively with teachers and other school personnel invite the entire school to participate in a team effort to create a culture and climate of safety, respect, and full citizenship for all students. It is therefore incumbent upon all school counselors to possess the knowledge and skills necessary to develop and implement programs to meet the challenges of today, and to help create a peaceful tomorrow in our schools.

RESOURCES

The following Web-based resources are but a small representation of available information on the Internet. Some of the resources are nonprofit sites and some are commercial. These sites offer a wide range of information, lesson plans, resources for purchase, available training, and K–12 programs. They cover topics of violence prevention, conflict resolution, peer mediation, and conflict and diversity. These materials can be used by counselors, teachers, parents, and administrators and incorporated into initiatives at multiple levels of service within a comprehensive school counseling program.

Conflict Resolution: www.clcrc.com/pages/conflict.html
Resolving Conflict Creatively Program: www.esrnational.org/about-rccp.html
Teaching Tolerance: www.splc.org/teachingtolerance/ttindex.html
Conflict Resolution Information Resource: www.crinfo.org
Teacher Talk: http://education.indiana.edu/cas/tt/v2i3/peer.html
Colorado School Mediation Project: www.csmp.org
Teacher Vision: www.teachervision.com/lesson-plans/lesson-3020.html
Mediation Network of North Carolina: www.mnnc.org/pg3.cfm
Top Ten Sites for Conflict Resolution and Peer Mediation:
    http://web.syr.edu/~nssonger/kristenandeterspe600.htm
Character Counts: www.charactercounts.org
Character Education Partnership: www.character.org
Peer Counseling and Assistance Resource Page:
    http://community-1.webtv.net/SoundBehavior/PeerAssistance
National Criminal Justice Reference Source: www.ncjrs.org
The Diary of Anne Frank: Tolerance and Conflict Resolution:
    www.ylt.org/AnneFrank/tolerance-web.htm
ERIC Clearinghouse on Urban Education: eric-web.tc.columbia.edu
Peace Education.com: www.peace-ed.org
Ten Web Sites for Exploring Conflict Resolution in the Classroom:
    www.education-world.com/a_curr/curr170.html
CRENet Conflict Education Resolution Network: www.crenet.org
Education for Peace: www.global-ed.org.e4p/resource.htm
Multicultural Mediation: The Diversity Factor: www.uconsultus.com/diversity.html
Conflict Resolution Consortium: www.colorado.edu/conflict
Conflict Resolution for Secondary Students:
    ericcass.uncg.edu/virtuallib/conflict/secondary.html
Conflict Resolution Education Network: www.crenet.org
National Curriculum Integration Project: www.ncip.org

REFERENCES

Bickmore, K. (1997). Preparation for pluralism: Curricular and extracurricular practice with conflict resolution. *Theory into Practice, 36* (Winter), 3–10.

Bickmore, K. (1999). Teaching conflict and conflict resolution in schools. In A. Raviv, L. Oppenhenheimer, & D. Bar-Tal (Eds.). *How children understand war and peace* (pp. 233–259). San Francisco, CA: Jossey-Bass Publishers.

Burgess, G., & Burgess, H. (1996). *Constructive confrontation theoretical framework.* Retrieved from: http://www.Colorado.EDU/conflict/peace/essay/con_conf.htm.

Burstyn, J. N. (2001). Violence and its prevention: A challenge for schools. In J. N. Burstyn, G. Bender, R. Casella, H. W. Gordon, D. P. Guerra, K. V. Luschen, R. Stevens, & K. M. Williams (Eds.), *Preventing violence in schools: A challenge to*

American democracy (pp. 1–12). Mahwah, NJ: Lawrence Erlbaum Associates, Publishers.

Carter, C. (1999). *Conflict mediation at school: Peace through avoidance?* Paper presented at the Annual Meeting of the American Educational Research Association, Montreal, Quebec, Canada.

Casella, R. (2001). What is violent about "school violence?": The nature of violence in a city high school. In J. N. Burstyn, G. Bender, R. Casella, H. W. Gordon, D. P. Guerra, K. V. Luschen, R. Stevens, & K. M. Williams (Eds.), *Preventing violence in schools: A challenge to American democracy* (pp. 15–46). Mahwah, NJ: Lawrence Erlbaum Associates, Publishers.

Christle, C. A., Jolivette, K., & Nelson, C. M. (2000). *Youth aggression and violence: Risk, resilience, and prevention* (Report No. E602). Arlington, VA: ERIC Clearinghouse on Disabilities and Gifted Education, Council for Exceptional Children (ERIC Document Reproduction No. ED449632).

Coleman, P. T., & Deutsch, M. (2000). *Cooperation, conflict resolution, and school violence: A systems approach.* (Choices Briefs No. 5). New York, NY: Columbia University, Institute for Urban and Minority Education.

Colorado School Mediation Project. (2000). *The whole school approach.* Retrieved from http://csmp.org/whole/whole.htm.

Compton, R. (2000). *Infusing and integrating conflict resolution into the school curriculum and culture.* Retrieved September 29, 2002, from http://www.crenet.org/research/infusing.htm.

Conflict Research Consortium. (1998a). *Denial of identity.* Retrieved September 29, 2002, from http://www.Colorado.EDU/conflict/peace/problem/denyid.htm.

Conflict Research Consortium. (1998b). *Domination conflicts.* Retrieved September, 29, 2002, from: http://www.Colorado.EDU/conflict/peace/problem/domination.htm.

Conflict Research Consortium. (1998c). *The denial of other human needs.* Retrieved September 29, 2002, from http://www.Colorado.EDU/conflict/peace/problem/needs.htm.

Conflict Research Consortium. (1998d). *Transformative mediation.* Retrieved September 29, 2002, from: http://www.Colorado.EDU/conflict/peace/treatment/tmedtn.htm.

Cutrona, C., & Guerin, D. (1994). Confronting conflict peacefully: Peer mediation in schools. *Educational Horizons, 72*(2), 95–104.

D'Andrea, M., & Daniels, J. (1996). Promoting peace in our schools: Developmental, preventive and multicultural considerations. *The School Counselor, 44,* 55–64.

Day-Vines, N. L., Day-Hairston, B. O., Carruthers, W. L., Wall, J. A., & Lupton-Smith, H. A. (1996). Conflict resolution: The value of diversity in the recruitment, selection, and training of peer mediators. *The School Counselor, 43,* 392–410.

Deutsch, M. (2001). *Practitioner assessment of conflict resolution programs.* (Report No. 163). New York, NY: ERIC Clearinghouse on Urban Education Teachers College, Columbia University (ERIC Document Reproduction Service No. ED 451277).

Education Trust. (1998). *The Education Trust state and national data book* (vol. 2). Washington, DC: Author.

Farrell, A. D., Meyer, A. L., & White, K. S. (2001). Evaluation of responding in peaceful and positive ways (RIPP): A school-based prevention program for reducing violence among urban adolescents. *Journal of Clinical Psychology, 30*(4), 451–463.

Flaherty, L. T. (2001). School violence and the school environment. In M. Shafii, & S. L. Shafii, (Eds.), *School violence: Assessment, management, prevention* (pp. 25–51). Washington, DC: American Psychiatric Publishing, Inc.

George, Y., Dagnese, D., Halpin, G., Halpin, G., & Keiter, R. (1996). *Peer mediation training: A solution to violence in schools.* Paper presented at the Annual Meeting of the Mid-South Educational Research Association, Tuscaloosa, AL.

Glasser, W. (2000). School violence from the perspective of William Glasser. *Professional School Counseling, 4*(2), 77–80.

Goodnough, G. E., & Pérusse, R. (2003). Developmental classroom guidance. In B. T. Erford (Ed.), *Transforming the school counseling profession* (pp. 121–151). Upper Saddle River, NJ: Merrill Prentice Hall.

Hanish, L. D., & Guerra, N. G. (2000). Children who get victimized at school: What is known? What can be done? *Professional School Counseling, (4)*2, 113–119.

Harris, I. M. (2001, April). *Challenges for peace education at the beginning of the twenty-first century.* Paper presented at the annual meeting of the American Educational Research Association, Seattle, WA.

Hazler, R. J. (1998). Promoting personal investment in systemic approaches to school violence. *Education, 119*(2), 222–231.

Hazler, R. J., & Carney, J. V. (2000). When victims turn aggressors: Factors in the development of deadly school violence. *Professional School Counseling, 4*(2), 105–112.

Henderson, N., & Milstein, M. M. (1997). *Resiliency in schools: Making it happen for students and educators.* Thousand Oaks, CA: Corwin Press, Inc.

Johnson, D. W., & Johnson, R. T. (1995a). *Reducing school violence through conflict resolution.* Alexandria, VA: Association for Supervision and Curriculum Development.

Johnson, D. W., & Johnson, R. T. (1995b). Teaching students to be peacemakers: Results of five years of research. *Peace and Conflict: Journal of Peace Psychology, 1*(4), 417–438.

Johnson, D. W., & Johnson, R. T. (1996). Teaching all students how to manage conflicts constructively: The peacemakers program. *Journal of Negro Education, 65*(3), 322–335.

Johnson, D. W., Johnson, R., Dudley, B., Ward, M., & Magnuson, D. (1995, Winter). The impact of peer mediation training on the management of school and home conflicts. *American Educational Research Journal, 32*(4), 829–844.

Jones, P. L. (1998). Values education, violence prevention, and peer mediation: The triad against violence in our schools. *Education Horizons, 76*(4), 177–181.

Lane, P. S., & McWhirter, J. J. (1992). A peer mediation model: Conflict resolution for elementary and middle school children. *Elementary School Guidance and Counseling, 27*(1), 15–23.

Lee, C. C., & Walz, G. R. (Eds.). (1998). *Social action: A mandate for counselors.* Alexandria, VA: American Counseling Association.

Leviton, S. C., & Greenstone, J. L. (1997). *Elements of Mediation.* Pacific Grove, CA: Brooks/Cole Company.

Lupton-Smith, H. S. (1996). The effects of a peer mediation training program on high school and elementary school students. *Dissertation Abstracts International Section A: Humanities and Social Sciences, 57*(2-A), 0589.

Michlowski, A. (1999). From conflict to congruence. *Kappa Delta Pi Record, 35*(3), 108–111.

Minden, J., Henry, D. B., Tolan, P. H., & Gorman-Smith, D. (2000). Urban boys' social network and school violence. *Professional School Counseling, 4*(2), 95–104.

Morse, P. S., & Andrea, R. (1994). Peer mediation in the schools: Teaching conflict resolution techniques to students. *NASSP Bulletin, 78*(560), 75–82.

Nieto, S. (1999). *The light in their eyes: Creating multicultural learning communities.* New York: Teachers College, Columbia University.

Opffer, E. (1997). Toward cultural transformation: Comprehensive approaches to conflict resolution. *Theory into Practice, 36*(1), 46–52.

Perlstein, R., & Thrall, G. (1996). *Ready to use conflict resolution activities for secondary school students*. West Nyack, NY: Center for Applied Research in Education.

Peterson, R., & Skiba, R. (2001, July/Aug.). Creating school climates that prevent school violence. *Social Studies, 92*(4), 167–175.

Prutzman, P., & Johnson, J. (1997). Bias awareness and multiple perspectives: Essential aspects of conflict resolution. *Theory into Practice, 36*(1), 26–31.

Ripley, V. V. (2003a). Conflict resolution and peer mediation in schools. In B. T. Erford (Ed.), *Transforming the school counseling profession* (pp. 297–316). Upper Saddle River, NJ: Merrill Prentice Hall.

Ripley, V. V. (2003b). Comprehensive school counseling program manual outline. In B. T. Erford (Ed.), *Transforming the school counseling profession* (pp. 494–498). Upper Saddle River, NJ: Merrill Prentice Hall.

Sandhu, D. S. (2000). Alienated students: Counseling strategies to curb school violence. *Professional School Counseling , 4*(2), 81–85.

Schwartz, D., & Proctor, L. J. (2000). Community violence exposure and children's social adjustment in the school peer group: The mediating roles of emotion regulation and social cognition. *Journal of Consulting and Clinical Psychology, 68*(4), 670–683.

Stanley, K. (2000, March/April). Invitational counseling and school violence. *ASCA Counselor, 37*(4), 6–7.

Stomfay-Stitz, A. M. (1994). Conflict resolution and peer mediation: Pathways to safer schools. *Childhood Education, 70*(5), 279–282.

Sweeney, B., & Carruthers, W. L. (1996). Conflict resolution: History, philosophy, theory, and educational applications. *The School Counselor, 43*(5), 326–344.

Thompson, S. M. (1996). Peer mediation: A peaceful solution. *School Counselor, 44*(2), 151–154.

Tremlow, S. T., Fonagy, P., & Sacco, F. C. (2001). A social systems–power dynamics approach to preventing school violence. In M. Shafii & S. L. Shafii (Eds.), *School violence: Assessment, management, prevention* (pp. 273–290). Washington, DC: American Psychiatric Publishing, Inc.

Tyrrell, F., Scully, T., & Halligan, J. (1998). Building peaceful schools. *Thrust for Educational Leadership, 28*(2), 30–33.

Wilburn, K. O., & Bates, M. L. (1997). Conflict resolution in America's schools: Defusing an approaching crisis. *Dispute Resolution Journal, 52*, 67–71.

WHAT IS THE COOLEST?

What is the coolest **music group?**_____

Who is the coolest **entertainer?**_____

What is the coolest **song?** _____

What is the coolest **music video?** _____

What is the coolest **TV show?** _____

Who is the coolest **sports personality?**_____

HANDOUT 8.2

WHAT IS CONFLICT?

Conflict is a natural part of life that occurs:

- **Within one's self**
    - an internal struggle over an issue/situation

- **Between two or more individuals**
    - a struggle within an established relationship
    - a struggle that may prevent the establishment of a relationship

- **Between two or more people who belong to the same group**
    - a struggle between two people who share a similarity of same group membership
    - a struggle that has the potential to involve members of the shared group

- **Between members of two different groups**
    - a more complex struggle involving multiple individuals and the group as a whole
    - a struggle that often involves past difficulties

- **Between two or more countries**
    - a very complex struggle involving multiple groups
    - a struggle with the potential to threaten world peace

CONFLICT OCCURS WHEN OUR NEEDS ARE NOT MET

Needs we all strive to meet include:

- **Identify**—Who are you?

- **Security/safety**—Freedom to thrive without threat

- **Control over one's own life**—Autonomy and self/group-determination

- **Recognition/belonging**—Part of the greater whole, acknowledgment of self/group

- **Fairness/justice**—Respect for self/group dignity, equal access and participation as part of the greater whole, lack of oppression

HANDOUT 8.4

THE CHARACTERISTICS OF CONFLICT

- **Not getting the whole story**—What information is missing?

- **Not getting the accurate information**—What is fact?

- **Stressful life events**—What else is going on at the same time?

- **Limited money, materials, and/or opportunities**—What barriers block access?

- **Not getting one's needs met**—What need or multiple needs are unmet?

TYPES OF CONFLICT

- **Tractable**—Usually the result of a simple misunderstanding

- **Intractable**—Based on different values, attitudes, beliefs, and worldviews held by different individuals/groups

HANDOUT 8.5

CONFLICT-RESOLUTION MODEL

- Define the problem

- Gather information

- Generate possible solutions

- Brainstorm the consequences of the decision

- Choose a solution

- Monitor the results

- Evaluate the results

PERSONAL INVENTORY

1. Which conflict category do you find yourself in most often?
   Check all that apply.

   ____ Conflict within myself

   ____ Conflict with another person

   ____ Conflict with a group of people

2. Which type of needs do you feel you have the most difficulty meeting?

   ____ Identity

   ____ Security/Safety

   ____ Control over Your Life

   ____ Recognition/Belonging

   ____ Fairness/Justice

3. Which of the following characteristics of conflict do you struggle with the most?
   Check all that apply.

   ____ Not getting the whole story

   ____ Not getting accurate information

   ____ Dealing with stressful life events

   ____ Limited money, materials, or opportunities

   ____ Not getting your needs met

4. Which type of conflict do you find yourself involved in the most?

   ____ Tractable

   ____ Intractable

AS WE CLOSE

Dear Group Member,

Please answer the questions below. Your input is very important to assist us in making groups a positive experience. Thank you.

1. What did you like most about the group?

2. What did you like least about the group?

3. What is the most important thing you learned in the group?

4. What would you change to make the group better?

5. Would you participate in a group again? Why/Why not?

FOLLOW-UP SURVEY

Just to Check in and See How You Are Doing!

Dear Former Group Member,

Please complete the following survey. Once again, your input is important. We want to know how you are doing since the group ended. Your response will help us learn how groups are benefiting students. Thank you.

1. **Please check the one that applies to you:**

   _____ a. Since the group ended, I have continued to apply the knowledge I learned.

   _____ b. I used the knowledge I gained shortly after the group ended, but I no longer use it.

   _____ c. I have not used the knowledge I gained since the group ended.

2. **Since I participated in the group,** I have shared the knowledge I gained with others to resolve conflict: yes / no

3. **Since participating in the group,** I have used my personal strengths and assets to help me resolve conflict: yes / no

4. **Since participating in the group,** I am more aware of others' needs in conflict situations: yes / no

5. **Since participating in the group,** I am more respectful of alternative points of view: yes / no

LOSS AND GRIEF IN THE SCHOOL SETTING

Susan Norris Huss, Bowling Green State University

INTRODUCTION

"I forgot my homework. I worked for two hours to get it done.
   I can't believe I left it home."
"My parents told me last night they are getting a divorce."
"I didn't make the basketball team."
"I really wanted to be the first chair trombone, but I didn't make it."
"My best friend will not talk to me."
"I have moved twice in six months."
"My grandfather died last night."
"Can you believe someone actually came to school with a gun!"
"I didn't get into the honors class. I should have been able
   to do that."
"I worked really hard on my grades the last two weeks.
   I cannot believe I only got a C in algebra."
"Can you believe all the damage that was done by the tornado that hit
   the school over the weekend?"
"Did you hear that Johnny's mom was shot and killed last night?"

These are all examples of loss and potential grief in a student's life and in the lives of all who function in a school. Loss and grief affect the entire school. The inability to cope with these losses can create barriers to learning for students.

As we review the Transforming School Counseling Inititiative's focus on closing the achievement gap (The Education Trust, 1999), the American School Counselor Association's (ASCA) National Standards for School Counseling Program's (Campbell & Dahir, 1997) personal/social domain, and ASCA's National Model (ASCA, 2003), we might ask, "How is loss and grief related to closing the gap and raising academic achievement for all children?" The answer is that many times we find that those who have not historically achieved as high as others in our schools are also those who have experienced more loss and therefore experienced more grief (for example, more parents incarcerated, more single-parent homes, more transient students) in their lives. With their lives compounded with multiple loss experiences, few coping skills, and a lack of comprehension about how these losses can affect their lives, children are in need of support systems to enable them to succeed (Moller, 2001). A comprehensive developmental school counseling program related to loss and grief can be part of a student's support system.

This chapter will demonstrate how a comprehensive developmental school counseling program can be a proactive response to loss and grief as a part of the daily life of students. This program can have a positive effect on the school's mission of increasing academic achievement for all students. A system-wide program of classroom guidance relating to loss and coping skills, specific group counseling interventions, and individual counseling strategies will be described. System-wide interventions and policies (for example, crisis response teams) will be presented.

Literature Review

Children and Grief

Grief occurs whenever there is a loss. It has been documented that one out of every twenty Americans under the age of fifteen loses one or both parents due to death. In a high school of eight hundred students, twenty-four will experience the death of a family member (Selekman, Busch, & Kimble, 2001). Every year, one in five families will move (McGlaufin, 1998). Add to this the everyday examples of loss of a friendship, place on a team, first chair in the orchestra, and belief in self from teasing, and it becomes obvious that loss is a universal phenomenon in the school setting.

Stages of Grief

The grieving process has been identified as having various stages or dimensions. Dimensions of the grieving process as described by Wolfert (1997) are similar to those described by Kubler-Ross (1969) but include dimensions unique to children. Wolfert's first dimension is the initial sense of shock or denial that generally occurs as a response to the information that a loss has occurred. Denial buffers children from fully experiencing the unexpected loss. Because of their lack of experience and level of emotional development, children may pretend that the loss has not occurred (Wolfert, 1997). Adults who do not understand how development interfaces with grief may be astonished at what appears to be a lack of feeling in children. The second stage of grieving relates to anger. In children, these emotions may be very intense and include hate, terror, and rage. Bringing these feelings out into the open and helping students express what they feel is an important part of this stage. The third stage is the bargaining stage.

In children, this stage often includes irrational beliefs about their ability to have prevented the death (for instance, "If I had been a better daughter he wouldn't have died."). The sense of loss children experience brings them to the fourth stage of grieving, often termed the sadness or depression stage. Fully experiencing sadness and loss is important for children to be able to move to the final stage of grief. This last stage, termed acceptance or resolution, occurs when children realize that the loss is permanent—the deceased person is not coming back. It is imperative that children understand that as they move toward acceptance, the person who died will always be a part of their life and they can continue to grow and remember the person who died. Counselors and others can help children commemorate the deceased in numerous ways (for example, with pictures, letters, poems, and so on).

Kubler-Ross's works, *On Death and Dying* (1969) and *On Children and Death* (1983), and Bowlby's (1980) *Attachment and Loss* indicate a recognition of the existence of children's ability to understand death and acknowledge the uniqueness of the related grieving issues of children. McGlauflin (1992) discusses the developmental nature of childhood bereavement as repetitive and cyclical in nature. It is described as repetitive because children often have to ask the same questions multiple times before they can clearly comprehend what is occurring. Childhood bereavement appears to be cyclical in that as the level of cognitive development changes, children reach new levels of understanding about the loss and there is renewed grieving at each level. As a result, the grieving process for children may last a relatively long time and recur more than in adults. Effective school counseling programs provide children with the skills necessary to cope with loss. In so doing, they take into consideration the child's level of cognitive development and the cyclical nature of childhood grief, also known as *maturational bereavement* (Johnson & Rosenblatt, 1981).

Because of maturational bereavement, the school counselor should explore what has happened previously in terms of loss experiences when a student is experiencing academic difficulties. In general, developmental milestones, anniversaries of the loss, and holidays are major sources of maturational grief. It is important to understand the difference between this maturational grief and pathological grief in children. Figure 9.1 lists some characteristics of normal bereavement for different ages; Figure 9.2 lists some characteristics of complicated or pathological bereavement. Pathological bereavement has been described as the intensification of grief to the level where the person is overwhelmed, resorts to maladaptive behavior, or remains interminably in the state of grief without progression of the mourning process toward completion (Horowitz et al., 1980). If the school counselor does not understand the concept of maturational grief, it might be easy to confuse it with pathological grief, since both can occur years after the loss incident.

Academic success has been widely reported to be negatively affected by unresolved grief (Goodman, 1987; Gray, 1988; Krupnick & Soloman, 1987; Sharpneck, 2001). As there is much support for the need for young people to have loss-coping skills (Lenhardt, 1997), it is appropriate for school counselors to look at the local in-house data to determine if those who are not being successful

---

EARLY ELEMENTARY

- Begins to comprehend finality of death but fails to understand it can happen to them
- Personifies death, usually as a monster
- Fears death is contagious
- Develops an interest in causes of death
- Maintains remnants of magical thinking
- May believe they caused the death

MIDDLE SCHOOL

- Understands the finality of death
- Experiences a wide range of emotions
- May see death as punishment for bad behavior
- Needs assurances that wishes do not kill
- Worries about who will care and provide for them
- Becomes interested in spiritual aspects of death
- Wants factual information; wants to know the mechanics of death

HIGH SCHOOL

- Thinks like an adult; can cognitively comprehend but emotionally unable to
- May feel guilt, anger, and even some responsibility for death
- May seek support of family or friends or may withdraw to themselves because of being unsure how to handle own emotions
- Begins to realize they and their loved ones will die some day

---

FIGURE **9.1**

SOME DEVELOPMENTAL PHASES IN UNDERSTANDING LOSS/DEATH

Sources: Developed from Worden (1996); Worden, J. W., & Silverman, P. R. (1996); and the Dougy Center (1998).

---

academically have experienced loss and, if so, to implement a plan to teach skills in this area. A method of disaggregating data around this issue is to examine the data related to students who are underachieving and determine if there have been major loss experiences in their lives (for example, moving, divorce, death, or major illness).

Jacobs, Harvill, and Masson (1994) support using group work as a valid intervention with bereaved children because of the efficacy of serving more than one child at a time and the multiple resources and viewpoints available in a group setting. Both small-group counseling and classroom guidance are beneficial, in part because of the phenomena of universality and commonality (Jacobs, Harvill, & Masson, 1994; Yalom, 1985). Huss and Ritchie (1999) reported that children who participated in bereavement groups indicated they felt their experiences had been normalized by interacting with other children in similar situations.

CAUSES OF COMPLICATED GRIEF

- Sudden or traumatic death or loss
- Social stigma of death
- Multiple losses
- Past relationship with deceased
- Grief process of caregiver
- Moving, divorce, disasters

CHARACTERISTICS OF COMPLICATED GRIEF

- Extended depression = Loss of interest in activities
- Inability to sleep
- Loss of appetite
- Fear of being alone
- Long-term regression
- Imitating the dead person for extended time
- Statements of wanting to join the dead person
- Withdrawal from friends
- School phobia or drop in school performance

FIGURE **9.2**

COMPLICATED GRIEF

WHOLE-SCHOOL INTERVENTIONS

A system-wide approach includes both prevention and intervention strategies. Prevention includes providing education to parents and teachers in a normative manner, in the absence of specific precipitating crises. A schoolwide prevention plan for teachers and parents follows.

Prevention

Teachers

Reid and Dixon (1999) found that most teachers require assistance when working with a child who has experienced death. Systemic interventions suggest that the training given to students should also be given to teachers so they are knowledgeable and able to provide appropriate responses when a loss occurs in the classroom. This can be done both by having teachers remain in the room during the classroom guidance activities and by offering in-service training designed specifically for teachers, administrators, and support staff.

Parents

Another component of a schoolwide plan is parent education. Parents benefit from knowing what is taught in classroom guidance sessions, both for their own information and for their use when their child experiences a loss. This parent education could be developed by collaborating with the parent stakeholders in the community through the PTA, parent council, guidance advisory committee, or a group of interested parents. Two interventions that might emerge from parental collaboration are (1) the regular provision of bereavement-related information in the school's newsletter and (2) a workshop for parents and teachers. An outline for a parent/teacher workshop follows.

OUTLINE FOR PARENT/TEACHER WORKSHOP

   I. Make introductions. In a workshop such as this, it is important for attendees to get to know each other. If it is a large group, have them turn to the people nearest them and introduce themselves. If the group is relatively small, ask each person to introduce him or herself. In either situation, get general information by asking participants to raise their hands related to ages of children and losses experienced (if any).

  II. Present purpose of workshop. Make a statement such as "This workshop is being offered to help you to understand what your children are learning about in the Loss-Coping Skills Unit. We at the school hope that by partnering with you, we may do an even better job of helping students develop these important life skills."

 III. Share rationale for unit for students. "The unit is part of the Comprehensive Developmental Counseling Program of the school district. It is based on the premise that we all experience loss on a daily basis. For instance, we experience minor losses all the time, such as losing our keys and losing our place in line. Students, too, experience minor losses regularly, such as when they misplace their homework. Many of us also experience more major losses, such as losing our job, experiencing divorce, or facing the death of a loved one. By understanding the stages of grief and feelings associated with them, we and our children can better cope with these losses. Learning these new skills helps all of us emotionally and also reduces a significant barrier to learning for students."

 IV. Teach the basics of the student unit.
   A. Loss as part of everyday life (Do one activity from student Lesson 1.)
   B. Feelings associated with loss (Do one activity from student Lesson 2.)
   C. Stages of grief (Do one activity from student Lesson 3.)
   D. Support systems/Summary (Do one activity from student Group Sessions 5 and 6.)
   E. It is important to provide time for questions during and after the workshop.

Note: This session may be shortened or expanded as time allows or as need dictates. This workshop could be done for the entire district or specific grade levels or buildings.

Intervention

Serious grief-inducing events will inevitably occur in schools. It is necessary to use teaming and collaboration to determine what is the best response and how to assist students. When a schoolwide crisis occurs, the response needs to collaboratively emerge from the crisis response team. Once decisions are made about the need (data driven), large group, small group, and individual interventions need to occur. Two specific examples will be described.

Brock (1998) provides a model for Classroom Crisis Intervention (CCI). He suggests the advantages of the CCI include not only that it is time efficient (the responders could not possibly see everyone individually) but that classroom intervention supports the normalcy of the responses and provides emotional support. For instance, if a middle school student commits suicide, the school needs to have a way to reach students and help them cope with the disaster. The school's crisis team might collaboratively decide that they need to provide classroom lessons in order to prevent possible copycat suicides and provide trauma support (Brock, 1998; Shen & Sink, 2002). Such a lesson has several parts. First, the school counselor or classroom leader needs to review the stages of grief with students and help them process their feelings, emphasizing that all feelings are normal. Next, it is helpful to help students identify how and from whom they can gain support. A key in copycat prevention work is to let students know that help is available for students through their support system, which includes the school counselor. The student who committed suicide chose not to use the support system, but surviving students need to use theirs if they become distressed.

Another example of system-wide intervention is when a student is diagnosed with a terminal illness. In this case, the school must collaborate with the student and family to decide how to handle many issues. These issues may include how to involve classmates in the situation, how much information should be shared, and how to channel expressions of support. A common mistake is to assume what is needed. Discussions with the student, and possibly the family, depending on the age of the student, should help determine the course of interventions the school will take. It is also the school counselor's responsibility to keep the needs of the entire student body in mind while working to provide appropriate interventions for the terminally ill student. School counselors must think systemically as well as individually.

These are just two examples of specific situations involving loss and grief that might occur in a school system. Having a crisis response plan in place that allows for flexibility of responses is the key to successfully addressing the ripple effect of crises in a school. The development of a good crisis response plan should be a priority in every school district (Watson, 2000).

CLASSROOM GUIDANCE ACTIVITIES

Loss-coping skills can be taught preventively in a classroom guidance program. McGlauflin (1998) suggests that it is important to provide an understanding and acceptance of grief not only to support the grieving children but also to teach non-grieving children that the grieving process is a natural and normal response to loss. Because children process information differently as they age, variations on these basic lessons can be taught at the early elementary, late elementary, middle, and high school levels. It is described here as a three-session unit but could be condensed into only two at the upper levels or expanded to six if needed at the elementary level. The first lesson teaches the central tenet of the program: that loss is part of living. Lesson 2 helps students to learn that the emotional feelings related to loss are normal and should not be considered debilitating. The normalization of these feelings enables students to not let them be barriers to their daily functioning and therefore to their academic growth. The third lesson introduces the stages of grief and assists students in understanding that emotional reactions are part of all losses, ranging from losing one's homework to having a grandparent die. This new understanding becomes the foundation for removing the barriers to learning that can occur when the feelings associated with bereavement are not understood.

LESSON 1: NORMALIZING LOSS

Personal/Social Development Standard A: Students will acquire the knowledge, attitudes, and interpersonal skills to help them understand and respect self and others.

Personal/Social Development Standard C: Students will understand safety and survival skills.

Competencies

- Students will understand change as a part of growth.
- Students will learn coping skills for managing life events.

Learning Objectives

- Students will be able to identify loss experiences in their life and the ways they coped with them.
- Students will be able to identify how their lives are different because of the loss experiences.
- Students will understand that loss is a part of life and does not need to create barriers to keep them from functioning or learning.

Materials: Paper, pens or pencils, colored markers or crayons (depending on level).

Developmental Learning Activity

Introduction: The counselor introduces the topic by asking questions such as "What loss might keep you from learning (getting your homework done)?" The counselor shares an insignificant loss experience from their life experience so students understand that loss can be a barrier to learning. The counselor asks students to share an experience until it is clear they understand the full spectrum of loss (for example, broken fingernail to best friend died).

Activity: The counselor has students create their own List of Losses. Some students may have difficulty getting started, and the counselor helps anyone who is stuck. Everyone should try to list at least fifteen (number can be adjusted depending on age).

The counselor asks students, "Was it difficult or easy to remember losses?" The response usually is that it was easy, and the counselor can follow with asking for reasons for it being so easy. After numerous responses the counselor draws the conclusion, if no one else already has, that loss is a part of everyday life.

The counselor asks students to circle the loss(es) that they had very strong feelings about; to put an X through the ones that if they had the same experience now, it would not bother them as much as it did then; and to underline those in which someone helped them.

Conclusion: To normalize the loss experience, after students have turned in their sheets, the counselor reads some of them aloud and asks if anyone else ever experienced those losses. After doing this for several minutes, the counselor discusses the similarities and explains that loss is, in fact, a part of life. The counselor tells students that the rest of the time together will be spent talking about what role loss plays and how we can manage the consequences and not let barriers to learning develop.

Assessment: Each week the counselor asks students to complete the sentence "Today I learned . . ." The counselor asks for a quick round the room response from everyone who chooses to share. The counselor keeps these to use at last session.

Lesson 2: Feelings

Personal/Social Development Standard A: Students will acquire the knowledge, attitudes, and interpersonal skills to help them understand and respect self and others.

Competency: Students will identify and express feelings.

Learning Objectives

- Students will express their feelings related to loss.
- Students will understand commonality of feelings related to loss (be it homework or parent) and commonality of feelings with others who have experienced similar events.
- Students will normalize their feelings related to loss.

Materials: 3 × 5 cards, large piece of newsprint, markers/crayons/pencils.

Developmental Learning Activities

Introduction: The counselor initiates a discussion about feelings (for younger elementary level, this would include being certain they understand what a feeling is) and the ways certain feelings can become barriers to being able to do well in school.

Activity: The counselor refers back to losses from Lesson 1 and asks students to list all the feelings associated with the losses they listed. This could be done in small groups, or as a large group, depending on age and size of class.

The counselor creates and posts one master list of feelings. Students raise their hand if they have ever had that feeling when experiencing a loss. This may generate some discussion (particularly when someone says they felt happy when someone died or moved out). The counselor indicates beside each feeling how many felt that way.

The counselor asks students the following process questions:

- Were any of you surprised at some of the words listed? Which ones? Why were you surprised? Would the person who experienced it like to share about that feeling?
- What did you learn from this activity? (Similar feelings no matter what the loss and same feelings as other felt.)

The counselor gives each student six 3 × 5 cards. They write three feelings (one on each card) they felt when they experienced a loss that was not too serious (for example, losing one's homework). The counselor asks one student to share one feeling; all others who wrote down that feeling then add their cards to the pile so all the same cards are together. Students do this again with a major loss, such as the death of someone.

Conclusion: The counselor asks the following process questions: "In comparing the sets of cards, did you find any differences? What were they? Why do you think they were different? Did you notice that the feelings were similar for each event? Could any of the feelings you experienced keep you from doing your best job in school? Would someone like to talk about how that might happen?" The counselor should validate that all feelings are OK. There should be no value judgment of any feeling expressed by anyone.

Assessment: Each week the counselor asks students to complete the sentence "Today I learned . . ." The counselor asks for a quick round the room response from everyone who chooses to share. The counselor keeps these to use at last session.

Follow-up: The counselor asks students to watch, between now and the next time they come to class, for when someone is experiencing a loss and to look for similarities between the feelings they observe and what had been discussed in class. The counselor will briefly introduce the next session by describing how there are similarities in the ways that we all react to loss and that we will be learning about that process the next time we meet.

LESSON 3: STAGES OF GRIEF

Personal/Social Development Standard C: Students will understand safety and survival skills.

Competencies

- Students will learn techniques for managing stress and conflict.
- Students will learn coping skills for managing life events.

Learning Objectives

- Students will learn what the grieving process is and what the stages of the grieving process are.
- Students will learn the feelings associated with each stage.
- Students will learn how the grieving process may create barriers to their learning and how to cope with this.

Materials: A diagram of stages (one for each student) (Handout 9.1), feeling cards from week before, pens or pencils.

Developmental Learning Activities

Introduction: The counselor reviews briefly the first two lessons and discusses the grieving process in general and how it helps with understanding, enduring pain, and moving forward.

Activity: The counselor will teach the stages of grief using age-appropriate information and examples. For lower grades the terms *understanding, grieving, commemorating,* and *going on* are appropriate. For upper grades use the following terms: *denial, anger, bargaining, depression,* and *acceptance.*

The counselor describes two low-severity loss experiences and has students share how each stage was demonstrated. Using feeling cards from the last lesson, students help the counselor categorize the feelings experienced with the different stages. This shows students both the similarities and the uniqueness of each individual and each circumstance.

Conclusion: The counselor asks and processes with students the following questions: "How are the loss experiences similar? Are there any major differences? How do you feel about understanding your feelings related to losses now? What have you learned that has helped you?" The counselor has students describe times when they have seen the various stages of grief. They look for commonalities in the responses.

Assessment: Each week the counselor asks students to complete the sentence "Today I learned . . ." The counselor asks for a quick round the room response from everyone who chooses to share. Using the "Today I learned . . ." statements from each session, students will add statements or phrases about what they learned to a mural. This continues the process of knowing the universality of their experience as well as helping them to collectively review what they have learned.

Note: During this activity there may be some unexpected and possibly inappropriate disclosures (for example, there might be an unusual family ritual related to death). The counselor needs to be prepared to respond to these disclosures.

SMALL-GROUP COUNSELING PLANS

For some students the classroom guidance lessons are sufficient to provide them with the coping skills needed. For others, additional levels of intervention such as group and/or individual counseling might be required. For example, these students might include those whose natural support system is limited due to having an incarcerated parent, being a foster child, or having a deceased parent. Other examples might be students who have experienced multiple losses. If students such as these are having difficulties academically, it is prudent to involve them in some additional interventions so that these barriers to learning can be addressed and ameliorated.

Small-group counseling is a recommended intervention for bereaved children. Pennells and Smith (1995) believe that family and individual work with bereaved children, while valid, may not address specifically the children's sense of isolation or give them needed peer support. Webb (1993) concludes that the use of group work is advantageous because it relieves the sense of isolation a child may feel, normalizes the death experience, and allows the child to see others in later stages of grief who have survived and gone on with their lives. The school is a particularly appropriate setting because it is part of the child's normal life. Having the group at the school helps to normalize children's experiences (Samide & Stockton, 2002).

Keitel, Kopala, and Robin (1998) recommend using groups in conjunction with regular death-education instruction. Small-group counseling can use classroom guidance curriculum as the basis for the sessions because the pertinent knowledge and skills have already been addressed. It may be necessary to reteach some of the concepts if the group happens to be made up of many students who did not receive the original classroom guidance curriculum. Generally, topics of discussion in the small group will be determined by the needs of the students. The following group counseling activities have been found to be successful in helping to normalize and process the feelings associated with the death of a loved one (Huss, 1997). This group is perhaps unique in that it maintains a focus on what is keeping the students from succeeding academically. The group membership here should be determined by disaggregating achievement data so as to serve students not succeeding in school who also have experienced a significant loss.

This unit concludes with the concept of a support system. The availability of support for children during bereavement is extremely important (Charkow, 1998). Often this support must come from people other than the family members, who are also grieving. It is helpful for a student to be able to specifically name those whom they can go to for support in specific instances. During this last session, students identify those people in their lives. They complete a diagram of those they have identified as their support system. Finally, they summarize what they have learned in the lessons and describe how they can use this knowledge in the future.

GROUP SESSION 1: TELLING OUR STORIES

Personal/Social Development Standard A: Students will acquire the knowledge, attitudes, and interpersonal skills to help them understand and respect self and others.

Personal/Social Development Standard C: Students will understand safety and survival skills.

Competencies

- Students will understand change as a part of growth.
- Students will learn coping skills for managing life events.

Learning Objectives

- Students will become acquainted.
- Students will help establish group rules.
- Students will share who has died.

Materials: Magazines, glue, scissors, file folders (all colors), colored markers/ pencils/crayons, and small ball or beanbag.

Activities

Introduction: The counselor explains the purpose of the group as being to assist members who have had a loved one die. The counselor tells students that there will be six sessions, what the times and places for the sessions are, and that the participants will assist in planning the last session.

Counseling Activity: The group starts with a discussion to establish the group rules. Typically, the following rules emerge from that discussion:

- One person speaks at a time.
- Each person has the right to pass.
- Each person is respected.
- What is said in the group stays in the group.
- Other rules as determined by the group.

These rules should be displayed and reviewed at each session.

To learn names of all participants, students toss a ball, saying, for example, "I am Susan Weeks and this is Seth Jones" as Susan tosses the ball to Seth. This is done several times until the names are learned.

Each participant, including the counselor, creates a folder that tells about himself or herself. In the center of the folder is a picture or word that relates to the person who died. The rest of the folder is covered with pictures that tell about themselves. The front may be decorated in any way, but the back needs to be left blank because it will be used for later activities. Magazine pictures and words as well as original drawings may be used. Discussion is encouraged during this time.

Often this activity does not get finished during the first session, but before the group ends each participant shares the picture in the middle of their folder that depicts the person who died and tells how that person died.

Conclusion: Students toss the ball to refresh memory about names, and the counselor emphasizes the rule about confidentiality.

Assessment: The ongoing creation of folders provides for authentic assessment.

GROUP SESSION 2: FEELINGS

Personal/Social Development Standard A: Students will acquire knowledge, attitudes, and interpersonal skills to help them understand and respect self and others.

Competency: Students will identify and express feelings.

Learning Objectives

- Students will become better acquainted.
- Students will express and begin to normalize their feelings about death.

Materials: Folders from first session, 4 × 6 cards, colored markers/pencils/crayons, group rules, small ball or beanbag, newsprint.

Activities

Introduction: The group goes twice around with the ball to remember and reinforce names. Then the counselor reviews group rules by having participants identify rules before putting them on display.

Counseling Activity: Students share information in folders. The counselor encourages each participant to share but does not force anyone.

The counselor begins a discussion about feelings, generates a list of feelings, and writes them on a large piece of newsprint. The counselor asks for a show of hands for each feeling, for students to indicate they have felt that way at some time. The counselor records the number of hands with checks by each word. The counselor discusses how many of them have had similar feelings.

Participants choose three of the feeling words they felt surrounding their significant loss and anytime since then. They put each feeling (in words) on one side of a card. Each participant will have three cards with one feeling word on each. Then they sort the cards so all similar cards are together. The counselor discusses the results in terms of similar feelings and the legitimacy of feelings.

Conclusion: Students share a completion of the sentence "Today I learned . . ." and record it on the back of their folder with the date.

Assessment: Group assessment is provided by the generated list of feelings.

GROUP SESSION 3: STAGES OF GRIEF

Personal/Social Development Standard A: Students will acquire the knowledge, attitudes, and interpersonal skills to help them understand and respect self and others.

Competency: Students will identify and express feelings.

Learning Objectives

- Students will learn the stages of grief and understand the grieving process.
- Students will learn about the feelings associated with grief.

Materials: File folders created in Session 1, feeling cards created in Session 2, and tagboard posters with stages of grief on them.

Activities

Introduction: The counselor reviews group rules.

Counseling Activity: The counselor will teach stages of grief using developmentally appropriate terms. (See Lesson 3.) The counselor does this through discussion with participants. Once all stages have been identified, the counselor discusses the *roller coaster effect*. The counselor helps participants identify the feelings associated with each stage by using the cards created in Session 2.

Conclusion: Students verbally share a completion of the sentence "Today I learned . . ." and record it on the back of their fold with the date.

Assessment: The ongoing creation of folders provides for authentic assessment.

Follow-up: Each participant is to bring a "memory object" with them for the next session. This should be something that reminds the participant of their significant loss. This could be a picture, keepsake, gift, food, or anything that shows the special significance of the relationship.

GROUP SESSION 4: MEMORIES

Personal/Social Development Standard C: Students will understand safety and survival skills.

Competencies

- Students will learn techniques for managing stress and conflict.
- Students will learn coping skills for managing life events.

Learning Objectives

- Students will have a nonthreatening environment to share about their significant loss.
- Students will explore the use of memories as a positive way to deal with grief.

Materials: Memory items brought by the participants, the book *The Tenth Good Thing about Barney* by Judy Viorst (1971), magazines, one large piece of construction paper, scissors, colored markers/pencils/crayons, glue, feeling cards created in Session 2, folders created in Session 1.

Activities

Introduction: The counselor reviews the group rules. The counselor discusses the importance of students' sharing memories during this session even though it may make them uncomfortable.

Counseling Activity: The counselor reads the book *The Tenth Good Thing about Barney.* Afterward, the counselor asks each participant to share the item they brought in and tell about it in terms of memories of the loved one.

The counselor places a large piece of construction paper in the middle of the table. Participants find pictures in magazines of things that serve as reminders of their deceased loved one, such as foods, hobbies, and interests. The counselor encourages them to draw pictures if none can be found. The counselor encourages each student to find ten, as was done about Barney in the book. All are placed on the big collage, and everyone shares at the end.

Conclusion: Participants select two feeling cards to describe their feelings today during the activities and share how they felt with the group. They record the two feelings they selected on the back of the folder.

Assessment: The collage and folder provide for authentic assessment.

Follow-up: The counselor encourages participants to begin to think about the last session of the group in terms of how to bring closure and how to celebrate.

GROUP SESSION 5: FAMILY

Personal/Social Development Standard A: Students will acquire the knowledge, attitudes, and interpersonal skills to help them understand and respect self and others.

Personal/Social Development Standard C: Students will understand safety and survival skills.

Competencies:

- Students will understand change as a part of growth.
- Students will learn coping skills for managing life events.

Learning Objectives

- Students will identify ways to discuss their feelings with their families.
- Students will gain comfort by discussing their feelings with their families.
- Students will recognize changes, for both better and worse, in families since the death.

Materials: Paper, colored markers, pencils, 4 × 6 cards, crayons, folders from Session 1.

Activities

Introduction: The counselor reviews group rules and activities from previous sessions.

Counseling Activity: Participants draw a picture of their family before the death occurred. On a second sheet, participants draw a picture of family since the death. The counselor discusses change by asking questions such as: "Has anyone changed? How have they changed? Do you have more responsibility? Can you talk with anyone about your deceased person? Could you before the death? Who were you closest to before the death? Who are you closest to in the family now?" The counselor helps participants identify some positive changes that have occurred, as well as the obvious negative ones.

Using the pictures, participants identify someone in their family they would like to be able to talk with about the person who died, their feelings, or just things in general. The counselor helps participants brainstorm ways to approach these people to talk. After a lengthy list is created, each participant puts on a card how they are going to try to approach the person during the next week, and then shares it with the group.

Conclusion: Participants give encouragement to each other for their week's task with a barrage of statements to each other such as "Go for it!" "Good luck!" "We will be pulling for you!" They record whom they plan to talk with and the date on the back of the folder. The counselor briefly discusses the final session. The counselor encourages participants to share any ideas that can be incorporated into the last session.

Assessment: The folder and the pictures provide assessment.

GROUP SESSION 6: MOVING ON

Personal/Social Development Standard A: Students will acquire the knowledge, attitudes, and interpersonal skills to help them understand and respect self and others.

Personal/Social Development Standard C: Students will understand safety and survival skills.

Competencies

- Students will understand change as a part of growth.
- Students will learn coping skills for managing life events.

Learning Objectives

- Students will develop constructive ways to deal with grief.
- Students will identify a support system.
- Students will evaluate the group experience.

Materials: Writing paper, pencils, markers, newsprint, folders from Session 1.

Activities

Introduction: The counselor reminds students that this is the last session. The counselor reviews group rules and what has occurred during the each of the sessions.

Counseling Activity: Each student shares how their planned conversation went. The counselor facilitates group encouragement and support. If discussions didn't go well, the counselor discusses with students whether and how to try again.

Each participant identifies additional people they can go to for support. Each draws a tree with numerous branches and puts the name of a person in their support system on each branch. The counselor reviews the importance of this support system when they need help.

The counselor distributes folders and briefly reviews them, particularly the back with their weekly additions. Participants identify ways they have grown and/or changed during the sessions.

The group brainstorms constructive ways of coping with grief, based on all they have learned during the sessions, and lists them on newsprint. The counselor may facilitate this by making suggestions if students have trouble starting. Then the group discusses the specifics of each suggestion. Each participant can relate how they used one of the suggestions and then identify one they plan to use in the future.

Conclusion: Participants will answer these questions and share with the group:

- What I liked most about this group was . . .
- Three things I learned are . . .
- I would recommend this group to another student because . . .
- One thing that is different because I participated in this group is . . .

Assessment: This is provided by the artifacts (collage, pictures, folder, and newsprint) that have been created during the group. Evaluation of the group experience is embedded in the final concluding activity.

Follow-up: The school counselor can monitor the academic and personal growth of the participants over time. Some will "move on" well. Others may need another group at a later time, and still others may benefit from individual counseling or referral.

INDIVIDUAL COUNSELING CONSIDERATIONS

Not all students respond to group counseling. The grief they are experiencing may be more complicated. In that case, individual counseling interventions are warranted. Parameters for individual counseling should be determined in advance as part of the school counseling program. In some schools, counseling programs limit individual counseling to three sessions. If more are needed, then a referral to an outside agency is made. It is difficult to be specific in this area. One session might be enough to determine that the student could benefit from group counseling. Or one session might be sufficient to help the student implement what they learned in classroom guidance. For individual counseling, the basic format should be to determine the intensity of the grief and its effect on academic achievement. Here again, the goal is to normalize an abnormal situation, accepting that grief is a normal reaction to a loss.

Kandt (1994) and Wolfert (1997) suggest several individual strategies for working with bereaved adolescents, which can be generalized and adapted to all ages. They include acknowledging the feelings associated with the loss and assuring the normalcy of the feelings expressed, thus giving permission for students to feel the way they do. It is necessary to provide a supportive and empathic environment in which to share feelings. If the loss is major (such as death of a parent) bibliotherapy, family trees, memory books, and journaling can help. Books can help students to understand the grieving process. The family tree helps the student evaluate the different roles and relationships family members play in their life. Memory books provide concrete objects to connect the student to the deceased and encourage sharing. The memory books can include photos and poetry about the deceased. Journal writing provides the opportunity to explore themes related to the grieving process. Relaxation techniques also can be taught to promote feelings of peace and well-being and to alleviate stress.

Individual counseling should be part of the responsive services provided by the school counselor. However, if it becomes apparent that a student needs ongoing counseling, a referral to an appropriate outside agency is appropriate. Generally, when symptoms are prolonged and intense to the point of being debilitating they are considered complicated and may require more time than a school counselor can provide. Figure 9.2 provides symptoms that could indicate the need for counseling beyond the time available in the school setting.

CONCLUSION

The comprehensive developmental counseling program that includes the mandates from the reform movements discussed in this book can very appropriately and effectively include loss-coping skills as a major component. This chapter shows how loss and grief in schools can be addressed using leadership, teaming and collaboration, and data-driven decision making. The connection between the personal/social domain and academic achievement was explored. The examples in this chapter make it clear that the expertise of all stakeholders needs to be employed when addressing grief and loss, a ubiquitous barrier to student learning.

REFERENCES

American School Counselor Association. (2003). *The ASCA National Model: A framework for school counseling programs.* Alexandria, VA: American School Counselor Association.

Bowlby, J. (1980). *Attachment and loss. Vol 4: Loss: Sadness and depression.* New York: Basic.

Brock, S. E. (1998). Helping classrooms cope with traumatic events. *Professional School Counseling, 2,* 110–116.

Campbell, C. A., & Dahir, C. A. (1997). *The national standards for school counseling programs.* Alexandria, VA: American School Counselor Association.

Charkow, W. B. (1998). Inviting children to grieve. *Professional School Counseling, 2,* 117–123.

Dougy Center. (1998). *How children grieve.* Retrieved October 14, 2002, from http://griefnet.org/KIDSAID/dougypage.html.

The Education Trust. (1999, September). *The transforming school counseling initiative.* Washington, DC: Author.

Goodman, R. A. (1987). *Life & loss: A guide to help grieving children.* Muncie, IN: Accelerated Development.

Gray, R. E. (1988). The role of school counselors with bereaved teenagers: With and without peer support groups. *School Counselor, 35,* 185–193.

Horowitz, M., Wilmer, N., Marmar, C., & Krupnick, J. (1980). Pathological grief and the activation of latent self-images. *American Journal of Psychiatry, 137,* 1157–1162.

Huss, S. N. (1997). The effect of peer bereavement support groups on the self-esteem, depression, and problem behavior of parentally bereaved children. *Dissertation Abstracts International* (UMI No. 9729145), *58*(64A), 1208.

Huss, S. N., & Ritchie, M. (1999). Effectiveness of a group for parentally bereaved children. *Journal for Specialists in Group Work, 27,* 186–196.

Jacobs, E. E., Harvill, R. L., & Masson, R. L. (1994). *Group counseling: Strategies and skills.* Pacific Grove, CA: Brooks/Cole.

Johnson, P. A., & Rosenblatt, P. C. (1981). Grief following childhood loss of a parent. *American Journal of Psychotherapy, 35,* 419–424.

Kandt, V. E. (1994). Adolescent bereavement: Turning a fragile time into acceptance and peace. *School Counselor, 41,* 203–211.

Keitel, M. A., Kopala, M., & Robin, L. (1998). Loss and grief groups. In K. C. Stoiber & T. R. Kratochwill (Eds.), *Handbook of group interventions for children and families* (pp. 159–171). Boston: Allyn & Bacon.

Krupnick, J. L., & Solomon, F. (1987). Death of a parent or sibling during childhood. In J. Bloom-Feshback, S. Bloom-Feshbach, & Associates (Eds.), *The psychology of separation and loss: Perspectives on development, life transitions and clinical practice* (pp. 154–178). San Francisco: Jossey-Bass.

Kubler-Ross, E. (1969). *On death and dying.* New York: MacMillan.

Kubler-Ross, E. (1983). *On children and death.* New York: MacMillan.

Lenhardt, A. M. (1997). Disenfranchised grief/hidden sorrow: Implications for the school counselor. *School Counselor, 44,* 264–271.

McGlauflin, H. (1992). How children grieve: Implications for counseling. In G. R. Walz, & J. C. Bleuer (Eds.), *Helping students cope with fears and crises* (Report No. ISBN-1-561-0-040-9). Ann Arbor, MI: Office of Educational Research and Improvement (ERIC Document Reproduction Service No. ED340987).

McGlauflin, H. (1998). Helping children grieve at school. *Professional School Counseling, 1,* 46–49.

Moller, B. (2001). A grieving child. *School Counselor Magazine, 39,* 14–17.

Pennells, M., & Smith, S. C. (1995). *The forgotten mourners: Guidelines for working with bereaved children.* Bristol, PA: Kingsley.

Reid, J. K., & Dixon, W. A. (1999). Teacher attitudes on coping with grief in the public school classroom. *Psychology in the Schools, 36,* 219–229.

Samide, L. L., & Stockton, R. (2002). Letting go of grief: Bereavement groups for children in the school setting. *Journal for Specialists in Group Work, 27,* 192–204.

Selekman, J., Busch, T., & Kimble, C. S. (2001). Grieving children: Are we meeting the challenge? *Pediatric Nursing, 27,* 414–418.

Sharpneck, J. D. (2001). The efficacy of group bereavement interventions: An integrative review of the research literature. *Dissertation Abstracts International, 61,* 6721.

Shen, Y., & Sink, C. A. (2002). Helping elementary-age children cope with disasters. *Professional School Counseling, 5,* 322–330.

Watson, J. A. (2000). The importance of having an effective school crisis response plan. *School Planning and Management, 39,* 4–6.

Webb, N. B. (1993). *Helping bereaved children: A handbook for practitioners.* New York: Guilford.

Wolfert, A. D. (1997). Death and grief in the school setting. In T. N. Fairchild (Ed.), *Crisis intervention strategies for school-based helpers* (pp. 199–244). Springfield, IL: Charles C. Thomas.

Worden, J. W. (1996). *Children and grief: When a parent dies* (ERIC document Reproduction Service No. ED405133).

Worden, J. W., & Silverman, P. R. (1996). Parental death and the adjustment of school-age children. *Omega: Journal of Death and Dying, 33*(2), 91–102.

Yalom, I. D. (1985). *Theory and practice of group psychotherapy* (3rd ed.). New York: Praeger.

HANDOUT 9.1

STAGES OF GRIEF

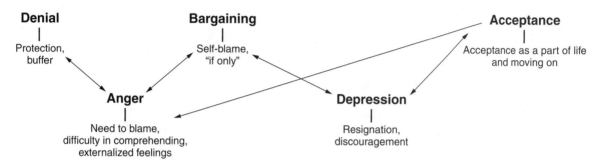

Note: Although there are identifiable stages of the grieving process, there is really no step-by-step progression. As the arrows in the diagram indicate, it is very fluid and may jump back and forth over time. Arriving at acceptance and even maintaining that stage for a while does not guarantee that one of the other reactions will not resurface.

ALCOHOL AND OTHER SUBSTANCE ABUSE: A COMPREHENSIVE APPROACH

CHAPTER

10

J. Kelly Coker, University of Nevada, Las Vegas

INTRODUCTION

A twelve-year-old seventh-grader is caught "huffing" glue on school grounds. A nine-year-old fourth-grader tells his teacher that his mom drinks "all day long." A sixteen-year-old freshman is returning to school after participating in an inpatient treatment program. All of these instances represent some of the alcohol and other drug (AOD) issues faced by school-aged youth. They also represent the types of AOD issues in which school counselors play a prominent role. This chapter discusses the role of the professional school counselor in addressing AOD issues in the school setting.

What are the common issues professional school counselors face regarding substance abuse? Examples include:

- Student's use and abuse of alcohol and other drugs
- Student's exposure to others' use and abuse of alcohol and other drugs
- Significant other's (for example, parent, sibling, other family member, close friend) use and abuse of alcohol and other drugs
- Personal issues faced by the counselor or other staff (for example, own use, family member use, family history of use) surrounding alcohol and other drug abuse
- School personnel's (for example, teachers, principals, other counselors, staff) use and abuse of alcohol and other drugs
- School policies and procedures governing student and faculty use of alcohol and other drugs

It is often difficult to find someone whose life hasn't been impacted in some way by alcohol and other drug use and abuse. An estimated 27.8 million children of alcoholics (COAs) live in the United States. Of those, about 11 million are under the age of eighteen (Center for Substance Abuse Prevention, 2002). As of 1996, it was estimated that 11 percent of the population of children under the age of

284

seventeen had at least one parent in the home dependent on alcohol or other illicit drugs and/or in need of treatment (National Household Survey on Drug Abuse [NHSDA], 1996). However, it is not always illicit drug use or alcoholism that impacts children. According to the same survey 50 percent of the population of children under the age of seventeen had one or more parents use cigarettes in the past month (NHSDA, 1996).

In addition to significant other use, children and adolescents are continuing to use and abuse substances at alarming rates. In one reported survey, almost one third of high school seniors met the accepted criteria of problem or binge drinking, defined as five or more consecutive drinks on at least one occasion in the previous two weeks (Bukstein, 1994). In another report, 27.9 percent of seniors, 21.1 percent of tenth-graders, and 13.4 percent of eighth-graders reported binge drinking behavior (Homonoff et al., 1994). In addition, although illicit drug use is declining, alcohol use among adolescents continues to be a problem and is beginning at increasingly younger ages (Guthrie et al., 1994). Peterson et al. (1994) found that 70 percent of adolescents reported they had used alcohol by the time they were twelve years old. In addition, the use of cigarettes among girls has risen sharply, and the use of marijuana has more than doubled since 1991 (St. Pierre et al., 1997).

These trends are troubling, particularly given the demonstrated links between problem drinking and serious health, social, and behavioral problems in youth. Problem drinking among youth and adolescents has a strong association with teenage pregnancy, delinquency, school misbehavior, aggressiveness, impulsiveness, and dropping out of school (Hawkins, Catalano, & Miller, 1992). In addition, problematic use of alcohol during childhood and adolescence directly increases the risk of accidents, homicides, and sexually transmitted diseases, including AIDS (Peterson et al., 1994).

This chapter provides professional school counselors with practical tools in their role as agents of prevention and intervention regarding AOD issues among youth. Organization of the chapter is as follows: first, recent and relevant literature regarding the history of prevention and effective prevention strategies; second, schoolwide intervention plans, including examination of school policies regarding AOD use and faculty in-service trainings; third, a three-lesson classroom guidance unit on the addictive process and addiction as a family disease for middle or high school students, followed by a six-lesson substance-abuse-prevention group for elementary-aged students; finally, individual counseling strategies focusing primarily on assessment.

LITERATURE REVIEW

The school counseling profession commonly accepts that prevention services are an integral part of comprehensive guidance programming (Gibson & Mitchell, 1999; Muro & Kottman, 1995; Schmidt, 2002). According to McLaughlin and Vacha (1993) the school counselor is uniquely equipped to function as a resource to the school regarding substance-abuse prevention and intervention as well as a liaison between the school, the family, and community institutions and programs. Still debatable in the profession, however, are what specific activities are included in prevention services, how much time is spent on such activities, and what level of direct involvement the school counselor should have in those activities. To help answer these questions, some focus and attention on the history of prevention in the schools as well as the evolution of prevention programs based in research is warranted.

History of Prevention

In the mid 1980s, over a billion dollars of the federal budget was allocated to fight the "war on drugs." Most money was spent, with little success, in attempting to reduce supply through law enforcement strategies. The government also allocated large amounts of funding to target prevention of substance use among youth. There was a strong "no use" message with a focus on learning to "just say no" to drugs.

In 1988, the U.S. Department of Education published a guide to help educators and counselors select appropriate drug prevention curricula. These recommendations were based primarily on the information dissemination model of prevention. The key message in prevention programs of the time was one of "no use/no tolerance," as evidenced in the following statement:

> While curricula can convey these themes in a variety of ways, it is essential that there be no confusion about the basic message: that drug, alcohol, and tobacco use will not be tolerated. The no-use message must be clear, consistent, and positively communicated throughout the materials, the lesson plans, the resources, and actual implementation at every grade level in the K-12 sequence. (U.S. Department of Education, p. 10)

Empirical evidence has not proven the efficacy of the no use/no tolerance program. According to Botvin and Botvin (1992), although the emphasis on information dissemination does increase knowledge, it has not decreased drug use.

Another prevention program that gained considerable momentum in the late 1980s was Drug Abuse Resistance Education (DARE). This program was started in 1983 by Daryl Gates, the former Los Angeles police chief, in response to the call for teaching students how to refuse and resist drug use. At the time of its development, no empirical examination existed for the components of the program or their effects on curbing substance use. The program was targeted primarily at fifth- or sixth-grade students, and curricula focused on information dissemination, refusal skills, decision making, alternatives to drug use, resistance to peer pressure, and self-esteem enhancement. The program gained national attention, and law enforcement agencies received large amounts of funding to implement the program.

During the mid 1990s researchers began investigating the effectiveness of DARE. Most studies showed that at best, short-term effects were positive and included factors such as enhanced self-esteem, better understanding of types of drugs, and an ability to discuss ways to say "no." Long-term outcomes, however, showed little to no effect on decisions to use or not to use. Major conclusions of studies examining DARE demonstrate that any effect the program has in deterring drug use disappears as students enter their senior year of high school (Kreft, 1998; Lynam et al., 1999).

The DARE program does seem to be responding to research regarding its effectiveness. At the time of this writing, DARE is pilot-testing a newly developed program targeted at middle-grade students that expands its current curriculum beyond teaching refusal skills to having students question their own assumptions about drug use (Zernike, 2001). Any preliminary or final results of the pilot-testing have not been published.

Traditional prevention programs such as DARE were designed to reduce substance use among youth by strengthening refusal skills and increasing awareness of the effects of drugs and alcohol. Who are the youth we are trying to reach with these programs? The term *at-risk youth* is common in the nomenclature of the educational environment.

Kids at Risk

What do we mean by the term *at-risk youth*? School counselors and other educators often use this label to identify children at risk for school failure or dropping out of school. Capuzzi and Gross (2000), in their book examining youth at risk, propose a broader view of at-risk youth. They suggest that the term *at-risk* refers to a set of causal/effect (behavioral) dynamics that can potentially place the young person in danger of some negative future event. This perspective moves beyond examining only the problematic behaviors, which might include such things as truancy, teenage pregnancy, and substance abuse, and encompasses an examination of causal factors that led to the development of the effect (behavior). From this perspective, we move from the scrutiny of substance-using behaviors themselves to an examination of risk and protective factors that lead to presence or absence of the substance-using behavior.

Risk and Protective Factors

One way to examine risk and protective factors that either contribute to or guard against substance-use behavior among adolescents is to break the factors down by six life domains. These six domains or combinations of the domains are supported in numerous prevention studies (Coker & Borders, 2001; Hawkins et al., 1992; Kumpfer & Turner, 1991). The six life domains are:

- Individual Risk and Protective Factors
- Society-Related Risk and Protective Factors
- Family Environment Risk and Protective Factors
- Community Environment Risk and Protective Factors
- School-Related Risk and Protective Factors
- Peer Association Risk and Protective Factors

(Department of Health and Human Services, 1996). Effective prevention programs and activities are those that work to enhance potential protective factors while focusing on a decrease of risk factors across the domains. Key risk and protective factors by the six life domains are outlined in Table 10.1.

TABLE 10.1   KEY RISK AND PROTECTIVE FACTORS BY THE SIX DOMAINS

Life Domain	Risk Factors	Protective Factors
Individual	Inadequate life skills, low self-esteem, emotional problems, favorable attitudes toward substance use, school failure, lack of school bonding, early antisocial behavior.	Positive social skills and social responsiveness, positive sense of self, attachment to parents and family, commitment to schools, involvement in positive community and school activities.
Family	Family conflict and violence, lack of cohesion, poor child supervision and discipline, family attitudes favorable to drug use, ambiguous or inconsistent rules, social isolation of family.	Positive bonding among family members, parenting that includes warmth, trust, and clear and consistent expectations, strong emotional support, parent involvement in school activities.
Peer	Association with peers who use or value substances, susceptibility to negative peer pressure, association with peers who reject mainstream activities, strong external locus of control.	Association with peers who value and are involved in school, recreation, religion, service, or other organized activities.
School	Lack of school bonding, lack of involvement in school-related activities, ambiguous or inconsistent rules regarding drug use and student conduct, harsh or arbitrary student management practices.	High expectations from school personnel, clear standards and rules for behavior, caring and supportive sense of community in school, youth participation, involvement, and responsibility in school tasks and decisions.
Community	Community disorganization, lack of cultural pride, lack of community bonding, attitudes favorable to drug use, availability of substances, inadequate youth services and opportunities for prosocial involvement.	Caring and supportive community members, high expectations of youth, opportunities for youth participation in community activities.
Society	Impoverishment, unemployment and underemployment, discriminations, pro-drug-use messages in the media.	Media literacy, decreased accessibility to substances, increased pricing through taxation, raised purchasing age and enforcement, stricter driving-while-under-the-influence laws.

Source: Adapted from *Here's Proof Prevention Works,* Department of Health and Human Services, 1999.

Two landmark studies have paved the way for a new view of effective prevention. In 1991, Kumpfer and Turner recognized that few theoretical models of substance use focus on the larger social environment in which use occurs. They suggested that the importance of the social environment could not be ignored in drug-abuse prevention. Kumpfer and Turner created the social ecology model that hypothesized that family and school climate affect a youth's self-esteem, which in turn predicts whether youth will develop bonds to school and peers, which will impact levels of drug use. With a sample of about 1,400 students, the researchers surveyed male and female adolescents on their perceptions of dimensions such as school climate, positive peer associations, self-report measures of lifetime use, and self-esteem. They also reported family climate as measured by family cooperation, liking of each parent, and mother and father's occupation/education level. Results indicated that the primary direct predictor of illegal alcohol and drug use is association with antisocial peers and involvement in antisocial acts. They also found that students with poor family or school climate do not appear to develop a positive sense of self or bond to their school, which can lead to association with antisocial peers.

In 1992, Hawkins, Catalano, and Miller conducted a groundbreaking study in the addiction/prevention field that is often used as a basis for developing prevention programs in schools. Hawkins et al. examined both risk and protective factors that could impact adolescents' decisions to use drugs and alcohol. They identified two categories of risk factors: broad societal/cultural (for example, media, laws, cultural expectations for use) and individual/interpersonal environments (for example, families, schools, classrooms, and peer groups). They suggested that recent prevention efforts had addressed only two risk factors: laws and norms, and social influences to use drugs. Social-influence resistance strategies had been used in many prevention programs of the time, but research indicates that these strategies have been markedly effective only when approached through peer-led training, as opposed to teacher- or other adult-led methods. On the other hand, prevention programs focusing on individual/interpersonal environments may have a greater chance of success.

Hawkins et al. (1992) concluded that prevention programs targeting early risk factors might hold the most promise for effective prevention. Early childhood education, programs for parents on family management, effective communication and discipline, and parenting skills have all shown correlations with reduced levels of substance use among youth. Studies have also shown that parental involvement is beneficial in increasing academic effort, grades, and attendance among students at risk for dropping out. Other factors such as bonding to school and involvement in alternative activities can guard against substance-use behavior (Hawkins et al.).

The two studies mentioned above, while broadening the base of potential causal factors, still took a "risk identification" approach to prevention. Other studies have examined the factors that are protective in nature and guard against substance-using behavior. Foundational in this focus on prevention was the longitudinal study conducted by Werner (1989) that examined youth responses to risk factors at different developmental stages. By examining a cohort of participants across a forty-year span, she concluded that more often than not, individuals in stressful, risky, or unhealthy situations have a human capacity for self-righting and will seek out and latch on to any positive, protective factors to help them do so. This tendency towards "self-righting," which became known as resiliency, has become a foundation for many research studies and prevention efforts in the past decade. Werner and her colleagues concluded that these protective factors exist within the individual, the family, and the community. From this perspective, the notion that "it's too late for him" or "she's too old" does not apply. To view all

children, particularly troubled or difficult children, as either resilient or potentially resilient can be difficult. It requires a true paradigm shift for both people and
institutions.

According to the Education Trust Transforming School Counseling Initiative (TSCI), the new vision of the professional school counselor includes
the roles of advocate and systems change agent. Consistent with this notion,
some prevention programs that adopt a resiliency perspective are focused on
changing the entire school community to develop a focus on fostering resilience
in all children. From this perspective, prevention efforts must extend beyond
the individual and include a focus on family, community, school environment,
and peer relationships. In the early 1990s prevention programs shifted focus.
For example, recommendations to build on resiliency and to create collaboration and communication among key players began. To this end, identification
of effective prevention programs that address identified risk and protective
factors is key.

Effective Prevention

Best practice for school counselors in choosing prevention activities is to utilize
prevention programs that have undergone empirical testing/validation and
have been shown to effectively enhance protective factors or decrease risk
factors within the six life domains (see Table 10.1). The Center for Substance
Abuse Prevention (CSAP) summarized eight prevention programs with validated, positive outcomes. While the discussion of each of these programs (and
others like them) is beyond the scope of this chapter, I will include a summary
of one of the school-based programs identified by CSAP as a model prevention
program (see Table 10.2). For more information on the recommended model
programs, visit the Center for Substance Abuse Prevention Web site at
www.samhsa.gov/csap/.

Future of Prevention

The new vision of substance-abuse prevention as a collaborative, systemic, and
long-term process suggests that the days of conducting one or two days of classroom guidance around prevention issues does not equate to "effective prevention."
According to Keys and Bemak (1997) classroom-based social competence programs have some short-term success but often fail to produce long-term results.
The authors go on to state that successful prevention efforts "need to be comprehensive, multifaceted, and integrated" (p. 25). This new vision dovetails nicely with
the Education Trust TSCI vision of school counselor as advocate, collaborator, and
team-builder. The school counselor can play an instrumental role in bringing about
systemic change that extends beyond individual, group, or even classroom interventions. In the next section, schoolwide prevention and intervention plans will be
explored.

TABLE 10.2 ACROSS AGES: A MODEL PREVENTION PROGRAM RECOMMENDED BY CSAP

Program Description	Risk Factors of Students	Protective Factors Enhanced	Outcomes and Evaluation
• School-based initiative • Target population: 6th grade • Four components include: 1. Elders mentoring youth 2. Youth performing community service 3. Classroom-based life skills curriculum 4. Activities for parents and family members • Mentors 55+ years were carefully recruited and trained • Students met with mentors in nursing homes and also provided community services to other elders in the home • The Positive Youth Development Curriculum was implemented in the classroom • Weekend events were held monthly involving youth, family members, and mentors	**Individual domain** • Already using alcohol or other drugs • Conduct problems • Economically disadvantaged **Family domain** • Child of a single parent • Child of a substance abuser **School domain** • Poor school performance • High absenteeism	**Individual domain** • Promotion of social competence **Family domain** • Enhanced communication with parents • Presence of a significant adult **Peer domain** • Responsible behavior modeled by peer group **School domain** • Increased motivation to succeed in school **Community domain** • Engagement of youth in positive activities outside school • Youth given useful and positively perceived role in the community	Based on a randomized pretest/posttest design with approximately 180 students participating over a 5-year period, the following outcomes were found: • Mentored youth (MPS) and youth in the limited treatment group (PS) had fewer days absent from school • MPS youth demonstrated improvement in their attitudes toward the future, school, and elders • MPS youth demonstrated large gains in their knowledge and perceived ability to respond appropriately to situations involving drug use • MPS youth gained more than PS and control youth in knowledge of community issues • MPS youth with involved mentors experienced gains in knowledge about the potential risks and consequences of substance use, increases in ability to respond appropriately to situation involving drug abuse, and reductions in days absent from school

Source: Adapted from *Here's Proof Prevention Works*, Department of Health and Human Services, 1999.

WHOLE-SCHOOL INTERVENTIONS

Given the support in the literature for schoolwide, systemic approaches to substance-abuse prevention (Keys & Bemak, 1997), it can be helpful for school counselors to examine the school's overall approach to substance-use issues. By assessing the school culture in terms of policies, discipline action taken, attitudes toward substance use, and identified needs of students, the school counselor can more accurately target interventions that serve the school as a whole.

Consider the following example: A high school in a small, rural school district has a policy that focuses on suspension and expulsion for infractions of the substance-use policy. Infractions include possession, intoxication, or suspicion of use. An investigation by the school counselor discovers that the same students are getting suspended and expelled again and again. From a proactive, systemic stand-point, the school counselor presents the findings of the investigation to school administrators, along with a suggestion to revisit the policy to include some opportunities for aid to students with substance-use issues. With the help of a local outpatient setting for teenagers, the policy is rewritten to include the option of attending a school-based drug intervention group for a first offense instead of suspension, and undergoing a mandatory substance-abuse assessment conducted by the outside agency for a second offense. These changes result in fewer infractions and more students being referred for treatment by the school. This represents one example of how a school counselor can impact the system to make changes regarding policy issues around substance abuse.

Another action that can lead to system-wide awareness regarding substance abuse is to find opportunities to inform the faculty as a whole of pertinent substance-abuse issues in the school. By offering a series of faculty in-service trainings on relevant substance-use information, the school counselor can impact change on multiple levels. First, faculty are more informed regarding issues such as profiles of users, "what to look for" characteristics of use, statistics of use in the school community, and ways to make appropriate referrals.

A frequent suggestion is that in addition to impacting systemic change by using available data, examining policies and procedures, and providing in-service trainings, school counselors think outside the "school only" focus. Prevention efforts that are targeted at families, communities, and students represent a more multidimensional focus and are more likely to show success (Keys & Bemak, 1997). Of course a school counselor does not impact this systemic, broad-based change alone. One way for school counselors to engage in program planning within a school-family-community context is to set up an advisory committee composed of school, family, and community representatives. This committee can provide information about student needs, information about existing resources, and brainstorming of appropriate interventions and programs for students.

Another system-change strategy outlined by Keys and Bemak (1997) is for school counselors to adopt both leadership and collaborative consultant roles. As leaders, school counselors can advocate for substance-use-focused counseling groups, guidance lessons, in-service trainings, identified referral sources, and changes in policies and procedures and for a system-wide focus on the importance of being preventative (proactive) versus reactionary (reactive). As a collaborative consultant, the school counselor forms partnerships with teachers, parents, and community members—not as the sole expert, but as an equal partner. This process allows for an examination of individual and system-level changes and encourages mutual goal setting, problem solving, decision making, planning for change, and evaluating results.

The school counselor as system-wide change agent regarding substance-use issues might be a new idea to some. Traditionally, school counselors have maintained more of a responsive role to substance-use issues, with the occasional substance-use-specific guidance lesson conducted in targeted classrooms. Working in a broader framework with other stakeholders will serve to better meet the needs of the student population while also relieving the school counselor of some of the duties they originally tackled alone.

This being said, the duties of classroom guidance and group counseling should not be minimized. The classroom is still a primary mode of reaching students and an important part of guidance programming. In addition, group counseling and the group interactive process have been shown to have significant curative results for students (O'Rourke & Worzbyt, 1996). Because of this, both a guidance unit and a group counseling unit that could be implemented by school counselors to address both substance-abuse prevention and intervention issues in schools will be presented. It is important to keep in mind that substance-use-focused school counseling programs work best when they are one part of an overall prevention program. Classroom guidance alone may not successfully deter substance use among students (Keys & Bemak, 1997).

CLASSROOM GUIDANCE ACTIVITIES

The following unit is designed to orient middle school and/or high school students to the addictive process and the impact of addiction on a family. School counselors could conduct the following unit in classes where concerns have been raised by teachers, principals, or parents about either student substance abuse or the impact of a family member's use. The material presented in the classroom guidance unit allows for a comprehensive examination of the impact of substance abuse on a family. Given the strong possibility that members of the participating classroom may have personal experiences with substance abuse in their own families, the counselor must exercise caution in the delivery of these activities and in follow-up activities.

LESSON 1: WHAT IS ADDICTION?

Personal/Social Development Standard C: Students will understand safety and survival skills.

Competency: Students will learn about the emotional and physical dangers of substance use and abuse.

Learning Objectives

- Students will be able to identify potential drugs of abuse.
- Students will understand the addictive process and the difference between use, abuse, and addiction.
- Students will begin thinking about addiction as a family disease.

Materials: Large paper and markers, or blackboard.

Developmental Learning Activity

Introduction: The counselor begins by discussing the fact that the information to be discussed over the next three lessons will focus around types of drugs, the process of addiction, and how addiction affects or impacts a family. The counselor shares with the participants that sometimes students will find they feel that some of the issues the group discusses are ones they are dealing with themselves. For this reason, the counselor encourages the students to share personal stories/issues/concerns with the counselor after the class. The counselor also reinforces the need to be respectful and keep information shared confidential, and says that everyone has a right to pass if they feel uncomfortable for any reason.

Activity: The counselor poses the question to the class: "When I say the word 'drug,' what kinds of substances do you think about?" The counselor writes a list on the blackboard based on student suggestions of all the substances that can be considered drugs. Examples of substances that are drugs are marijuana, alcohol, tobacco, cocaine, LSD, heroin, caffeine, inhalants, aspirin, cough syrup, painkillers, and designer "club" drugs.

The counselor writes the following definition on the board: "A drug is a substance, not primarily used as food, that when taken into the body will change the way a person's mind or body functions." The counselor asks for class reactions to the definition. Using caffeine as an example, ask the class how the use of this drug will change the way a person's mind or body functions (for example, heart beats faster; peps you up; wakes you up; makes you more alert; too much can make you feel nervous, shaky, irritable).

The counselor explains to the class that different drugs affect the body in different ways. Some drugs are designed to help us when we are sick by fighting diseases and relieving pain. Some drugs (cocaine, tobacco, caffeine, and the like) make the systems in our body speed up, and other drugs (alcohol, painkillers, and the like) make the systems in our body slow way down. It is important to say that all drugs, even those designed to help us, can be very dangerous.

The counselor asks, "Why do people take drugs?" The group discusses student responses. Reasons could include: because they are sick and need medicine; because they are curious about what the drugs will do to them; because they are lonely, scared, upset, and think the drug will make them feel better; because their friends tell them to; because their bodies are addicted and they feel like they need the drug.

The counselor next asks, "Which drug or drugs do you think people are most likely to become addicted to?" The group discusses student responses. The counselor shares the following facts:

- Alcohol is the most commonly used illicit substance among youths aged twelve to twenty. In 2001, 28.5 percent of people ages twelve to twenty reported using alcohol in the last month. Nearly one in five adolescents engaged in binge drinking (having five or more drinks in a row at one time) in the last month (National Household Survey on Drug Abuse, 2003).
- An estimated 27.8 million children of alcoholics (COAs) live in the United States. Of those, about 11 million are under the age of eighteen (Center for Substance Abuse Prevention, 2002).
- As of 1996, it was estimated that 11 percent of the population of children under the age of seventeen had at least one parent in the home dependent on alcohol or other illicit drugs and/or in need of treatment (National Household Survey on Drug Abuse, 1996).
- According to the same survey (NHSDA, 1996), 50 percent of the population of children under the age of seventeen had one or more parents use cigarettes in the past month.

In summary, alcohol and tobacco remain the most widely used and abused substances in the U.S. today, although use of marijuana, inhalants, and "designer drugs" such as Ecstasy is on the rise.

The counselor shares with the class that it is widely accepted in the addictions field that not everyone who uses drugs or alcohol becomes addicted, but that young people are more likely to move from use to abuse to addiction in a shorter span of time than are adults. According to the disease model of addiction, the path of addiction can be represented by a continuum of stages starting with recreational use and leading to compulsive use and possibly death (see Overhead 10.1). The counselor asks, "As you look at the stages of the disease, what kinds of losses or consequences might someone experience along each stage? Also pay attention to where you might fall along this continuum with any substance use."

- In the **recreational stage,** use usually occurs in a social setting among friends who are also using. Use tends to be limited to infrequent social situations and involves small to moderate amounts of the chemical being used. Even at this stage, however, there could be consequences. What might some of them be? (Possible answers: getting sick; getting in trouble for use; making unwise decisions under the influence.)
- In the **circumstantial stage,** use is motivated by a desire to obtain a specific effect in a specific situation (use is more of a planned activity). For example, someone's drinking wine at the end of a long day to help unwind; a truck driver's taking amphetamines to stay awake for driving. What might be some consequences you might see at this stage? (Possible answers: blackouts; DUI; passing out; vomiting.)
- In the **intensified use stage,** psychoactive chemicals are taken daily or almost daily, usually in low to moderate doses. Use is motivated by a need to achieve relief from a persistent problem (anxiety or depression) or

to maintain a desired level of performance. Consequences here might include what? (Possible answers: more DUI; functioning impaired for work, school, home; blackouts; using more to feel normal; increased tolerance; experiencing some withdrawal symptoms.)

- The **compulsive stage** is the most dangerous. Use is characterized by daily or almost daily use of high doses of the chemical. Use of the chemical becomes the most important thing in the user's life, around which all other activities are organized, usually to the user's detriment. What might be consequences suffered here? (Possible answers: loss of job; loss of family; expulsion from school; lack of social support; isolated use to feel normal; serious physical and psychological symptoms.)

- According to the disease model, once users pass into compulsive use, they have reached the point of no return, and will not be successful in returning to recreational use.

Conclusion: The counselor reviews the model and asks students to get into groups and generate questions or concerns they may have as a result of learning about this model.

Assessment: The group discusses the questions/concerns that students generate.

Follow-up: The counselor tells the class that the next lesson will involve looking at what happens when someone in a family abuses or becomes addicted to alcohol or other drugs.

Depending on time available, the following lesson could be broken into two separate lessons.

LESSON 2/3: ADDICTION AS A FAMILY DISEASE

Personal/Social Development Standard C: Students will understand safety and survival skills.

Competency: Students will learn about the emotional and physical dangers of substance use and abuse in the family.

Learning Objectives

- Students will understand the concept of addiction as a family disease.
- Students will understand the roles of an addicted family including chief enabler, hero, scapegoat, mascot, and lost child.
- Through two activities, students will experience the different roles in an addicted family.

Materials: Large paper and markers or blackboard, Family Role signs, masking tape. (In preparation for the activity, create six signs with the following words: "Drug," "Chief Enabler," "Hero," "Scapegoat," "Mascot," "Lost Child.")

Developmental Learning Activity

Introduction: The counselor begins by reinforcing the need to be respectful and reminding the group that everyone has a right to pass if they feel uncomfortable for any reason. The counselor also reminds students that they should discuss any personal concerns generated by the lesson with the counselor after class.

The counselor begins by defining key terms in an alcoholic family (Wegsheider, 1981):

> *Addict/alcoholic*—People who are physically and/or psychologically dependent on alcohol or other drugs. In other words: Alcoholics feel like they need alcohol in their bodies most of the time just to feel normal.
>
> *Enabling/Chief Enabler*—The tendency to help chemically affected persons maintain their patterns of abuse by blocking opportunities for them to experience consequences of their actions. In other words: People in a family may lie, cheat, cover-up, or fix problems for the alcoholic person (mediating, lying, self-sacrifice, blaming others, and so on.). The chief enabler is often a spouse or oldest child.
>
> *Hero*—The Hero in a chemically affected family is usually a very high achiever, does well in school, sports, and other activities. The purpose of the Hero in the family is to take the focus off of the addict by giving the family something to be proud of. The Hero is often an oldest child.
>
> *Scapegoat*—The Scapegoat in a chemically affected family often acts out, gets in trouble at home and school, might have legal problems or substance abuse problems as well. The purpose of the Scapegoat in the family is to take the focus off of the addict by being in trouble all of the time. The Scapegoat is often a middle child.
>
> *Mascot*—The Mascot in a chemically affected family is funny, seeks attention through humor, is often the "class clown" in school. The purpose of the Mascot is to take the focus off of the addict by being funny and providing comic relief in the family. The Mascot is often a middle or youngest child.
>
> *Lost Child*—The Lost Child in a chemically affected family is usually withdrawn and a loner. The Lost Child doesn't get in trouble at home or school, but also doesn't speak up when he/she needs help. The purpose of the Lost Child is to provide relief because they are one less thing the family has to worry about.
>
> *Recovery*—When the addicted person and the family members recognize the problem and decide to stop. This usually requires the help of counselors, therapists, or psychologists. Recovery can take a very long time.

Activity 1: The Family Sculpture: The counselor explains to the class that one way to see how the different roles play out in a chemically affected family is to create a sculpture of the family and to see how each person is affected by and copes with the addict's use. The counselor asks for six volunteers from the class to help sculpt the "Tip family." The counselor explains that in this family there is a father who is addicted to alcohol, a mother, and four children.

The volunteer who plays the "father" stands in the front of the class with the sign "DRUG" held up in front of his face. This represents that since he is addicted, the father is primarily focused on using alcohol and nothing else. The counselor asks the class to discuss some of the possible consequences of this addiction (loss of job, loss of family, and so on).

The volunteer who plays the "mother" holds the sign "Chief Enabler." The counselor asks the class what the mother might be doing to enable the father's drinking (calling in to work for him to tell his boss he's sick, buying him alcohol, and so on). The counselor asks the class where the "Chief Enabler" might be standing in relationship to the father in the sculpture. (Most likely very close and probably facing him; as his focus is on his drug, her focus is on keeping him out of trouble.)

The volunteers who play the other family roles (Hero, Scapegoat, Mascot, and Lost Child) are then placed in the sculpture. For each placement, the counselor has the class share what activities each child might be involved in from their role in the family and how they might be placed in the sculpture. Physical distance, levels of power represented by standing, sitting, and the like can all convey the experiences of the members of the family.

The counselor asks the volunteers to hold their poses in the sculpture and asks the class to comment on what they see. Processing questions could include:

- "Which child seems most affected by the addiction? How can you tell?"
- "How aware is the father of what is going on with his family?"
- "How aware is the mother of what is going on with her family?"
- "Do any of the children seem to be following in either their mother's or father's footsteps? How can you tell?"

Finally, the counselor asks the class how the picture might change if the father entered into recovery and worked on trying to stop drinking. The counselor resculpts the picture based on the comments of the students.

The counselor explains that just as addiction affects every member of the family, so does recovery. Recovery can be scary because everyone in the family has to reexamine their roles and make changes, too.

The counselor reminds students that if they or someone they know is affected by someone else's substance use, it is not their fault, but it is okay to talk about it with a trusted adult such as a teacher or counselor. Often children in these situations feel they are alone, and they are surprised to find out how many other people experience the same kinds of things.

Activity 2: The Balancing Act: This might be done instead of or in addition to the previous activity. It could be conducted on the same day or a different day.

The counselor makes a large rectangle on the floor with the tape. The counselor invites one person to volunteer to be the addicted member of the family. The counselor and the volunteer can decide if the volunteer will be a mother, father, sister, brother, grandparent, or other member. It doesn't really matter since any one of those people could be an addict.

The counselor tells the addicted person they are standing on a raft in shark-infested waters. The counselor asks the chemically addicted person to stand in the middle of the raft and tells them the raft is very unstable, and it wouldn't take much for it to become unbalanced and knock them into the water.

Now the counselor asks someone to come up and play the chief enabler. The counselor explains that this is the person in the family who is working the hardest to cover up for the addict's behavior. Again, it could be a mother, father, sister, brother, grandparent, or other family member.

The chief enabler and the addict stand in opposite corners of the raft. The counselor explains to the chief enabler that it is his or her job to keep the raft in balance. (It's good to set some ground rules here, that no one can knock another person off the raft or physically touch or grab the addict.)

The addicted person starts moving from corner to corner of the raft while the chief enabler attempts to keep the raft in balance. The counselor explains through this process that the addict is primarily concerned with himself or herself and getting the next drink/drug, and doesn't really care if the raft is balanced or not.

The chief enabler, meanwhile, is calling work to say the addicted person won't be in, cleaning up vomit, keeping the kids away so they don't get in trouble, reorganizing their own work schedule to take care of the addict, finishing the homework assignment, and generally lying to everyone outside the family.

After a while, the chief enabler gets tired, and finds they need help in keeping the raft in balance. The counselor invites another volunteer to represent another family member (parent, son, daughter, brother, sister, or other).

The chief enabler and the other family member must stay together while keeping the raft in balance. Again, the user isn't concerned with their efforts, but they must work harder than ever. The counselor explains some of the things the other family member might be doing to help (skipping football practice to take care of the addicted person, getting in trouble more themselves to take the focus off the addicted person, and so on).

The counselor talks about the balance of power. It now takes two people to balance out the user's behavior.

The counselor keeps adding members to the raft, up to four. The addict speeds up to make keeping up harder and harder. The counselor looks for evidence of the raft "tipping."

The counselor talks about how eventually it becomes almost impossible to keep covering up for the user. The counselor suggests that the family members have a discussion about what they want to do. They can do anything that doesn't involve grabbing or pushing or touching the addict without permission from him/her.

The counselor asks them to implement their strategy. Some strategies might include: All family members "abandon ship" and take their chances with the sharks (representing not getting help, but abandoning the addict for possibly more and bigger problems); all family members go to the middle of the raft and invite the addicted person to either join them or fall in (representing getting help even if the addicted person won't); all family members join hands and try to form a ring around the addict in the center of a raft (representing an intervention or attempting to help the addict while also helping themselves); some family members seek help (go to the middle), some leave the family (jump off the raft), and some continue enabling (keeping the raft in balance). Some families might invite someone else onto the raft to help them with the problem (counselor, preacher, friend, other family member, and so on.) This is typical in families where there is little agreement for what needs to happen.

Conclusion: The counselor processes the experience by discussing how the activity might really reflect the dynamics of addiction as a family disease. It is important to reinforce that when a family member is addicted, it is not the other members' fault. Instead, the other family members can recognize that they ARE NOT responsible and can choose to stop enabling or can seek help themselves even if the addicted person won't.

Assessment: At the end of the activities the counselor discusses the main points, looking for understanding among the class.

Follow-up: The counselor takes time at the end of the unit for processing of strong feelings or emotions that students may feel and reminds the students they can come talk about any personal issues that have arisen as a result of the classroom guidance unit.

SMALL-GROUP COUNSELING PLANS

The following group guidance unit, "Four-Fold Prevention," is grounded in research regarding risk and protective factors (Coker & Borders, 2001; Hawkins et al., 1992; Kumpfer & Turner, 1991), and is designed to enhance environmental factors that have been shown to guard against problem drinking and substance-using behavior. It was designed and pilot-tested by the author with fourth-grade students in a small-group environment with positive results (Coker, 2001). Both observational and quantitative data were gathered during the pilot study. Both sets of data supported the efficacy of the program. For the qualitative analysis, ongoing observational data were gathered after each group meeting with participants. Participants were also interviewed after the program for their reactions to the experience, and their responses and writings in the student journal were examined for relevant information.

Quantitative data were gathered by comparing scores on a pretest/posttest instrument made up of items from the National Education Longitudinal Study. Questions on the instrument assessed perceptions of parental support, parental control, school climate, opportunities for involvement in community-based activities, and exposure to drug and alcohol use among students (U. S. Department of Education, 1996).

Examples of quantitative results include the following. In reference to the feature of the four-fold program involving community-based activities, the participant group reported an increase from 9 percent to 22 percent for involvement in team sports between pretest and posttest. For the control group, the corresponding percentages actually decreased over the six-week period of this program from 63 percent to 14 percent.

For the feature regarding relationships with parents, the percentage of students in the participant group who indicated they had talked to their parents about school-related activities increased from 18 percent to 33 percent, and the percentage of students who indicated they counted on their parents to help them solve problems rose from 18 percent to 55 percent. In contrast, the percentage of students in the control group who indicated they had talked to their parents about school-related activities increased only from 13 percent to 14 percent, and the percentage of students who indicated they counted on their parents to solve problems actually dropped from 63 percent to 57 percent. For other results concerning the efficacy of this program, please see Coker (2001).

Although tested in a small-group environment, the program could also be successfully utilized with students from fourth through sixth grades in either a small-group or a classroom environment. The entire student workbook is available as Handout 10.4. In order to test the efficacy of the program, the counselor may wish to use an instrument to determine changes in student perceptions of parental involvement, school climate, community involvement, and relationships with peers. The instrument used by the author in the pilot study can be used as a pretest/posttest instrument to assess the impact of the group on the participants (see Handout 10.3).

GROUP SESSION 1: FOUR-FOLD PREVENTION: UNDERSTANDING DRUGS AND IDENTIFYING SUPPORT

Personal/Social Development Standard C: Students will understand safety and survival skills.

Competency: Students will learn about the emotional and physical dangers of substance use and abuse.

Learning Objectives

- Students will gain an understanding of the definition of "drug" and successfully identify substances that can be defined as "drugs."
- Students will identify team members for participation in the program.

Materials: Blackboard; Handout 10.1, Information for Student Support Team Members (3 copies per student); Handout 10.4, Student Journal.

Activities

Introduction: The counselor gives an overview of the six-session group. The group brainstorms substances considered "drugs."

Counseling Activity: The counselor defines "drugs" and their effects ("A drug is a substance, other than food, that when taken into the body will change the way a person's mind or body functions."). Then the counselor leads a discussion with the participants on why people take drugs.

The counselor asks the students about the different attitudes that exist about drugs.

The counselor discusses "social support" and what it means. The counselor asks participants to identify members of their social support team by completing sections 1 and 2 of Student Journal (Handout 10.4).

Conclusion: The counselor reviews information on drugs. The counselor asks students to share within the group whom they plan on asking to be on their support team.

Follow-up: Students ask chosen members to serve on their support team and give team members the description of the program (Handout 10.1). Students complete section 3 in Student Journal for next time.

GROUP SESSION 2: FOUR-FOLD PREVENTION: STUDENT-FRIENDLY SCHOOLS

Personal/Social Development Standard C: Students will understand safety and survival skills.

Competency: Students will learn about the emotional and physical dangers of substance use and abuse.

Learning Objective: Students will gain an understanding of the definition of a "student-friendly school."

Materials: Blackboard, Student Journal (Handout 10.4), paper/pencils.

Activities

Introduction: The counselor asks students to reflect on the process of what it was like to ask people to be part of their support teams. What kind of responses did they get? They then share with the other group members who they selected to be the members of their social support teams.

Counseling Activity: The counselor generates discussion regarding the positive qualities of team members. Then the counselor asks students to go to section 4 of their journals. Together, the group brainstorms ideas for what makes a school "student-friendly" and generates a list of the characteristics of a student-friendly school. In journal section 4, students add to the list the names of people who work at school who help to make it student-friendly.

Conclusion: The counselor helps students to summarize the two sessions thus far. The counselor tells students they'll be interviewing the school team members about their attitudes about drugs and alcohol. The counselor helps them get ready for their interview.

Follow-up: Between sessions, students interview school team member using sections 5–7 in their journals. This will assist students to get a better sense of how to make their school more student-friendly.

GROUP SESSION 3: FOUR-FOLD PREVENTION: SCHOOLS AND HOME

Personal/Social Development Standard C: Students will understand safety and survival skills.

Competency: Students will learn about the emotional and physical dangers of substance use and abuse.

Learning Objectives
- Students will generate letters to the principal outlining suggestions for a student-friendly school.
- Students will gain an understanding of the importance of communicating with parents about drugs and alcohol.

Materials: Blackboard, Student Journal (Handout 10.4), copies of Student Journal section 8.

Activities

Introduction: The counselor discusses the experience of working with their school team member. Students share what they learned from their school team members about student-friendly schools. The counselor lists these on the board.

Counseling Activity: Students break into smaller groups. Using the list generated from the group members, each group selects three ideas to make their school more student-friendly. Each group puts the suggestions in a letter to the principal.

    The counselor engages participants in a discussion about communicating with their parents. The counselor asks, "How many of you have ever talked with an adult family member about drugs?" The counselor leads a discussion highlighting the importance of talking about drugs and alcohol with parents.

Conclusion: The counselor summarizes the group's work today. The counselor tells the group that before the next group, they will be interviewing a family member about family drug use policy.

Follow-up: Using journal sections 9–11, group participants conduct family member interview with their family team member.

GROUP SESSION 4: FOUR-FOLD PREVENTION: COMMUNITY

Personal/Social Development Standard C: Students will understand safety and survival skills.

Competency: Students will learn about the emotional and physical dangers of substance use and abuse.

Learning Objectives

- Students will identify safe, fun community activities.
- Students will identify opportunities in their communities for involvement in "safe fun" activities.
- Students will identify people in their communities who can be of help.

Materials: Vignettes of safe and unsafe activities (Handout 10.2), blackboard, Student Journals (Handout 10.4).

Activities

Introduction: The counselor discusses the interviews the group members did with a family member (journal section 9). The counselor asks volunteers to share their family's alcohol and other drugs (AOD) policy (journal section 11).

Counseling Activity: The counselor asks students to get into smaller groups. Each group receives a vignette to rehearse and act out (Handout 10.2).

Next the groups do the scenes for the larger group. After each vignette, the larger group determines if the activity was "safe" or "unsafe."

The full group generates a list of safe and fun activities they can be part of in their communities.

The group brainstorms opportunities for community involvement and discusses leaders in their community.

Conclusion: Students complete section 12 of the Student Journal.

Follow-up: The counselor helps students decide whom in the community they would like to interview about drugs, alcohol, and kids. Before the next meeting, participants use journal sections 13 and 14 to guide their interviews.

GROUP SESSION 5: FOUR-FOLD PREVENTION: FRIENDS

Personal/Social Development Standard C: Students will understand safety and survival skills.

Competency: Students will learn about the emotional and physical dangers of substance use and abuse.

Learning Objectives
- Students will discuss attitudes about drugs with a partner in the group.
- Students will work on final project with a small group.

Materials: Blackboard, reference materials, poster board, markers and pencils, extra paper, Student Journal (Handout 10.4).

Activities

Introduction: The counselor asks group members to share the community activities with the class (journal, section 14).

Counseling Activity: The counselor has students work with a partner; each conducts the "friend interview" in section 15 of the Student Journal. The counselor processes these interviews in the larger group.

Students break into smaller groups. As a group, they will prepare a presentation. They need to decide whether their presentation will be a skit, a poster, or a lecture on some aspect of drugs or alcohol. They complete section 16 of their journals.

The counselor provides information fact sheets and creative materials to the groups. They spend the remainder of the time preparing their presentations.

Conclusion: The group cleans up materials. The counselor tells students that they'll be making their presentations next time.

Follow-up: The counselor asks participants to invite their team members to presentations for next week.

GROUP SESSION 6: FOUR-FOLD PREVENTION: BRINGING IT ALL TOGETHER

Personal/Social Development Standard C: Students will understand safety and survival skills.

Competency: Students will learn about the emotional and physical dangers of substance use and abuse.

Learning Objectives

- Students will work cooperatively to convey important information about drugs and alcohol.
- Students will synthesize experiences during the "Four-Fold Prevention" project.

Materials: Student Journal (Handout 10.4), projects, posters.

Activities

Introduction: The counselor asks students to introduce any team members who are attending the presentations to the class.

Counseling Activity: Small groups present their final projects to the group and to invited team members.

Conclusion: The counselor thanks students for participating in the program and asks them to fill out section 17 of the Student Journal. The counselor reminds students that they will be completing a posttest instrument the following week.

Follow-up: Students take posttest instrument the following week; the counselor compares to pretest results (Handout 10.3).

INDIVIDUAL COUNSELING CONSIDERATIONS

The school counselor might be involved in numerous counseling-related tasks regarding substance use issues. These might include counseling with children and adolescents who feel the impact of someone else's substance abuse, students who self-refer for their own use, and students who are referred by someone else because there are concerns about possible substance use/abuse. In the first two situations, counselors will usually rely on known counseling strategies and skills such as normalizing the student's situation, giving the student an avenue to discuss their concerns, building a caring and trusting relationship with the student, and making recommendations or referrals on a case-by-case basis. Whether students are self- or other-referred for counseling regarding their own substance use, it is helpful to conduct a comprehensive substance-abuse assessment to determine the level of the concern and to make appropriate recommendations or referrals. The following assessment interview is based on the bio-psycho-social model of substance abuse, which suggests that it is the interactions of biological, psychological, cognitive, social, developmental, and environmental variables that help to explain addictive behavior (Fisher & Harrison, 2000).

Beginning the Interview

Be sure to begin with adequate joining skills. You want to set up a nonthreatening and nonjudgmental environment. This example refers to alcohol use; substitute other substance-use concerns as appropriate.

(If referred due to evidence of use)

- "Tell me what happened in your own words."
- "Can you tell me what happened today before school?"
- "What brings you here?"
- "My purpose today is to ask some specific questions about your use, so you and I can come up with some strategies to keep (this event) from happening again."

(If referred due to suspicion of use)

- "The reason you are here today is because someone who cares about you is worried about your drinking."
- "My purpose today is to ask some specific questions about your use, so you and I can determine if there's any cause for concern. The more honest you are with me, the more I'm able to make a realistic determination."

(With resistance)

- "Let's not focus on you right now. I want you to just think about drinking in general. What do you see as some of the pros, or benefits, to drinking? What are some of the cons, or drawbacks, to drinking?" (Write out and discuss.)
- "I'd like you to graph how you think you've performed both socially and academically throughout school." (Excellent, Very Good, Good, Fair, Poor)
- Discuss "peaks" and "valleys," have the student describe what was going on.

Substance-Use History

- "Tell me about your drinking."
- "How often do you use alcohol?"
- "Besides alcohol, what other drugs have you tried?"
- "When you drink (or drink and use, if indicated) is it usually with friends, family, or alone?"
- "When you drink (or drink and use, if indicated) how much do you use?"
- "Do you remember the first time you used alcohol? Tell me what happened." Then, "How would you compare your use then with your use now?"
- "I'd like you to take a minute to map your substance-use history. Starting in kindergarten and ending in the grade you're in now, indicate at specific points on this timeline when you first tried a particular substance, and indicate what the substance was."

Family History

- "Tell me about your family."
- "Tell me about your relationship with your parents. Would you call it excellent, very good, just okay, or terrible?"
- "Have there ever been any problems in your family that you know of with alcohol and other drugs?"
- "Are there any other problems or issues in your family that are of concern for you right now?"
- "Do your parents know about your use?"
- (If use is known) "What was your mother/father/grandparent's reaction to the fact that you drink alcohol? Were they surprised? Were they angry? What did they do?"
- (If use is not known) "How do you think your parents/family would react if they knew you drank alcohol?"

Social History

- "Tell me about your friends . . . you don't have to tell me who they are if you don't want to."
- "What do you do with your friends for fun?"
- "Do any of your friends use drugs or alcohol?"
- "What kinds of activities are you involved in?" or "What kinds of activities did you used to be involved in?"

Educational History

- "How would you describe school?"
- "If you weren't in school today talking to me, what would you rather be doing?"
- "How do you think you do academically in school? What's your best subject and your worst subject?"
- "Who's your favorite teacher?"

- "If you think back over the years, what was your favorite grade to be in and why?"
- (If caught using at school) "Other than now, how many times do you think you've been in trouble of one kind or another at school?"

Problems with Substance Use

- Conduct CAGE assessment:
  "Have you ever felt the need to CUT down on your drinking?"
  "Have you ever felt ANNOYED by someone criticizing your drinking?"
  "Have you ever felt bad or GUILTY about your drinking?"
  "Have you ever had a drink first thing in the morning or throughout your school/work day to steady your nerves?" (EYE-OPENER)
- "What's the worst thing that's ever happened while you were drinking?" (Good to balance with "What's the best thing?")
- "Have you ever not been able to remember what happened while you were under the influence of alcohol?"
- "Have you ever gotten sick or passed out as a result of using alcohol?"
- "Have you ever done anything while under the influence of alcohol you regretted later?"

(The more yes answers to the above, the more indication of misuse/abuse.)

Supplemental Assessment Instruments

- Michigan Alcohol Screening Test (MAST)
- Substance Abuse Subtle Screening Inventory-3 (SASSI-3)

Closing the Interview

- **If mild to moderate concern for level of use,** "I appreciate your honesty today, and I believe that in general, you have a pretty good handle on things. However, the fact that you got in trouble today suggests to me that you might at least want to begin to look at how your substance use and misuse is affecting your day-to-day life. Would you be interested in joining a group here at school to talk more about substance use?"
- **If moderate to high concern for level of use,** "I appreciate your honesty today. I must admit that I'm feeling concerned about the amount of alcohol/drugs you are using and the kinds of consequences you are experiencing. (Give examples.) I recommend that you talk to a counselor outside of school who works specifically with kids your age who are experiencing some problems with their use."
- **If high to very high concern for level of use,** "I appreciate your honesty today. I must admit that I'm very concerned about the amount of alcohol/drugs you are abusing and the kinds of consequences you are experiencing. (Give examples.) I'm going to recommend to your parents that you talk to a counselor outside of school who works specifically with kids your age who are experiencing some problems with their use as well."

The purpose of the substance-abuse assessment is to obtain information that will guide the school counselor toward the next appropriate steps. It is not designed as a diagnostic tool, nor does the assessment provide all information necessary to determine the need for treatment. In general, the more positive responses the counselor receives regarding relevant risk factors, the stronger the cause for concern. Once the assessment interview has been conducted, the school counselor makes decisions regarding involvement of parents, involvement of school officials, school-based interventions (for example, individual counseling, group counseling), or referrals for a more in-depth assessment and possibly treatment. The school counselor's role in any of these activities should be active versus passive, proactive versus reactive, and whenever possible, systemic versus individual. Of course, specific strategies and interventions to deal with a variety of substance abuse issues among youth are beyond the scope of this chapter. McClanahan et al. (1998) does recommend that when possible, school counselors seek opportunities to enhance their training and expertise in more specialized prevention and intervention strategies.

CONCLUSION

Numerous ethical and legal issues are to be considered in making determinations about appropriate interventions for substance-abuse-affected youth. A detailed understanding of the American Counseling Association's Code of Ethics, the American School Counselor Association's Ethical Standards for School Counselors, and the Code of Federal Regulations, specifically CFR 42–Part 2, is vital in working with youth and substance abuse issues (American Counseling Association, 1995; American School Counselor Association, 1998; Federal confidentiality regulations, 1989). Of course, ongoing consultation and supervision with other colleagues in substance-abuse-specific mental health settings is also recommended.

The school counselor is a vital element in promoting system-wide, comprehensive prevention as well as intentional intervention strategies. As advocates, change agents, leaders, and collaborative consultants, school counselors can pave the way for systemically implemented prevention and intervention strategies that work to meet the needs of all students.

RESOURCES

Books

Department of Health and Human Services. (1999). *Here's proof prevention works.* (DHHS Publication No. SMA 99-3300). Washington, DC: U.S. Government Printing Office.

SASSI Institute. (1997). *SASSI scales: Clinical feedback*. Bloomington, IN: Author.

Selzer, M. L. (1971). Michigan Alcoholism Screening Test: The quest for a new diagnostic instrument. *American Journal of Psychiatry, 127,* 1653–1658.

Web Sites

National Clearinghouse for Alcohol and Drug Information: http://www.health.org/
National Institute on Drug Abuse: http://www.nida.nih.gov
U.S. Dept. of Education: Safe and Drug Free Schools:
    http://www.ed.gov/offices/OESE/SDFS/

REFERENCES

American Counseling Association. (1995). *Code of ethics and standards of practice*. Annapolis Junction, MD: Author.

American School Counselor Association. (1998). *Ethical standards for school counselors*. Alexandria, VA: Author.

Botvin, G. J., & Botvin, E. M. (1992). Adolescent tobacco, alcohol, and drug abuse: Prevention strategies, empirical findings, and assessment issues. *Developmental and Behavioral Pediatrics, 13*, 290–301.

Bukstein, O. G. (1994). Treatment of adolescent alcohol abuse and dependence. *Alcohol Health and Research World, 18*, 296–301.

Capuzzi, D., & Gross, D. R. (Eds.). (2000). *Youth at risk: A prevention resource for counselors, teachers, and parents* (3rd ed.). Alexandria: American Counseling Association.

Center for Substance Abuse Prevention. (2002). *SAMHSA Clearinghouse*. Retrieved February 20, 2002, from http://www.samhsa.gov/centers/csap/csap.html

Coker, J. K. (2001). Four-fold prevention: Strategies to prevent substance abuse among elementary school-aged children. *Professional School Counseling, 5*(1), 70–74.

Coker, J. K., & Borders, L. D. (2001). An analysis of environmental and social factors affecting adolescent problem drinking. *Journal of Counseling & Development, 79*(2), 200–208.

Department of Health and Human Services. (1996). *Understanding Substance Abuse Prevention—Toward the 21st Century*. (DHHS Publication No. SMA 99-3300). Washington DC: U.S. Government Printing Office.

Federal confidentiality regulations. (1989, March/April). *Student Assistance Journal*, 55–57.

Fisher, G. L., & Harrison, T. C. (2000). *Substance abuse: Information for school counselors, social workers, therapists, and counselors* (2nd ed.). Needham Heights: Allyn & Bacon.

Gibson, R. L., & Mitchell, M. H. (1999). *Introduction to counseling and guidance* (5th ed.). Upper Saddle River, NJ: Prentice Hall.

Guthrie, B. J., Loveland-Cherry, C., Frey, M. A., & Dielman, T. E. (1994). A theoretical approach to studying health behaviors in adolescents: An at-risk population. *Family Community Health, 17*, 35–48.

Hawkins, J. D., Catalano, R. F., & Miller, J. Y. (1992). Risk and protective factors for alcohol and other drug problems in adolescence and early adulthood: Implications for substance abuse prevention. *Psychological Bulletin, 112*, 64–105.

Homonoff, E., Martin, J., Rimpas, D., & Henderson, M. (1994). It takes a village to raise a child: A model of training for prevention of youth abuse of alcohol and other drugs. *Child and Adolescent Social Work Journal, 11*, 53–61.

Keys, S. G., & Bemak, F. (1997). School-family-community linked services: A school counseling role for changing times. *The School Counselor, 44*, 255–263.

Kreft, I. G. (1998). An illustration of item homogeneity scaling and multilevel analysis techniques in the evaluation of drug prevention programs. *Evaluation Review, 22*(1), 46–77.

Kumpfer, K. L, & Turner, C. W. (1991). The social ecology model of adolescent substance abuse: Implications for prevention. *International Journal of the Addictions, 25,* 435–463.

Lynam, D., Milich, R., Zimmerman, R., Navak, S., Logan, T., Martin, C., Leukefeld, C., & Clayton, R. (1999). Project DARE: No effects at 10-year follow-up. *Journal of Consulting and Clinical Psychology, 67,* 590–593.

McClanahan, K. K., McLaughlin, R. J., Loos, V. E., Holcomb, J. D., Gibbins, A. D., & Smith, Q. W. (1998). Training school counselors in substance abuse risk reduction techniques for use with children and adolescents. *Journal of Drug Education, 28*(1), 39–51.

McLaughlin, T. E., & Vacha, E. F. (1993). Substance abuse prevention in the schools: Roles for the school counselor. *Elementary School Guidance & Counseling, 28*(2), 124–129.

Muro, J. J., & Kottman, T. (1995). *Guidance and counseling in the elementary and middle schools.* Dubuque: Brown & Benchmark.

National Household Survey on Drug Abuse (NHSDA). (1996). Retrieved February 20, 2002, from http://www.samhsa.gov/oas/NHSDA.

National Household Survey on Drug Abuse (NHSDA). (2003). Retrieved July 15, 2003, from http://www.samhsa.gov/oas/2k3/UnderageDrinking/UnderageDrinking.htm.

O'Rourke, K., & Worzbyt, J. C. (Eds.). (1996). *Support groups for children.* Philadelphia: Taylor & Francis.

Peterson, P. L., Hawkins, J. D., Abbott, R. D., & Catalano, R. F. (1994). Disentangling the effects of parental drinking, family management, and parental alcohol norms on current drinking by black and white adolescents. *Journal of Research on Adolescents, 4,* 203–227.

Schmidt, J. J. (2002). *Counseling in schools: Essential services and comprehensive programs* (4th ed.). Needham Heights: Allyn & Bacon.

St. Pierre, T., Mark, M., Kaltreider, D., & Aikin, K. (1997). Involving parents of high-risk youth in drug prevention: A three-year longitudinal study in boys and girls clubs. *Journal of Early Adolescence, 17*(1), 21–50.

U.S. Department of Education. (1988). *Drug prevention curricula: A guide to selection and implementation.* (GPO Publication No. 249-884/00803). Washington, DC: U.S. Government Printing Office.

U.S. Department of Education, Office of Educational Research and Improvement. (1996). *National education longitudinal study of 1988 (NELS:88). Research framework and issues.* (Working Paper No. 96-03). Washington, DC: Author.

Wegscheider, S. (1981). *Another chance: Hope and health for the alcoholic family.* Palo Alto, CA: Science and Behavior Books.

Werner, E. E. (1989). Children of the garden island. *Scientific American, 260*(4), 106–111.

Zernike, K. (2001, February 15). Antidrug program says it will adopt a new strategy. *New York Times.* Retrieved June 1, 2001, from http://www.nytimes.com.

PATH OF ADDICTION

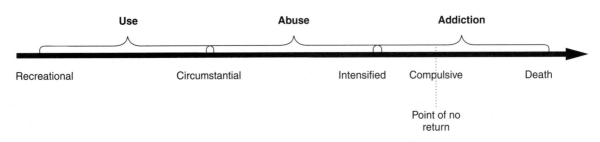

HANDOUT 10.1

INFORMATION FOR STUDENT SUPPORT TEAM MEMBERS

Four-Fold Prevention Project

Dear _____:

You are being asked to serve on a "support team" for _____. This student is involved in a prevention program being conducted at _____ school.

Description of Program

Four-Fold Prevention is a 6-session substance-abuse program is designed to:

- Help students identify supportive role models in their environment
- Help students to begin to communicate with these role models about alcohol and other drugs
- Identify opportunities for positive involvement with peers both in the school and in the community

Students are asked to identify one adult in the community, one parent or guardian, one school employee, and one peer to serve on their "support team." Each week, students will be responsible for completing a short activity with one team member. As a team member, you are asked to take the time to participate with the student on their activity. If you feel you cannot fulfill this obligation, please tell the student so he or she can select another team member.

If you have any questions, please don't hesitate to call.

Sincerely,

(Counselor's name)

(Counselor's contact information)

HANDOUT 10.2

VIGNETTES FOR GROUP SESSION 4

Vignette 1: Bored after School

Molly and Wanda are hanging out at Molly's house after school. Since Molly's mother works, no one else is home yet. Both Molly and Wanda complain that they are bored. They try to come up with ideas of what to do, but nothing sounds good to them.

Molly:	"We could watch TV?"
Wanda:	"Nah, we always do that. Besides, there's nothing on right now."
Molly:	"Well, we could go ride our bikes?"
Wanda:	"Nope. Too cold outside."
Molly:	"Okay, maybe we could call somebody else and see what they are doing!"
Wanda:	"Probably nothing, just like us."
Molly:	"Well what do you want to do, Wanda?"
Wanda:	"I don't know. Hey! Doesn't your Mom have a liquor cabinet?"
Molly:	"Yeah, so . . . "
Wanda:	"So why don't we see what's inside?"

1. What should Molly do?

2. What could Molly say to Wanda?

3. Is Wanda's suggestion to see what's inside Molly's mother's liquor cabinet a "safe" or "unsafe" activity?

4. What could Molly and Wanda do for fun instead?

Vignette 2: Helping Mrs. Carmike

Two brothers, Jamie and Hector, always run errands for their parents. The boys live down the road from a small grocery store run by Mrs. Carmike. Usually, the two boys just grab the items they need to buy and head home. But today is different . . .

(Jamie and Hector see Mrs. Carmike trying to lift a heavy box by herself.)

Jamie: "Be careful, Mrs. Carmike! That looks heavy!"

Hector: "Here, let us help you."

(The two boys help Mrs. Carmike put the box on a shelf.)

Mrs. Carmike:	"Thank you, boys! I didn't realize how heavy that was, and my back isn't as strong as it used to be."
Jamie:	"That's all right. My brother and I are both really strong."
Hector:	"Yeah."
Mrs. Carmike:	"Yes, I can see that. I sure could use two strong boys to help me out around the store on the weekends. Would you two be interested?"
Jamie:	"Wow, really?"
Hector:	"That would be great! We are always looking for things to do on the weekends."

1. Would helping Mrs. Carmike at the store be an example of a "safe" or "unsafe" activity?

2. Other than money, what would be benefits to working at the store for Jamie and Hector?

314

Vignette 3: The Older Kids

Jane and Mark have always been good friends. They live on the same street, go to the same school, and have been in the same class for many years. Lately, Mark has noticed that Jane doesn't talk to him like she used to. He has started to worry about his friend.

Mark: "Hey Jane. You want to come over to my house after school? A bunch of us are getting together to play basketball."

Jane: "Thanks but no thanks. I'm meeting some other kids at the mall after school today."

Mark: "Really? Who are you meeting?"

Jane: "Oh, you wouldn't know them. They are just some older kids from the high school I met through my sister. They are really cool."

Mark: "So, what do you do when you get together with them?"

Jane: "You know, just hang out . . . cruise the mall . . . smoke . . . the usual stuff."

Mark: "Wait a minute! Did you say smoke? What are you smoking?"

Jane: "Gosh, you sure are nosy! If you want to know so bad, why don't you come with me and try it?"

1. Do you think what Jane is doing with the older kids is "safe" or "unsafe"?

2. What could Mark say to his friend?

3. Should Mark go with Jane to meet her friends? Why or why not?

HANDOUT 10.3

FOUR-FOLD PREVENTION PROJECT

Thank you for taking the time to fill out this survey. Before you begin, please answer the following questions about yourself:

(Check one)

I am a: _____ boy

_____ girl

(Fill in the blank)

I am _____ years old.

(Check all that apply)

I live with my:

_____ Mother/female guardian

_____ Father/male guardian

_____ Stepmother

_____ Stepfather

_____ Other relative

_____ Other adult not related to me

Please read the following questions and **put a check mark beside the best answer for each.** There are no right or wrong answers. If you have a question, please raise your hand and I will help you. Thank you for your cooperation!

1. In the last three weeks, which of the following things have you talked about with your parents or guardians? (Check all that apply)
   a. ____ Classes you enjoy at school
   b. ____ School activities or events that you are interested in
   c. ____ Things you have studied in class
   d. ____ None of these things

2. In the last three weeks, which of the following things have your parents or guardians done? (Check all that apply)
   a. ____ Talked to your teacher or counselor
   b. ____ Visited your classes
   c. ____ Been to a school event such as a play, concert, sport competition, honor ceremony, or science fair where YOU participated
   d. ____ None of these things

3. Are the following statements mostly true for you and your parents, or mostly false for you and your parents?
   • My parents trust me to do what they expect without checking up on me.
     a. ____ True
     b. ____ False
   • I count on my parents to solve many of my problems for me.
     a. ____ True
     b. ____ False

4. In the last three weeks, which of the following things have your parents or guardians done? (Check all that apply)
   a. ____ Checked on whether you have done your homework
   b. ____ Had you do work or chores around the home
   c. ____ Limited the amount of time you can spend watching TV
   d. ____ Limited the amount of time for hanging out with friends on school nights
   e. ____ None of these things

5. I often don't know why I am supposed to do what my parents tell me to do.
   a. ____ True
   b. ____ False

6. Which of the following activities have you participated in outside of school in the last three weeks? (Check all that apply)
   a. ____ Boy or Girl Scouts
   b. ____ Youth groups at church
   c. ____ Hobby clubs
   d. ____ Boys' clubs or girls' clubs
   e. ____ Team sports
   f. ____ 4-H club
   g. ____ YMCA or other youth group
   h. ____ Summer programs/summer camp
   i. ____ I have not participated in any activities outside of school
   j. ____ Other: _____

7. Are you aware of activities for young people in your neighborhood or community?
   a. ____ Yes
   b. ____ No

8. Is there at least one adult who is not your parent whom you feel like you can talk to?
   a. ____ Yes
   b. ____ No

9. Check the reasons you have talked to a counselor at your school in the last three weeks.
   a. ____ To talk about things you've studied in class
   b. ____ Because you've gotten in trouble for something at school
   c. ____ For counseling on personal problems
   d. ____ I have not talked to a counselor about any of these things at school in the last three weeks.

10. Check the reasons you have talked to a teacher at your school in the last three weeks.
    a. ____ To talk about things you've studied in class
    b. ____ Because you've gotten in trouble for something at school
    c. ____ To talk about personal problems
    d. ____ I have not talked to a teacher about any of these things at school in the last three weeks.

11. Check the things that you think are problems at your school.
    a. ____ Fighting among students is a problem.
    b. ____ Stealing is a problem.
    c. ____ Breaking school property is a problem.
    d. ____ None of these things are problems at my school.
    e. ____ Other: _____.

(continued)

12. How many of the following statements do you agree with about your school and your teachers? (Check all that apply)
    a. ____ Students get along well with teachers at my school.
    b. ____ There is real school spirit at my school.
    c. ____ Rules for behavior are strict at my school.
    d. ____ Rules are fair at my school.
    e. ____ The teaching is good at my school.
    f. ____ Teachers are interested in students at my school.
    g. ____ When I work hard on schoolwork, teachers praise my efforts.
    h. ____ Most of my teachers really listen to what I have to say.

13. Check the activities you have participated in during the last three weeks at school. (Check all that apply)
    a. ____ Sports
    b. ____ Band or chorus
    c. ____ After school program
    d. ____ School plays
    e. ____ Other school activity: _____

14. How many times in the last three weeks have you been around another person about your age who was smoking cigarettes?
    a. ____ More than 3 times
    b. ____ More than 1 time
    c. ____ 1 time only
    d. ____ None

15. How many times in the last three weeks have you been around another person about your age who was drinking alcohol?
    a. ____ More than 3 times
    b. ____ More than 1 time
    c. ____ 1 time only
    d. ____ None

16. I have at least one good friend that I spend time with.
    a. ____ Yes
    b. ____ No

17. Check the things that are important to your good friend(s). (Check all the things that are important)
    a. ____ My friends think it is important to study and get good grades.
    b. ____ My friends think it is important to be liked by others.
    c. ____ My friends think it is important to study in school.
    d. ____ My friends think it is important to go to school every day.
    e. ____ My friends think it is important to go to church or synagogue.
    f. ____ My friends think it is important to be involved in sports or other activities.
    g. ____ My friends think it is important to listen to what parents say.
    h. ____ My friends think it is important to not drink or use drugs.
    i. ____ My friends don't think any of these things are important.

Thank you for taking the time to fill out this survey. DO NOT put your name on this survey. Let me know if you have any questions.

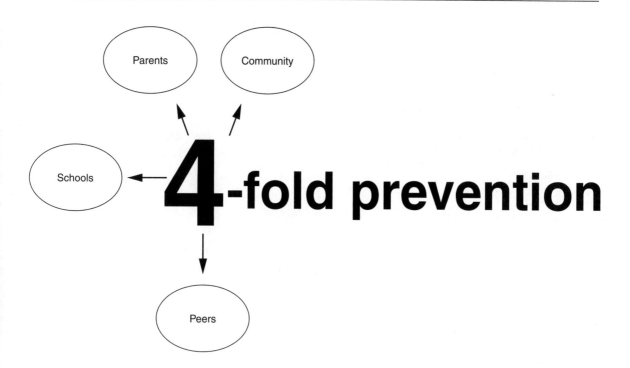

(continued)

STUDENT JOURNAL

THIS JOURNAL BELONGS TO: _____

Section 1: My Support Systems

Put two to three names in each circle to represent adults you feel you can trust, talk to, turn to for help, ask questions to, and have fun with!

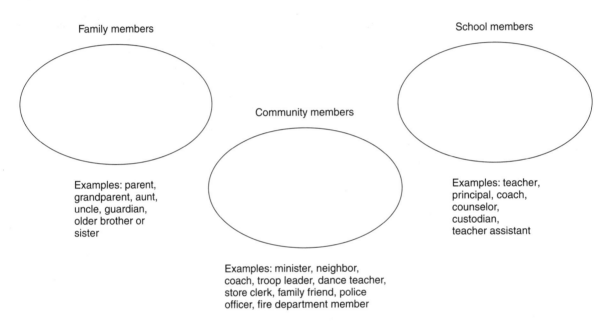

Family members

Examples: parent, grandparent, aunt, uncle, guardian, older brother or sister

Community members

Examples: minister, neighbor, coach, troop leader, dance teacher, store clerk, family friend, police officer, fire department member

School members

Examples: teacher, principal, coach, counselor, custodian, teacher assistant

Section 2: My SST

List the people you have decided to ask to be part of your social support team:

- Community Member: _____
- School Member: _____
- Family Member: _____
- Classmate Member: _____

Be sure to give each member of your team the description of the program!

Section 3: What Is a Drug?

A drug is:

_____

_____

Some common drugs are:

_____

_____

Some effects of drugs on the body are:

_____

_____

Section 4: Student-Friendly Schools

What are some characteristics of a "student-friendly" school?

_____

_____

Who are the people at your school that help to make it "student-friendly"?

_____

_____

Section 5: School Member Interview

School Member's Name: _____

1. Why do you think some adults drink or use drugs?

_____

_____

2. Why do you think some kids drink or use drugs?

_____

_____

3. What should schools do to educate students about drinking and drug use?

_____

_____

4. What should parents do if their kids drink or use drugs?

_____

_____

5. What should kids do if their friends drink or use drugs?

_____

_____

(continued)

Section 6: Student-Friendly Schools

Talk about the following questions as you and your school team member brainstorm ideas for a "student-friendly" school. Look back at section 4 for ideas.

- Why do students like to come to school?
- Do students feel like they can talk to their teachers?
- Do students feel like they can talk to the counselor?
- Do students feel like they can talk to the principal?
- Do students feel safe in this school?
- What could the school do to make learning here more fun?
- What could the school do to make students feel listened to?
- What could the school do to make students feel safer?

Section 7: What Are Your Ideas?

Based on your discussion with your school support team member about student-friendly schools, answer the following questions:

1. What could the school do to make learning here more fun?

_____

_____

2. What could the school do to make students feel listened to?

_____

_____

3. What could the school do to make students feel safer?

_____

_____

_____   _____
School Member Signature   Student Signature

Section 8: Dear Principal,

Dear _____ ,
(name of principal)

It is very important to be in a school where students feel safe and listened to, and where learning is fun! Here are three suggestions to help make our school even more student-friendly than it already is:

1. _____

_____

2. _____

_____

3. _____

_____

Thank you for reading our suggestions for a more student-friendly school.
Sincerely,

Section 9: Family Member Interview

Family Member's Name: _____

1. Why do you think some adults drink or use drugs?

_____

_____

2. Why do you think some kids drink or use drugs?

_____

_____

3. What should schools do to educate students about drinking and drug use?

_____

_____

4. What should parents do if their kids drink or use drugs?

_____

_____

5. What should kids do if their parents drink excessively or use drugs?

_____

_____

Section 10: Family AOD Policy

Make a list of the rules and expectations in your family about alcohol and other drug (AOD) use for the next year (see example below for ideas). List ideas for how to talk about drugs and alcohol in your family. Have everyone in the family sign and date the contract.
Example of family contract:

As a child in this family I agree to:

1. Remain free of alcohol and other drugs.
2. Call home if I need help or a safe ride.
3. Talk with my family if I'm worried about a friend's use of drugs or alcohol.

(continued)

As a parent in this family I agree to:

1. Always come get you if you need help or a safe ride.
2. Remain free of drugs.
3. Not drink and drive.
4. Be understanding and available to talk with you and your friends when you are having problems.

Date: _____ Student: _____ Family Member: _____

Section 11: My Family AOD Policy

As a child in this family I agree to:

1. _____
2. _____
3. _____
4. _____

As a parent or guardian in this family I agree to:

1. _____
2. _____
3. _____
4. _____

Date: _____   Student: _____
Family Member: _____   Family Member: _____
Family Member: _____   Family Member: _____

Section 12: Community Resources

Give three examples of safe, fun things to do in your community:

1. _____
2. _____
3. _____

Name at least five people in your community who can help you if you have a problem or a concern:

1. _____
2. _____

3. _____

4. _____

5. _____

Section 13: Community Opportunities

Name: _____

1. Why do you think some adults drink or use drugs?

   _____

   _____

2. Why do you think some kids drink or use drugs?

   _____

   _____

3. What should community members do if kids in their neighborhood drink or use drugs?

   _____

   _____

4. What should parents do if their kids drink or use drugs?

   _____

   _____

5. What should kids do if an adult they know drinks excessively or uses drugs?

   _____

   _____

Section 14: Community Member Interview

Along with your community team member, answer the following questions:

1. What do kids in your neighborhood do after school?

   _____

   _____

2. What do kids in your neighborhood do on the weekends?

   _____

   _____

3. What could community members do to make your neighborhood safer?

   _____

   _____

(continued)

4. What could community members do to make your neighborhood more fun for kids?

_____

_____

5. If you could design an after-school program for kids in your neighborhood, what would it be like?

_____

_____

6. List at least 2 community-based activities you would like to be involved in OR list 2 activities you already are involved in:

1. _____   2. _____

Section 15: Friend Interview

1. Why do you think some adults drink or use drugs?

_____

_____

2. Why do you think some kids drink or use drugs?

_____

_____

3. What should schools do to educate kids about drinking and drug use?

_____

_____

4. What should parents do if their kids drink or use drugs?

_____

_____

5. What should community members do if kids in their neighborhood drink or use drugs?

_____

_____

6. What should kids do if their friends drink or use drugs?

_____

_____

Section 16: AOD Presentation

Student Presenters: _____

Title of presentation: _____

Presentation style: (check one)

❑ Poster presentation

❑ Skit

❑ Lecture

Summary of presentation:

_____

_____

_____

_____

_____

_____

Section 17: Final Thoughts

The thing that was most helpful during this program was:

_____

_____

The thing that was least helpful during this program was:

_____

_____

The thing I remember the most about this program was:

_____

_____

THANK YOU FOR BEING A PART OF FOUR-FOLD!

Source: Developed by J. Kelly Coker, Ph.D., 4505 Maryland Parkway, Box 453003, University of Nevada, Las Vegas, Las Vegas, NV 89052.

STRESS MANAGEMENT: THE SCHOOL COUNSELOR'S ROLE

Vicki Brooks, Lewis and Clark College

INTRODUCTION

The events of the past several years have created a new world for today's youth. Children and adolescents are exposed to violence on TV, to bullying, harassment, and shootings in schools and neighborhoods, and to unexpected disasters. The issue is not whether individuals experience stress but rather how stress is perceived (Massey, 1998). Seaward (2002) defines stress as "the inability to cope with a threat (real or imagined) . . . which results in a series of physiological responses and adaptations" (p. 4). Twenty-first-century stress is considered to be "hitting a fever pitch in every nation . . . a global epidemic" (p. 13). All five domains of holistic health are affected by stress: physical, social, emotional, mental, and spiritual (Massey, 1998).

Physical reactions include the flight-or-fight syndrome, shaking, nausea, and headaches (Balch & Balch, 1997; Seaward, 2002). Emotional and social responses are evidenced in irritability, crying, difficulty in identifying fears, and withdrawal from friends and family. Confusion, lack of concentration, and difficulty in making appropriate decisions are symptoms of mental and emotional reactions to stress. Re-involvement with religion or disbelief and distrust in God for doing such a terrible thing can signal a spiritual reaction.

Children and adolescents experience daily occurrences of stress. The question is not will children and adolescents be stressed, but rather, how can school counselors help students better manage stress.

LITERATURE REVIEW

"I cannot and should not be cured of my stress, but merely taught to enjoy it."

Hans Selye (Seaward, 2002, p. 2)

Research on the effects of stress on the body began in the 1950s with Hans Selye (Seaward, 1994). Original research focused on adults. Recently research has identified and evaluated children's and adolescents' stress and coping strategies.

Children and Stress

School appears to be one of the major stressors in young children's lives (de Anda & Bradley 1997; Romano, 1997). Students identify major school stressors as tests, grades, and performing in front of others (Romano, 1997). Upper elementary children voice concern about losing a best friend and being picked last for an activity or team (DeWolfe & Saunders, 1995). During stressful times, if a child has support from others and effective problem-solving skills, social success and adjustment naturally follow (Dubow et al., 1991).

Leading sport psychologist Terry Orlick's research includes enhancing children's lives via life-skills training. Orlick applies performance-enhancement research, such as visualization and imagery, to children's learning and development of positive coping strategies. Orlick (1993) states: "the ultimate goal with children is to teach them relevant mental skills that will enhance their quality of life and endure over the lifetime" (p. 9).

Comprehensive life-skills programs teach children to utilize stress controls (for example, breathing) in real-life situations (Gilbert & Orlick, 1996). Results indicate children manage homework better, have fewer headaches, and sleep better at night. Advocates for children have long argued the need for stress-management and life-skills classes (Romano, 1992; Romano & Miller, 1996; Omizo & Omizo, 1992). An inclusive curriculum teaches children to identify stress, talk about feelings associated with stress, and apply positive problem-solving strategies (DeWolfe & Saunders, 1995).

Adolescents and Stress

Middle school children are continually on a roller coaster. Volatility of this age group increases participation in dangerous and inappropriate risk-taking behaviors. To manage the transition, adolescents need effective coping strategies (Chapman & Mullis, 1999).

Stress-management programs have been developed and administered to middle school children (McCraty et al., 1999). Curriculum content includes teaching children to disengage from stressful events and reframe situations using positive visualization. Simultaneously, the children are peer-teachers of the program. Upon conclusion of the comprehensive two-year program, children report feeling happier and more in control of their lives.

The family teaches and models problem-solving skills. If the structure is less than supportive, appropriate coping strategies can be absent or maladaptive. Problematic behaviors can be born out of negative responses to stress. Additionally, the inability to effectively cope with stress leads to a heightened sense of despair. Left unchecked, despair can lead to destructive behavior patterns such as impulsivity, promiscuity, drug and alcohol use and abuse, and increased absenteeism (Kashani et al., 1997).

Adolescents with high self-esteem utilize more positive coping strategies (for example, focusing on changing the situation or changing one's perception of the problem) (Chapman & Mullis, 1999). Social activities and support can be as important as academic programs for healthy development of youth (Dumont & Provost, 1999). Across grades, females' self-esteem ratings remain lower than males (Byrne, 2000). By the ninth grade, females report increased anxiety and fear at a level higher than males (Gullone & King, 1993). By the twelfth grade, females move from problem-solving to emotion-based (e.g., support seeking) coping strategies (Frydenberg & Lewis, 1993).

Adolescent coping strategies do not differ markedly between countries (Piko, 2001). Generally, females use passive methods of coping and males choose a direct approach. Males view the stressful situation as a challenge and take immediate action (Petersen, Sarigiani, & Kennedy, 1991). Piko (2001) suggests differences are due to socialization techniques. Society accepts aggression from males but expects females to present a more resigned demeanor. Of note: Drinking or substance abuse is reported by adolescents to be risk-taking or sensation-seeking behavior rather than a coping strategy (Piko, 2001).

Moving through adolescence challenges problem-solving capabilities (Frydenberg & Lewis, 1991). Educators report an increase in the number of students lacking strategies for effective management of social and emotional issues. Hence, many schools and districts are including curriculums specific to fostering social and emotional skill development (McCraty et al., 1999). By learning positive stress-management strategies, adolescents acquire resources for navigating transitional stages ahead.

Special Populations and Stress

Disabled Populations

Students with individualized educational plans (IEP) have in place documentation regarding academic and social concerns. As the learning environment becomes more complex during school-level transitions (elementary to middle and middle to high) stress levels increase (Wenz Gross & Siperstein, 1998). When transitioning to the next school level, children with disabilities report increased difficulty understanding and following directions. Frustration with a new system increases stress and lowers feelings of self-efficacy. Academic success has been found to correlate with feelings of self-worth (Wenz Gross & Siperstein, 1998).

Children with disabilities perceive daily hassles as more stressful than life events (Boyce, Marshall, & Peters, 1999). Daily stressors include time management, time on task, an increased awareness of the disability, and peer relationships. Peer relationships become paramount during adolescence; however, a child with a disability has difficulty in making and sustaining friendships during these years. Social-skills training can assist a child with a disability in developing positive peer relationships (Geisthardt & Munsch, 1996).

If the parent or caregiver perceives the child's disability as embarrassing and has minimal support, the parental stress level is high (Duis & Summers, 1997). As one would surmise, families with a child with a disability have increased parental and child-related stress. Lower incidences of child-related stress occur when the family uses outside resources. Parent-related stress is lowest when support includes both external and internal sources. The degree of the handicapping condition is a predictor for the level of stress expressed by both parent and child (Duis & Summers, 1997).

Children and adolescents with disabilities have the capacity to utilize journal or diary work when communicating about stress (Boyce et al., 1999). Writing as an intervention tool provides a nonintrusive pathway for beginning dialogue via the student's own words. Interventions with students with disabilities include group or classroom guidance activities for developing skills in (1) time management, (2) friendships, (3) self-advocating, (4) decision making, (5) identifying stressors, and (6) positive coping techniques. Educational teams should also include the parents as helpers to support acquisition of positive skill development (Wenz Gross & Siperstein, 1998).

Economically Marginalized Populations

Poverty is "the extent to which an individual does without resources" (Payne, 2001, p. 16). Approximately 17 percent of children in the United States live in poverty (Payne, 2001). Insufficient fundamental resources (for example, housing, food) have significant implications on emotional, social, and physical well-being. Living without resources brings a sense of disconnection from the neighborhood, school, and community. Children and adolescents without a sense of belonging exhibit behaviors directly affecting well-being (Vissing, 1996). These behaviors include isolation, anger, depression, confusion, and anxiety (Igoa, 1995).

School counselors are key connections in school success for children who are marginalized. Sensitivity to basic needs (for example, paper/pencil) can help reduce these children's anxiety. Keeping children engaged in education affords the opportunity for cessation of generational poverty.

Assessment of the child's and family's available resources assists school personnel in providing options. Community networks are essential when aligning families with support services. Knowing available resources and laws provides the school counselor positive strategies to assist in reducing the child's and family's stress.

Gifted and Talented Populations

Gifted students, even at a young age, demonstrate a deep desire to understand the universe. Gifted children have a propensity for asking existential questions and are quick to identify injustices and inequities present in the world. These topics make for easy discussion with adults. However, when the student innocently asks questions or shares ideas with peers, the responses can vary from apathy to hostility, leaving the child to feel different and misunderstood (Webb, 2002).

Gifted and talented students report feeling different and isolated from peers. Constant pressure to perform to excessively high standards and the need to hide their giftedness in order to belong contribute to the exceptional child's anxiety (Silverman, 1993). Exceptional students report more performance dissatisfaction than nongifted populations.

Intensity, sensitivity, and perfectionism are traits found in gifted children. The normal classroom does not readily embrace such characteristics. Again, the exceptional child feels different. These feelings compound the child's stressful life and can contribute to underachievement, withdrawal, depression, and suicidal ideation (Silverman, 1993; Webb, 2002).

Journal entries provide a rich forum for discussions. Keen analytical abilities make the gifted child an ideal student to learn decision-making skills and strategies. The educational community, working collaboratively with parents, should address the emotional, social, physical, and spiritual needs of the exceptional child while challenging the intellectual (Swassing, 1998). Teaching the exceptional child effective strategies for managing stress is key to success. "Counseling for this group should be focused on prevention, a proactive role" (National Association for Gifted Children, 2002, p. 1).

WHOLE-SCHOOL INTERVENTIONS

School Climate and Stress

If children and adolescents feel powerless to effectively manage or create positive change, acting out behaviors (impulsivity, angry outbursts) can result (Kashani et al., 1997). Youth lacking control in their life can create an unsafe, hostile, and even violent atmosphere. Recent episodes of school violence bring to the forefront the need for long-term solutions for environmental stressors. Feeling cared for and belonging to one's environment have been shown to reduce risky behaviors such as drinking, sex, or violent activities (McCraty et al., 1999).

When school goals reflect effort and learning of subject matter, students exhibit a willingness to work within the system's structure (Kaplan & Midgley, 1999). Students demonstrate positive effort and enthusiasm when mastery rather than competition between classmates is the learning goal (Roeser, Midgley, & Urdan, 1996; Slavin, 2000). If students' perception of the school climate is competitive rather than collegial, problem-solving strategies can be maladaptive in nature (Kaplan & Midgley, 1999). School environments conducive for learning reduce competition between classmates and increase cooperative learning opportunities.

For students who reside in a family or community in which violence is prevalent, the psychosocial environment of the school can provide the safe place necessary for healthy development and learning (Massey, 1998). School counselors are perfectly posed to ask the school climate questions. For example: Is the school climate emphasizing respect for others, thereby reducing stress? How can we develop a school climate of collaboration rather than competition?

Faculty and Staff Development for Stress Reduction

Faculty and staff also need healthy coping skills. How and what we teach to students reflects who we are as individuals (Palmer, 1998). Positive self-care seminars for faculty and staff can enhance morale and reduce stress. Teachers who participate in health promotion programs have (1) less absenteeism, (2) more effective teaching methods, and (3) an overall heightened sense of personal health and well-being (Massey, 1998). An emotionally healthy faculty and staff are positive role models for children and families.

Ideas to share *with administrators* to reduce faculty and staff stress levels (Long, 1998):

- Recruit volunteers to help with staff and faculty workload
- Encourage responsible delegation
- Model caring behavior and respect confidences
- Publicize and share individual accomplishments . . . frequently!
- Encourage self-care (for example, exercise, pursuing outside interests); foster quiet time
- Share future visions and directions for the school community

Ideas for *faculty and staff* in-service topics (Seaward, 1994; 2002):

- Positive self-talk; assertiveness training
- Creative problem solving
- Effective communication
- Time management
- Relaxation and imagery techniques
- Importance of exercise and proper nutrition
- Development of individual programs

Please see Resources and References for books and Web resources.

Schoolwide Stress-Reduction Intervention Plan

Step 1: Building the Case

First steps include consultation with counseling department members to present areas of concern (for example, school climate issues). Counselors can make a PowerPoint or similar presentation of results from a brief survey conducted with students during lunch period (random sampling of ten to twenty students per grade level).

Step 2: Gaining Administrative Support

After departmental support is gained, counselors schedule a meeting with the building administration. Include in the discussion survey data, school counseling department support, and recommendations for the development of a schoolwide team.

Step 3: Identifying the Team

Membership should represent all stakeholders (administrators, teachers, students, staff, volunteers, parents, and other community members). If possible, the team should consist of eight to ten members. With careful selection of members and organized meetings, the team can effect positive change in the school.

Step 4: Using Meetings and Agendas

All meetings should have an agenda with suggested time allocations per item. Include in the first meeting department and administrative support, survey results, and team purpose. Provide examples of other schools' efforts and successes.

Step 5: Getting It Done

The team needs to have a mission and purpose. Give all team members a direct voice in developing and implementing action plans (short- and long-term goals). Remember, the team will go through the same parallel process all groups experience: forming, storming, norming, working, and adjourning. Keep the administration informed of team movement. Establish regular check-ins via meeting dates.

Step 6: Sharing Successes

When the project is complete, recognize team members' contributions via television, radio, and school and local newspapers. Share with the school and community outcomes and future considerations. Celebrate successes with a closure party, inviting team members, faculty, staff, administrators, and local media.

CLASSROOM GUIDANCE ACTIVITIES

School Counselors as Leaders, Advocates, and Collaborators in Reducing Stress

School counselors are well positioned to be advocates for creating healthy learning environments. Advocacy includes establishing goals for a positive school climate promoting stress reduction, enhancing individual self-worth, and encouraging cooperative learning. Schools are ideal for the delivery and integration of prevention and intervention curricula.

Students, whether elementary or secondary, can identify stress. Hence, successful stress-reduction strategies can begin in elementary school and continue each year (Gilbert & Orlick, 1996; Romano, 1992). Sharing curricula information with parents and teachers fosters support and collaboration. The following classroom and small-group counseling lessons are examples of proactive educational models to help children identify, understand, and reduce stress. They can be used at all levels with modifications and changes in language.

LESSON 1: UNDERSTANDING HOW STRESS AFFECTS THE BODY

Personal/Social Development Standard C: Students will understand safety and survival skills.

Competency: Students will learn techniques for managing stress and conflict.

Learning Objectives: After the class activity and counselor-led instruction, students will demonstrate knowledge, skills, and understanding of:

- The definition and categories of stress
- Physiological responses to stress
- Stress-producing situations

Materials: Body Response to Stress (Handout 11.1), information provided in the Stress Management chapter, flipchart with pens or chalkboard and chalk.

Developmental Learning Activity

Introduction: The counselor begins the lesson by asking students to describe if/when they have felt their heart pump very hard (other than through exercise). The counselor writes responses on the board with single/double word bullets. Next, the counselor asks for identification of emotions associated with the incidents (for example fear, nervousness, or excitement). Briefly, the counselor summarizes by identifying the incidents as stressors and emphasizes stress creates reactions in the body. The reactions (called flight or fight) are a result of the brain's responding to the perceived stressor. The counselor addresses responses listed on the board and helps students identify each as flight or fight.

The counselor writes on the board the three types of stress: Instant, Daily, and Life Events. Examples: Instant: car wreck, loud noise; Daily: taking a test, giving a speech; Life Events: moving, serious illness. Finally, the group explores definitions of stress. Eustress is good stress (for example, winning a prize) and distress is negative stress (for example, failing a test).

Activity: The counselor gives students Handout 11.1, Body Response to Stress, and discusses the body's sensory sites and connections to the brain.

Next, the counselor presents the body's response to a stressful event. This should include the following information:

- Sympathetic nervous system definition: This involuntary system is responsible for secreting chemicals to increase heart rate, breathing, and blood flow to muscles. The main chemical is adrenaline secreted from the adrenaline gland located on top of the kidneys.
- Sympathetic nervous system function: The brain reacts to the event and sends information via the sympathetic nervous system to the body to be ready to fight or flee. Hence, we become tense and ready to go.

Students break into small groups and share personal situations in which adrenaline was experienced. One student in each group records responses. Students come back to large group, and the counselor lists the most frequent response from each group on the board/chart.

The counselor addresses recovering from stress. This should include the following information:

- Parasympathetic nervous system definition: This involuntary system is responsible for secreting chemicals to maintain homeostasis in the body (for example, relaxation). The main chemical is acetylcholine, which decreases heart rate, breathing, and muscle tension, thus neutralizing the sympathetic nervous system's chemicals.

- Parasympathetic nervous system function: This brings the body back to a balanced state in order for body functions (for example, digestion) to return to normal.

Students break into small groups and share personal situations in which recovery from stress was experienced. One student in each group records responses. Students come back to large group, and the counselor lists on the board the most frequent response from each group.

Finally, the counselor briefly explains prolonged effects of stress on the body. This should include the following information: After prolonged stress, the body begins to experience total fatigue. Fatigue involves the following:

- No energy
- Inability to respond to everyday events
- Sickness
- Need for a lot of rest to get back to normal (weeks or months)

Remaining in large group, students relate experiences or situations in which this level of fatigue has been experienced or observed in others.

Conclusion: The counselor summarizes the lesson, asking students to record in notebooks situations (that is, Instant, Daily, or Life) in which effects of stress on the body have been experienced. The counselor asks students to be alert to and identify stressful situations between now and the next meeting.

Assessment: Via class discussion, written summaries, and/or a pre-post curriculum or daily test, the school counselor will determine students' knowledge and understanding of categories of stress, physiological effects of stress on the body, and identification of stressful situations.

Follow-up: In the following lessons, students will build upon today's information by utilizing a good decision-making model for reducing stress.

LESSON 2: MAKING GOOD CHOICES/DECISIONS

Personal/Social Development Standard C: Students will understand safety and survival skills.

Competencies

- Students will learn techniques for managing stress and conflict.
- Students will apply effective problem-solving and decision-making skills to make safe and healthy choices.

Learning Objectives: After the class activity and counselor-led instruction, students will demonstrate knowledge, skills, and understanding of:

- Positive and negative techniques for coping with stress
- Steps involved in making good choices/decisions

Materials: Chalkboard, chalk, Model for Making Good Choices/Decisions (Handout 11.2).

Developmental Learning Activity

Introduction: The counselor quickly reviews the last lesson. The counselor asks students to record in notebooks a recent stressful experience and their body's response to the event.

Activity: Students move to small groups to discuss a time when a difficult situation was handled poorly (negative coping strategy). One student in each group records responses. After moving back to large group, small group recorders share two negative responses generated in small group. The counselor records responses on the board.

In the large group, the counselor asks students to share other options (positive coping) to be used in place of the identified negative strategies. The counselor records responses on the board across from negative responses. The counselor should make sure responses include talking with a friend, taking a time-out, or making a better decision.

Making good choices/decisions is the core of this lesson. The group brainstorms decision-making styles (for example: not making a decision, delaying the decision, or allowing others to make the decision). The counselor discusses how the various styles can either reduce or create additional stress.

Next, the counselor asks students to quietly identify and record their personal mode of decision making.

The counselor gives students Handout 11.2, Model for Making Good Choices/Decisions. The counselor reviews the model with students, explaining the steps. During the first step, the school counselor needs to address the issue of peer pressure: What it is, how does it feel, and is it a stressor?

Conclusion: The counselor asks students to summarize ideas regarding positive and negative coping strategies and making good choices/decisions. The counselor asks students to identify a current stressful situation and be ready to apply the Making Good Choices/Decisions model to help in resolution.

Assessment: Via class discussion, small group sharing, and/or a pre-post written test, the school counselor can determine students' knowledge and understanding of positive coping strategies, negative coping strategies, and making good choices/decisions.

Follow-up: The next class lesson will focus on the application of the Making Good Choices/Decision Model to a current stressful situation.

LESSON 3: REAL-LIFE CHOICES/DECISIONS

Personal/Social Development Standard C: Students will understand safety and survival skills.

Competencies

- Students will learn techniques for managing stress and conflict.
- Students will apply effective problem-solving and decision-making skills to make safe and healthy choices.

Learning Objectives: After the class activity and counselor-led instruction, students will demonstrate knowledge, skills, and understanding of:

- Criteria necessary for making a good choice/decision
- Application of Model for Making Good Choices/Decisions to a current situation

Materials: Chalk, chalkboard, Model for Making Good Choices/Decisions (Handout 11.2).

Developmental Learning Activity

Introduction: The counselor tells students that for the lesson today, work will continue with making good choices/decisions. At the conclusion of the last class, students were asked to identify a current stressful situation and be prepared to reference the issue during class. If they cannot identify a current stressor, the counselor allows them to use a recent past stressful event.

Activity: The counselor refers to the Model for Making Good Choices/Decisions handout from the previous lesson. The counselor carefully walks students through the model, allowing time to fill in the boxes according to the identified stressful situation.

When students have completed the model's Steps 1–3, they identify a partner and share those steps. During Step 4 each partner acts as the responsible adult. Students may share and rework previous steps if necessary. Then they begin work on Step 5 with partner.

The counselor assigns the completion of Step 5 and Step 6 as homework.

Conclusion: The large group brain storms ideas of applying the model to future situations.

Assessment: Via class discussion, partner sharing, and/or a pre-post written test, the school counselor can determine student's understanding of evaluating the spectrum of choices and decisions to be made (Steps 1 through 3) and the importance of talking it out (Step 4).

Follow-up: At a follow-up only meeting, students will partner-share Steps 5, 6, and 7. If necessary, partners will discuss moving from Step 7 back to Steps 1 through 3.

Throughout the comprehensive school counseling guidance activities, the Model for Making Good Choices/Decisions can be applied across the curriculum.

SMALL-GROUP COUNSELING PLANS

H.A.H. Group (Handling All Hassles)

In this six-session group counseling unit, the first three group sessions parallel the classroom guidance activities above, but are modified for a psychoeducational group counseling format. Individuals participating in the group have either self-identified or been selected because the topic is stress management. It is best to limit group membership to six to eight individuals and to hold meetings once a week for six weeks.

GROUP SESSION 1: STRESS, THE BODY, AND YOU

Personal/Social Development Standard C: Students will understand safety and survival skills.

Competency: Students will learn techniques for managing stress and conflict.

Learning Objectives: After the group session, students will demonstrate knowledge, skills and understanding of:

- The definition and categories of stress
- Physiological responses to stress
- Stress-producing situations

Materials: Body Response to Stress (Handout 11.1), information provided in the Stress Management chapter, flipchart with pens or chalkboard and chalk. Students will create personalized stress workbook that will include handouts from the meetings and self-reflections (Handout 11.3).

Activities

Introduction: The counselor explains to students that the purpose of the group is to have fun, learn about stress, and develop positive lifetime coping strategies. The counselor discusses group ground rules and establishes norms for group participation.

Counseling Activity: The counselor presents the information from classroom Lesson 1. The counselor should modify classroom didactic style to include processing among group members. The counselor should allow time to share personal ideas, experiences, or feelings about the topic and provide time for students to write in journals/workbooks.

Conclusion: The counselor invites students to reflect and respond to the day's activities. The counselor collects notebooks to store in a secure location. The counselor establishes goals for next meeting.

Assessment: The counselor asks participants to write a one-sentence summary addressing what was learned today, then reviews summaries to ensure goals and objectives are being addressed.

GROUP SESSION 2: MAKING DECISIONS

Personal/Social Development Standard C: Students will understand safety and survival skills.

Competencies

- Students will learn techniques for managing stress and conflict.
- Students will apply effective problem-solving and decision-making skills to make safe and healthy choices.

Learning Objectives: After the group session, students will demonstrate knowledge, skills, and understanding of:

- Positive and negative techniques for coping with stress
- The steps involved in making good choices/decisions.

Materials: Model for Making Good Choices/Decisions (Handout 11.2), personalized stress workbook including handouts from the meetings and self-reflections.

Activities

Introduction: The counselor asks students to recall and discuss some of the content from the first session. In a quick check-in, students take thirty seconds to share how they are doing (example: on a 1–10 scale with 10 being super, how are you today?). This information will allow the school counselor to quickly frame the day's lesson with an overall group rating.

Counseling Activity: The counselor presents the information from classroom Lesson 2. The counselor should modify classroom didactic style to include processing among group members. The counselor should allow time to share personal ideas, experiences, or feelings about the topic and to write in journals/workbooks.

Conclusion: The counselor invites students to reflect and respond to the day's activities. The counselor collects notebooks to store in a secure location. The counselor establishes goals for next meeting.

Assessment: The counselor asks participants to write a one-sentence summary addressing what was learned today, then reviews summaries to ensure goals and objectives are being addressed.

GROUP SESSION 3: MANAGING STRESS: PRACTICING A DECISION-MAKING MODEL

Personal/Social Development Standard C: Students will understand safety and survival skills.

Competencies

- Students will learn techniques for managing stress and conflict.
- Students will apply effective problem-solving and decision-making skills to make safe and healthy choices.

Learning Objectives: After the class activity and counselor-led instruction, students will demonstrate knowledge, skills, and understanding of:

- Criteria necessary for making a good choice/decision
- Application of Making Good Choices/Decisions model to a current situation.

Materials: Model for Making Good Choices/Decisions (Handout 11.2), personalized stress notebook.

Activities

Introduction: The counselor reminds students that one of the goals last week was to learn about positive and negative coping strategies. The counselor asks, "How many of you were able to cope positively?" Students share examples.

Counseling Activity: The counselor presents the information from classroom Lesson 3. The counselor should modify classroom didactic style to include processing among group members. The counselor should allow time to share personal ideas, experiences, or feelings about the topic and record in journals/ workbooks.

Conclusion: The counselor invites students to reflect and respond to the day's activities. The counselor collects notebooks to store in a secure location. The counselor establishes goals for next meeting.

Assessment: The counselor asks participants to write a one-sentence summary addressing what was learned today, then reviews summaries to ensure goals and objectives are being addressed.

GROUP SESSION 4: MAKING "I" STATEMENTS

Personal/Social Development Standard C: Students will understand safety and survival skills.

Competency: Students will learn coping skills for managing life events.

Learning Objectives: After the class activity and counselor-led instruction, students will be able to:

- Identify and discuss the segments of a complete "I" statement (for example, feeling identification).
- Make "I" statements during partner scenario role plays.

Materials: Flipchart with pens or chalkboard and chalk.

Activities

Introduction: After check-ins and/or icebreakers, the counselor begins by introducing the concept of "I" statements.

Counseling Activity: The counselor makes clear that "I" statements omit the word *you*. The purpose of the "I" statement is to have ownership of the feeling(s) without placing blame on others while stating the problem or issue and, when possible, advocating for an alternative solution. An "I" statement merely states the feeling, names the situation or circumstances creating the feeling, and offers a potential solution (optional).

Using an example (either student generated or predetermined), the counselor demonstrates an effective "I" statement:

I_____ *(name the feeling)* because_____ *(situation)*.
I wish_____ *(alternative)*.

An example: I feel *angry* because *I was at school by 4:30 P.M. and no one else came.* I would have liked *a phone call or something* to let me know what was happening.

Initially students may be uncomfortable with "talking this way." The group can generate scenarios for the counselor to role play, thus providing examples before they begin working in pairs.

The group begins by using pregenerated scenarios (for example, situations the counselor has directly observed via working with students). One partner takes the part of the person creating the problem (for example, not making the phone call) and the other partner is the responder (generating the "I" statement). Partners switch roles after each scenario. If time permits, partners can generate original scenarios. The school counselor might also ask students to switch partners.

The counselor should allow time after each role play for the students to process the following:

- How it felt to make the "I" statement
- How it felt to receive the "I" statement
- What, if anything, could have been done differently

Conclusion: The counselor asks for discussion on the following statement: Speaking up (that is, "I" statements) can reduce or eliminate stress. If appropriate and time allows, the counselor can ask students for any specific examples.

The counselor can assign students to practice making five "I" statements with a friend and five at home with a parent or sibling before the next group meeting. Students should make written notations of what happened, how it felt for them, and what the outcome was, and make suggestions or ideas for improvement (if appropriate).

Assessment: Via role plays and discussion, the school counselor will determine the students' knowledge and understanding of the "I" statement content and purpose and students' application of "I" statements to their own lives.

Follow-up: The counselor reminds students there are two remaining group meetings. At the next meeting, the counselor will begin group by asking members to share a successful "I" statement situation.

GROUP SESSION 5: STRESS, FOOD, AND EXERCISE

Personal/Social Standard C: Students will understand safety and survival skills.

Competency: Students will learn techniques for managing stress and conflict.

Learning Objectives: After the group activities, students will be able to:

- Identify and discuss examples of healthy and unhealthy foods
- Identify and discuss examples of how food is or is not used when stress is present
- Identify and discuss examples of how exercise is or is not used during stressful times
- Make healthy choices (food and exercise) when under stress in their daily lives

Materials: Flipchart with pens or chalkboard and chalk.

Activities:

Introduction: The counselor begins the group by asking students to share a successful "I" statement situation (assignment from last meeting). The counselor can make notations or highlights on the flipchart.

The counselor explains that today's group focuses on healthy and unhealthy choices made during stress, specifically in the areas of food and exercise. The goal for today is not an in-depth understanding of nutritional or exercise impact upon the body, but rather to develop an awareness of food and exercise use and misuse during stressful times. The counselor records each activity's highlights on the flipchart or chalkboard.

Counseling Activity: The counselor asks for examples of good nutrition (for example, what makes up a good breakfast?). The counselor should make sure to highlight the concept that simple sugars (for example, sugar-coated cereals, candy bars) are examples of poor nutrition because they are quickly "burned," leaving the individual in a low glucose (sugar) state. Complex sugars and/or carbohydrates (for example, fruits, shredded wheat, bread) provide more nutrition and "burn" longer in the system. The counselor refers to the Body Response to Stress diagram (Handout 11.1).

The counselor asks students to share examples of foods eaten during stressful situations. For example, when studying for a test do they eat candy, drink colas, or crave pizza? Or do they undereat or not eat at all?

The counselor asks the group to discuss examples of the use and misuse of exercise during stress. The counselor should make sure to highlight the following: Under stress some individuals become sedentary, and others become overactive. (Students can refer to the Body Response to Stress diagram).

Conclusion: The counselor asks for discussion on the following statement: Healthy choices about food and exercise can reduce or eliminate stress.

The counselor can assign students to keep a stress, food, and exercise log over the next week (for example, tempted by a friend to make an unhealthy choice of eating a candy bar before the final exam). Additionally, Session 4 "I" statements could be incorporated.

Assessment: Via group discussion, the school counselor will determine students' knowledge and understanding of potential healthy and unhealthy food and exercise choices when under stress and students' application of healthy food and exercise choices to their own lives when under stress.

Follow-up: The counselor reminds students the next meeting is the final group meeting. At the next meeting, the counselor will begin group by asking members to share a successful healthy choice/decision regarding food and/or exercise made during the last week. (This could include the use of an "I" statement.)

GROUP SESSION 6: PUTTING IT ALL TOGETHER

Personal/Social Standard C: Students will understand safety and survival skills.

Competency: Students will learn techniques for managing stress and conflict.

Learning Objectives: Upon completion of group participation, students will be able to:

- Define stress
- Identify everyday and life stressors
- Identify body responses to stress
- Identify, discuss, and demonstrate an understanding of the long-term effects of stress
- Identify, discuss, and apply the model for Making Good Choices/Decisions
- Identify, discuss, and apply additional healthy choices for stress reduction

Materials: Flipchart with pens or chalkboard and chalk.

Activities

Introduction: The counselor begins the group by asking students to share a successful healthy choice/decision regarding food and/or exercise made during the last week. (This could include the use of an "I" statement.) The school counselor can make notations or highlights on the flipchart.

The counselor explains that today's group focuses on students' sharing knowledge, skills, and understandings garnered from the five previous meetings.

Counseling Activity: The counselor asks students to share:

- An important concept or idea gleaned over the past five weeks
- How, or if, they have incorporated the concept into their life
- What, if any, goals they might be thinking about setting from the knowledge gained via the group participation

Conclusion: The counselor asks students to share one "wish" they would give to the group particular to the focus of the group: stress. For example: I wish everyone in the group the ability to identify major stressors in their lives, or I hope everyone can make good "I" statements. The counselor should be prepared to give the first example to set the tone.

The counselor allows students the opportunity to share any final thoughts or ideas. If a pretest was given, the counselor should allow time for the posttest.

Follow-up: Solicit participant feedback regarding group format and information and activities. Plan a lunch time reunion of the H.A.H. group. The school counselor could also create a pre/post-participation questionnaire evaluating knowledge, understanding, and skill level regarding weekly topics. Longitudinal data could be obtained via follow-up questionnaires administered at intervals: two weeks, one month, and two months.

INDIVIDUAL COUNSELING CONSIDERATIONS

Solution-focused approaches are ideal when working with children and adolescents on stress-management issues. Solution-focused counseling asks the student to identify: (1) when the problem did not exist (exceptions to today), (2) what resources were present at the time (assets, positive coping strategies), (3) the "magic wand" question (if things could be different what would you like to see), and (4) how would you know they were different (measurable outcome). Simply stated, the student should identify: what do I want to be different (goal), how am I going to get there (plan), and how will I know when I get there (measurable outcome)? For example:

- Problem: lack of sleep
- What I want to be different: feel more rested; not sleep in my classes (goal)
- When the problem did not exist: when I was doing my homework after school and getting help on the hard subjects; going to bed by 10:00 P.M (assets, positive coping strategies)
- Plan #1: start doing homework right after school rather than later in the evening (positive strategy)
- Plan #2: ask my parent(s) to check homework; access teachers after school who can help (assets)
- I will know I reached my goal when: I get four nights of adequate sleep (measurable outcome).

CONCLUSION

Without adequate coping skills and strategies, children and adolescents can succumb to the physical and mental effects of continued stress. Eventually the effects are observed in the overall quality of life. Difficulty in concentrating, unhappiness, poor relationships, hypersensitivity, frequent illness, and exhaustion can be symptoms of high stress (Kaplan, 1990; Seaward, 2002).

School counselors are in a unique position to advocate for schoolwide, systems-level preparations and interventions such as those described in this chapter. Further, as direct service providers, they can present classroom, group, and individual interventions oriented to helping equip youth with the tools they need in order to cope and thrive in the twenty-first century. Hopefully, when a child or adolescent appears in the school counselor's office, rather than the counselor's asking (silently, of course), "What is wrong with this child?" the question can become "What stressors are occurring in this young person's environment that are influencing the current issue?"

RESOURCES

Books

Childre, D. L. (1996). *Teaching children to love: 80 games and activities for raising balanced children in unbalanced times*. Boulder Creek, CO: Planetary Publications.

Kottman, T., Ashby, J. S., & DeGraaf, D. (2001). *Adventures in guidance: How to integrate fun into your guidance program*. Alexandria, VA: American Counseling Association. Resources for activities (for example, humor, fun, and trust building). Each lesson includes goals, objectives, materials needed, and sample personalization and application processing questions.

Meeks, L., & Heit, P. (2003). *Totally awesome strategies for teaching health: A K–12 curriculum guide, lesson plans, and teaching masters for implementing the National Health Education Standards*. New York, NY: McGraw-Hill.

Oregon School Counselor Association. (2000). *Crosswalk: Oregon common curriculum goals and the National Standards for School Counseling Programs*. Salem, OR: Oregon Department of Education, Office of Student Services. Web site at http://wvi.com/~osca/. Telephone 503-378-5585. Good resource demonstrating alignment of National Standards for Comprehensive School Counseling Programs with state classroom grade-level expectations.

Web Sites

Humor: www.comics.com
Kindness: www.actsofkindness.org
Inspiration: www.geocities.com/hollywood/hills/2844/qp.htm
    www.followyourdreams.com

www.successnet.org/library2.htm
www.quoteland.com
www.bartleby.com/100

Eric Clearinghouse on Disabilities and Gifted Education: http://ericec.org. 1110 North Glebe Road, Arlington, Virginia 22201; 1-800-328-0272. Additional web addresses for gifted and talented: www.giftedbooks.com; www.sengifted.org; www.nfgcc.org (National Foundation for Gifted and Creative Children); www.nagc.org (National Association for Gifted Children); www.gifteddevelopment.com.

Stress Management and Emotional Wellness Links: www.imt.net/~randolfi/StressLinks.html. Excellent resource links (for example, relaxation techniques; cognitive approaches including humor; situational approaches including time management; social support; kids and stress): www.stresstoughness.com.

REFERENCES

Balch, J. F., & Balch, P. S. (1997). *Prescription for nutritional health* (2nd ed.). Garden City Park, NY: Avery Publishing Co.

Boyce, G. C., Marshall, E. S., & Peters, M. (1999). Daily stressors, coping responses and uplifts of adolescents with disabilities. *Education and Training in Mental Retardation and Developmental Disabilities, 34*(4), 406–417.

Byrne, B. (2000). Relationships between anxiety, fear, self-esteem and coping strategies in adolescence. *Adolescence, 35*(37), 201–215.

Chapman, P. L., & Mullis, R. L. (1999). Adolescent coping strategies and self-esteem. *Child Study Journal, 29*(1), 69–77.

de Anda, D., & Bradley, M. (1997). A study of stress, stressors and coping strategies among middle school adolescents. *Social Work in Education, 19*(2), 87–98.

DeWolfe, A., & Saunders, A. M. (1995). Stress reduction in sixth-grade students. *Journal of Experimental Education, 63,* 315–329.

Dubow, E. F., Tisak, J., Causey, D., Hryshko, A., & Reid, G. (1991). A two-year longitudinal study of stressful life events, social support, and social problem-solving skills: Contributions to children's behavioral and academic adjustment. *Child Development, 62,* 583–599.

Duis, S. S., & Summers, M. (1997). Parent versus child stress in diverse family types: An ecological approach. *Topics in Early Childhood Special Education, 17*(1), 53–73.

Dumont, M., & Provost, M. A. (1999). Resilience in adolescents: Protective role of social support, coping strategies, self-esteem and social activities on experience of stress and depression. *Journal of Youth and Adolescence, 28*(3), 343–363.

Frydenberg, E., & Lewis, R. (1991). Adolescent coping styles and strategies: Is there functional and dysfunctional coping? *Australian Journal of Guidance and Counseling, 1,* 35–42.

Frydenberg, E., & Lewis, R. (1993). Boys play sports and girls turn to others: Age, gender and ethnicity as determinants of coping. *Journal of Adolescence, 16,* 252–266.

Geisthardt, C., & Munsch, J. (1996). Coping with school stress: A comparison of adolescents with and without learning disabilities. *Journal of Learning Disabilities, 29*(3), 287–296.

Gilbert, J. N., & Orlick, T. (1996). Evaluation of a life skills program with grade two children. *Elementary School Guidance & Counseling, 31*(2), 139–151.

Gullone, E., & King, N. J. (1993). The fears of youth in the 1990s: Contemporary normative data. *Journal of Genetic Psychology, 154*(2), 137–153.

Igoa, C. (1995). *The inner world of the immigrant child.* Mahway, NJ: Lawrence Erlbaum Associates, Inc.

Long, L. J. (1998). Less stress in school. *Education Digest, 63*(9), 37–38.

Kaplan, L. S. (1990). *Helping gifted students with stress management.* (ERIC Document Reproduction Service No. ED321493). Retrieved March 28, 2002, from www.kidsource.com.

Kaplan, A., & Midgley, C. (1999). The relationship between perceptions of the classroom goal structure and early adolescents' affect in school: The mediating role of coping strategies. *Learning & Individual Differences, 11*(2), 187–212.

Kashani, J., Suarez, L., Allan, W., & Reid, J. (1997). Hopelessness in inpatient youths: A closer look at behavior, emotional expression, and social support. *Journal of the American Academy of Child and Adolescent Psychiatry, 36*(11), 1625–1631.

Massey, M. S. (1998). *Promoting stress management: The role of comprehensive school health programs.* Washington, DC: ERIC Clearinghouse on Teaching and Teacher Education (ERIC Document Reproduction Service No. ED421480).

McCraty, R., Atkinson, M., Tomasino, D., Goelitz, J., & Mayrovitz, H. N. (1999). The impact of an emotional self-management skills course on psychosocial functioning and autonomic recovery to stress in middle school children. *Integrative Physiological & Behavioral Science, 34*(4), 246–268.

Meeks, L., & Heit, P. (1992). *Comprehensive school health education: Totally awesome strategies for teaching health.* Blacklick, OH: Meeks Heit Publishing.

Meeks, L., Heit, P. & Page, R. (1996). *Comprehensive school health education: Totally awesome strategies for teaching health.* Chicago: Everyday Learning Corporation.

National Association for Gifted Children. (2002). *Recent research on guidance, counseling and therapy for the gifted: Affective issues and the gifted series.* Retrieved March 28, 2002, from www.nagc.org/CounGuide.

Omizo, M. M., & Omizo, S. A. (1992). Promoting wellness among elementary school children. *Journal of Counseling & Development, 71*(2), 194–198.

Orlick, T. (1993). *Free to feel great: Teaching children to excel at living.* Carp, Ontario: Creative Bound.

Palmer, P. (1998). *The courage to teach: Exploring the inner landscape of a teacher's life.* San Francisco, CA: Jossey-Bass, Publisher.

Payne, R. K. (2001). *A framework for understanding poverty.* Highlands, TX: aha! Process, Inc.

Petersen, A. C., Sarigiani, P. A., & Kennedy, R. E. (1991). Adolescent depression: Why more girls? *Journal of Youth and Adolescence, 20,* 247–271.

Piko, B. (2001). Gender differences and similarities in adolescents' ways of coping. *Psychological Record, 51*(2), 223–235.

Roeser, R. W., Midgley, C., & Urdan, T. C. (1996). Perceptions of the school psychological environment and early adolescents' psychological and behavioral functioning in school: The mediating role of goals and belonging. *Journal of Educational Psychology, 88,* 408–422.

Romano, J. L. (1992). Psycho-educational interventions for stress management and well-being. *Journal of Counseling & Development, 71*(2), 199–202.

Romano, J. L. (1997). Stress and coping: a qualitative study of 4th and 5th graders. *Elementary School Guidance & Counseling, 31*(4), 273–282.

Romano, J. L., & Miller, J. P. (1996). Stress and well-being in the elementary school: A classroom curriculum. *School Counselor, 43*(4), 268–276.

Seaward, B. L. (1994). *Managing stress: Principles and strategies for health and well being.* Boston, MA: Jones & Bartlett Publishers.

Seaward, B. L. (2002). *Managing stress: Principles and strategies for health and well being* (3rd ed.). Sudbury, MA: Jones & Bartlett Publishers.

Silverman, L. K. (1993). *Counseling the gifted and talented.* Denver, CO: Love Publishing.

Slavin, R. E. (2000). *Educational psychology: Theory and practice.* Needham Heights, MA: Allyn & Bacon.

Swassing, R. (1998). *From the editor, Ohio Association for Gifted Children.* Retrieved March 28, 2002, from www.sengifted.org/editor.

Vissing, Y. M. (1996). *Out of sight out of mind: Homeless children and families in small-town America.* Lexington: University Press of Kentucky.

Webb, J. T. (2002). *Existential depression in gifted individuals: Supporting emotional needs of the gifted.* Retrieved March 28, 2002, from www.giftedbooks.com.

Wenz Gross, M., & Siperstein, G. N. (1998). Students with learning problems at risk in middle school: Stress, social support and adjustment. *Exceptional Children, 65*(1), 91–100.

BODY RESPONSE TO STRESS

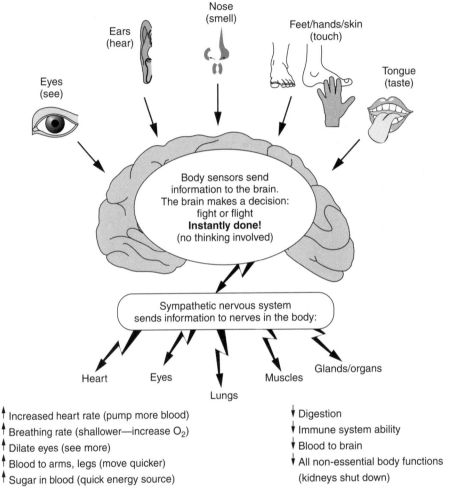

Nose
(smell)

Ears
(hear)

Feet/hands/skin
(touch)

Eyes
(see)

Tongue
(taste)

Body sensors send
information to the brain.
The brain makes a decision:
fight or flight
Instantly done!
(no thinking involved)

Sympathetic nervous system
sends information to nerves in the body:

Heart   Eyes   Muscles   Glands/organs

Lungs

↑ Increased heart rate (pump more blood)
↑ Breathing rate (shallower—increase O_2)
↑ Dilate eyes (see more)
↑ Blood to arms, legs (move quicker)
↑ Sugar in blood (quick energy source)

↓ Digestion
↓ Immune system ability
↓ Blood to brain
↓ All non-essential body functions
   (kidneys shut down)

After stress is over, the body returns to normal via parasympathetic nerves
—or—
If stress continues over time, the body's systems are without a good blood
supply and essential nutrients. The results:

- **sleep patterns are interrupted**
- **vulnerable to sickness**

- **poor digestion**
- **body is run-down**

MAKING GOOD CHOICES/DECISIONS

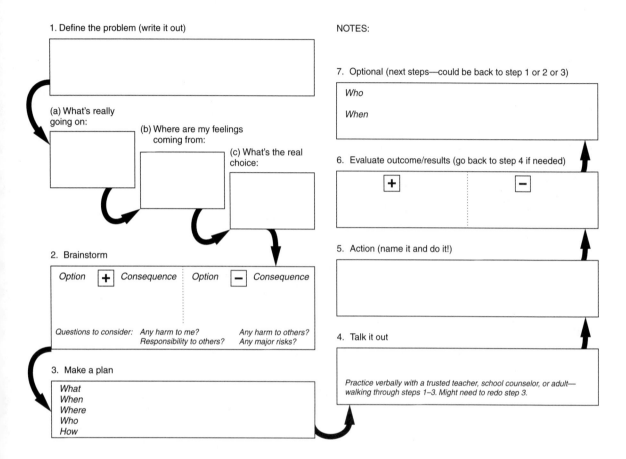

1. Define the problem (write it out)

(a) What's really going on:

(b) Where are my feelings coming from:

(c) What's the real choice:

2. Brainstorm

Option **+** Consequence   Option **−** Consequence

Questions to consider: Any harm to me?   Any harm to others?
                         Responsibility to others?   Any major risks?

3. Make a plan

What
When
Where
Who
How

NOTES:

7. Optional (next steps—could be back to step 1 or 2 or 3)

Who

When

6. Evaluate outcome/results (go back to step 4 if needed)

+   **−**

5. Action (name it and do it!)

4. Talk it out

Practice verbally with a trusted teacher, school counselor, or adult—walking through steps 1–3. Might need to redo step 3.

HANDOUT 11.3

SAMPLE WORKBOOK PAGE

I notice I am stressed when:

1. _____

2. _____

Better strategies for coping with stress include:

1. _____

2. _____

My goals for the next week are:

1. _____

2. _____

SCHOOL COUNSELORS AS LEADERS AND ADVOCATES IN ADDRESSING SEXUAL HARASSMENT

Carolyn B. Stone, University of North Florida

INTRODUCTION

Sarah, a fifth-grade student, reported to her teacher that the boys were snapping the girls' bra straps on the playground. The teacher told her that the boys were "best ignored. Try wearing two blouses or a sweater over your blouse, and this will discourage them."

Sandy, a seventh-grader, reported to her assistant principal that boys were deliberately rubbing their bodies up against her and other girls in the crowded hallways during class changes. The assistant principal told her that there was nothing that could be done unless Sandy could give her the names of the boys, and then she would discipline them.

Rolanda, an eleventh-grader, confided to her friends that the four boys who had lockers near hers had pictures of Playboy centerfolds up in their lockers and have made comments to her such as "I bet this is how you look with your clothes off." Rolanda's friends told her not to "make a big deal out of it" and to "just ignore it."

Martin's teacher overheard his friends laughing at him for being cornered on a bus by a girl who aggressively grabbed at his "private parts," taunting him that there was nothing there. When Martin's teacher asked him about the incident, he begged her not to confront the girl or tell on her. The teacher told him that she had no choice but to confront the girl with the information that was related to her.

How can school counselors exercise a leadership and advocacy role in the above scenarios? School counselors in their advocacy role can empower students with the knowledge and support needed to participate in a fair, equitable, and hospitable school environment. As human behavior specialists, school counselors can be instrumental in helping to heighten awareness of the sexual harassment problem and assist in establishing a safe school environment. More importantly, the school counselor can be an advocate and a source of strength for the individual student who needs help in confronting and dealing with sexual harassment.

Defining and responding to sexual harassment is not easy, as males and females often have different ways of looking at sexual harassment (Marczely, 1999; Moore & Rienzo, 1998; Rowell, McBride, & Nelson-Leaf, 1996). Sexual harassment is further complicated for school counselors because as many as 90 percent of students (Harris/Scholastic Research, 1993) do not tell a school official that they have been victimized. Recommendations, suggestions, and interventions included in this chapter can help school counselors foster a more equitable and healthier school climate. Through leadership and advocacy, school counselors can negate the emotional costs of sexual harassment by encouraging victims to come forth and supporting victims when they do seek help.

LITERATURE REVIEW

Definition and Prevalence

Sexual harassment has become a subject of social and educational policy debate and discourse. Recent legislation and court rulings give counselors a legal definition of sexual harassment and support counselors to serve as advocates against student-on-student harassment. In 1997, the U.S. Department of Education's Office of Civil Rights, the office that governs Title IX implementation, issued the definition of sexual harassment under Title IX as "sufficiently severe, persistent, or pervasive that it adversely affects a student's education or creates a hostile or abusive educational environment and the conduct must be sexual in nature" (U.S. Department of Education, Office of Civil Rights, 1997, p. 12036). Title IX of the Education Amendments was enacted by Congress in 1972 and is a federal mandate against sex discrimination in education, in which gender can no longer influence educational opportunities.

Consistently, three elements appear in definitions of sexual harassment: (1) the behavior is unwanted or unwelcome, (2) the behavior is sexual or related to the gender of the person, and (3) the behavior occurs in the context of a relationship where one person has more power, such as the informal power one student can have over another (Moore & Rienzo, 1998; Sandler, 1994).

In 1993, the American Association of University Women (AAUW) defined sexual harassment as "unwanted and unwelcome sexual attention" and commissioned a study of 1,600 teens to provide a profile of the problem of sexual harassment in schools in terms of the educational, emotional, and behavioral impact of sexual harassment (Harris/Scholastic Research, 1993, p. 6). This research, aimed at examining equity in educational access and preparation, uncovered a significant problem in sexual harassment. The study, commonly referred to as Hostile Hallways, indicated that four out of five students have experienced some form of sexual harassment in school, with both males and females as targets, although girls experienced more harassment and suffered graver consequences (Harris/Scholastic Research).

Thirty-one percent of girls experienced harassment "often," compared to 18 percent of boys. Thirteen percent of girls and 9 percent of boys reported being "forced to do something sexual at school other than kissing" (Bryant, 1993, p. 10).

An examination of student-on-student sexual harassment lawsuits from 1994 to 1999 provides additional insight. Twenty-two of the twenty-seven complaints were female targets against male perpetrators, two cases were males against males, and three were female targets with both male and female perpetrators. All age levels from elementary to secondary were involved, and the conduct ranged from verbal harassment to rape (Sullivan & Zirkel, 1999).

Sexual harassment is infrequently reported. In the Hostile Hallways study, fewer than 10 percent of the students who said they were a victim of sexual harassment told an adult at their school, and fewer than 25 percent told a parent or other family member. Sixty-three percent of harassed students said they told a friend, and 23 percent of harassed students said they told no one (Harris/Scholastic Research, 1993).

With 80 percent of students experiencing sexual harassment and fewer than 10 percent of that number reporting the harassment to an adult at school, what advocacy is needed? What can be done to help students who are harassed? Recent court rulings have given school counselors legal muscle to encourage students to come forward, to support students who have been harassed, and to contribute toward changing hostile school climates into healthy ones. Following is a brief chronology of court cases and laws that inform school counselors' practice.

School Counselors Given Legal Muscle to Intervene

Throughout the 1990s, sexual harassment in schools was on the national consciousness and on the agendas of school-board policy makers. The 1990s opened with the U.S. Supreme Court decision in *Franklin v. Gwinnett County Public Schools* (1992), in which the court drew a parallel between teacher-on-student sexual harassment and supervisor-to-subordinate harassment found in the workplace (Marczely, 1999). The *Franklin* ruling established a precedent for a number of subsequent court cases in which plaintiffs successfully sought to extend the Supreme Court's findings in *Franklin* from teacher-on-student sexual harassment to student-on-student sexual harassment (Zirkel, Richardson, & Goldberg, 1995). Sullivan and Zirkel (1999) examined twenty-one cases brought under Title IX following *Franklin* and found that twenty of the cases recognized Title IX as providing a statutory basis for a claim of student-on-student sexual harassment.

The U.S. Supreme Court in *Davis v. Monroe County Board of Education* (1999) has given sexual harassment an even more prominent place on the national agenda. The *Davis* case, in combination with Title IX of the Education Amendments of 1972 and other legislation and case law, established that public schools can be forced to pay damages for failing to stop student-on-student sexual harassment. The *Davis* case is predicted to be a defining court case, cited and exercised in subsequent litigation, defining the potential economic impact of sexual harassment on school districts that do not establish or strengthen their district's posture against sexual harassment. School districts can no longer ignore sexual harassment or give it cursory attention. *Davis* demands advocacy against known sexual harassment (Biskupic, 1999; *Davis v. Monroe County Board of Education*, 1999; U.S. Department of Education, Office of Civil Rights, 1997; Van Boven, 1999).

In the *Davis* case a fifth-grade girl, L. Davis, reported sexual abuse behaviors by G.F. to her teachers for five months. Her mother also contacted the teacher and the principal (Van Boven, 1999, p. 33). The principal allegedly stated, "I guess I'll have to threaten him a bit harder," but at no time was G.F. disciplined for his actions against L., and it was only after three months of complaints that any effort was made to separate L. and G. F.'s desks (Zirkel, 1999, p. 172). The complaint alleged that L. was unable to concentrate on her studies (her previously high grades dropped), and her father found a suicide note. The abuse continued until Mrs. Davis filed a complaint with the Monroe County, Georgia, Sheriff Department, and G. F. pleaded guilty to sexual battery. Then Mrs. Davis filed a $1 million lawsuit under Title IX's prohibition of sex discrimination in schools (*Davis v. Monroe County Board of Education*, 1999).

Justice Sandra Day O'Connor, writing for the majority in the Supreme Court's 5 to 4 ruling in favor of Mrs. Davis, emphasized a relatively stringent standard of proof for plaintiffs. According to the Supreme Court, liability may be imposed "only where the funding recipient is deliberately indifferent to sexual harassment, of which the recipient has actual knowledge" (Biskupic, 1999, p. A.1). The plaintiff must show harassment that is "so severe, pervasive, and objectively offensive that it can be said to deprive the victims of access to the educational opportunities or benefits provided by the school. It is not enough to show . . . that a student has been teased or called offensive names" (Biskupic, 1999, p. A.1).

The *Davis* case clearly encourages school officials to offer students more protection against sexual harassment or face monetary damages. Therefore, school counselors enter the new millennium with legal support to exercise a leadership/advocacy role to assist individual victims and to help establish an educational environment that is safe and free from sexual harassment.

School District Responsibilities

School counselors, as part of the school's leadership team, can help implement the responsibilities as outlined by the 1997 U.S. Department of Education's Office of Civil Rights (OCR). The OCR's policy guide declared that student-on-student sexual harassment is illegal and that school districts must adopt and publish a policy against sexual harassment that includes statements that it is illegal. The policy must include grievance procedures providing resolution of complaints of harassment based on sex. School districts are not required to adopt a separate policy prohibiting sexual harassment, but the district's policy must apply to sexual harassment. If the school district's general Title IX policy does not make students aware of conduct that constitutes sexual harassment, then the policy will be considered ineffective (U.S. Department of Education, Office of Civil Rights, 1997).

A hostile environment exists in the school's programs or activities if "the school knows or should have known of sexual harassment, and the school fails to take immediate and appropriate corrective action" (U.S. Department of Education, Office of Civil Rights, 1997, p. 12049). A hostile environment is created if conduct of a sexual nature is "sufficiently severe, persistent, or pervasive to limit a student's ability to participate in or benefit from the education program or to create a hostile or abusive educational environment" (U.S. Department of Education, Office of Civil Rights, 1997, p. 12041). "Title IX does not require schools to take responsibility for the actions of other students but does require school districts to respond to student actions with corrective measures" (ACA, 1997b, p. 8). Corrective measures translate into fair and equitable grievance procedures that provide:

- Directions to students and parents for filing complaints
- Adequate, reliable, and impartial investigation of complaints, including the opportunity to present witnesses and other evidence
- Notice of the outcome of the complaint
- Assurances that the school will take steps to prevent recurrences of any harassment and to correct its discriminatory effects on the complainant (U.S. Department of Education, Office of Civil Rights, 1997)

Investigation of complaints by school officials has historically been neglected. Sullivan and Zirkel (1999) analyzed twenty-seven sexual harassment cases involving students and were "startled by the number of people the victims of harassment notified without obtaining suitable resolution. School districts in the cases to date would have difficulty escaping liability due to the number of staff the target notified" (p. 618). Liability is strong when school officials are notified and ignore complaints. The imperative to act that comes from the highest court in the land gives school counselors an entrée into advocacy that is not always provided in other social justice issues.

School Counselors Advocating for Victims of Sexual Harassment

Through the hypothetical case of Yolanda, we will examine a school counselor's leadership and advocacy role in sexual harassment. To illuminate our role in sexual harassment, we will examine legislation, case law, and recommendations from the Office of Civil Rights. In context of the "Yolanda" case, the discussion will center on the school counselor's legal and ethical obligations to students and to parents, as well as the legal and ethical complications of confidentiality with minors in schools.

The Case of Yolanda

Yolanda is a seventh-grader who is a victim of sexual harassment. Yolanda maintained above-average grades until the middle of her seventh-grade year, which brought a marked change in grades and attitude. Yolanda, who was very well developed for a thirteen-year-old, was constantly hounded by a group of boys who made comments about her breasts and other sexually suggestive remarks. Yolanda's locker was near the group of boys, and she started to carry her books around all day to avoid the locker area and only visited when she thought the majority of the boys would be gone. Yolanda's math teacher, Ms. Rodriquez, overheard Yolanda talking to her friends about the harassment; her friends were telling Yolanda not to make a big deal about it as she would only "give them [the boys] the attention they wanted." Ms. Rodriquez did not want to tell anyone about Yolanda's predicament because she felt this would be betraying information she learned by accident. Ms. Rodriquez decided to spend more time talking to Yolanda and encouraging her to discuss her situation. After four weeks in which Yolanda revealed nothing about her harassment, Ms. Rodriquez became more concerned and decided to talk to Yolanda's counselor; she feared the harassment explained recent changes in Yolanda such as disinterest in her studies, flat affect, and withdrawn and sullen demeanor. This was not the Yolanda that Ms. Rodriquez had enjoyed all year.

Mr. Estes, the school counselor, began to learn the truth of the girl's misery when Yolanda confided that it was impossible to go through a day without harassment; lately it had progressed to physical touching from a boy who grabbed her and pressed his body against hers while making groaning and moaning sounds. Yolanda explained that the harassment was witnessed by more than twenty students and that she was very embarrassed but tried to save face by laughing it off and taunting the boy that he was not man enough to satisfy her. Yolanda said she felt "dirty" making such a retort, but in her mind it was preferable to looking weak and wounded.

At first, Yolanda confided in Mr. Estes that she hated this kind of attention. When Mr. Estes explained that he would have to report the harassment to the administration, Yolanda tried to divert this by saying she liked the attention and that she liked each of these boys individually: "They are okay. They only act like big jerks when they get in a group." Yolanda was emphatic that she did not want to make a big deal out of the situation. When Mr. Estes explained that he really had no choice but to report the boys whose names Yolanda had supplied, Yolanda became angry. "You tricked me. You got me to tell you my secrets and now you are going to blab it everywhere." Mr. Estes spent time trying to reduce Yolanda's fear and resistance, and he discovered that Yolanda felt that these were tough boys who would hurt her if she got them into trouble because she told on them. Yolanda then tried another tactic by declaring she was responsible for bringing the harassment on herself by encouraging the boys' attention and by going out of her way to be near them.

Yolanda fits the profile of the harassed student, experiencing a wide range of emotions and vacillating between wanting to be free of the harassment and enduring it rather than risk being labeled a "snitch" or a "narc." Avoiding school, self-blame, helplessness, and self-doubt are familiar chords among victims of sexual harassment (Fischer, Schimmel, & Kelly, 1999; Webb, Hunnicutt, & Metha, 1997). Yolanda's confusion and pain highlight the seriousness of sexual harassment. Once regarded as innocuous horseplay, teasing, or boys-will-be-boys behavior, sexual harassment is now widely understood to be destructive and illegal.

School Counselors' Responsibilities

As school counselors develop and implement intervention strategies and support students who are victims of sexual harassment, they must consider difficult, legitimate legal and ethical questions. Below are four major issues in the form of questions that Yolanda's school counselor may face. The questions are designed to examine the complexities of protecting students' confidentiality while adhering to the OCR guidelines of Title IX legislation.

1. Yolanda requested that Mr. Estes not report the boys as harassers. **Must Mr. Estes report the harassment?** The counselor must engage in a delicate balance between the obligation to protect the confidences of the harassed student and the responsibility to help the administration stop the sexual harassment. Yolanda's counselor is required by law to report the sexual harassment. "A school has actual notice of sexual harassment if an agent or responsible employee of the school receives notification" (U.S. Department of Education, Office of Civil Rights, 1997, p. 12037). It is not necessary that the counselor or any other person notified be in a position to take appropriate steps to end the harassment or prevent its recurrence, but Title IX requires that harassment be reported to school officials who have the responsibility to take appropriate action. School officials have been given notice whenever they "knew" of the behavior. In a confidential counseling conference, if a student victim of sexual harassment confides in the counselor, then this constitutes "notice" and triggers the school's responsibility to take "corrective action" (ACA, 1997b, p. 9).

2. Yolanda requested confidentiality. **Can Mr. Estes keep Yolanda's confidence?** Students deserve assurances that their confidences in a counseling relationship will not be breached. Without the safety of a confidential, secure environment in which trust can be established and maintained, students may not seek help. The primacy of confidentiality, clear in the code of ethics and standards of practice for the American Counseling Association (ACA, 1997a, B.1) and the American School Counselor Association (ASCA, 1998, A.2.b), instructs this school counselor to protect Yolanda's privacy unless disclosure is in her best interest or is required by law. Must Yolanda be identified by name in a report of the harassment? The Office of Civil Rights (OCR) recognizes that declining to honor a student's confidentiality may discourage reporting of harassment; therefore, OCR promotes protecting confidentiality. On the other hand, OCR realizes that withholding the name of the victim may interfere with the investigation and infringe on the due process rights of the accused. In the context of each situation, school counselors and school administrators will need to strike a balance to honor an alleged victim's request for confidentiality if this can be done "consistently with the school's obligation to remedy the harassment and take steps to prevent further harassment" (U.S. Department of Education, Office of Civil Rights, 1997, p. 12037). The school counselor in this situation will want to educate Yolanda about the legal requirement for school counselors to report sexual harassment and if absolutely necessary, encourage Yolanda to allow her identity to be known to aid in addressing sexual harassment. A student's request for confidentiality should be respected even if this hinders the investigation. The school should make every effort to address the grievance despite being unable to identify the victim, but sometimes the investigation must be sacrificed to protect the

victim. Depending on the seriousness of the harassment and the age of the victim, the identity of the harassed may as a last resort have to be revealed. For example, given what we currently know in the hypothetical case of Yolanda, there is no overriding reason for revealing her identity against her wishes. However, if Yolanda was being stalked by a sexual harasser and her physical safety was in question, the duty to protect her from clear, imminent danger might outweigh the duty to protect her confidences.

3. What if Mr. Estes reports the boy who grabbed Yolanda, the boy vehemently denies the accusation, and the boy's parents demand full disclosure of the incident to include the name of the accuser? **Must he give Yolanda's name to the boy and his parents at this juncture?** If Yolanda continued to insist on anonymity and there were no other accusers known and willing to come forth, then the appropriate response might be to forgo disciplinary action against the accused as the alleged harasser could not respond to the charges. In short, Yolanda's confidentiality needs might outweigh the need for disciplinary action against the accused. Other strategies would have to be implemented, such as holding a schoolwide sexual harassment workshop, surveying students to see how widespread the problem is, and responding to the survey results by implementing prevention measures. In this situation, the school might still be able to effectively respond to the harassment and prevent harassment of other students (U.S. Department of Education, Office of Civil Rights, 1997).

4. **Should Yolanda's parents be informed?** What is the counselor's legal and ethical responsibility to Yolanda's parents? Yolanda's academic and emotional well-being appear to be compromised by the harassment. The school counselor's obligation to Yolanda extends beyond Yolanda to include her parents, teachers, administrators, and other students (ASCA, 1998). Section B of the ASCA ethical standards suggests that to facilitate the maximum development of the counselee, school counselors should collaborate and establish a cooperative relationship with parents (ASCA, 1998). Consistent with professional codes, judicial decisions have historically protected parental rights. The Supreme Court of the United States continues to assert parents' legal ability to raise their children and to provide guidance in the values and decisions governing their children. Courts generally have vested the rights of minors in their parents. In 1979, the United States Supreme Court declared: "We have recognized three reasons justifying the conclusion that the constitutional rights of children cannot be equated with those of adults: the peculiar vulnerability of children; their inability to make critical decisions in an informed, mature manner; and the importance of the parental role in child rearing" (Huey & Remley, 1988, p. 96).

The school setting considerably complicates the issue of confidentiality (American School Counselor Association, 1986; Corey & Corey, 1997; Huey & Remley, 1988; Isaacs & Stone, 1998) as parents send students to school for academics; when individual counseling enters into the education picture, tension develops between a parent's right to be the guiding voice in their children's lives and a student's right to privacy in the counseling arena (Huey & Remley, 1988; Isaacs & Stone, 1998; Salo & Shumate, 1993). If Yolanda's counselor decides to continue to work with her in the absence of parental knowledge of the true nature and extent of the problem, the counselor must be ready to defend his or her decision that Yolanda was mature enough to make such decisions without parental involvement and that no clear danger existed for her. School counselors have to discern between the maturity level of minors and their confidentiality needs and parents' rights to govern their children with full knowledge of the critical issues their children are facing. To further illustrate these points, the following three sections contain schoolwide interventions that school counselors can spearhead, strategies for school counselors to employ in responding to individual victims, and lesson plans to use in classroom guidance and small-group counseling.

WHOLE-SCHOOL INTERVENTIONS

The challenge for school counselors is to help create an environment free of sexual harassment and to encourage students to report harassment when it does occur. School counselors cannot take on the task of eliminating sexual harassment from their school; but as part of the leadership team of the school, they can be another set of eyes and ears, contributing greatly to the initiative by identifying harassment and collaborating and teaming with the internal and external members of their school community to eliminate harassment. Following are recommendations for the school counselor, in the role of leader and advocate, to help school administrators, teachers, and others implement schoolwide prevention programs and effectively respond to sexual harassment:

1. Working through your supervisors and other stakeholders, collaborate to implement a school district and school site policy protecting all students against sexual harassment, to include a sexual orientation clause to protect gay, lesbian, bisexual, and transgendered youth. Elements of an effective sexual harassment policy should include:
   a. A code of conduct with a strong *no tolerance* statement that explains the commitment to maintain an educational environment free of fear and intimidation
   b. A clear statement that sexual harassment will result in disciplinary action
   c. Examples of specific sexual harassment behavior
   d. Legal definitions and the applicable laws
   e. A statement of confidentiality that explains that the victim's identity will remain confidential to the extent possible and explains the circumstances under which confidences will be breached, for example, duty to protect the victim or other potential victims
   f. The name of at least one person of each gender to contact if students feel they have been a victim of sexual harassment (preferably school counselors)

    g. Detailed grievance procedures and contact information for the complaint manager

    h. A statement regarding training for staff and students (Bryant, 1993; Minnesota Department of Education, 1993; Moore & Rienzo, 1998; Strauss & Espeland, 1992; Webb et al., 1997)

2. Work with other stakeholders to adopt a plan for dissemination of the sexual harassment policy and other information on sexual harassment. Use forums such as student assemblies, club meetings, bulletin boards, brochures, and the code of conduct.

3. Publicize widely that the school counseling office is a safe place for students to come and talk if they feel they are being sexually harassed.

4. Implement a series of classroom guidance lessons on respecting differences in others. Include in the series education about bullying, name calling, and sexual harassment. Provide strategies to help students understand how to identify, prevent, and report all kinds of harassment, including sexual harassment. The primary objectives of these lessons would be to increase students', appreciation for diversity, ability to advocate for themselves and others, and willingness to report harassment.

5. Work with perpetrators in small groups. Help them understand the emotional costs to victims of sexual harassment.

6. Provide periodic on-site sexual harassment workshops for staff. All school personnel should be educated about:

    a. Identifying harassment

    b. Reporting harassment, including reporting procedures and an understanding of the school district's sexual harassment policy and grievance procedures

    c. Establishing a school and classroom climate that does not foster or tolerate harassment

    d. Implementing and developing schoolwide and classroom interventions

7. Contact Parents and Friends of Lesbians and Gays (PFLAG), an international support group, and see whether they have a local chapter. Use this support group as a resource for information about other local resources and support groups to assist students and their parents. Encourage school officials to allow written information on bulletin boards and in brochures detailing support groups and community activities for all minority groups, to include questioning and gay, lesbian, bisexual, or transgendered students. (It is less threatening to school officials to have a bulletin board that gives referral resources in the community for support groups for a number of minority groups. In this context, gay, lesbian, and bisexual groups are one more minority group in the information exchange.)

8. Implement violence prevention activities. Students across Colorado returned to school wearing tiny patches that had the single word "respect." The patch was designed to promote harmony among the school cliques exposed in the Columbine High School shooting.

9. Help develop and disseminate strategies to avoid victimizing students twice. It is critical that the identity of the harassed be protected. Educators who confront perpetrators must do so without revealing the time, place, or type of harassment that the victim confided. Techniques such as positioning an adult where they can observe the harassment will allow an introductory comment such as "Ms. Jones observed you pulling at a student's bra" rather than "We have information from a student that you are pulling at her bra and making lewd remarks to her about her breasts." If there is a choice between calling the harasser in and risking the identity of the harassed, then it may be in the victim's best interest that the student be stopped by using another approach besides direct confrontation. The bottom line is that the primary responsibility is to the well-being of the victim. If students feel that they are risking more by telling then by just enduring the harassment, then the problem will not be addressed.

CLASSROOM GUIDANCE ACTIVITIES

Following are three classroom guidance lessons suitable for upper elementary and middle school and six small-group sessions for high school. All of these lessons can be adapted to use in large or small groups.

LESSON 1: NAME CALLING, TEASING, BULLYING, AND SEXUAL HARASSMENT

Personal/Social Development Standard C: Students will understand safety and survival skills.

Competency: Students will learn about the relationship between rules, laws, safety, and the protection of individual rights.

Learning Objectives

- Students will feel the effects of discrimination and/or being privileged.
- Students will describe how discrimination or privilege made them feel.
- Students will identify ways in which people are different.
- Students will identify ways in which people discriminate or try to hurt others who are different from them, such as name calling, teasing, bullying, harassment, and sexual harassment behaviors.
- Students will begin to understand the emotional impact of sexual harassment.

Materials: Small blue cutouts of a star, small red cutouts of a stop sign, chalkboards or whiteboards.

Developmental Learning Activity

Introduction: The counselor starts this lesson by explaining to the class that there will be a discussion of how people are alike and how they are different. The people with blue stars will be favored, but this is not revealed to the students in advance. Proceed by following the steps below.

Activities: The counselor begins by handing half the class red stop signs and half the class blue stars. The counselor has all the students with blue stars sit in the front of the room and starts talking about how people are alike and how they are different. The counselor calls only on students with blue stars, reinforces them, and ignores or extinguishes the efforts to participate of the students with red stop signs. This continues for five to ten minutes.

The counselor then asks the red stop sign students to describe how they felt about the treatment they and their fellow students received. The same question follows with the blue stars. The counselor discusses the difference in feelings of the two groups, the unfairness of the situation, and the fact that this is how some people experience life because they are victimized for being "different."

The counselor labels two classroom boards *Hurtful Actions or Words* and *Respectful Behaviors or Words*. In groups of five, students come to the boards and list ways in which they or their classmates have hurt other people with words or actions. Students then go to the board and write words or actions that demonstrate respect for others.

A student records all the words on paper so that they can be used in a follow-up lesson.

In small groups of five, the students discuss the words and actions recorded and how they believe the recipient of these words and actions felt. Back in the full group, they report their findings.

From the list under "Follow-up," the counselor adds to the discussion any actions or words they have not included.

Conclusion: The counselor leaves the students with the impression that discrimination and bullying are not innocuous horseplay but emotional hurt.

Assessment: The counselor starts the next classroom guidance lesson by asking the students to recap the words they labeled *Hurtful Actions or Words* and *Respectful Behavior or Words*. The counselor then rereads the words the students identified and adds any new ones to the list. Assessment is determined by the retention and carry-over from the previous lesson.

Follow-up: From the list of hurtful actions or words, the teacher asks students to identify the words that denote sexual harassment and to group these words together, because this is going to be the topic of the next class that the school counselor comes in to conduct. The school counselor starts the second lesson in the series using these words as the starting point for defining sexual harassment. Some examples of hurtful actions or words that become sexual harassment are:

- Telling sexual jokes
- Showing nude pictures

- Calling a classmate gay, lez, fag, a he/she, and the like
- Starting or spreading rumors about a student that are sexual in nature
- Writing messages about students that are sexual in nature on textbooks, chalk boards, bathroom walls, and the like
- Passing notes to or about a student that are sexually suggestive in nature
- Rubbing, touching, blocking
- Leering and suggestive expressions that are sexual in nature and unwanted
- Asking for sexual favors
- Tugging at another's clothes in a sexually suggestive way
- Trying to pull another's clothes off or down

LESSON 2: DEFINING SEXUAL HARASSMENT

Personal/Social Development Standard C: Students will understand safety and survival skills.

Competencies

- Students will learn about the relationship between rules, laws, safety, and the protection of individual rights.
- Students will learn the difference between appropriate and inappropriate physical contact.

Learning Objectives

- Students will help define sexual harassment.
- Students will identify sexual harassment behaviors.
- Students will identify the emotional impact on the recipient of sexual harassment.

Materials: Paper, pencils, classroom boards.

Developmental Learning Activity

Introduction: The counselor introduces this lesson by reviewing the points from Lesson 1 and by encouraging the students to recap the words they labeled Hurtful Actions or Words that could be defined as sexual harassment. If the students do not remember the words, the counselor refreshes their memory by reading the list the counselor and the students generated during Lesson 1.

Activities: Students will revisit the words from Lesson 1 that describe sexual harassment. Using the classroom boards, students in groups of five take a few minutes to add to the list of words or actions denoting sexual harassment. The counselor facilitates, adding and discussing areas of sexual harassment that have not been named.

Students then work in their groups of five and come up with a definition for sexual harassment, using the terms they have learned. After the breakout group, students reconvene in the large group, and with the counselor facilitating, students contribute to defining sexual harassment.

Using the information students have supplied, the counselor helps students understand that sexual harassment is difficult to define, as it depends on the person being harassed—that is, what is appropriate for one person may be harassment to another person; when the behavior is unwelcome, then it is harassment.

The counselor shares and discusses with the students the three elements of sexual harassment: (1) the behavior is unwanted or unwelcome, (2) the behavior is sexual or related to the gender of the person, and (3) the behavior occurs in the context of a relationship where one person has more power, such as the informal power one student can have over another (Sandler, 1994).

Conclusion: The counselor uses the classroom board to write a developmentally appropriate definition of sexual harassment, and the students copy the definition and explain it to someone who was not in the class.

Assessment: To start the next classroom guidance lesson, the counselor will ask the students to define sexual harassment.

Follow-up: The teacher will ask the students to give the reaction of the person to whom they explained their definition of sexual harassment. Students will be asked to begin thinking about how they can make their school an environment free of sexual harassment and to be prepared to share their ideas during the next class lesson.

LESSON 3: THE PSYCHOLOGICAL IMPACT OF SEXUAL HARASSMENT

Personal/Social Development Standard C: Students will understand safety and survival skills.

Competencies

- Students will learn about the relationship between rules, laws, safety, and the protection of individual rights.
- Students will learn the difference between appropriate and inappropriate physical contact.
- Students will demonstrate the ability to assert boundaries, rights, and personal privacy.

Learning Objectives

- Students will disclose sexual harassment they have experienced, inflicted, or observed.
- Students will label the emotions experienced by victims of sexual harassment.
- Students will identify ways to stop sexual harassment.

Materials: Paper, pencils, large sheets of paper.

Developmental Learning Activity

Introduction: The counselor recaps Lesson 2 and reminds the students that they were to be ready to give ideas about how they can make their school an environment free of sexual harassment. The counselor explains that the lesson will focus on the students' ideas but that first the class will talk about the emotional costs to victims of sexual harassment.

Activities: The counselor asks the students to write a letter to someone who has sexually harassed them or whom they have sexually harassed. In the letter, students will explain what the harassment was and how the harassment made them feel, and ask the perpetrator to stop the behavior. Students are not to reveal any identifying information. Students can write a fictitious letter if they feel they have never harassed or been a victim of sexual harassment.

The counselor asks students to volunteer to read their letters to the class. The counselor facilitates helping students label the emotions heard in the letters and identify the harassing behaviors. The counselor lists the emotions and behaviors on the board as they are identified.

The counselor discusses the students' experiences regarding what they wrote. The counselor should place particular attention on how it feels or might feel to be the recipient of such behavior.

In groups of five, students brainstorm how they can help stop sexual harassment in their school and record their answers on large paper, which they then post on the walls. The counselor processes what has been written by taking the answers and summarizing their ideas. The counselor can then determine to what extent the students have grasped the information.

Conclusion: The counselor asks students to take a few minutes to reflect on what they learned and then in one sentence to share aloud how they can contribute to making their school environment harassment free.

Assessment: Learning will be assessed by the verbal responses students give to making their school environment harassment free. Disciplinary referrals for sexual harassment behaviors will be reduced for the participating grade levels.

Follow-up: The teacher will ask students to sign a commitment that they will try to implement the ideas for making their environment free of sexual harassment.

SMALL-GROUP COUNSELING PLANS

The following six small-group counseling lessons are designed to work with high school perpetrators who have been targeted for small-group counseling intervention because they have at least one discipline referral in a six-month period for sexual harassment. The group is developmental and helps the perpetrator (1) define sexual harassment, (2) label behaviors that are harassing, (3) identify the emotions experienced by victims, (4) confess to their own harassing behavior, and (5) sign a contract to cease sexually harassing others.

GROUP SESSION 1: FLIRTING AND SEXUAL HARASSMENT

Personal/Social Development Standard C: Students will understand safety and survival skills.

Competencies

- Students will learn the difference between appropriate and inappropriate interactions and physical contact.
- Students will demonstrate the ability to assert boundaries, rights, and personal privacy.

Learning Objectives

- Students will identify the difference between flirting and sexual harassment.
- Students will identify how flirting makes the recipient feel.
- Students will identify how sexual harassment makes the recipient feel.

Materials: Paper, pencil, classroom board or two chart tablets.

Activities

Introduction: The counselor begins the group by providing informed consent for the group. The counselor should stress:

- the need for students to respect one another's confidences
- the limits of confidentiality
- the fact that confidentiality in a group cannot be guaranteed
- the importance of their not revealing the name or any identifying information about any student that they have victimized

It is very important to stress at the beginning of each group meeting how critical confidentiality is in a group such as this one. The counselor explains that the group was formed because each group member had a discipline referral for sexual harassment and that the purpose of the group is to educate them about the emotional costs to victims, to have them take ownership of their behavior, and to have them cease sexually harassing others.

Counseling Activities: On a classroom board or chart tablet the counselor writes the word *Flirting* and on another the words *Sexual Harassment*. Students in groups of five come to the boards and write down words that describe how a person feels who is the recipient of flirting and the recipient of sexual harassment.

The counselor compares and contrasts the difference between sexual harassment (unwanted behavior) and flirting. For example, sexual harassment is behavior that makes you feel bad, unattractive, degraded, powerless, invaded, demeaned, angry, sad, self-doubt, withdrawn, stressed, threatened, and the like. Flirting by contrast is behavior that can make you feel good, attractive, complimented, positive, flattered, happy, confident, valued, praised, and so on.

The counselor shares and discusses with the students the three elements of sexual harassment: (1) the behavior is unwanted or unwelcome, (2) the behavior is sexual or related to the gender of the person, and (3) the behavior occurs in the context of a relationship where one person has more power, such as the informal power one student can have over another (Sandler, 1994).

Conclusion: The counselor asks students to relate the knowledge they gained to their own personal experience as a perpetrator. The counselor cautions students not to reveal any identifying information about their victims.

Assessment: At the beginning of the second small-group counseling session, students will be able to articulate the differences between sexual harassment and flirting. Students will be able to write the three elements of sexual harassment as defined during the small-group lesson.

Follow-up: The counselor asks students to be alert to sexual harassment during the interim period between small-group Session 1 and Session 2 and to make mental notes of harassment they are observing. Students should understand they will be asked to contribute to the group the descriptions of the harassment they witnessed.

GROUP SESSION 2: THE CASE OF YOLANDA

Personal/Social Development Standard C: Students will understand safety and survival skills.

Competency: Students will identify the difference between appropriate and inappropriate interactions and physical contact.

Learning Objectives

- Students will identify sexual harassment behaviors in the school environment.
- Students will become trained observers, identifying behaviors that recipients of the behavior would likely define as sexual harassment.
- Students will discuss a hypothetical case to illuminate behaviors that constitute sexual harassment and to begin to understand the implications for victims.

Materials: Paper, pencils, the story of Yolanda, the description of *Davis v. Monroe County Board of Education* (from this chapter).

Activities

Introduction: The counselor begins by having the students describe to the group the harassment they observed in the hallways, bus, classrooms, and other places. (During the previous lesson, students were asked to be alert to sexual harassment during the interim period between group meetings).

Counseling Activity: The counselor reads or retells the case of Yolanda. Yolanda fits the profile of the harassed student, experiencing a wide range of emotions. The students label the emotions they believe Yolanda was experiencing.

Conclusion: The counselor helps the students develop a plan of action for reporting sexual harassment.

Assessment: Students can appropriately identify sexually harassing behaviors as well as the corresponding emotions felt by the victim.

Follow-up: Students will be asked to identify at least one adult they trust and can turn to in the event of sexual harassment involving themselves or others.

GROUP SESSION 3: TAKING RESPONSIBILITY

Personal/Social Development Standard C: Students will understand safety and survival skills.

Competencies

- Students will learn about the relationship between rules, laws, safety, and the protection of individual rights.
- Students will learn the difference between appropriate and inappropriate physical contact.
- Students will demonstrate the ability to assert boundaries, rights, and personal privacy.

Learning Objectives

- Students will be empathetic toward peers who have experienced sexual harassment.
- Students will provide appropriate responses to reports of sexual harassment from peers.

Materials: Paper, pencils, Dangerous Words (Handout 12.1).

Activities

Introduction: The counselor begins the lesson by discussing the fact that sexual harassment is rarely reported. The counselor asks the students to reflect on how many times they have participated in harassing behaviors that went unreported. The students discuss why they believe their victims did not always report.

Counseling Activities: The counselor leads a discussion of the way peers often advise their classmates to deal with harassment, which rarely includes reporting the harassment. The counselor has students discuss sexual harassment reactions they hear peers give one another, such as "ignore them and they will stop," "don't make a big deal out of it," "they are just fooling around," "boys will be boys." Students discuss why these were dangerous messages for Yolanda and other victims of harassment.

The counselor passes out Dangerous Words (Handout 12.1). The group compares, the students' list with this list. Students offer ideas as to why they believe the words inhibit students from getting help. Students then replace dangerous messages with more appropriate and effective ways to respond to harassment, such as "if it makes you feel uncomfortable then the action is inappropriate," "sexual misconduct of any nature is not tolerable."

Conclusion: The counselor will provide further examples of appropriate responses to harassment.

Assessment: Discipline referrals for sexual harassment will be reduced for the participants.

Follow-Up: Students will educate one or more peers about appropriate responses to their classmates who have both participated in and experienced sexual harassment.

GROUP SESSION 4: THE EMOTIONAL COSTS

Personal/Social Development Standard C: Students will understand safety and survival skills.

Competencies

- Students will learn about the relationship between rules, laws, safety, and the protection of individual rights.
- Students will learn the difference between appropriate and inappropriate physical contact.
- Students will demonstrate the ability to assert boundaries, rights, and personal privacy.

Learning Objectives

- Students will identify sexual harassment.
- Students will describe the emotional toll on the victim.

Materials: Handout 12.2.

Activities

Introduction: The counselor has students review what they have learned in the group thus far.

Counseling Activities: The counselor passes out Handout 12.2, which are the case studies presented at the beginning of this chapter. The counselor helps the group analyze each case study to decide whether the scenario involves sexual harassment. Using the scenarios, students respond as to why or why not they believe the action involves sexual harassment. Then the students speculate as to how the action made the victim feel.

Conclusion: Students identify the range of emotions experienced by victims of sexual harassment.

Assessment: Discipline referrals for sexual harassment will be reduced for the participants.

Follow-up: The counselor will speak to each student individually to get feedback as to what the student is learning from the group sessions as well as the steps to take in the event of sexual harassment on oneself or others.

GROUP SESSION 5: WRITING AN APOLOGY

Personal/Social Development Standard C: Students will understand safety and survival skills.

Competencies

- Students will learn about the relationship between rules, laws, safety, and the protection of individual rights.
- Students will learn the difference between appropriate and inappropriate physical contact.
- Students will demonstrate the ability to assert boundaries, rights, and personal privacy.

Learning Objectives

- Students will personalize sexual harassment by identifying their own sexual harassment behaviors.
- Students will learn to begin to understand the emotional toll on victims and the range of emotions experienced by victims by beginning to project how their victim may have felt.

Materials: Paper and pencils.

Activities

Introduction: The counselor asks each student to describe a time when they sexually harassed another student. Students should be cautioned not to use the victim's name or any identifying information that would reveal the victims identity. The counselor asks students to project how they believe their actions impacted the victim.

Counseling Activity: Students write an apology letter to someone they feel they harassed, to include how they believe they made the victim feel. Willing students can be asked to share their letter with the group.

Conclusion: The counselor assists the students in viewing sexual harassment from the victim's perspective.

Assessment: Students will discontinue harassing behaviors as evaluated by self-report.

Follow-up: Before the next group meeting, students will deliver the letter of apology they wrote to their victim.

GROUP SESSION 6: STOP THE HARASSMENT

Personal/Social Development Standard C: Students will understand safety and survival skills.

Competencies

- Students will learn about the relationship between rules, laws, safety, and the protection of individual rights.
- Students will learn the difference between appropriate and inappropriate physical contact.
- Students will demonstrate the ability to assert boundaries, rights, and personal privacy.

Learning Objectives

- Students will describe their own sexually harassing behaviors.
- Students will contract to stop their part in sexual harassment.

Materials: Sample contracts (Handout 12.3).

Activities

Introduction: The counselor introduces the concept of a contract or commitment to cease hurting classmates through sexual harassing behaviors.

Counseling Activities: The counselor passes out Handout 12.3, the sample contract. Students have an opportunity to tailor their contract by deciding if they want to add or delete anything on their personal contract.

The counselor asks students to decide whether the contract is something that they can adhere to before they sign it.

The counselor discusses with students specific procedures to ensure that they have fulfilled their contract.

Conclusion: Students sign a contract to cease harassing behaviors.

Assessment: Discipline referrals for sexual harassment will be reduced for the participants.

Follow-up: The counselor will make contact with each student during the course of the coming weeks to see is the student is keeping the contract. The counselor will determine whether additional assistance is needed and begin to take steps to aid each individual student.

INDIVIDUAL COUNSELING CONSIDERATIONS

Following are recommendations for the school counselor in the two-prong role of (1) helping school administrators and teachers correctly respond to sexual harassment and (2) supporting individual students who have been victimized.

1. Stay current on laws, ethical standards, and school district policies regarding sexual harassment and counseling minor clients. Consult with professional colleagues when faced with an ethical dilemma.
2. Acquire professional development through counseling organizations, workshops, and literature on counseling strategies and legal and ethical issues involving confidentiality with minors and sexual harassment.
3. Encourage students to involve their parents if they have been sexually harassed. If students express fear in telling their parents, assist them in developing strategies for coping with their parents' reactions. Offer to be available for a joint conference or subsequent parent consultation.
4. On the school counseling office door display the pink triangle "safe place" stickers supplied by GLSEN or other support symbols to send a message to the school community that the school counselor is an "ally" to heterosexual and gay, lesbian, bisexual, and transgendered students.
5. Develop strategies to help students ease into the discussion of sexual harassment. For example, have students respond to verbal or written questions in which sexual harassment is but one of a number of questions and is given the same weight as other questions.
6. Continue to enhance collaboration between families and the school. Routinely involving parents helps facilitate communication in tougher times.

CONCLUSION

School counselors in their advocacy role can empower students with the knowledge and support needed to participate in a fair, equitable, and hospitable school environment. Title IX, as used in the *Davis* case, gives counselors support to serve as advocates against student-on-student harassment. As human behavior specialists, school counselors can be instrumental in helping to heighten the awareness of the sexual harassment problem and assist in establishing prevention and intervention plans. More importantly, the school counselor can be an advocate and a source of strength for the individual student who needs help in confronting and dealing with sexual harassment. The legal and ethical complications of working with minors in schools continue to pose daily dilemmas, and never more so than in sexual harassment issues. Respecting students' confidences requires school counselors to balance the rights of minors with the rights of their parents and the need to protect other students from potential abuse. Legal rulings and the ASCA and ACA codes for ethical behavior offer suggestions and guidance in the complexities of confidentiality. However, it is ultimately the responsibility of the school counselor to determine the appropriate response for the individual student who puts trust in the security of the counseling relationship.

RESOURCES

Web Site Resources for Sexual Harassment

American Counseling Association (http://www.counseling.org/): Contains updated information regarding code of ethics and standards of practice for all counselors.

Committee for Children (www.cfchildren.org): Devoted to promoting safety, well-being, and social development of children; offers programs in bullying and child abuse prevention, including sexual harassment by peers.

Office of Civil Rights (www.ed.gov/offices/OCR/sexharassresources.html): Provides resources for addressing sexual harassment; provides schools with practical guidance to help protect students from harassment and violence.

Adams & Keese Education Law Online (http://education.arlaw.com): Legislative updates, reports, and research on education policy issues (current and archives), IDEA, Education Hot Spots section, the National School Board Resource.

Find Law/Law Crawler (www.lawcrawler.com): Governmental information: search state government servers, government departments, U.S. codes, federal regulations, Supreme Court and circuit cases, as well as search worldwide.

United States Department of Education (www.ed.gov/databases/ERIC_Digests/ed315709): A digest supplied by ERIC concerning the ethical and legal issues involved with school counseling, including ethical standards, confidentiality issues, and legal aspects of the profession.

Safe Learning (www.safe-learning.com): Provides creative resources for education; includes programs for crisis planning and emotional learning; promotes gun-, drug-, and bully-free schools; includes discussion forums for teens.

American School Counselors Association (www.schoolcounselor.org/ethics/specific.htm): Code of ethics and standard of practice.

Street Law Online (http://www.streetlaw.org/): Contains current information and links involving school violence, laws relative to education, and more.

Internet Legal Services (www.legalethics.com/index.law): Ethical opinion for each of the states; offers direct links to a variety of subjects, including: confidentiality rules, ethic opinions, and disciplinary contact information.

NEA Safe Schools Now (http://www.nea.org/issues/safescho/): Information and resources for ensuring and maintaining safe school environments.

School Counselors (http://www.school-counselors.com/): Devoted to helping school counselors meet the needs of students and families; offers consulting services, original publications, fact papers, e-newsletter, and other related resources.

Gay, Lesbian and Straight Education Network (http://www.glsen.org): Gay and lesbian rights in the schools.

Center for Law and Education (www.cleweb.org): Current federal legislation and national issues.

Information on teasing and bullying (http://www.teasingvictims.com): Provides resources and activities for parents and students.

American Counseling Association (http://www.counseling.org/resources/pracguide.htm):
Assists professional decision making through the use of a good moral systemic
approach.

REFERENCES

American Counseling Association (ACA). (1997a). *Code of ethics and standards of
practice*. Alexandria, VA: Author.

American Counseling Association (ACA). (1997b). *Sexual harassment in the schools.
Background on Title IX of the education amendments of 1972 and guidance issued by
the Office of Civil Rights*. Alexandria, VA: Author.

American School Counselor Association (ASCA). (1986). *The school counselor and
confidentiality*. Alexandria, VA: Author.

American School Counselor Association (ASCA). (1998). *Code of ethics and standards of
practice*. Alexandria, VA: Author.

Biskupic, J. (1999, May 25). Davis v. Monroe County Board of Education et al.
Washington Post, A.1.

Bryant, A. L. (1993). Hostile hallways: The AAUW survey on sexual harassment in
America's schools. *Journal of School Health, 63*, 355–357.

Corey, G., & Corey, M. (1997). *Issues in ethics in the helping profession* (5th ed.). Pacific
Grove, CA: Brooks/Cole.

Davis v. Monroe County Board of Education et al. 120 F.3d 1390. (Supreme Court,
May 24, 1999).

Fischer, L., Schimmel, D., & Kelly, C. (1999). *Teachers and the law*. New York,
NY: Addison Wesley Longman.

Franklin v. Gwinnett County Public Schools. 503 U.S. 60, 68. (1992).

Harris/Scholastic Research. (1993). *Hostile Hallways: The AAUW Survey on Sexual
Harassment in America's Schools*. Washington, DC: AAUW Educational Foundation.

Huey, E., & Remley, T. (1988). Confidentiality and the school counselor: A challenge for
the 1990s. *School Counselor, 41*, 23–30.

Isaacs, M. I., & Stone, C. B. (1998). School counselors and confidentiality: Factors
affecting professional choices. *Professional School Counseling 4*, 258–266.

Marczely, B. (1999). Mixed messages: Sexual harassment in the public schools. *Clearing
House, 72*, 315.

Minnesota Department of Education. (1993). *Sexual harassment to teenagers: It's not
fun—it's illegal*. St. Paul, MN: Department of Education.

Moore, M., & Rienzo, B. (1998). Sexual harassment policies in Florida school districts.
Journal of School Health, 68, 237–242.

Rowell, L. L., McBride, M. C., & Nelson-Leaf, J. (1996). The role of school counselor in
confronting peer sexual harassment. *School Counselor, 43*(3), 196–207.

Salo, M. M., & Shumate, S. G. (1993). Counseling minor clients. *ACA Legal Series, 4*, 73–78.

Sandler, B. (1994). *Educator's guide to controlling sexual harassment*. Washington,
DC: Thompson Publishing Group.

Strauss, S., & Espeland, P. (1992). *Sexual harassment and teens*. Minneapolis, MN: Free
Spirit.

Sullivan, K., & Zirkel, P. (1999). Student to student sexual harassment: Which tack will the
Supreme Court take in a sea of analyses? *West Education Law Reporter, 132*,
609–628.

U.S. Department of Education, Office of Civil Rights. (1997). *Sexual Harassment Policy Guidance: Harassment of Students by School Employees, Other Students, or Third Parties*. 62 Fed. Reg. 12034–12051.

Van Boven, S. (1999, January 25). Playground Justice. *Newsweek*, 33.

Webb, D. L., Hunnicutt, K. H., & Metha, A. (1997). What schools can do to combat student-to-student sexual harassment. *NASSP Bulletin, 81*, 72.

Zirkel, P. (1999). Courtside: More harassment. *Kappan, 81*(2), 171–172.

Zirkel, P., Richardson, S. N., & Goldberg, S. S. (1995). *A digest of Supreme Court decisions affecting education* (3rd ed.). Bloomington, IN: Phi Delta Kappa.

DANGEROUS WORDS

Don't make a big deal out of it.

Boys will be boys.

He/she is just flirting. They do not know any other way to get your attention.

Ignore him/her and they will leave you alone.

Don't react. That is what he/she is trying to get you to do.

He/she treats everyone that way.

It's a cultural thing. That is how they are in his/her culture.

Where is your sense of humor? Can't you take a joke?

He is just fighting raging hormones. He will settle down.

He/she probably just has a crush on you.

Don't give them the attention they want.

HANDOUT 12.2

Scenario 1

Sarah, a fifth-grade student, reported to her teacher that the boys were snapping the girls' bra straps on the playground.

Scenario 2

Sandy, a seventh-grader, reported to her assistant principal that boys were deliberately rubbing their bodies up against her and other girls in the crowded hallways during class changes.

Scenario 3

Rolanda, an eleventh-grader, confided to her friends that the four boys who had lockers near hers had pictures of Playboy centerfolds up in their lockers and have made comments to her such as "I bet this is how you look with your clothes off."

Scenario 4

Martin's teacher overheard his friends laughing at him for being cornered on a bus by a girl who aggressively grabbed at his "private parts," taunting him that there was nothing there.

HANDOUT 12.3

This is a sample contract for students to cease sexual harassment behaviors. It is a guideline. You are encouraged to make changes to personalize a contract of your own.

I _____ recognize sexual harassment behaviors.
     (name of student)

I understand how hurtful and long-lasting these behaviors can be to individuals and the community. I promise to stop sexually harassing others and I am willing to encourage proper behavior in others to counteract sexual harassment.

_____

Signed

Index

TO THE OWNER OF THIS BOOK:

We hope that you have found *Leadership, Advocacy, and Direct Service Strategies for Professional School Counselors* useful. So that this book can be improved in a future edition, would you take the time to complete this sheet and return it? Thank you.

School and address: _____

_____

Department: _____

Instructor's name: _____

1. What I like most about this book is:_____

_____

_____

2. What I like least about this book is: _____

_____

_____

3. My general reaction to this book is: _____

_____

_____

4. The name of the course in which I used this book is: _____

_____

5. Were all of the chapters of the book assigned for you to read? _____

   If not, which ones weren't? _____

6. In the space below, or on a separate sheet of paper, please write specific suggestions for improving this book and anything else you'd care to share about your experience in using this book.

_____

_____

_____

OPTIONAL:

Your name: _____ Date: _____

May we quote you, either in promotion for *Leadership, Advocacy, and Direct Service Strategies for Professional School Counselors*, or in future publishing ventures?

Yes: _____ No: _____

Sincerely yours,

Rachelle Pérusse

Gary E. Goodnough